Internal Audit Practice from A to Z

Internal Audit and IT Audit

Series Editor: Dan Swanson

A Guide to the National Initiative
for Cybersecurity Education (NICE)
Cybersecurity Workforce Framework (2.0)
Dan Shoemaker, Anne Kohnke, and Ken Sigler
ISBN 978-1-4987-3996-2

A Practical Guide to Performing
Fraud Risk Assessments
Mary Breslin
ISBN 978-1-4987-4251-1

Corporate Defense and the Value
Preservation Imperative:
Bulletproof Your Corporate
Defense Program
Sean Lyons
ISBN 978-1-4987-4228-3

Data Analytics for Internal Auditors
Richard E. Cascarino
ISBN 978-1-4987-3714-2

Fighting Corruption in a
Global Marketplace:
How Culture, Geography, Language
and Economics Impact Audit and Fraud
Investigations around the World
Mary Breslin
ISBN 978-1-4987-3733-3

Investigations and the CAE:
The Design and Maintenance
of an Investigative Function
within Internal Audit
Kevin L. Sisemore
ISBN 978-1-4987-4411-9

Internal Audit Practice from A to Z
Patrick Onwura Nzechukwu
ISBN 978-1-4987-4205-4

Leading the Internal Audit Function
Lynn Fountain
ISBN 978-1-4987-3042-6

Mastering the Five Tiers of
Audit Competency:
The Essence of Effective Auditing
Ann Butera
ISBN 978-1-4987-3849-1

Operational Assessment of IT
Steve Katzman
ISBN 978-1-4987-3768-5

Operational Auditing:
Principles and Techniques
for a Changing World
Hernan Murdock
ISBN 978-1-4987-4639-7

Securing an IT Organization
through Governance,
Risk Management, and Audit
Ken E. Sigler and James L. Rainey, III
ISBN 978-1-4987-3731-9

Security and Auditing of Smart Devices:
Managing Proliferation of
Confidential Data on Corporate
and BYOD Devices
Sajay Rai, Philip Chukwuma, and Richard Cozart
ISBN 978-1-4987-3883-5

Software Quality Assurance:
Integrating Testing, Security, and Audit
Abu Sayed Mahfuz
ISBN 978-1-4987-3553-7

The Complete Guide to
Cybersecurity Risks and Controls
Anne Kohnke, Dan Shoemaker,
and Ken E. Sigler
ISBN 978-1-4987-4054-8

Cognitive Hack: The New Battleground in
Cybersecurity ... the Human Mind
James Bone
ISBN 978-1-4987-4981-7

Internal
Audit Practice
from A to Z

Patrick Onwura Nzechukwu

CRC Press
Taylor & Francis Group
Boca Raton London New York

CRC Press is an imprint of the
Taylor & Francis Group, an **informa** business
AN AUERBACH BOOK

First published 2017 by Auerbach Publisher

Published 2019 by CRC Press
Taylor & Francis Group
6000 Broken Sound Parkway NW, Suite 300
Boca Raton, FL 33487-2742

First issued in paperback 2021

ISBN-13: 978-1-4987-4205-4 (hbk)
ISBN-13: 978-0-367-56795-8 (pbk)

Library of Congress Cataloging-in-Publication Data

Names: Nzechukwu, Patrick Onwura, 1969-
Title: Internal audit practice from A to Z / Patrick Onwura Nzechukwu.
Description: 1 Edition. | Boca Raton : CRC Press, 2016. | Includes bibliographical references and index.
Identifiers: LCCN 2016019259 | ISBN 9781498742054
Subjects: LCSH: Auditing, Internal.
Classification: LCC HF5668.25 .N94 2016 | DDC 657/.458--dc23
LC record available at https://lccn.loc.gov/2016019259

Visit the Taylor & Francis Web site at
http://www.taylorandfrancis.com

and the CRC Press Web site at
http://www.crcpress.com

This book is dedicated to the glory and majesty of the Almighty God (God the Father, God the Son, and God the Holy Spirit).

Contents

List of Figures

List of Tables

Preface

Three major situations inspired me to engage in this book project on internal auditing. First, as the head of internal audit in my organization (Continental Shipyard Ltd., a joint venture partner of the Nigerian Ports Authority), I discovered that I could not lay my hands on any textbook on internal auditing authored by a Nigerian. Secondly, I was motivated by the scandals of major corporations in the United States in the early 2000s and the Asian economic crisis of 1998, to put up a research work that would assist internal auditors, corporations, professionals, academia, and industry players, including students, investors, and general public desiring general knowledge and a good understanding about the practice of internal auditing. The third motivation stems from my inability to find a textbook that captures all aspects of internal audit practice.

It was on this premise that our research effort inspired the development and production of this book, which we believe augments relevant legislative pronouncements and standards in the fight against management fraudulent manipulation of financial reports and other operations. Also, the corrupt and fraudulent practices in public organizations, particularly in developing economies, like Africa, some parts of Asia, South America, etc., with so much executive impunity and compromised legislative and judicial arm seating, has propelled the development of this book.

This book comprises nine chapters: Introduction, Internal Audit Procedure and Techniques, Internal Audit Charter, Managing the Internal Audit Function, Internal Audit Practice Layout, Internal Audit Documentation and Reporting, Internal Audit Peer Review, What the Standards Say, and Internal Control Checklist.

Chapter 1 (Introduction) is designed to lay the foundation of the subject title, including background, definition, and scope of study.

Chapter 2 (Internal Audit Procedure and Techniques) is designed to enlighten readers on the procedures and techniques adopted in arriving at internal auditors' conclusions and recommendations.

Chapter 3 (Internal Audit Charter) is designed to enlighten the general public of the content of the standard document containing the purpose, objectives, functions and authority, scope, and general rules of engaging the internal auditor.

Chapter 4 (Managing the Internal Audit Function) is designed to educate readers and practitioners on the general organization of the internal audit function.

Chapter 5 (Internal Audit Practice Layout) is designed to show readers and practitioners the general flow or phases of internal audit practice.

Chapter 6 (Internal Audit Documentation and Reporting) is designed to show readers and practitioners the types of forms and documents used at various stages/ phases of internal audit practice, and the types of reports generated or generatable from the process.

Chapter 7 (Internal Audit Peer Review) is incorporated to inform readers that though the internal auditor is the watchdog to every organization, it has also another function of watching over its activities.

Chapter 8 (What the Standards Say) is an innovation introduced to briefly look at regulators of the internal audit profession and some of their pronouncements.

Chapter 9 (Internal Control Checklist) is bonus chapter to assist internal auditors to know the possible control elements in each functional area of any organization.

This research compilation was started in 2011. The first and second printed but unpublished versions were reviewed by the Institute of Chartered Accountants of Nigeria (ICAN) in 2012 and 2014, respectively, with high commendations and recommendations. ICAN recommendations formed the bedrock of the final output of this work. The tortuous journey of this work was not without a couple of misfortunes and disappointments, the major being a system crash where the majority of the work was lost. The original intention of this work was to produce two books: a study part and a practice part; however, because of the system crash, the entire work on the study park was lost.

Finally, this book is the author's contribution to the accountancy profession and a reference material to the internal audit function, practitioners, and captains of industries. I appreciate questions and consultations on any part of this work. I also ask for constructive criticisms and suggestions that would be useful for future editions through my e-mail (patrickonsult@hotmail.com; patrickonsult@gmail.com).

Acknowledgments

Special thanks go primarily to the Almighty God, who, in 2010, gave me the inspiration and insight to fill a gap existing in the system I was operating and to add back to the society that has impacted my life in different ways.

My special thanks go to the following people: Adel Rosario, project manager at Manila Typesetting Company, for your immense contribution in typesetting and layout of this book, particularly your scholarly contributions to some oversight cases of the author; Jay Margolis, project editor at CRC Press, Taylor & Francis Group, for your timely interventions in knotty areas in the production process; Delroy Lowe, project coordinator at CRC Press, Taylor & Francis Group, your encouragement and guidance at the manuscript stage is not forgotten; Rich O'Hanley of CRC Press, Taylor & Francis Group, you made the signing of this contract possible; your understanding to my peculiar situation and concession granted to me was highly appreciated.

It is pertinent to recognize my former employers, CONTEC Global Ltd. and Continental Shipyard Ltd., Equinox Petroleum & Petro-Chemical Co. Ltd. (Equinox Resources Ltd.), and Green Circle Network Africa Limited; you all gave me the platform and requisite experiences to leverage on academic and research efforts. It is equally important to note that it was during my employment as the head of internal audit at Continental Shipyard Ltd. that the idea to write this book was conceived.

I especially recognize and thank the Institute of Chartered Accountants of Nigeria (ICAN), which, through its desire for excellence, made me conceive the idea of taking this project beyond our national boundaries to become an internationally oriented document.

I also specially thank the erudite scholars and seasoned professionals and practitioners in the persons of Chief Oyedokun Godwin Emmanuel, a seasoned author and renowned fraud examiner and forensic accountant; Prince Niyi Adeniji, author of several auditing text books and associate director at WYSE Associate (ICAN tuition house); and Kenneth Afam, internal auditor at Nigerite Limited. These professionals reviewed the first version of this book; their words ignited a fire in my bones and rejuvenated the lubricants in my joints for this tortuous five years of research work.

I recognize my fellow authors from around the globe, whose works played a great source of materials and also greatly enriched my knowledge of the subject.

How can I forget you, my kindhearted and caring sister, Patience Odunze, a vessel of honor God has used and is still using to uplift not only my family members but also the lowly esteemed members of our community in love and charity. You have supported me materially and spiritually before, during, and even after the completion of this work through your sacrificial giving.

My special thanks also go to my amiable wife, Christiana Omaebi Nzechukwu, whose patience and dexterity covered so many gaps that were created as a result of my commitment to long-term projects, and consequently added to the peace of mind I needed to work assiduously day and night to put together this piece of work. In a similar manner, I recognize the role played by my princesses and angelic daughters, Ugo, Amarachi, and Chijiderem, who, through their necessary noise, kept the spirit alive whenever the spirit was willing but the flesh was weak. I thank the Almighty God, who at the twilight of the production of this book gave me a crown of glory through a newborn baby boy by the name of Samuel C.A. Nzechukwu, whose birth on the 28th of June gave me more hope to leave an enduring legacy.

Let me equally pay tribute to my brothers-in-law, Victor and Roland Mgbonozu, who at one point or the other sacrificially released their Internet facility for my research effort and information gathering. This, in no small measure, contributed to the success of this work, particularly at the early phase.

How can I forget my spiritual earthly father, Rev. Best Chimdiebere, and his amiable wife, Charity Chimdiebere, the chief shepherd of Word Exploits Assembly International Church; his words of encouragement and spiritual outpouring have become a beacon of hope and exceeding great pleasure at a time the world seemed crumbling around me.

I also recognize and thank you, my sweet mother, Regina Ijego Odunze, for your care, love, and prayers.

Finally, I want to use this opportunity to thank the late Prof. A.B. Okoro and his surviving family members; it was his foresight and good nature that kept my education ambition alive. May God grant his gentle soul eternal rest in Jesus's name, Amen!

If I have not mentioned your name, it is not an indication that your role is not important or not appreciated, but that I must limit the presentation to an acceptable volume. Please forgive me if your name is not mentioned.

About the Author

Patrick Onwura Nzechukwu (Fmr. Odunze) was born in Jos, Plateau State of Nigeria, in 1969, of Igbo parents.

He completed his primary education at Ndionyemobi Primary School, Oguta LGA, Imo State of Nigeria, in 1981. He completed his high school (secondary school) education in 1986. He earned a national diploma in accountancy from Federal Polytechnic, Bauchi, in 1990, and a higher national diploma in accountancy from Yaba College of Technology in 1994. He qualified as a chartered accountant in 2001 from the Institute of Chartered Accountants of Nigeria and earned his master's in business administration in 2002. He also earned certification in Oracle 8i Database Administration in 2002 and a certificate in computer appreciation in 1995.

He started his work career in 1995 after completing the compulsory one-year National Youth Service Corps with Equinox Petroleum & Petrochemical Co. Limited. In 2002, he joined Continental Transfert Technique Limited (CONTEC Global Ltd.), an international consultancy firm for Nigeria Immigration Service's Combined Expatriate Residence Permit and Aliens Card (CERPAC) project, as an assistant accounts manager. In 2003, he was appointed production manager in charge of a CERPAC production center. In 2004, he was appointed as an internal auditor. Later in 2005, he became the accounts manager in charge of all CERPAC branches, including the head office (admin). In 2010, he had a stint with Continental Shipyard Limited, a joint venture partner with the Nigerian Ports Authority, as the internal audit manager. It was while in this employment that the idea of writing a book in internal auditing was conceived. Later in 2011, he joined Hitachi/Green Circle Network Africa Ltd. as the group financial controller. He held this office until 2012, when he established his consultancy firm, Patrickonsult Limited.

Nzechukwu is a good researcher with interest on filling gaps in trending global economic issues. This trait was demonstrated when he noticed that there was no textbook by a Nigerian on internal auditing, maybe because the emphasis has been on external auditing, which has legislative backing. At that time, corruption has driven the economy almost into recession. Also, internationally, there was a high level of business manipulation by managements in advanced economies, particularly in the United States. These discoveries gave rise to the writing of the first textbook on internal auditing in Nigeria by a Nigerian. The book was structured into two parts: the practice part and the study part. The practice part is being released first, and the study part will follow later.

Nzechukwu has written an unpublished textbook on forensic accounting, *Forensic Accounting, A Mirror to Financial Undercutting.*

Besides his professional accounting background, he also engaged in management consulting, with particular interest on the balanced scorecard (BSC) methodology. This prompted his research on and writing of an unpublished textbook on BSC, *Balanced Scorecard, A Tool Achieving Vision and Mission Statements.*

Nzechukwu has written some articles published in LinkedIn, Facebook, ResearchGate, Academic.edu, and Global Research & Development Services (GRDS), including the following:

1. Enterprise risk management (ERM) and internal auditing (IA)—the case of dual change agents to eradicate corruption in Nigeria
2. Strategy and operational/process excellence transformation consultancy programs
3. Business intelligence for oil and gas, construction/manufacturing companies, SME and conglomerates, government agencies and NGOs, etc.
4. Balanced scorecard overview
5. DasukiGate, a case of zero level project management (PM) in the Nigerian military
6. Balanced scorecard (BSC): strategy clarification, implementation and performance management, etc.

In furtherance to its consulting work and to fulfill its vision of assisting corporate entities attain Fortune company status, Patrickonsult Limited was incorporated in 2012. The company is a partnership with some foreign firms to form a consortium of international firms. The consortium firm was established in pursuit of the vision of assisting corporate entities in Nigeria to attain Fortune company status through service delivery and training in corporate governance, risk management and compliance, strategy, and operational transformation excellence, among others. It organizes training and certifications on BSC, Lean Six Sigma, big data predictive analytics, net promoter score, leadership development, and project management, among others. The consultancy specializes on the strategy and process excellence transformation domain.

Chapter 1

Introduction

1.1 Background Information

The year 2001 witnessed a series of large financial information frauds in the United States of America, in particular, and in other big economies of the world. Mostly involved are Enron Corporation, at one time one of the world's largest accounting firm; Arthur Andersen; the telecommunications company WorldCom; Qwest; and Sunbeam. Others include Adelphia Communications Corporation, Peregrine Systems, Tyco International, among other well-known corporations. A summary of the scandals of some of these companies is provided in this chapter. These scandals highlighted the need to review the effectiveness of accounting standards, auditing regulations, and corporate governance principles. In some cases, management manipulated the figures shown in financial reports to indicate a better economic performance. In other cases, tax and regulatory incentives encouraged the over-leveraging of companies and decisions to tolerate extraordinary and unjustified risks.

As the big economies of the world are collapsing today owing to wrong financial indices hatched and produced over a period of time by corporate entities, we have taken time to study the causes and dynamics of the failures of these great companies, and the measures being put in place to forestall future occurrences. We have come to terms that as wealth is being transferred from these failed economies to growing economies, it is pertinent to pay heed to the reasons for their failures and the measures being advanced to arrest future occurrences, in order to avoid being caught in the same web that engulfed these great economies.

Adelphia Communications Corporation (former NASDAQ ticker symbol ADELQ): Adelphia, a Greek word meaning *brothers*, was a cable television company with headquarters in Coudersport, Pennsylvania. Adelphia was the fifth largest cable company in the United States before filing for bankruptcy in 2002 as a result of internally motivated fraud and corruption cases. It was founded in 1952 by John Rigas in the town of Coudersport, which remained the company's headquarters until it was moved to Greenwood Village, Colorado, shortly after filing for bankruptcy.

Enron Corporation (former New York Stock Exchange ticker symbol ENE): Enron was an American energy, commodities, and services company based in Houston, Texas. It was one of the world's leading electricity, natural gas, communications, and pulp and paper companies, with a statement of revenues of nearly $101 billion in 2000. Enron was recorded to have approximately 22,000 staff in its employment before it went into bankruptcy in late 2001. *Fortune* magazine named Enron "America's Most Innovative Company" for six consecutive years. At the end of 2001, it was discovered that its reported financial position was sustained substantially by institutionalized, systematic, and creatively planned accounting fraud. This was later interpreted to what is known today as the "Enron scandal." With this assertion, Enron has gone down in the annals of history as an *emblem* of willful corporate fraud and corruption. This scandal was responsible for the dissolution of one of the five largest accounting firms in the world at that time, Arthur Andersen (Slucom, 2001; BBC News, 2002; Dan, 2002; Murphy, 2002; Bethany and Peter, 2003; CNN, 2005; Egan, 2005; Fox News, 2006; Pasha, 2006).

Peregrine Systems Inc.: Peregrine is an enterprise software company founded in 1981 that sold enterprise asset management, change management, and Information Technology Infrastructure Library (ITIL)–based IT service management solutions. As a result of an accounting scandal and subsequent bankruptcy, Peregrine was acquired by Hewlett-Packard (HP) in 2005. HP now markets the Peregrine products as part of its IT Service Management Solutions, within the HP Software Division portfolio.

These scandals also brought into question the existing accounting practices and activities of many corporations in the United States and contributed substantially to the creation of the Sarbanes–Oxley Act of 2002.

In a related development, ever since the Asian economic crisis of 1998, the call for risk management has become the single most important answer or survival tool kit for industries. For internal auditors, this has broadened their roles; their focus and approach in considering the audit function has undergone radical change. In assessing the adequacy and effectiveness of internal controls, internal auditors no longer only determine controls and test their effectiveness, but have evolved into examining the business objectives first and identifying the associated risks before proceeding to assess the business control. Today, internal auditing has progressed from compliance- to risk-based auditing (Zarkasyi, 2006).

It was on this premise that our research effort inspired the development and production of a document (Nzechukwu, 2011) that we believe would augment relevant legislative pronouncements and standards in the fight against managerial fraudulent manipulation of financial reports and other operations. Also, the corrupt and fraudulent practices in public organizations, particularly in developing economies, like Africa and some parts of Asia, South America, etc., with so much executive impunity and compromised legislative and judicial arm-seating, have propelled the development of this book.

Traditionally, people understand internal audit as an activity of a self-imposed internal check and also supposedly an activity that involves going around telling people what they are doing wrong. The traditionalist internal auditors tend to see themselves as revered personalities sneaking around at odd times in order to catch people indulging in wrongdoing. However, the truth remains that even if one sees it from a narrow sense, the contribution of internal audit activity is of great importance in that an effective internal audit system leads to improved accountability, ethical and professional practices, effective risk management, and improved quality of output, as well as supports decision making and performance tracking.

Historically, it has always been held that internal auditing is confined to merely financial activities, that is, ensuring that the accounting and allied records have been properly maintained, and the assets management system is in place in order to safeguard the assets and also to see whether policies and procedures are in place and are duly being complied with. However, with changing times, this concept has undergone a radical change with regard to its definition and scope of coverage. The modern approach suggests that it should not be restricted to financial issues alone but also on issues such as cost–benefit analysis, resource utilization and their deployment, matters of propriety, effectiveness of the management in enterprise-wide risk management, corporate governance and control processes, etc. Internal auditing has always been viewed as an integral part of organizational governance, and increasingly as an instrument for improving the performance of the organization, in both the private and public sectors.

Internal auditing is an assessment tool that provides a reliable indicator of the integrity of your organization's system and processes, and their capacity to support your objectives. Audits help an organization identify problems, risks, good practices, and opportunities that would better serve its customers. The information obtained from well-conducted audits is a company asset that far outweighs the modest investment in time, training, and other costs associated with the audits. The manner in which the organization values and uses this asset is partially dependent on the quality of the audits. Hence, executive management, through visible support and allocation of resources, has primary responsibility for ensuring the effectiveness of the internal audit program. On the other hand, auditors have the responsibility for good stewardship of management's support, as demonstrated by their commitment to good auditing practices and the production of meaningful audit reports (Robitaille, 2007).

Internal audit practice is one big area being advanced to be strengthened by corporate bodies to ensure quality and reliable financial reporting; sound corporate governance and virile internal control system; effective enterprise-wide risk management; and adherence to relevant legislations, standards, policies, and procedures.

Every successful audit is based on a comprehensive planning under an atmosphere of constructive participation and communication between the auditee and the auditor.

As indicated in the publication of AuditNet, LLC (2014), every audit project is unique; however, the audit process is similar for most engagements and generally consists of four phases: planning (also called survey or preliminary review), fieldwork, audit report, and follow-up review. It is important to involve the client/auditee at each phase of the audit process. It is equally important to note that, as in any special project, internal auditing results in a certain amount of time being diverted from the auditee's usual routine; hence, one of the key objectives in the audit program is to minimize this time diversion and avoid disrupting ongoing activities.

1.2 Definition

1.2.1 Meaning of Internal Auditing

The International Auditing Standard, ISA 610 (2007), *Considering the Work of Internal Audit*, issued by the Auditing and Assurance Standards Board, defines internal audit as follows:

> *Internal audit* means an appraisal activity established within an entity as a service to the entity. Its functions include, amongst other things, monitoring internal control.

According to Nigerian Standards on Auditing, NSA 26 (2013), *Considering the Work of Internal Audit*, internal auditing is defined as follows:

> An appraisal activity established or provided as a service to the entity. Its functions include, amongst other things, examining, evaluating and monitoring the adequacy and effectiveness of internal control. (p. 546)

However, the Institute of Internal Auditors (IIA; 2010) has developed the globally accepted definition of *internal auditing* as follows:

> Internal auditing is an *independent, objective assurance* and *consulting* activity designed to *add value* and improve an organization's operations. It helps an organization accomplish its objectives by bringing a *systematic, disciplined approach* to evaluate and improve the effectiveness of risk management, control and governance processes.

An internal auditor can

- Make an objective assessment of operations and share ideas for best practices
- Provide guidance for improving controls, processes and procedures, performance, and risk management

Also, the International Organization of Supreme Audit Institutions (INTOSAI), a worldwide affiliation of governmental entities, has adopted the IIA definition of internal auditing. INTOSAI strongly advocates for the establishment of independent internal audit units in public entities, which it has enunciated in

- ISSAI 1610—*Using the Work of Internal Auditors*
- INTOSAI Guidance for Good governance: INTOSAI Govs 9100–9230

INTOSAI Gov 9100, among other things, recommends that internal auditors should use the Professional Practices Framework issued by the IIA.

The scope of internal audit activity encompasses the wider concepts of corporate governance and risk management—recognizing that control exists in an organization to manage risk and promote effective governance.

In this definition, two types of internal audit services have been contemplated and defined by the IIA as follows:

- *Assurance Services*—an objective examination of evidence for the purpose of providing an independent assessment of risk management, control, or governance processes for the organization. ISO 31000:2009 is a process that provides a level of confidence that the objectives will be achieved within an acceptable level of risk.
- *Consulting Services*—advisory and related client activities, the nature and scope of which are agreed upon with the client, and which are intended to add value and improve an organization's operations.

Throughout this book, all references to *internal audits* will encompass both of these services.

According to the Virgin Islands (2015), in the public sector, the main objective of the internal audit department is to determine that those entrusted with public resources are establishing and maintaining effective controls to

1. Accomplish goals and objectives in the most efficient and economical manner
2. Comply with applicable laws and regulations
3. Safeguard public resources
4. Assess the accuracy and reliability of financial information

Thus, internal audit activity can play an important role and support the board and management in fulfilling an essential component of their governance mechanisms. The internal auditor provides analyses, appraisals, recommendations, counsel, and information concerning the activities reviewed. The internal auditor can suggest ways for reducing costs, enhancing revenues, and improving profits.

Furthermore, according to ISO 19011 (2002), the cost of failing an environmental/quality management systems audit can take a number of forms: companies can lose valuable contracts or prized certifications; they may have to pay for an expensive range of improvements demanded by a client; they may experience an erosion of efficiency; etc.

BS EN ISO 19011:2002 therefore offers guidelines for quality and/or environmental management systems auditing. It is intended that by using this new standard, organizations can save time, effort, and money by

- Avoiding confusion over the objectives of the environmental or quality audit program
- Securing agreement of the goals for individual audits within an audit program
- Reducing duplication of effort when conducting combined environmental/quality audits
- Ensuring audit reports follow the best format and contain all the relevant information
- Evaluating the competence of members of an audit team against appropriate criteria

Whatever the reason for the audit (e.g., certification, internal review, contract compliance, etc.), however, it is intended that organizations can move efficiently through the process by applying the guidelines.

1.2.2 Four Resources

Within one single standard, there are now four critical decision/support resources for the efficient planning, conduction, and evaluation of quality and/or environmental audits:

- A clear explanation of the principles of management systems auditing
- Guidance on the management of audit programs
- Guidance on the conduct of internal or external audits
- Advice on the competence and evaluation of auditors

1.2.3 Internal Audit Function

Wasonga (2013) states that an internal audit function is expected to maximize its assurance provision to the board, the audit committee and management, and at the same time contribute to the continuous improvement strategies of the organization without compromising or impairing its objectivity and independence.

The internal auditor's role also involves providing guidance and expert advice in diverse areas, including, but not limited to, corporate governance, enterprise-wide risk management, fraud policies and prevention, and information technology systems, in addition to its traditional area of internal controls (Wasonga, 2013).

1.3 Scope

As stated earlier, every audit project is unique; however, the audit process is similar for most engagements and generally consists of four phases: planning (sometimes called survey or preliminary review), fieldwork, audit report, and follow-up review.

The scope of this work covers the planning, management, conduct, documenting, and communicating results of internal audits against enterprise procedures in order to verify that they are effectively implemented and maintained and to identify areas for improvement.

This book also covers the comprehensive nature of the internal audit charter and the structure of an internal audit function. We shall also consider the general procedures adopted in carrying out internal audit practice.

In doing this, we shall consider internal audit planning (survey or preliminary review), internal audit fieldwork, internal audit report, and internal audit follow-up review. We also attach *templates* for practical knowledge.

We shall equally attempt to show a typical structure of internal audit function with lines of reporting. This shall show recommended skills and personal attributes of an internal auditor, among others.

We shall make attempt to x-ray the current practice of internal auditing in developing economy with Nigeria as a reference point, using Nigerian Standards on Auditing publications vis-à-vis recommended best practices by the International Standards for the Practice of Internal Auditing, including the most recent International Standards for the Professional Practice of Internal Auditing.

The scope of this book shall attempt to consider possible checklists of a standard internal control system.

Finally, as a bonus, we shall also review extensively the internal audit peer review procedure, and the forms and templates for presenting reports.

This book is the author's contribution to the accountancy profession, the internal audit sub-branch, practitioners, and captains of industries, as a reference material. I appreciate questions and consultations on any part of this work. I also call for constructive criticisms and suggestions that would be useful for future editions through e-mail (patrickonsult@hotmail.com or patrickonsult@ gmail.com).

References

AuditNet, LLC. (2014). The-internal-audit-process-from-a-to-z-how-it-works. Retrieved July 1, 2014 from: http://www.auditnet.org/audit-library/the-internal-audit-process-from-a-to-z-how-it-works.

BBC News. (2002). Andersen guilty in Enron case. Retrieved from: http://news.bbc.co.uk/1/hi/business/2047122.stm.

Bethany, M., and Peter, E. (2003). The smartest guys in the room: The amazing rise and scandalous fall of Enron. Published by Portfolio, Penguin Books, Limited, Penguin Group (USA) Inc. ISBN 10: 1591840082/ISBN 13: 9781591840084.

CNN. (2005). Tapes: Enron plotted to shut down power plant. Retrieved from: http://www.cnn.com/2005/US/02/03/enron.tapes/.

Dan, A. (2002). Enron the incredible. Retrieved from: http://www.forbes.com/2002/01/15/0115enron.html.

Egan, T. (2005). Tapes show Enron arranged plant shutdown. *The New York Times*. Retrieved from: http://www.nytimes.com/2005/02/04/national/04energy.html?ex=1107666000&en=01449ebf62df572e&ei=5070.

Fox News. (2006). Fast facts: Timeline of Enron Corp. Published by Associated Press. Retrieved from: http://www.foxnews.com/story/2006/05/25/fast-facts-timeline-enron-corp.html.

Institute of Internal Auditors. (2010). *Definition of Internal Auditing*. Institute of Internal Auditors.

International Auditing Standard 610. (2007). *Considering the Work of Internal Audit*. Issued by the Auditing and Assurance Standards Board (AUASB).

ISO 19011. (2002). Guidelines for quality and/or environmental management systems auditing. Retrieved from: http://www.iso14000-iso14001-environmental-management.com/iso-19011.htm.

Murphy, D. (2002). GE completes Enron Wind acquisition; Launches GE Wind Energy *Desert Sky Wind Farm*. Retrieved from: http://webcache.googleusercontent.com/search?q=cache:dYornY3Jt5IJ:www.desertskywind.com/news05022002.htm+&cd=1&hl=en&ct=clnk&gl=ng.

Nigerian Standards on Auditing 26. (2013). *Considering the Work of Internal Audit*. Nigerian Auditing Standards Committee (NASC). The Institute of Chartered Accountants of Nigeria.

Nzechukwu, O. O. (2011). *Internal Audit Practice, How It Works from A to Z*, p. 3.

Pasha, S. (2006). Skilling comes out swinging. Retrieved from: http://money.cnn.com/2006/04/10/news/newsmakers/enron_trial/index.htm.

Robitaille, D. (2007). The basics of internal auditing; *Quality Digest*. Software Copyright 2006 QCI International. Retrieved December 19, 2015 from: http://www.qualitydigest.com/june07/articles/06_article.shtml.

Slucom, T. (2001). Blind faith: How deregulation and Enron's influence over government looted billions from Americans. Public Citizen's Critical Mass Energy and Environment Program 215 Pennsylvania Ave. S.E. Washington, D.C. 20003; ©Public Citizen. All rights reserved.

Virgin Islands. (2015). Internal Audit Department; Virgin Islands (British) VG1110; Copyright 2015 by Government of the Virgin Islands. Retrieved November 27, 2015 from: http://www.bvi.gov.vg/departments/internal-audit-department.

Wasonga, J. K. (2013). Managing the internal audit function. *The Annual Internal Audit Conference*. Retrieved November 2015 from: http://www.icpak.com/wp-content/uploads/2015/09/Managing-the-Internal-Audit-Function.pdf.

Zarkasyi, W. S. (2006). Internal audit techniques, traditional vs progressive approach. *Jurnal Ekonomi dan Bisnis Terapan*. Volume 2, No. 1 February 2006.

Chapter 2

Internal Audit Procedure and Techniques

2.1 Introduction

Contrary to an external audit, which focuses on determining whether financial statements conform to generally accepted accounting principles, an internal audit focuses on uncovering internal control weaknesses and evidence of fraud, waste, or abuse. Internal audit procedures and techniques are veritable instruments for effective risk management implementation (Lohrey, 2015). As with any other process, internal auditing requires planning, definition, consistent implementation, and control to be effective. According to ISO 19011 (2011), internal auditing is one of the elements that make your quality management system (QMS) complete. It fits comfortably into the *check* component of your plan–do–check–act (PDCA) cycle in the overall organizational functions, while on its own it replicates the PDCA cycle in the exercise of its function. The person in charge of the internal auditing program asks management to support the endeavor. In exchange for the trust and confidence implicit in this support, auditors strive diligently to provide valuable information that management can utilize for strategic planning and other decision making. What follows are some of the practices that will help your organization reap benefits from its internal auditing program. Although the comments are directed primarily at the first-party (or internal) audit, most of the tips are equally valid for second- and third-party audits (Robitaille, 2007).

2.2 Internal Audit Procedure and Objectives

The main objective of an internal audit assignment is to assess and, when necessary, improve by recommendation, the effectiveness of internal business controls, risk management plans, and overall business processes. A typical audit procedures starts by assessing current processes and procedures. Auditors then analyze and compare results against internal control objectives to determine whether the audit results comply with internal policies and procedures as well as federal and state laws and regulations; finally, the auditors compile an audit report to present to the board of directors or to the audit committee, the CEO, and other stakeholders related to the audit assignment.

The process for internal audits is as shown in Figure 4.1 of this book. The audit process shall be consistent with the requirements of ISO 19011 (2011), ISO 27001 (2005; Regalado [2012]), and other relevant standards. ISO 19011 identifies 13 steps to audit process (be it a first-, second-, or third-party audit) as summarized hereunder:

1. **Initiate the audit:** To start, the auditor must initiate the audit by contacting the process owner to be audited and ensuring the audit will be feasible. This is important to make sure someone is available to present evidence when you want to audit, rather than try to make a surprise appearance.
2. **Review the documents:** You then need to review the documents for the process. This will help you to know how big of an audit it will be; this knowledge is critical for the next step.

   According to Regalado (2012) in ISO 27001 (2005), the two steps above are described as general procedure where an Information Security Management System audit program shall be created that contains all scheduled and potential audits for the whole calendar year. Internal audits shall be scheduled twice a year or as the need arises. Only competent personnel who are truly independent of the subject area shall perform audits. All members of the internal audit team shall be appointed by the information security management representative, who may double as the lead auditor. The lead auditor shall supervise the activity of the audit team, and an audit notification memo is sent to the department/section to be audited at least three working days in advance of the audit.
3. **Develop audit plan:** The purpose of the document review is to develop your audit plan of what will be audited, who will do the auditing, when it will happen, and who will be audited. Here, you decide how the audit will be split up if more than one auditor will be used, and how much time will be dedicated to each process in the audit.
4. **Assign work to auditors per plan:** Larger audits may assign work among several auditors, with each taking more than one process to audit. In this way, you can shorten the amount of time that an audit disrupts the processes, such

as having three auditors working for one day rather than one auditor working for three days.

5. **Prepare working papers:** The assigned auditor then prepares the audit working papers that will identify what the auditor wants to verify, what questions to ask, and what they expect as evidence. This will be drawn from the QMS documentation and the ISO 9001 standard.

6. **Determine the audit sequence:** The next step is to determine the sequence of audit from the opening meeting through presenting audit findings. If done right, the sequence of process audits can help make the audit flow easier. Some examples are starting a large audit with a review of internal control and corrective actions, which will give you an idea of what weaknesses have already been identified, or ending the audit with a review of documentation records and training records, because the process audits will have identified records to review, making this easier.

7. **Conduct opening meeting:** The audit begins with an opening meeting. This is to reiterate to the auditees that this is not a surprise audit, and is being done to verify conformance rather than to find fault. Some fine tuning of the audit times can be done at the opening meeting, as well as making sure that everyone understands the scope and extent of this particular audit.

8. **Review documents and communicate:** After the meeting, any documents immediately presented by the auditee should be reviewed to gather relevant information that might not have been available before (an example would be a process improvement that is being used on a trial basis but is not yet in the documentation). A general rule is that communication should be maintained throughout the audit.

9. **Carry out the audit:** This step is often thought of as the actual audit. The auditor asks the questions, and collects the records and observations that will demonstrate if the processes meet the QMS requirements. Again, it is important to remember that an auditor is there to try to verify that a process conforms to the requirements set out, not to dig until fault is found.

10. **Generate audit findings:** After the auditor finishes the verification, they must generate the audit findings and prepare any audit conclusions to be presented. If all is found to be conforming, then there will be no corrective actions presented; if not, then the corrective actions need to be properly prepared. It is equally important to highlight best practices in a process as it is to identify any shortcomings. Some companies also use a process of having internal audits identify opportunities for improvement, which the process owner can review and accept if they wish.

11. **Present findings and conclusions:** The findings and conclusions are then presented, normally at a closing meeting, in order for the process owners to understand and ask questions as well as present clarification if something was misunderstood in the audit.

12. **Formally distribute audit report:** The final findings are formally written and distributed in an audit report. This gives everyone an easy reference on actions needed, as well as providing a record of the outcome of the audit.
13. **Follow-up on actions/corrective actions:** Probably the most important part of an audit is for the auditor to follow-up on any actions, as a way of ensuring remedial action is taken and completing the audit. Without follow-up of corrections and corrective actions, the same problems could be found continually during subsequent audits, which defeats the purpose of the audit.

2.3 Internal Audit Planning

Like any other managerial exercise, internal audit work requires planning, which involves the setting up of the internal audit objectives and means of achieving them. It involves a careful arrangement of activities to be carried out in the auditee's department/client's organization.

Before the start of each year, the internal audit plan shall be distributed to the managers of the entities or units to be audited with the assignments being distributed to the planned audit leaders and auditors. In the case of publicly quoted companies, audit plans are approved by the audit committee or board of directors/reporting authority. The internal audit plan will focus on risk areas derived from the auditor's risk assessment of the enterprise (Institute of Chartered Accountants of Nigeria—ICAN, 2013).

During the planning stage of the audit, the auditor notifies the client of the audit, discusses the scope and objectives of the examination in a formal meeting with organization management/manager of the department, gathers information on important processes, evaluates existing controls, and plans the remaining audit steps.

The auditor creates a checklist that consists of all procedures applicable to the entity being audited, with comments, where applicable, of findings during the previous audit.

At the preparation stage, any audit team member can provide the audit leader with support in relation to the planning and proposed scope of the audit.

At least one week before the audit, the audit leader shall confirm to the head of the audit unit or the chief audit executive (CAE) that the preparations for the audit are completed, and also agree with the manager of the entity to be audited on the date, time, and scope of the audit.

It is important to note that audits may be delayed or deferred with the agreement of the audit leader and the manager of the entity to be audited. However, it is expected that where the audit is delayed for more than two weeks beyond the planned date or rescheduled, the audit leader shall inform the head of the audit unit, and provide the reasons for the delay.

2.4 Audit Conduct

According to ESCC 11100 (2005), the audit leader shall chair an opening conference with auditors and the auditee's members. At this conference, the audit leader shall

1. Review the scope and reference point of the audit
2. Explain the planned activities and schedule
3. Identify and agree on any amendment or revisions to planned activities

It is pertinent to note that during the audit, the auditors are expected to use the already prepared checklists as a guide to help them in confirming compliance and identifying areas of improvement.

The auditors are to document all findings and noncompliances identified in the course of the audit using internal audit finding reports, as they are detected. The auditor shall obtain confirmation from the individuals being audited in the case of any noncompliance.

An Internal Audit Finding Record is provided in Section 6.3.6.5 (Format A, B and C).

The audit, and all associated findings, are to be extracted from the interview of relevant staff and the review of documentary evidence of conformance or non-conformance to the procedure under consideration. Audit members shall note all documentary evidence and pass same to the audit leader. Note that lack of required documentary evidence shall, in itself, form a nonconformance.

At the end of the audit, the audit leader shall

a. Collate and organize the results from each auditor
b. Chair a closing conference with the auditors, the manager of the entity being audited, and, if desired, the members of the entity audited

At the closing meeting/conference, the audit leader shall

a. Review all findings of the audit
b. Review all observations, nonconformances, and recommendations for corrective/preventive action from the audit
c. Correct any erroneous information resulting from the audit
d. Agree with the manager of the entity being audited with the factual information documented in the audit records
e. Agree with the manager of the entity being audited on all corrective/preventive actions and their schedule for implementation

It may not be practically possible to identify all suitable corrective/preventive actions immediately. Where this happens, the audit leader and the manager of the entity being audited shall agree on a plan of activities to define and on the necessary corrective/preventive actions, and this is not expected to exceed two weeks after the closing conference of the audit.

Where the audit leader and the manager of the entity being audited are unable to reach an agreement on remedial action, or where applicable, there is no budget authority, regarding the audit findings for appropriate corrective or preventive actions for an identified deficiency, then this shall be immediately reported to the head of the audit department. In such circumstances, the head of the audit department shall resolve the disagreements directly with the manager of the audited entity. But where this is not possible, the head of the audit department shall refer the issue to progressively higher-level authorities in the hierarchy until a satisfactory solution is agreed.

2.4.1 Assessment Techniques

These are techniques designed to ensure internal auditors fully understand internal control procedures and determine whether employees are complying with internal control instructions.

2.4.1.1 Preliminary Phase Assessment Techniques

Customarily, auditors try to avoid or minimize disrupting the daily workflow by starting the internal audit process using an indirect assessment technique. These include reviewing existing documentations such as flowcharts, office manuals, and departmental control policies. Another common assessment technique at this phase of auditing is creating audit trails that trace specific processes from start to finish.

2.4.1.2 Fieldwork Phase Assessment Techniques

Techniques in the second phase, including one-on-one interviews and process observations, are techniques internal auditors use if audit trails or document reviews do not fully answer the auditor's questions.

The audit tools and techniques at this level include

- Computer-assisted audit technique (CAAT)
- Electronic work papers
- Continuous/real-time auditing
- Risk-based audit planning
- Control self-assessment
- Other electronic communication
- Institute of Internal Auditors (IIA) quality assurance review tools
- Benchmarking
- Analytical review
- Process mapping applications
- Flowchart software

- Statistical sampling
- Total quality management techniques
- Balanced scorecard (BSC) or similar framework
- Process modeling software
- Data mining
- Data analytics (business intelligence/descriptive analytics, predictive analytics, and prescriptive analytics)

While we shall describe some tools and techniques as part of subsequent chapters, we shall concentrate only on balanced scorecard, data mining, and data analytics tools in this chapter.

2.5 Documentation of Audit Results

Following the audit, the audit leader shall prepare an audit report, following the structure defined in Sections 6.4.3.1 (Internal Audit Report [Appendix C]) through 6.4.3.5 (Action Plan Template).

The audit leader shall ensure that all audit finding reports are numbered sequentially.

Within one month of the audit, the audit leader shall review the audit report with the manager of the audited entity to ensure it is correct and complete, and then distribute the audit report to the appropriate recipients.

2.6 Audit Conduct Analysis

The head of the audit unit is responsible for monitoring the conduct of audits and shall assess the implementation of the internal audit program to verify whether

1. Audits are conducted as scheduled in the internal audit plan.
2. The auditors are competent based on their training, technical experience, and any previous audits.
3. The auditors are implementing audits according to the procedure.
4. Audit results are properly documented in audit reports and audit finding reports.
5. Corrective and preventive actions are implemented as agreed.

2.7 Audit Findings, Follow-Up and Closure

According to ESCC 11100 (2005), it is the responsibility of the manager of the audited entity to ensure that the agreed corrective/preventive actions are implemented as intended. When the planned corrective/preventive action has been implemented, the manager of the audited entity shall inform the relevant audit leader, who shall in turn verify the implementation action and update the audit finding report log accordingly.

When the corrective or preventive actions are not implemented by the agreed deadline, the audit leader shall inform the head of the audit unit, who shall then verify either the effectiveness of all corrective/preventive actions at the time of action closure or the next internal audit, as appropriate.

2.8 Internal Auditing Process: A Collaborative Effort

According to AuditNet LLC (2014), during each stage in the audit process— planning (sometimes called survey or preliminary review), fieldwork, audit report, and follow-up review—the client/auditee has the opportunity to participate in the process. It has been observed that the process works best when client management or the auditee and the internal audit team have a solid working relationship founded on clear and continuing communication.

As a result, many clients/auditees tend to extend this working relationship beyond the particular audit. Once the audit department has worked with management in this way on a project, it should have an understanding of the distinctive characteristics of the client/auditee unit's operations. As a result, it can help appraise the feasibility of making further modifications in their operations.

2.9 Balanced Scorecard (BSC) in Internal Audit Department

Why a BSC?

A BSC is a *framework* that helps organizations *translate strategy into operational objectives* that drive both *behavior* and *performance.*

It is a strategy-focused approach to performance management that includes nonfinancial and financial performance measures of efficiency and effectiveness that are derived from the organization's vision and strategy. It *balances* the following:

- External measures for shareholders and customers with internal measures for internal business processes, innovation, and learning and growth
- Outcome measures (lagging indicators) and measures of future performance (performance drivers or leading indicators)
- Objective and subjective performance measures

Remember: What can't be measured can't be managed, and what gets measured gets done!

We shall, in this study, concentrate on the BSC as it relates or cascades to the internal audit department rather than the organization as whole.

2.9.1 Terminologies

According to eXample Consulting Group (2015), some of the commonly used terms in a BSC include the following.

Strategy: Refers to how management plans to achieve the organization's objectivity. It is an expression of what the organization must do to get from one reference point to another reference point. Strategy is expressed in terms of mission statements, vision, goals, and objectives. Strategy is usually developed by the top level of the organization and executed by lower levels in the organization.

Perspectives: Different views that drive the organization. Perspectives provide a framework for measurement. The four common perspectives in a BSC are financial (final outcomes), customer, internal processes, and learning and growth.

Cause–effect relationship: The natural flow of business performance from a lower level to an upper level within or between perspectives. For example, training employees on customer relations leads to better customer service, which, in turn, leads to improved financial results. One side is a leader or driver, producing an end result or effect on the other side.

Goal: An overall achievement that is considered critical to the future success of the organization. Goals express where the organizations want to be. What we must achieve to be successful.

Examples:

- Microsoft: A computer on every desk and every home
- Motorola: Attain Six Sigma quality; win Baldridge Award; Achieve USD 10 billion revenues by 2020
- Twitter: Become the pulse of the planet

Strategic theme (area): Strategic themes are the main, high-level business strategies that form the basis for the organization's business model. They apply to every part of the organization and define what major strategic thrusts the organization will pursue to achieve its vision—a major strategic thrust for the organization such as maximizing shareholder value or improving efficiency of operations.

Examples:

- Operational excellence
- Service excellence
- Breakthrough innovation
- Strategic partnering
- Strategic outsourcing

Strategic maps: A logical framework for organizing a collection of strategic objectives over the BSC perspectives. Everything is linked to capture a cause–effect relationship. Strategy maps are the foundation for a BSC.

Objective: What specifically must be done to execute the strategy? What is critical to the future success of the strategy? What the organization must do to reach its goal. Action statements linked to execution of strategy. Specific outcomes are expressed in measurable terms (*not* activities).

Examples:

- Reduce cycle time
- Improve employee motivation
- Enhance asset/equipment availability
- Launch new products
- Outsource support tasks

Measures: Indicators and monitors to track performance.

Measurement: A way of *monitoring and tracking* the *progress of strategic objectives*. Measurements can be *leading* indicators of performance (leads to an end result) or *lagging* indicators (the end results).

Examples:

- Defect percentage
- Customer satisfaction score
- Employee retention percentage
- Asset uptime percentage
- Order to delivery cycle time
- Project management to schedule (deviation)

Target: An expected level of performance or improvement required in the future. Desired level of performance and timelines.

Examples:

- Staff retention to 80%
- Cash to cash cycle 30 days
- Productivity 85%
- Customer satisfaction score 4.2 (average)

Programs: Major initiatives or projects that must be undertaken in order to meet one or more strategic objectives.

Examples:

- Six Sigma
- Talent management

- Employee engagement
- Customer relationship management
- Service turnaround improvement
- E-learning

Mission: Why we exist; why we are in business.

Vision: What we want to be in the future; our picture of the future or desired future state.

Initiatives: Planned actions to achieve objectives.

2.9.2 Benefits of a BSC

According to ISACA and IIA (2013), the key benefits of BSCs are

- Describing and clarifying the departmental strategy and strategic themes
- Communicating departmental strategies and priorities throughout the department
- Aligning performance measures of efficiency and effectiveness to departmental and corporate strategy
- Identifying leading indicators that drive outcome performance measures in internal auditing departments
- Identifying cause-and-effect linkages between performance measures
- Enhancing the usefulness of benchmarking performance measures from the Global Audit Information Network (GAIN)
- Focusing departmental activities on value-added services and other corporate strategies and priorities
- Using performance measures as a continuous improvement tool

2.9.3 Performance Measures for Internal Auditing

The IIA attribute standards 1311 states that internal assessments should include

a. Ongoing reviews of the performance of internal audit activity
b. Periodic reviews performed through self-assessment or by other persons within the organization, with knowledge of internal audit practices and the standards.

On September 29, 2005, the IIA released Practice Advisory (PA) 1311-2: Establishing Measures to Support Review of Internal Audit Activities Performance. PA 1311-1 suggests using analysis of performance measures as one method for conducting these reviews.

To establish effective performance measurements, the CAE should establish a measurement process that

- Identifies critical performance categories to measure, e.g., internal customer expectations. This advisory suggests the use of the following categories based on a BSC approach:
  - **Stakeholder expectations** of audit committee, executive management, etc.
  - **Internal audit process** including risk assessment, planning, and audit methodologies
  - **Innovation and capabilities** that include the use of technology, training, and industry knowledge
- Identifies performance category strategies and measurements. Strategies are typically based on methods to comply with IIA Standards, other professional standards, and stakeholder expectations.
- Provides an effective ongoing performance measurement and reporting process.
- Links to strategies and includes specific baseline and target measurements to monitor progress.

Implementing the use of performance measures, as a method of ongoing review, is one element of the internal audit activity's internal assessment process. Another key element is periodic self-assessment of the internal audit activity's compliance with the standards.

2.9.3.1 Identifying Critical Performance Categories

The CAE should identify key performance measurement categories such as stakeholder expectations, audit processes, and innovation and capabilities of internal audit.

Stakeholders could include the audit committee, executive management, external government bodies and regulators, and the external auditors. Audit processes could include risk assessment, planning, and audit methodologies. Innovation and capabilities could include effective use of technology, training, and industry knowledge.

In the next step, the CAE should determine what objectives to meet in each of the above categories, using the mission, strategy, and organization of the activity. It is important to ensure that the applicable IIA Standards and laws and regulations are identified as guidelines for setting strategies. In addition to the IIA Standards, there may be other applicable professional standards.

The performance measure selected by an internal audit activity will depend on the resources available to collect the necessary data in a systematic way. We shall consider some suggested performance indicators as listed in Appendix B of IIA's attribute standard 1311.

2.9.3.2 *Identifying Performance Category Strategies and Measurements*

In identifying performance category strategies and measurements, the IIA Standards, other applicable professional standards; the corporate and internal audit activity mission and strategy, laws and regulations; and the internal audit activity charter will provide an effective foundation for determining the appropriate strategies for each category of performance. Performance category strategies and measurements are based on this foundation and an analysis of stakeholder expectations.

Stakeholder expectations: Typically the key stakeholders for the internal audit activity are divided into internal and external stakeholders.

Internal stakeholders may include

- Board/audit committee
- Senior and operating management

On the other hand, external stakeholders may include

- Regulators
- External audit

The CAE should identify all relevant stakeholders and perform an assessment of their expectations (and corresponding priorities) and any identified gaps. Assessments can be performed via interviews, facilitated sessions, and questionnaires. As gaps are identified, the CAE is encouraged to develop an appropriate action plan. The expectations among stakeholders may need to be reconciled and validated. In doing this, consideration should be given to

- The extent of regulation for the organization or audit activity
- The relationship with the key internal and external stakeholders
- The nature of the organization (e.g., publicly versus privately held)

Internal audit processes: The IIA Performance Standards should be considered in identifying performance measurement categories in internal audit processes. Examples of internal audit process categories and potential areas to measure in each category are as follows:

- **Risk assessment/audit planning**
  - Are measures in place to ensure that key risk areas are being addressed?
  - Are measures in place to ensure that appropriate managers are involved in the risk assessment and audit planning processes?
  - Percentage of resources allocated to addressing audit committee risk concerns and percentage allocated to addressing senior management risk concerns.

  - Areas where risk concerns have been mitigated/addressed (reduced partially, i.e., from severe to moderate) by effective internal audit evaluation and comment.
  - Extent to which the audit committee, senior management, and external auditor believe the internal audit has effectively addressed risk concerns.
- **Planning and performing the audit engagement**
  - Are measurements in place to ensure that appropriate audit plans are established for each engagement that include scope, objectives, timing, and resource allocations?
  - Are measurements in place to ensure that audits are performed in accordance with established audit methodologies and working practices?
- **Communication and reporting**
  - Is feedback obtained from key stakeholders on the quality, level of detail, and frequency of audit communications?
  - Does the internal audit activity measure the degree that key recommendations are implemented?

Innovation and capability: The IIA Attribute and Performance Standards should be considered in identifying performance measurement categories related to the internal audit activities' innovation and capability. Examples of innovation and capability categories and potential areas to measure in each category are as follows:

- **Training**
  - Are measurements in place to ensure that audit staff receive sufficient training (hours of training per staff, completion by staff of critical training subjects, etc.)?
  - Is audit staff satisfied with training measured?
- **Use of technology**
  - Have goals been established for staff training in the use of technology? Are measures in place to ensure these goals are achieved?
  - Have goals been established for using technology to effectively support audit testing and analysis? Are measures in place to ensure these goals are achieved?
- **Industry knowledge**
  - Are measures in place to ensure that the staff has sufficient knowledge of industry, business, operations, and key functions (e.g., measuring the completion of orientation sessions, audit projects in key areas, working in the operations)?

A pictorial representation of performance categories and related measures relevant to internal audit activity is shown in Figure 2.1.

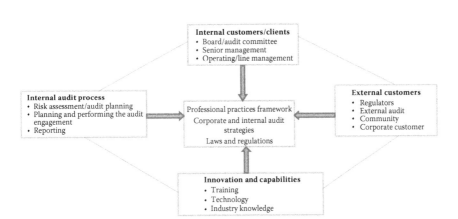

Figure 2.1 Performance categories and related measures relevant to internal audit activity.

2.9.3.3 Reasons for Performance Measurement

McMaster University's discussion paper on *performance indicators* stated some reasons for performance measurement as follows:

1. To clarify the mission and vision of the organization
2. To assist in translating its strategy into measurable objectives
3. To allow the organization to measure progress
4. To understand what improves results
5. To improve accountability and decision making
6. To align operational activities and resources with strategic objectives
7. To encourage dialogue
8. To share understanding of activities planned to deliver objectives
9. To give clear communication of expectations to all organizational levels

2.9.3.4 Creating an Effective Performance Measurement and Reporting Process

The CAE should establish a measurement process that drives behavior that supports established audit activity goals/objectives and that provides an appropriate assessment of achievement of those goals/objectives (Figure 2.2). An effective ongoing process would include

- Performance measures that are aligned with the IIA Standards, key strategic objectives, and applicable laws and regulations. These measures can be both qualitative and quantitative. Measurement points should be clear, measurable, achievable, realistic goals or standards.
- Consistent processes for gathering, summarizing, and analyzing measurement data and providing timely feedback.

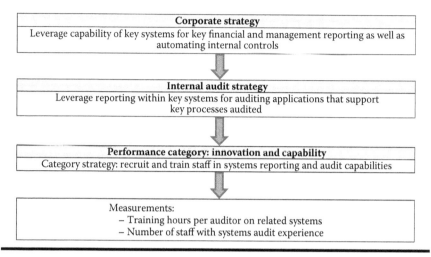

Figure 2.2 Determining appropriate performance measurements for innovation and capabilities by CAE.

- Processes to ensure measures are kept current with changing expectations, conditions, priorities, and objectives.
- Reporting of the results of the measurement process to department management and key stakeholders.
- Annual reporting on the effectiveness of the internal audit activity to the audit committee.

2.9.3.5 Strategic Questions to Address

In designing your metrics and performance measures, they must address the following questions:

1. What is the value proposition of your team?
2. How do we make the performance indicator transparent to our stakeholder?
3. How can your team fulfill unmet and changing customer/client needs?
4. How will your team innovate its offerings?
5. How will your team manage its brand?
6. How will your team achieve and measure operational excellence?
7. How will your team partner strategically both internally and externally?
8. How will your team communicate strategically within the department and to clients to build and reinforce its brand and communicate its value proposition?
9. How will your team truly engage employees in achieving the mission and strategy of the department?
10. Are we in a position to establish professional/national/regional standards in some categories?

2.9.3.6 Evaluation of Current Internal Auditing Performance Metrics (Table 2.1 and Figure 2.3)

Table 2.1   Evaluation of Current Internal Auditing Performance Metrics

Performance Measurement Category	*Departmental Metrics*	*Poor–Less than Adequate*	*Adequate– Good*	*Very Good– Excellent*
Financial				
Customer/client				
Internal process				
Learning and growth				
Innovation				
Employee				
Information technology				
Supplier/vendor				

Source: Adapted from ISACA and IIA (2013). A balanced scorecard framework for internal auditing. Orange County Chapter.

Note: Consider current department metrics (what are they?), and rate each item for your team according to the categories provided.

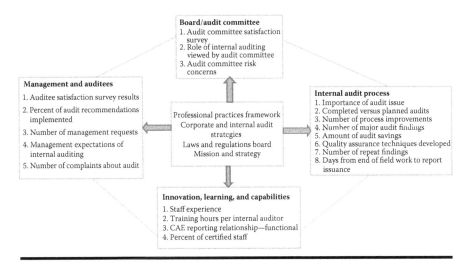

Figure 2.3   Balanced scorecard framework for internal auditing department with measures considered most important by CAEs. (Adapted from ISACA and IIA (2013). A balanced scorecard framework for internal auditing. Orange County Chapter.)

2.9.4 Steps to Create a BSC

Step 1—Identify what your customers/clients want
Step 2—Assess internal audit's capabilities
Step 3—Develop strategic objectives
Step 4—Identify performance measures
Step 5—Identify targets and initiatives
Step 6—Develop a strategic map
Step 7—Develop a scorecard for each category

2.9.4.1 Step 1—Identify What Your Customers/Clients Want

A BSC provides a framework to develop performance measures that incorporate the attributes, deliverables, and capabilities of internal audit key stakeholders value, as well as related shortcomings or advancements in these areas (Table 2.2).

Seek feedback as to the following:

■ The purpose and responsibility of internal auditing and whether that is understood by different levels within the organization and all the stakeholders
■ Adequacy of internal audit independence and objectivity
■ Target deliverables and expectations of the internal audit activity

Table 2.2 Internal Auditing Value Proposition = Product/Service Attributes (Functionality, Quality, Time, Cost) + Departmental Image + Customer Relationship

Customer Value Proposition	
Basic Requirements	*Differentiators*
Efficiency	Specialized experts
Objectivity	Best practices knowledge
Technical competence	Specialized teams
Professional standards	Thought leader
Due professional care	
Independence	
Knowledge of company and industry	

Source: Adapted from ISACA and IIA (2013). A balanced scorecard framework for internal auditing. Orange County Chapter.

- Current or planned business priorities and correlation of those with the activity's scope, as appropriate
- Current shortcomings or gaps, if any, of the internal audit activity
- Quality and sufficiency of communication from internal audit activity
- Current level of satisfaction, or lack thereof, with the frequency and nature of engagements planned and performed
- Current level of satisfaction, or lack thereof, with the internal audit activity's resources
- Changing needs of business, related risks, and ability of internal auditing to provide assurance and consulting services

2.9.4.2 Step 2—Assess Internal Audit's Capabilities

We advise that the IIA's Internal Audit Capability Model be utilized or referred to in assessing internal audit capabilities.

What Is the Internal Audit Capability Model?

- A communication vehicle—a basis for communicating what is meant by effective internal auditing and how it serves an organization and its stakeholders, and for advocating the importance of internal auditing to decision makers.
- Framework for assessment—a framework for assessing the capabilities of an internal auditing activity against professional internal audit standards and practices, either as a self-assessment or an external assessment.
- Road map for orderly improvement—a road map for building capability that sets out the steps an organization can follow to establish and strengthen its internal auditing activity.

The Internal Audit Capability Model is a valuable tool that the organization can use to

- Determine its internal audit requirements according to the nature, complexity, and associated risks of its operations
- Assess its existing internal audit capabilities against the requirements it has determined
- Identify any significant gaps between those requirements and its existing internal audit capabilities and work toward developing the appropriate level of internal audit capability (Figure 2.4 and Table 2.3)

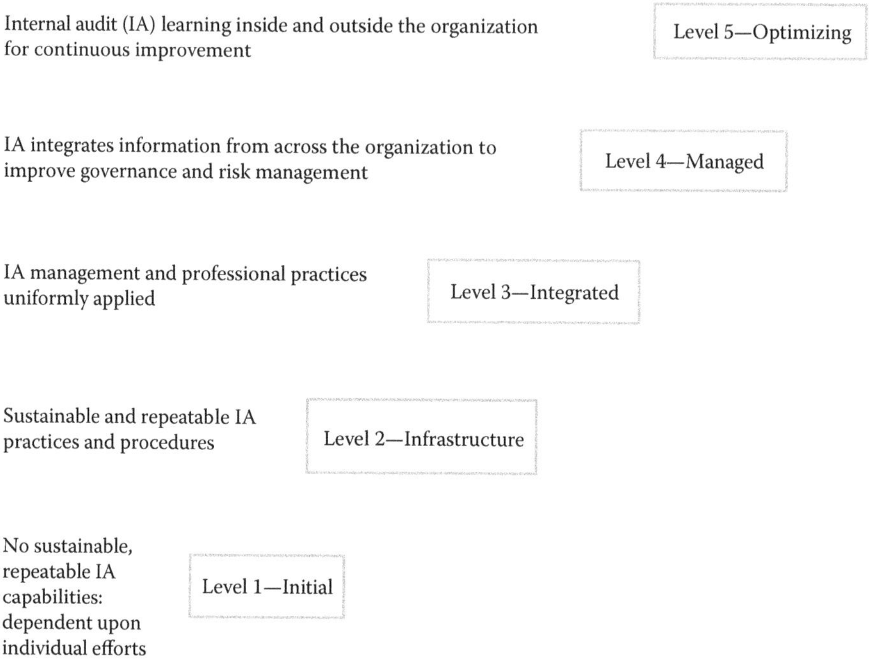

Internal audit (IA) learning inside and outside the organization for continuous improvement

Level 5—Optimizing

IA integrates information from across the organization to improve governance and risk management

Level 4—Managed

IA management and professional practices uniformly applied

Level 3—Integrated

Sustainable and repeatable IA practices and procedures

Level 2—Infrastructure

No sustainable, repeatable IA capabilities: dependent upon individual efforts

Level 1—Initial

Figure 2.4   Internal audit capability levels. (Adapted from ISACA and IIA (2013). A balanced scorecard framework for internal auditing. Orange County Chapter.)

Table 2.3　Internal Audit Capability Model Matrix

	Services and Role of Internal Auditing (IA)	*People Management*	*Professional Practice*	*Performance Management and Accountability*	*Organizational Relationships and Culture*	*Governance Structure*
Level 5—Optimizing	IA recognized as key agent of change	Involvement with professional bodies, workforce projection	Continuous improvement in professional practices, strategic IA planning	Reporting of IA effectiveness	Effective and ongoing relationships	Independence, power, and authority of the IA activity
Level 4—Managed	Overall assurance on governance, risk management, and control	IA contributes to management development, IA activity supports professional bodies, workforce planning	Audit strategy leverages organization's management of risk	Integration of qualitative and quantitative performance measures	CAE advises and influences top-level management	Independent oversight of the IA activity, CAE reports to top-level authority

(Continued)

Table 2.3 (Continued) Internal Audit Capability Model Matrix

	Services and Role of Internal Auditing (IA)	People Management	Professional Practice	Performance Management and Accountability	Organizational Relationships and Culture	Governance Structure
Level 3—Integrated	Advisory services, performance/value-for-money audits	Team building and competency, professionally qualified staff, workforce coordination	Quality management framework, risk-based audit plans	Performance measures, cost information, IA management reports	Coordination with other review groups, integral component of management team	Management oversight of the IA activity, funding mechanisms
Level 2—Infrastructure	Compliance auditing	Individual professional development, skilled people identified and recruited	Professional practices and processes framework, audit plan based on management/stakeholder priorities	IA operating budget, IA business plan	Managing within the IA activity	Full access to the organization's information, assets, and people; reporting relationships established
Level 1—Initial	Ad hoc and unstructured; isolated single audits or reviews of documents and transactions for accuracy and compliance; outputs dependent on the skills of specific individuals holding the position; no specific professional practices established other than those provided by professional associations; funding approved by management, as needed; absence of infrastructure; auditors likely part of a larger organizational unit; no established capabilities; therefore, no specific key process areas					

Source: Adapted from ISACA and IIA (2013). A balanced scorecard framework for internal auditing. Orange County Chapter.

2.9.4.3 Step 3—Develop Strategic Objectives

Consider the identified value propositions and critical success factors for each area of the BSC (audit committee, external customers, internal audit processes, innovation and capabilities, and management) and develop strategic objectives to leverage strengths, address weaknesses, harvest opportunities, and attack threats (SWOT) (Figure 2.5).

On the basis of the customer needs, prepare a listing of strategic objectives (e.g., Table 2.4).

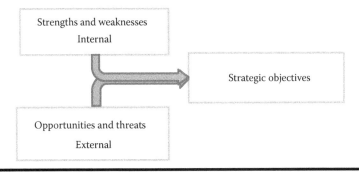

Figure 2.5 SWOT analysis. (Adapted from ISACA and IIA (2013). A balanced scorecard framework for internal auditing. Orange County Chapter.)

Table 2.4 Board/Audit Committee Metrics Scorecard

Objectives	Measure	Schedule	Rating
Internal audit will have appropriate level resources to perform the fiduciary responsibility	Staff head count, rotations, and turnover	1	
Internal audit will appropriate professional qualifications and competencies to perform their duties	Staff experience and qualifications Staff certification Staff training	2 3 4	
Internal audit identifies key issues and works with management to facilitate/cause corrective action(s) to be taken	Agreed action summary	5	
Internal audit provides appropriate coverage to all aspects of the company's business activities	Audit plan completion	9	

Source: IIA—A Balanced Scorecard for Internal Audit Departments.

2.9.4.4 Step 4—Identify Performance Measures

Consider the identified strategic objectives and develop one or more performance measures for each objective. Performance measures can either be objective or subjective, as well as either leading or lagging indicators of performance. In addition, they should reflect the mandate and role of the internal audit activity (Figure 2.6).

Why measure performance? Because "what gets measured gets done."

Some Suggested Performance Measures
Stakeholder expectations:

- At least 70% of the time is spent on direct audit hours.
- Over a three-year cycle, at least 1000 hours will be spent on
  - Compliance audits
  - Consulting
  - Information technology audits
  - Performance measurement
  - Operational auditing
  - Risk management
  - Value for money audits
- Fraud investigations are concluded within 60 days of an employee being suspended.
- Client survey is conducted for every operational audit, and results are summarized for the audit committee.

Internal audit processes:

- An in-depth risk assessment will be conducted every three years.
- Risk assessment profile will be updated annually.

Figure 2.6 Process of developing performance measures. (Adapted from ISACA and IIA (2013). A balanced scorecard framework for internal auditing. Orange County Chapter.)

- Over a three-year cycle, some aspects of every department will be audited even if no activity is identified in risk assessment ranking.
- All audit assignments over 50 hours have an audit plan.
- Audit projects are within 10% of the approved budget or maximum of 50 hours over budget.
- Operational audit reports are issued within six weeks after exit interview.
- Final reports are issued two weeks after management responses are received.
- Management implements over 75% of the recommendations within two years of audit report issuance.
- Management accepts over 90% of the recommendations in the audit reports.

Innovation and capabilities:

- All staff at associate level and higher will have at least one auditing designation (CIA, CFE, CFI, CISA, etc.).
- At least 10% of the staff time is spent on professional development.
- All staff proficiently use data analysis tools (ACL, IDEA, etc.).
- Staff understand the role of legislation, regulation, policy, directives, and program procedures in relation to employees and the public.

Vital performance measures:

- Staff experience
- Role of internal auditing viewed by the audit committee
- Management expectation of internal auditing
- Percentage of internal audit recommendations implemented
- Internal auditor education levels
- Auditee satisfaction survey
- Importance of audit issue
- Training hour per internal auditor
- Audit committee satisfaction survey results
- CAE reporting relationships—functional

Others include

- IIA professional standards
- Budgets
- Customer surveys
- GAIN benchmarks

Figure 2.7 shows an example of leading and lagging indicators associated with several critical performance categories.

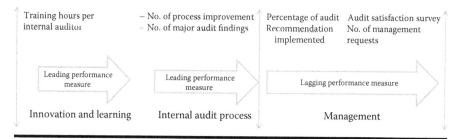

Figure 2.7 Leading and lagging indicators with critical performance categories. (Adapted from ISACA and IIA (2013). A balanced scorecard framework for internal auditing. Orange County Chapter.)

2.9.4.5 Step 5—Identify Targets and Initiatives

Performance measures driven by strategic objectives should similarly drive targets and their corresponding initiatives (Figure 2.8).

Prepare a listing of the targets and initiatives for internal audit and its related performance measure (Table 2.5).

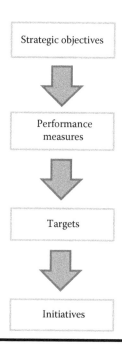

Figure 2.8 Process of developing targets and initiatives. (Adapted from ISACA and IIA (2013). A balanced scorecard framework for internal auditing. Orange County Chapter.)

Table 2.5   Example Audit Committee Metrics

Strategic Objective	Performance Measures	Frequency/ Type	Responsible
The audit function maintains independence with the organization	Reporting to appropriate level of management determined by organizational structure/reporting lines	On-going— leading (on changes from current status	CD
Internal audit provides adequate coverage to all appropriate aspects of the organization's business activities	Annual and long-term plans and risk assessment reviews Comparison of planned to actual coverage	Annual— leading Annual— lagging	LD
Internal audit identifies key issues and works with management to facilitate/cause corrective action to be taken	Analysis of issues raised by tier, issues closed, issues remaining open/past due date	Quarterly— lagging	LD

Source: IIA—A Balanced Scorecard for Internal Audit Departments.

2.9.4.6 Step 6—Develop a Strategic Map (Figure 2.9)

What are the benefits of strategy mapping?

- Strategy maps are used to develop strategic objectives for key strategic themes.
- Strategic objectives are linked and organized within the four perspectives of the BSC.
- Performance measures for strategic objectives are identified, and baseline performance and targets are established.

Key point: Performance measures are specific, measurable, attainable, relevant, and time bound.

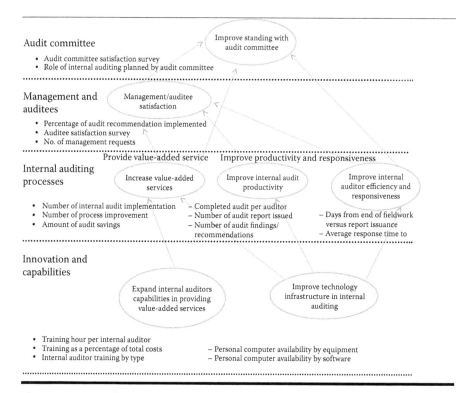

Figure 2.9 Develop a strategic map.

2.9.4.7 Step 7—Develop a Scorecard for Each Category

For each critical performance category, develop a scorecard noting the relevant performance measures to be communicated (Table 2.6).

Closing—How to Ensure Success

A good performance measurement system for internal auditing departments should have certain characteristics, as follows:

- Performance measures are driven by mission, vision, and strategy.
- Performance measures should represent a balanced set of performance measures that reflect operational effectiveness and strategy.
- Performance measurement systems should include
  - Cause and effect linkages (strategic map)
  - Leading indicators (performance drivers)
  - Linkages to outcome performance measures (lagging indicators)
- Performance measures should be unique/customized to a department.
- Performance measurement systems require continuous refinement.

Table 2.6 Critical Performance Category: Audit Committee

Strategic Objective	Performance Measure	Targets	Initiatives
Internal audit provides appropriate coverage to all aspects of the company's business activities	Audit plan completion	X # of operational audits	
Internal audit will have appropriate professional qualifications and competencies to perform their duties	Staff experience and qualifications Staff certifications Staff training	X years of average experience X% of staff certified X hours of training per auditor	
Internal audit will have appropriate levels of resources to perform their fiduciary responsibilities	Staff head count, rotations, and turnover	X FTEs % of YTD turnover versus prior year	Development of rotational staff
Internal audit should meet the expectations of various constituencies, including: the AC, BU management, audit staff, external auditors, and regulators	Employee survey results Client survey results Regulator feedback External auditor analysis Audit committee survey/feedback	Overall average score greater than X Advise AC of scores greater than 2 std. deviations from mean	
Periodic evaluation of the internal audit function	Results of internal self-assessment	Remediation of findings identified during self-assessment	

Source: Adapted from ISACA and IIA (2013). A balanced scorecard framework for internal auditing. Orange County Chapter.

■ Leadership at the top is crucial for setting a clear message that metrics are key to success.
■ Metrics should be made available to all appropriate persons, including all auditing members, so that improvements in performance can be made.
■ Quality metrics should be specific and appropriate for each organization and should be based on the organization's goals and strategic plan.
■ Quality measures do not necessarily measure productivity. Rather, they measure performance against a standard.
■ Accurate audit data must be maintained by auditors, and standards must be established so that the measures apply equally to everyone.
■ Quality measures should be visually displayed so that they can easily be analyzed.

Did we answer all the strategic questions?

2.10 Technology-Based Audit Techniques

Internal auditors always strive to improve the efficiency and effectiveness of business processes. Internal audit organizations created or helped create various frameworks such as the Committee of Sponsoring Organizations of the Treadway Commission (COSO), Control Objectives for Information Technology (COBIT), and the International Professional Practices Framework (IPPF), to standardize the profession and share best practices. The organizations also created guidance within these frameworks for the use of automated tools to help with the efficiency and effectiveness of the auditing process itself.

Technology-based audit techniques, in particular, play a part in the audit process. The IPPF references technology-based audit techniques as noted in Figure 2.10.

Figure 2.10 Business process relationships. (Retrieved from *International Journal of Business Intelligence Research*, 3(3), 42–53, July–September 2012 43; Business Intelligence in Audit. Copyright 2012, IGI Global.)

According to IIA (2011) Standards, "Internal auditors must have sufficient knowledge of key information technology risks and controls available and technology-based audit techniques to perform their assigned work. However, not all internal auditors are expected to have the expertise of an internal auditor whose primary responsibility is information technology auditing" (Standard 1210.A3).

Again, the IIA (2011) Standards state that, "In exercising due professional care internal auditors must consider the use of technology-based audit and other data analysis techniques" (Standard 1220.A2).

According to IIA (2011), technology-based audit techniques are defined as "any automated audit tool, such as generalized audit software, test data generators, computerized audit programs, specialized audit utilities, and computer-assisted audit techniques (CAATs)."

Usually, in a noninformation technology audit, technology-based audit and data analysis techniques are applied during the enterprise-wide risk assessment, project- or process-specific risk assessments, and CAATs for automated tests of transactions. The procedures can range from limited analytical review up to automated scripts that identify processing exceptions in real time. According to the IIA 2010 Common Body of Knowledge (CBOK) report titled "Core competencies for today's internal auditor," the worldwide use of analytical review is about 65% and the adoption rate for CAATs is less than 50% (Bailey, 2010, as cited in Leticia, 2012).

According to Leticia (2012), the tools used for technology-based audit and data analysis techniques vary widely and include software packages such as Microsoft Excel, Access, and Structure Query Language (SQL), and generalized audit software such as Audit Command Language (ACL), IDEA, and Oversight. It has been identified that Microsoft suite is by far the most utilized software by internal audit. Internal auditors not only use Microsoft products for analysis, but also for documentation.

However, the growing volume of data in contemporary businesses and the ever-growing expectations of various stakeholders from the internal audit function is shifting technology-based audit to data mining and analytics.

2.10.1 Data Mining in Auditing

2.10.1.1 Introduction

Finding a needle in a haystack: Fraud, noncompliance, and inefficiencies exist in virtually every organization and cost businesses billions of dollars each year. The difficulty is finding them, and if you cannot find them, you cannot prevent or resolve them. Thus, the *finding a needle in a haystack* analogy fits the situation well. Supposing you have lots of needles in the haystack, you want to be sure you have found them all. Each needle is different and ranges from knitting needles to hypodermic—some are easier to find, others are harder. The haystack is huge, and simply hunting through the whole thing yourself would be impossible and just looking around the edges is unlikely to uncover any needles. What you really need is an automatic hay-sorting machine, where you can throw in the entire haystack, and the machine spits out just the needles! But of course you will need to tell the machine how to differentiate a needle from hay or any other debris in the stack (maybe they are magnetic or they have a high density), but once you have done that, the machine will sift through much more quickly and accurately than a person, or even an army of people could. This is what data mining tools do; they allow you to work with huge amounts of data and distill them down to just the things that you might be interested in (TeamMate Analytics, 2014).

What is data mining? Simply put, data mining is the practice of examining large amounts of existing databases with the intent to generate new information. Data mining, sometimes called knowledge discovery, is the analysis of data for relationships that have not previously been discovered.

Data mining is a broad area that integrates techniques from several fields, including machine learning, statistics, pattern recognition, artificial intelligence, and database systems, for the analysis of large volumes of data. It is the process of extracting hidden knowledge from large volumes of raw data. It is a process used by companies to turn raw data into useful information. By using software to look for patterns in large batches of data, businesses can learn more about their customers and develop more effective marketing strategies as well as increase sales and decrease costs.

In this section, we will explore some applications of data mining techniques as an auditing tool, fraud detection scheme, and instrument for investigating improper payments. We will also compare the general auditing software with the data mining software, for the purpose of showing the superiority of the modern data mining technology.

According to John and James (2006), we are drowning in data but starving for knowledge. Some researchers are of the opinion that the volume of information stored doubles every year using disk storage per person, a way to measure the growth in personal data. Edelstein and Millenson (2003 as cited in John and James, 2006) estimated that the number has dramatically grown from 28 MB in 1996 to 472 MB in 2000.

Data mining appears to be the most promising solution for the dilemma of dealing with too much data but very little knowledge. By using pattern recognition technologies and statistical and mathematical techniques to sift through warehoused information, data mining helps analysts recognize significant facts, relationships, trend, patterns, exceptions, and anomalies. The use of data mining can enhance a company's position by creating a sustainable competitive advantage. Data warehousing and mining is the science of managing and analyzing large database and discovering unique patterns (Wang, 2003, 2005; Olafsson, 2006, as cited in John and James, 2006).

Data mining involves searching through databases for correlations or other nonrandom patterns. Data mining has been extensively used by statisticians, data analysts, the management information systems community, and a host of other professionals for further insight into a data warehouse. Recognizing patterns of data in order to discover valuable information, new facts, and relationships among variables are important in making business decisions that would best minimize costs, maximize returns, and create operating efficiency. In accounting and auditing functions, as companies are accumulating vast amounts of complex electronic data in different forms, the use of data mining has been growing. Data mining allows accountants or auditors to analyze data in many different ways and summarize relationships. Data mining analysis sorts through data and reveals the information accountants or auditors need.

2.10.1.2 Data Mining as an Auditing Tool

What are data mining tools? Data mining tools are used in many different fields, including scientific research, engineering, marketing, and business decision making to find patterns, interrelationships, and anomalies in data. One very common application for data mining tools is auditing. Data mining, as applied to auditing, can also be known as data analytics, data analysis, or CAATs. By applying defined rules and methods to data, mining can uncover interesting information hidden within it. For auditors, this information can be used to recommend changes in the business that can improve efficiency, reduce fraud, recover cash, strengthen controls, and ensure compliance (TeamMate Analytics, 2014).

John and James (2006) opine that as online systems and high-technology devices make accounting transactions more complicated and easier to manipulate, the use of data mining in the auditing profession has increased significantly in recent years. Since auditing involves "the accumulation and evaluation of evidence about information to determine and report on the degree of agreement between the information and established criteria" (Sirikulvadhana, 2002, p. 4, as cited in John and James, 2006), independent auditors conduct audit work to make certain that the financial statements or assurance of risk management of a company conform to the Generally Accepted Accounting Principles/IPPF/Generally Accepted Government Auditing Standards as the case may be. This process is known as attest function. Through CAATs, data mining makes this process more accurate and reliable.

The New York State Society of Certified Public Accountants (2005, as cited in John and James, 2006) recognizes three basic approaches to data mining: mathematical-based methods, distance-based methods, and logic-based methods.

■ **Mathematical-based methods**

These methods make use of neural networks, which are networks of nodes modeled after a neuron or neural circuit that mimics the human brain. These neural networks are used in the auditing profession in many different ways, such as risk assessment, finding errors and fraud, determining the going concern of a company, evaluating financial distress, and making bankruptcy predictions.

- **Distance-based methods**

  These methods use clustering to put large sets of data into groups and classifications based on attributes. These methods are not as commonly used in auditing; they are used more in the marketing field, but can sometimes be used for auditing.

- **Logic-based methods**

  This approach uses decision trees to organize data. The areas of auditing that the logic-based method is most commonly used for are bankruptcy, bank failure, and credit risk.

Data mining approaches are used to make auditing easier by organizing and analyzing data in a more efficient and effective way.

2.10.1.3 Why Is Data Mining Better than Traditional Auditing Methods?

According to TeamMate Analytics (2014), the role of the auditor has always included reviewing and testing controls and processes in order to provide management with a level of assurance about their efficiency and effectiveness. Traditional methods of testing generally rely on sampling, but with the ever-increasing volumes of data that organizations are processing, sampling is no longer adequate. To go back to our *finding needle in a haystack* analogy, the haystack may contain hundreds of thousands of hay stalks. Sampling 100 stalks at random is unlikely to result in one of them having a needle. Also, with sampling, you can never find all needles; you may stumble on one or two needles if you are lucky, but you need that automatic hay-sorting machine to find them all and eliminate sampling risk altogether. Sampling can also be very time consuming and monotonous; even sifting through a sample of 30 manually can be laborious. However, you can *mine* hundreds of thousands of items in seconds. To be able to find and report on every anomaly in the data is incredibly powerful. It also allows you to calculate the total financial impact of any issues found, so management and stakeholders sit up and take notice, then the resolution is quicker and easier and sometimes cash can be recovered for the organization.

2.10.1.4 Applications of Data Mining

Some of the areas data mining could be applied to include continuous auditing, fraud detection, improper payments, going concern status, etc.

- **Continuous auditing**

  The growing volume of data and technology enhancement has changed the auditing being performed in the accounting profession. Traditionally, financial auditing is performed periodically, usually on an annual basis. Unfortunately for the traditionalist, this high volume of financial data is continuously flowing through the electronic circuit in the form of processed data that require to be harnessed. Also, there is growing demand by stakeholders of financial information (statements) for more timely and forward-looking information. To solve this problem, a growing number of auditing firms start using *continuous auditing*. It is "a methodology in auditing that enables independent auditors or internal auditors to provide written assurance on a subject matter using a series of auditors' reports issued simultaneously within a short period of time after the occurrence of events underlying the subject matter" (Zhao et al., 2004, p. 389, as cited in John and James, 2006). Zhao et al. posit that since so many transactions are being recorded electronically, without the use of paper documentation, continuous auditing allows for "real-time assurances from an independent auditor that the information is secure, accurate, and reliable." Data mining is therefore one of the tools that can make continuous auditing a possibility. On his part (as cited in John and James, 2006), Mr. Shire, the CEO of PriceWaterhouseCoopers, said that "the Internet, stakeholders' demands for real-time financial information, new corporate value drivers, global stock trading, 24-hour business news, and security, needs for electronically transmitted information are fundamentally changing the way we do business."

■ **Going concern status**

One of the major of areas of auditing is making predictions about the going concern of a company. Auditors are required by auditing standards to assess the status of a company and make a prediction as to whether it is able to continue operating as a going concern. Determining the going concern status of a company is a very difficult task, so auditors have been trying to come up with statistical methods to help make it easier. It has been identified that data mining is one of the ways to solve this problem. One of the elaborate surveys that demonstrated this fit was the one posted in an article by Koh (2004, p. 462, as cited in John and James, 2006), "Going concern prediction using data mining techniques." Here 165 going concern companies and 165 non–going concern companies were used in a study to assess the effectiveness of data mining in determining going concern. Decision trees, neural networks, and regression were used to test the sample. The results found that the usefulness of data mining to determine whether a company is a going concern was very high. The decision tree model had an accuracy rate of 95%; the regression model had an accuracy rate of 94%; and the neural network model had an accuracy of 91%. All three models were able to predict which companies were going concerns.

■ **Fraud detection**

Fraud detection is a constant challenge for any business; however, implementation of data mining techniques has been shown to be cost-effective in many business applications related to auditing, such as fraud detection, forensics accounting, and security evaluation. Randall Wilson (as cited in

John and James, 2006), director of fraud at RGL in St. Louis, agreed that the growth in computer forensics has been nothing short of unbelievable, especially in the area of employee misappropriation. He has picked up countless cases of collusion between employees and outside vendors, complete with fraudulent invoices. Clearly, there has been an increase in the opportunities for fraud and, consequently, increased opportunities for catching fraud. Wilson explained that what has happened in the business world has triggered a rise in fraudulent activities. As a result, his company is doing more data mining, simulation, fraud detection, and prevention (Kahan, 2005, as cited in John and James, 2006).

There are two applications of data mining that can be used to detect fraud, and these include outlier analysis and Benford's law analysis.

In *outlier analysis*, the data that are very different from the rest of the data (outliers) are identified. The outliers can be the result of errors or something else like fraud. This analysis identifies these deviations that are not the norm and have a higher risk of being fraudulent. *Benford's law analysis* is a technique that allows the auditor to quickly assess data in ways that will detect potential variances. Benford's law was named after Dr. Frank Benford, who was a physicist working for General Electric in the 1930s. He discovered that, within a large enough universe of numbers that were naturally compiled, the first digits of the numbers would occur in a logarithmic pattern. This analysis concludes that if numbers do not follow the Benford pattern, then something abnormal has happened with the data, which could lead to detecting fraud.

■ **Improper payments**

Improper payments are a widespread and significant problem that is receiving increased attention by governments, including federal, state, Local Government Area (LGA), and foreign governments, and by private sector companies as well. Some of these payments may include unintentional errors, such as duplicate payments and miscalculations, payments for unsupported or inadequately supported claims, payments for services not rendered, payments to ineligible beneficiaries, and payments resulting from outright fraud and abuse by program participants or employees. Some examples of improper payments in the federal government sector include those related to contractors and contract management; health-care programs such as Medicare and Medicaid; financial assistance benefits such as food stamps and housing subsidies; and tax refunds. There could be many causes of improper payments, ranging from fraud and abuse, poor program design, inadequate internal controls, and simple mistakes and errors.

The consequences of improper payments could be threatening to both public and private sectors of the economy. In the private sector, improper payments most often present an internal problem that threatens profitability; in the public sector, they can translate into serving fewer recipients or represent wasteful spending or a higher relative tax burden that prompts questions and criticism from the legislative arm of government with an oversight function over the executive arm, the media, and even the taxpayers themselves.

In the United States, the Office of Management and Budget (OMB) has estimated that at least $35 billion is improperly spent each year. The deputy director of OMB said recently that just cutting away of improper or erroneous payments could save the federal government $100 billion over the next 10 years (United States General Accounting Office, 2002, as cited in John and James, 2006). These problems could be solved using data mining solution.

Data mining analyzes data for relationships that have not previously been discovered. As a tool in managing improper payments, applying data mining to a data warehouse allows an organization to efficiently query the system to identify questionable activities, such as multiple payments for an individual invoice or to an individual recipient on a certain date. This technique allows personnel who are not computer specialists, but who may have useful program or financial expertise, to directly access data, target queries, and analyze results. Queries can also be made through data mining software, which includes prepared queries that can be used in the system on a regular basis.

The challenges of using data mining to address the problem of improper payments include establishing a data set of known fraudulent payments, a target population of nonfraud, and a method by which to leverage the known fraud cases in the trailing of detection models. As is typical in fraud detection, the set of known cases was very small relative to the number of nonfraud examples. Thus, the researchers have had to devise methods to reduce false alarms without drastically compromising the sensitivity of the models.

The first step is to obtain the data needed to perform the analysis. For the most part, actual transactions are used; however, for some of the transactions, source documents may have to be used to recreate those transactions. The results are a data set of fraudulent payment candidates that will be used to develop models predicting similar transactions. The challenge for the data mining effort is to predict suspicious payments using a very small set of known fraudulent payments relative to a larger population of nonfraudulent payments.

The next step is to transform the data. Experts in identifying vendor payment fraud hypothesized dozens of potentially useful transformations of known information that might be useful indicators of fraud. Examples of data transformations made in this step include setting flags that identify

1. Payments addressed to a post office box or suite number
2. Invoices from the same vendor paid to multiple addresses
3. Invoices from multiple vendors paid to the same address
4. Invoices from the same vendor were not sequential based on date submitted

5. Vendor addresses matching employees' addresses
6. Highest paid vendors on a comparative basis
7. Changes in aggregate amounts paid to vendors over time
8. Payments made under various approval limits
9. Payments of employee salaries and bonuses not in agreement with master file data or to terminated employees

Although a single fraud/nonfraud binary label for the output variable can be used, multiple fraudulent payment types can be identified to comprise the different styles of payments in the known fraud data.

The third step is to analyze the relationships and patterns in the data by application software. The different levels of analysis that are available in data mining are artificial neural networks, genetic algorithms, decision trees, nearest neighborhood method, rule induction, and data visualization. In general, the relationships sought are classes, clusters, associations, and sequential patterns. These relationships allow the data to be mined according to predetermined groups, logical relationships, and associative relationships. This allows the data to be mined according to certain criteria; that is, when improper payments are likely to occur or what categories of vendors are more likely to receive improper payments. This also allows for the prevention of improper payments by mining the data to anticipate patterns and trends (John and James, 2006).

Other areas of data mining application in auditing include

■ Looking for payroll fraud, such as phantom employees
■ Identifying expense fraud or abuse
■ Finding journal entries that manipulate financial reporting
■ Highlighting orders not billed to customers
■ Exposing failures in purchasing controls
■ Extracting suppliers with short credit terms or customers with excessive credit limits that reduce working capital, etc.

2.10.1.5 General Auditing Software versus Data Mining Software

Under the COSO framework, internal control is broadly defined as a process, effected by an entity's board of directors, management, and other personnel, designed to provide reasonable assurance regarding the achievement of four core business objectives that make every business strive:

■ Effectiveness and efficiency of operations
■ Reliability of financial and management reporting
■ Compliance with laws and regulations
■ Safeguarding of assets

Management is responsible for designing and implementing internal control, which comprises five critical components:

- Control environment
- Risk assessment
- Risk-focused control activities
- Information and communication
- Monitoring activities

Management establishes policies, processes, and practices in these five components of internal control to help the organization achieve the four specific objectives listed above. It is the responsibility of internal auditors to perform audits to evaluate whether the five components of internal control are present and operating effectively, and if not, provide recommendations for improvement. Again, under the COSO enterprise risk management framework, an organization's strategy, operations, reporting, and compliance objectives all have associated strategic business risks, which are the negative outcomes resulting from internal and external events that inhibit the organization's ability to achieve its objectives. It is the responsibility of management to assess and manage risk as part of their ordinary course of business activities. It is, however, the responsibility of the internal auditors to evaluate each of these activities, or focus on the overarching process used to manage risks entity wide.

An effective internal control system has become a stringent requirement under the Sarbanes–Oxley Act of 2002. Internal auditors use software for a variety of auditing tasks. Also, internal auditing professional standards require the function to evaluate the effectiveness of the organization's risk management activities.

These deductions have necessitated the need for internal auditors to be proficient in the use of internal audit software. As auditors become more proficient in the software and as technology keeps on changing, auditors will continue to use software applications more and more.

2.10.1.5.1 Generalized Audit Software (GAS)

According to John and James (2006), GAS is the most common software that auditors use. Auditors use GAS to automatically perform overall auditing processes. GAS was originally developed in-house by professional auditing firms to "provide auditors the ability to access, manipulate, analyze, and report data in a variety of formats. The basic features of GAS are data manipulation (including importing, querying, and sorting), mathematical computation, cross-footing, stratifying, summarizing, and file merging. It also involves extracting data according to specification, statistical sampling for detailed tests, generating confirmations, identifying exceptions, and unusual transactions and generating reports" (Sirikulvadhana, 2002, p. 18, as cited in John and James, 2006). Auditors also use GAS for risk assessment, high-risk transactions and unusual items continuous monitoring, fraud detection, key performance indicators tracking, and standardized audit program generation.

GAS provides auditors with many incentives. It offers all-in-one features that are designed to support the entire audit process, which includes data access, project management, and all audit procedures. All GAS packages are designed to process tremendous amounts of transactions. It can also be customized to support specific audit procedures so that auditors do not need to make adjustments to the program before using it and are able to understand how the program works more easily. Most GAS software is user-friendly and has high presentation capability. As a result, little or no technical skills are required to use GAS.

Many companies use GAS to reduce the expense of having an extensive professional staff. Most auditing firms rely on GAS a lot because of the high return on investment that the packages offer as compared to the expense of having a professional staff. However, although audit features such as sorting, querying, aging, and stratifying are built into GAS packages, auditors are still required to observe, evaluate, and analyze the results. "Consequently, GAS can reduce the degree of professional staff requirements, but cannot replace any level of professional staff" (John and James, 2006, p. 5).

2.10.1.5.1.1 Examples of GAS Software

The commonly use GAS software include Audit Command Language (ACL), Interactive Data Extraction and Analysis (IDEA), DB2 Intelligent Miner for Data, DBMiner, Microsoft Data Analyzer, SAS Enterprise Miner, SAS Analytic Intelligence, and SPSS. The most popular GAS package that is purchased by auditors is Audit Command Language (ACL) because it is convenient, flexible, and reliable. ACL appears most commonly used for data-access, analysis and reporting. The interactive capability of ACL allows auditors to test, investigate, and analyze results in a short period of time. Auditors can easily download their client's data by connecting their laptops to the client's system for further processing. This allows the auditor to view the client's files, steps, and results at any time. Similar to other GAS software, ACL is not able to deal with complex data. It does have an open database connectivity to reduce this problem; however, some files are still too complex. As a result, auditors face control and security problems.

2.10.1.5.2 Data Mining Software

Although GAS is widely used by auditors today, data mining can present to these users more extensive conclusions. Data mining software offers auditors automated capabilities to discover useful information. The software has the ability to handle complex problems that are limited by the human brain. Data mining is scalable and can handle an unlimited amount of data in the data warehouse or any size problem. Data mining can uncover interesting information hidden in the accounting transactions that when performing normal work, auditors may not come across. It can be used even when the auditors do not know what they are looking for.

2.10.1.5.2.1 Some Drawbacks of Data Mining   Data mining software requires a lot of technical skills; the auditors should be able to understand the differences between various types of data mining algorithms to choose the right one to use. They should possess only the ability to use the software but also the ability to interpret the results. Although data mining is useful for handling complex problems, sometimes the complexity of the outcome is too difficult for the auditor to understand. Another challenge is the difficulty in determining how the system came up with the results since data mining is done automatically. This is a major problem for auditors because "the audibility, audit trails, and replicability are key requirements in audit work" (Koh, 2004, p. 476, as cited in John and James, 2006, p. 6). Another problem that auditors find when using data mining software is the lack of interoperability between different data mining algorithm methods. The software tends to focus on a single method and utilizes only a few techniques that cannot integrate with other software. Finally, although data mining is becoming cheaper, it is still expensive compared to other software. Besides paying for the software itself, users must incorporate the cost of preparing the data, analyzing the results, and training auditors to use the software.

The automation ability of data mining indicates that it could greatly enhance the efficiency of auditors and also replace the level of involvement required by these professionals. However, although data mining can be a highly proficient tool for auditors, it has not yet been widely adopted by these users. GAS packages still tend to be more widely used due to their low cost, high capabilities, and user-friendliness.

2.10.1.5.2.2 Types of Data Mining Software   There is wide range of data mining software packages that auditors can use. The software can be classified according to their level of sophistication, which ranges from low-end to high-end data mining tools. The more sophisticated data mining tools handle complex tasks by using multiple methods and algorithms, including wizards and editors for data preparation, and can incorporate scalability and automation. On the other hand, low-end data mining tools are not difficult to use and can provide the capability to query, summarize, classify, and categorize data. However, the software is not sophisticated enough to recognize patterns.

Some examples of high-end data mining software include CART, WizSoft, Clementine, Enterprise Minder, and Oracle Darwin. These tools are used in complex cases with enterprise-scale database management systems such as Oracle or DB2. Oracle Darwin is mostly used for activity-based costing, cost–benefit analysis, and credit analysis, while Enterprise Minder and Clementine are primarily used by marketing companies for trend analysis, customer retention, and product/market analysis. Though used extensively by marketing companies, Clementine is used by auditors for fraud detection and credit scoring. Notwithstanding its complexity,

Clementine has a visual programming interface that simplifies the data mining process.

CART, which stands for Classification and Regression Trees, is used by auditors to assess the financial risk of a business entity. Auditors use CART to find hidden patterns in data to develop decision trees that can be used to predict the entity's financial risk. On the basis of these results, auditors can predict the likelihood that a business will fail, as well as the overall business risk of trading partners, corporate affiliates, investment partners, and takeover targets.

WizSoft is software based on mathematical algorithms and is used for both data mining and data auditing. It features six products: WizWhy, WizRule, WizSame, WizDoc for Office, WizDoc for Web, and WizCount for Reconciliation. WizWhy is another data mining tool that is used for fraud detection. The software learns patterns of previous cases of fraud to detect new fraud incidents. WizRule is an auditing and cleansing application that reveals the rules in the data and automatically indicates auditing rules that are being broken. WizSame reveals records that are duplicated, such as duplicate payments, two customer names that differ by one letter, or two addresses that are synonymous. "WizCount bank and account reconciliation reveals all the matching transactions, thus leaving out the nonreconciled records. WizCount makes use of several sophisticated mathematical algorithms that quickly cover the enormous number of one-to-one, one-to-many, and many-to-many matching possibilities, and reveal the right ones" (WizSoft, 2005, as cited in John and James, 2006).

Microsoft Excel is an example of low-end data mining software that is used with database systems to build assessments. It is used for a variety of audit applications, including tests of online transactions, sampling, internal control evaluation, and specialized fraud procedures. Special software add-ins, such as risk and sensitivity analyzers, can be used to make accounting management easier. Also, PivotTables can be created in Excel to summarize large amounts of data.

Using any of these data mining packages can assist auditors with complex transactions in large volumes. As transactions are made, recorded, and stored electronically, all of the tools are capable of capturing, analyzing, presenting, and reporting the data. Manipulating complicated data through data mining gives auditors the opportunity to analyze information that is beyond their human capabilities (John and James, 2006).

2.10.2 Analytics in Internal Auditing

According to RapidMiner (2015), data analytics or simply analytics refers to the skills, technologies, applications, and practices for continuous iterative exploration, evaluation, and investigation of data or business operations to gain hindsight, insight, and foresight for decision making.

According to Daniel (2012), analytics is best captured by what IBM calls an *analytics triangle*, which categorizes different types of business analytics based on the types of questions the user is trying to answer.

- The base of the triangle is *descriptive analytics* and answers the questions, What has happened in my business? Why has it happened? What do I know about my customers, competitors, suppliers, etc.? Examples of this are business intelligence (BI), reporting, advanced visualizations, etc.
- The middle of the triangle is *predictive analytics* and answers the questions, What is likely to happen? What is likely to be true about my customers, competitors, suppliers, etc.? Examples of this are forecasting, regressions, data mining, most big data applications, simulations, etc.
- The top of the triangle is *prescriptive analytics* and answers the questions, What should I do? What is the best course of action given what I know and what I think will happen? Examples of this are optimization, mathematical programming (LP, MIP, QP, CP, etc.), heuristic algorithms, etc.

From the above, analytics consists of three major areas: BI or descriptive analytics, predictive analytics, and prescriptive analytics.

> Essentially, business intelligence, predictive analytics, and prescriptive analytics are interconnected solutions 'doing what they can' to help companies get the most out of this new intimate knowledge. (WealthEngine Team, 2015, para 5; see Figure 2.10)

2.10.2.1 Business Intelligence (BI)

According to WealthEngine (2015), Gartner defines BI or descriptive analytics as "An umbrella term that includes the applications, infrastructure and tools, and best practices that enable access to and analysis of information to improve and optimize decisions and performance." Another name for BI is decision support solution. By Gartner's chart in Figure 2.11, we can answer the question, "What happened?"

BI is a data-driven decision-making tool. It includes the generation, aggregation, analysis, and visualization of data to inform and facilitate business management and strategizing.

BI focuses on using a consistent set of metrics to measure past performance and guide business planning. Business intelligence consists of querying, reporting, online analytical processing (OLAP), and can answer questions including "what happened," "how many," and "how often."

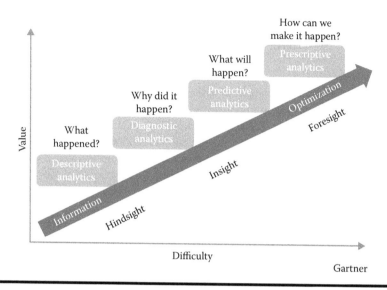

Figure 2.11   Relationship between analytics (Gartner's chart). (Retrieved from WealthEngine Team (2015). Business intelligence vs predictive analytics vs prescriptive analytics. Copyright 2016 WealthEngine.)

2.10.2.2 Predictive Analytics

"Firms have spent many years building enterprise data warehouses (EDWs) and using business intelligence (BI) tools to report on the business. But predictive analytics is different—advanced statistical, data mining, and machine learning algorithms dig deeper to find patterns that traditional BI tools may not reveal" (Mike Gualtieri, Forrester Research, as cited in WealthEngine, 2015). Predictive analytics goes a step further than BI, by using algorithms to find patterns and develop probabilities to predict similar future outcomes.

By Gartner's chart above, we can look for a cause–effect relationship, to answer the questions, "Why did it happen?" and "What will happen?"

2.10.2.3 Prescriptive Analytics

From descriptive and predictive analytics was born prescriptive analytics, which is basically exactly what it sounds like. Prescriptive analytics uses the knowledge gained through predictive analytics to build actionable, predictive models capable of prescribing healthier, more robust, and successful action (Table 2.7).

Gartner describes prescriptive analytics as "the final frontier in big data analytics, where companies can finally turn the unprecedented levels of data in the enterprise into powerful action."

Table 2.7 Prescriptive Analytics and Business Intelligence Compared

Item	*Business Intelligence*	*Advanced/Predictive Analytics*
Orientation	Review	Future
Types of questions	What happened? When? Who? How many?	What will happen? What will happen if we change this one thing? What's next?
Methods	Reporting (KPIs, metrics) Automated monitoring/ alerting (thresholds) Dashboards Scorecards OLAP (cubes, slice and dice, drilling) Ad hoc query Data mining (but uses sets of known outcome)	Predictive modeling Data mining Text mining Multimedia mining Descriptive modeling Statistical/quantitative analysis Simulation and optimization
Uses big data	Yes	Yes
Data types	Structured and some unstructured data	Structured and unstructured data
Knowledge generation	Manual	Automatic
Users	Business users	Data scientist, data analyst, IT, Business users
Business initiatives	Reactive	Proactive

Source: RapidMiner (2015). Summarizing the differences between business intelligence and advanced analytics. RapidMiner Blog. Copyright 2015 RapidMiner.

2.10.2.4 Why Analytics in Internal Auditing?

In the context of internal auditing, analytics is the analysis of a large population of data to obtain insights and improve business performance, reduce risk, and maximize business value.

> Applying analytics to the internal audit process can facilitate moving beyond the traditional Internal Audit activities toward an environment of more sophisticated risk analysis and monitoring. (Deloitte, 2015)

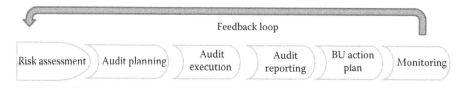

Figure 2.12 Analytics has a role to play throughout the IA lifecycle. (Adapted from EY (2014). Harnessing the power of data: How IA can embed data analytics and drive more value, p. 2. Insights on governance, risk and compliance. Copyright 2014 EYGM Limited.)

As the business landscape for most organizations becomes increasingly complex and fast paced, there is a growing movement toward leveraging advanced business analytic techniques to refine the focus on risk and derive deeper hindsight, insights, and foresight into the organization. Leading internal audit functions are embracing recent enhancements in data mining technology and data visualization tools to deliver results more dynamically, efficiently, and effectively in response to risk, dive deeper into organizational data, and deliver profound hindsight, insights, and foresight. Business analytics holds incredible promise to enhance the internal audit process. Key to delivering on this promise is asking the right questions, embedding analytics into the culture of the internal audit function, and aligning the analytics implementation with the planning process and overall organizational operational as well as strategic objectives (Figure 2.12).

According to EY (2014), traditional internal auditing focuses on what could go wrong. Auditors attempt to understand the population and build a representative sample that can be extrapolated. The sample might not be properly representative, and the resulting audit might miss critical areas and fail to identify all relevant issues.

With the advent of analytics, the internal auditor can examine an entire population of data using various analytics techniques (e.g., descriptive [BI], predictive [advanced], or prescriptive) and focus on potential issues. By looking through unprecedented amounts of data from internal and external sources, for instance, individual items at the transaction level, the internal auditor can identify and focus on attributes that previously were out of reach, and discern relationships and correlations that were never before visible.

However, to derive the above advantages and benefits, the internal audit function must acquaint itself with the knowledge of this great tool.

One of the biggest challenges that the internal audit process faces today is the expectation of the C-suite and audit committee that internal audit should support the business by delivering deeper insight and greater value more efficiently and effectively. Some of the more challenging expectations of internal audit include

■ Being more efficient and achieving more with less
■ More effectively identifying and responding to risk

- Delivering more robust and effective analysis of key issues
- Providing more meaningful actionable insights
- Driving change within the business

Obviously, the solution to these challenging expectations lies in the application of analytic techniques to the internal audit process. As a matter of fact, it is believed that analytics will bring about transformation to the internal audit function. One example of this is the use of analytic techniques to evaluate compliance with controls, business rules, and organizational policies that can deliver long-term cost savings and increase internal audit efficiency. This will allow Internal Auditors to focus their efforts away from traditional Internal Auditing processes, which is riddled with monotonous manual exercise and toward the areas of greatest benefit to the organization.

By applying analytic tools and techniques, internal auditors can help stakeholders obtain deeper insight into their data, systems, and processes and gain the ability to ask—and answer—new and more complex questions about their business. Example, instead of asking "what do we need to do?," they can graduate into asking "what do we need to know?" Instead of simply asking "what happened?," companies that employ analytics can look forward and gain insight and foresight into what might happen, and they can formulate new questions to ask in order to get the information they need to model the future.

2.10.2.5 Benefits of Analytics in Internal Auditing

According to Lalit and Joe (2014), the benefits and value of analytics in internal auditing covers:

- Company expectations: Maximizing the use of technology to increase coverage, quality, and business impact, while managing a finite audit budget. That is, increase coverage, quality, and business impact.
- Competitive landscape: Competitors continue to strengthen their capabilities and seek new talent, that is, it has established competitive advantage in industry.
- Value/relationship: Insights open the door for deeper discussion on issues and develop/strengthen relationships.
- Talent development and appeal: Effective integration of analytics will strengthen the business skills of auditors, that is, strengthen the business and technical skills of auditors.
- Audit/business partnership: Innovation and resulting methods could be ultimately transitioned into the business, that is, cultivate an audit/business partnership.
- Regulatory expectations: Audit needed to get stronger assurance and quantifiable results.

- Data discovery and presentation: Gaining effective insight through advances in visualization capabilities. *Audit by sight* results in increased risk coverage.
- Agile analytics: Alternative modeling and analytic techniques that can tackle audit objectives in hours instead of weeks, resulting in efficient audit cycle time.
- Unstructured data integration: Emerging methods to collect, organize, structure, and search massive amounts of data not found in traditional databases results in insight in real-time or *right-time*.
- Enhanced audit management: Collaborative project management technology integrated into audit planning, execution, and reporting builds a learning organization and manages risk/return.

2.10.2.6 Approach Comparison (Table 2.8)

According to Lalit and Joe (2014), our approach using analytics provided significant up-lift to the organization and demonstrated tangible benefits over traditional audit approaches.

Table 2.8 Approach Comparison

Item	Traditional	Using Analytics
Risk assessment	• Broader interviews with business stakeholders • High-level review of processes	• Focused discussions on anomalous areas and regions • Targeted, risk-driven assessments that result in clear objectives
Control testing	• Sample 10–25% transactions • Review is limited to process level coverage	• Analyze 100% and sample only high-risk anomalies • Identify instances of potential fraud and policy violations by their specific criteria
Repeatability	• Insight with minimal reusability and heavy manual editing	• Leave behind scripts and dashboard for ongoing monitoring by business

2.10.2.7 Analytics Maturity Model (Table 2.9)

According to EY (2014), harnessing the power of data, the maturity model as shown below provides a useful way to measure an organization's progress in the journey of analytics. Companies that have no formal approach and no readily available analytics tools are in the initial phase. In the second phase, the analytics are repeatable but not formalized in the system, and they are not applied consistently or correctly. Companies tend to move smoothly from the first/initial phase to the second phase; the third phase, the defined phase, presents a more significant challenge.

Companies in the defined phase have an established analytics methodology, and they enforce their analytics policy. When Internal Audit management champions analytics, it becomes a key step toward the managed phase, where the analytics methodology is institutionalized and management understands the business issues and root causes. The final phase is the optimized phase, where the IA function is locked into continuous improvement and continual monitoring.

Table 2.9 Internal Auditing (IA) Analytics Maturity Model

Initial	Repeatable	Defined	Managed	Optimized
No formal analytics approach, procedures or methodology	Recognized as a value added to the audit	Enforced analytics policy	Methodology is institutionalized	Practices evolved in the first four phases are used to continually improve analytics processes, procedures, and results
Performed occasionally at best	Not yet institutionalized	Established analytics methodology	Management involved in the ongoing analytics efforts	Advanced tools are used
Tools are not readily available	Relies on a central group or a single person	Use of analytics championed by IA management	Management understands business issues and root causes	
Dependent on skills of limited number of subject-matter resources	Tools are available, but not applied consistently or correctly	Quality of analytics results are evaluated	Re-performance of analytics procedures	
		Understanding of the business meaning of analytics procedures and results	Advanced tools are used	

Source: Adapted from EY (2014). Harnessing the power of data: How IA can embed data analytics and drive more value, p. 4. Insights on governance, risk and compliance. Copyright 2014 EYGM Limited.

References

AuditNet, LLC. (2014). The-internal-audit-process-from-a-to-z-how-it-works. Retrieved July 1, 2014, from: http://www.auditnet.org/audit-library/the-internal-audit-process-from-a-to-z-how-it-works.

Daniel. (2012). Business analytics vs business intelligence? *Timo Elliot Blog*, December 5, 2012 at 20:43. Retrieved February 4, 2016, from: http://timoelliott.com/blog/2011/03/business-analytics-vs-business-intelligence.html.

Deloitte, R. A. (2015). Adding insight to internal audit: Reinforcing the transformation of Internal Audit through data analytics. Copyright 2015 Deloitte & Touche. Creative Solutions at Deloitte, Johannesburg (810062/lie). Retrieved February 4, 2016, from: http://www2.deloitte.com/content/dam/Deloitte/za/Documents/risk/ZA_AddingInsighttoAuditwhitepaper_180915.pdf.

ESCC 11100. (2005). *Internal Audit Procedure for the ESCC*, Issue 1, pp. 7–10. European Space Agency (https://escies.org).

EY. (2014). Harnessing the power of data: How IA can embed data analytics and drive more value. Insights on governance, risk and compliance. Copyright 2014 EYGM Limited. Retrieved February 4, 2016, from: http://www.ey.com/Publication/vwLUAssets/EY-internal-audit-harnessing-the-power-of-analytics/$FILE/EY-internal-audit-harnessing-the-power-of-analytics.pdf.

eXamplecg. (2015). eXample Consulting Balanced Scorecard Introductory Session; eXampleCG Balanced Scorecard Overview. eXample India, Mumbai HQ, India. © 2015 eXample Consulting Group. All rights reserved. About us: http://www.examplecg.com/about-us.html.

Institute of Chartered Accountants of Nigeria—ICAN. (2013). NSA 10(ISA 315): Identifying and assessing the risk of material misstatement through understanding the entity's Business and Environment, pp. 209–257. ICAN, Lagos, Nigeria.

ISACA and IIA. (2013). A balanced scorecard framework for internal auditing. Orange County Chapter. Retrieved January 15, 2016, from: https://chapters.theiia.org/Orange%20County/IIA%20OC%20Presentation%20Downloads/2013-12-%20The%20Balanced%20Scorecard.pdf.

ISO 19011. (2011). 13 Steps for ISO 9001 Internal Auditing using ISO 19011, Quality Management System. Academy. Copyright 2015 EPPS Services Ltd. Retrieved December 19, 2015, from: http://advisera.com/9001academy/knowledgebase/13-steps-for-iso-9001-internal-auditing-using-iso-19011/.

John, W., and James, G. S. (2006). Data mining in auditing attest function. In: *6th Global Conference on Business and Economic*. Gutman Conference Center, USA. Yang Montclair State University, New Jersey, USA.

Lalit, T., and Joe, H. (2014). Internal audit analytics: Take advantage of your data. In: *ISACA Rhode Island Chapter; 2014 Annual General Meeting*. Copyright 2013 PricewaterhouseCoopers LLP. Retrieved February 4, 2016, from: http://www.isaca.org/chapters1/rhode-island/Documents/ISACA%20SEMINAR_May%202014_PWC.pdf.

Leticia, R. W. (2012). Business intelligence in audit. *International Journal of Business Intelligence Research*. Copyright 2012, IGI Global. Retrieved February 24, 2016, from: http://www.igi-global.com/article/business-intelligence-audit/69968.

Lohrey, J. (2015). *Demand Media: Audit Procedures & Techniques for an Internal Audit*. Houston Chronicle, Texas. Copyright 2015 Hearst Newspapers, LLC. Retrieved December 12, 2015, from: http://smallbusiness.chron.com/audit-procedures-techniques -internal-audit-74403.html.

RapidMiner. (2015). Summarizing the differences between business intelligence and advanced analytics. *RapidMiner Blog*. Copyright 2015 RapidMiner. Retrieved February 4, 2016, from: https://rapidminer.com/summarizing-differences-business-intelligence-advanced -analytics/.

Regalado, R. O. (2012). ISO 27001 Security: Model ISMS Internal Audit Procedure. Copyright © 2012, Richard O. Regalado and ISO27k Forum, some rights reserved. Retrieved December 20, 2015, from: http://www.iso27001security.com/ISO27k_ISMS _internal_audit_procedure_v3.docx.

Robitaille, D. (2007). The basics of internal auditing. *Quality Digest*. Software Copyright 2006. QCI International. Retrieved December 19, 2015, from: http://www.quality digest.com/june07/articles/06_article.shtml.

TeamMate Analytics. (2014). Data mining tools in auditing. Posted by TopCAATson. Retrieved February 4, 2016, from: http://www.topcaats.com/data-mining-in-auditing/.

WealthEngine Team. (2015). Business intelligence vs predictive analytics vs prescriptive analytics. Copyright 2016 WealthEngine. Retrieved February 4, 2016, from: https:// www.wealthengine.com/resources/blogs/business-intelligence-vs-predictive-analytics -vs-prescriptive-analytics.

Chapter 3

Internal Audit Charter

3.1 Introduction

The Internal Audit Charter also refers to as terms of reference, spells out the purpose, authority, and responsibility of the internal audit function of any organization. The charter provides the framework for the conduct of the internal audit function in any organization, as approved by the chief executive/board/council on the advice of the audit committee. The charter also provides a basis for the appraisal of the operations of the internal audit function and acts as a formal written agreement with management and the board/council/minister, as the case may be, about the role and responsibility of the internal audit within the organization.

According to the standards, the purpose, scope, authority, and responsibility must be clearly stated in an internal audit charter. A typical internal audit charter should outline the following information:

1. Mission/purpose and objectives
2. Scope
3. Roles and responsibilities of management
4. Roles and responsibilities of internal auditors
5. Relationship with external auditors
6. Relationship with audit committee
7. Authority of internal auditors
8. Independence and objectivity
9. Internal audit report and monitoring
10. Confidentiality
11. Organization and resources of the internal audit function

12. Internal audit plan
13. Periodic assessment (quality assurance and improvement program)
14. Approval and amendment of the charter
15. Conclusion

3.2 Mission/Purpose and Objective of Internal Audit

The purpose of the internal audit function is to provide an independent and objective review and advisory service to

■ Provide assurance to the chief executive/board/council/minister, as the case may be, that the financial and operational controls designed by management to manage the organization's risks and achieve its objectives are operating in an efficient, effective, ethical, and economic manner
■ Assist management in improving the organization's business performance

The board or council, in seeking to ensure effective corporate governance and adoption of world best practice, establishes an audit committee to enhance the overall effectiveness of the internal control of the organization. The audit committee in the discharge of its responsibilities should establish an internal audit function.

Internal auditing is an independent, objective assurance and consulting activity designed to add value and improve the organization's operations. It helps the organization accomplish its objectives by bringing a systematic and disciplined approach to evaluate and improve the effectiveness of risk management, internal control, and corporate governance process. It ensures that the

■ Organization's assets are safeguarded.
■ Information given to management is accurate, timely, and reliable.
■ Organization's policies and procedures adopted by management and external laws and regulations are complied with.
■ Resources are used efficiently, effectively, and economically.
■ Operations and programs are being carried out as planned, and results are consistent with the organization's objectives.

ROSNEFT (2014) identifies key objectives of the internal audit structural units to include but not limited to

■ Supporting the executive bodies of the organization and its employees in developing and monitoring the procedures and activities aimed to streamline the company's internal control, risk management, and corporate governance systems by assessing the internal control, risk management, and corporate governance systems, and also to ensure

- Reliability and integrity of information on financial and business operations of the organization
- Efficiency of the organization's operating performance
- Identification of internal reserves for improvement of financial and business operations of the organization
- Safety of the company's property (hardware and software)

■ Coordinating activities with the external auditor, audit committee, and the entities providing consulting services in the area of risk management, internal control, and corporate governance of the organization

■ Independent audit of the quality management system (including capital construction quality management and compliance with ISO international standards)

■ Audit of compliance with applicable legal provisions and internal regulations of the company related to the insider information and observance of the organization's code of business ethics by the members of executive bodies and employees of the organization

■ Preparing and submitting to the board of directors, audit committee, and executive management of the organization the reports on the internal audit

■ Improving the quality of audits and timely response to changes associated with the organization's business development

The aim of an internal audit is to assist management at all levels with information about the establishments and maintenance of adequate internal control over all activities, and to ensure that these activities can be carried out efficiently and effectively.

Internal auditing assists management to meet its responsibilities effectively by evaluating financial, managerial, and operating information; making recommendations for improvement of systems and procedures; and providing other information aimed at promoting effective control by reducing risk at a reasonable cost. Internal auditing expresses an independent opinion on the measures that management and the council have taken regarding internal control. Internal auditing will form an opinion on whether internal control measures are sufficient for the organization's needs and whether such measures work effectively.

Internal auditing considers risks in general, monitors activities on the terrain of risk management, and makes recommendations to the management and the audit committee to reduce or eliminate the risk.

3.3 Scope of Internal Audit Activity

Internal audit reviews cover all programs and activities of the entire organization, including those of associated entities as provided for in relevant business agreements, memorandum of understanding, or contracts. Internal audit activity encompasses the review of all financial and nonfinancial policies, procedures, and operation, including support service to departments, sections, and units.

The scope of the internal audit work will be conducted in accordance with the Institute of Internal Auditors' Standards for the Professional Practice of Internal Auditing. These include the following:

- Evaluating the reliability and integrity of financial and nonfinancial information
- Evaluating internal controls systems established by the organization to ensure that policies, plans, procedures, laws, and regulations are complied with
- Determining whether sufficient controls exist for securing assets, and verifying the existence of the assets where necessary
- Evaluating the effectiveness and efficiency with which administrative procedures are carried out
- Determining whether the organization's activities and processes are completed in accordance with set targets, and whether activities were performed as previously planned

The extent and frequency of internal audits will depend on varying situations, such as results of previous audits, relative risks associated with activities, materiality concept, adequacy of the system of internal control, compliance issues, and availability of resources to the internal audit department.

3.4 Role and Responsibility of Management

Management is responsible for ensuring that systems of internal control are in place, effective corporate governance and enterprise risk management are established and implemented and followed in all areas, compliance is maintained, and fraud risks are identified and mitigated. This provides assurance that financial information and other management information are reliable, that corporate resources are used efficiently and effectively, and that the potential for fraud is minimized.

Management provides a written response to report recommendations issued by internal audits within the time frames requested. Management is responsible for addressing issues identified by implementing recommendations or agreed-upon corrective action plans.

3.5 Role and Responsibility of the Internal Audit Function

The internal audit activity is established by the board of directors, audit committee, or highest level of governing body (as identified in any organization, private or public). The internal audit activity's responsibilities are defined by the board or governing body as part of their oversight function.

The scope of internal auditing covers, but is not limited to, the examination and evaluation of the adequacy and effectiveness of the corporate governance, enterprise-wide risk management, and internal controls, as well as the quality of performance in carrying out the assigned tasks to achieve the organization's stated goals and objectives.

According to University of Swaziland (n.d.), for internal audit to fulfill stake-holders' expectations as stated above, internal audits shall have the following responsibilities:

- Assessing the adequacy and efficiency of the internal control, risk management system, and corporate governance
- Developing a flexible risk-based annual audit schedule, and obtaining inputs and approval from executive management and the audit committee
- Planning and performing audits and reviews as noted on the audit schedule and within their terms of reference
- Carrying out comprehensive examinations/audits of the audited entity performance, which imply the documentary and physical checking of the legitimacy of financial and business operations, reliability and correctness of their reflection in the accounting (financial) reporting, and follow-up control of financial and business operations of the audited entity
- Providing consultations to the executive bodies of the company on the issues related to risk management, internal control, and corporate governance (subject to retaining independence and objectivity of internal audit)
- Performing special administrative requests, special projects, and investigations due to allegations of fraud, theft, waste, abuse, etc., as requested by management, and recommending control improvement
- Providing internal audit recommendations to management for improvements to the system of risk management, internal control processes, and governance processes
- Preparing written internal audit reports on the results of the audit engagement to the management and the audit committee, and evaluating the organization's plans or actions to correct reported concerns
- Reporting all internal audit findings to the appropriate level of management and audit committee
- Performing internal operational services, and/or financial auditing of programs, departments, and accounts that come under the budget authority of the organization
- Proactively consulting with the departments, units, sections, and committees to provide internal control consideration
- Coordinating internal audit services with external auditors and other outside auditing firms to seek to avoid redundancies and to ensure maximum coverage in the audit effort

- Maintaining appropriate professional development to ensure that the internal audit staff has the skills and abilities to perform internal audit assignments
- Keeping the audit committee and management aware of emerging trends regarding internal controls, risk management, governance, and internal auditing
- Striving to comply with the International Standards on the Professional Practice of Internal Auditing

3.6 Relationship with External Auditors

It is a statutory requirement that organizations appoint an independent firm of chartered accountants to audit the financial statements of their organizations and to provide an independent opinion on the state of affairs of the financial statements so audited; they also render other special services.

On the other hand, the objectives of the internal auditor differ from that of the external auditor, and focus on the adequacy and effectiveness of systems and the correctness of management reports rather than certifying financial statements. However, the tasks of the two groups overlap in certain aspects, and some of the ways in which the internal auditor and the external auditor achieve their respective objectives are similar. An internal audit coordinates its activities with those of the organization's independent external auditors to ensure that maximum audit coverage is achieved at minimum cost.

3.7 Relationship with Audit Committee

In public organizations where there is statutory requirement for an audit committee, the audit committee acts on behalf of the council or the board on audit-related matters and advises both council/board and the management. The committee reports to the council/board in connection with the oversight of the independent appraisal activities performed through the internal audit function, to ensure efficiency, effectiveness, and economy of operations of the organization. Today's audit committee requires a reasonable degree of financial literacy, independence, and knowledge about risk management, corporate governance, and internal control. Also, individual audit committee members must be deeply dedicated, vastly experienced, and highly qualified in order to effectively carry out their diverse responsibilities. Moreover, as internal auditing's contribution to effective corporate governance and enterprise-wide risk management has progressively and increasingly been recognized and valued; the audit committee's understanding of internal audit value, processes and procedures, strengths and weaknesses, and opportunities has increased significantly. As a result, best practice requires that the audit committee includes in its charter the scope of its relationship with the internal audit function toward enhancing its oversight function, thereby strengthening the internal audit activities. In the same vein, an internal audit can also be an important resource for the audit committee's improvement by furnishing it with timely and relevant information on new legislation and regulations, thereby fulfilling the role of educator to audit committee members. Thus, as the popular *Igbo* adage says, "if the right hand watches the left hand, the left hand also watches the right hand"; this is true in this circumstance.

The internal audit function reports directly to the audit committee of council/board. All reports of the internal audit function are provided to the audit committee by the internal auditor or chief audit executive (CAE).

According to the IIA (n.d.), to provide adequate oversight of internal auditing, the audit committee should have the following oversight checklist:

1. The audit committee should engage in an open, transparent relationship with the head of internal audit (HIA) or CAE.
2. The audit committee should review and approve the internal audit charter annually.
3. As a result of discussions with the HIA/CAE, the audit committee should have a clearer understanding of the strengths, weaknesses, potentials, and possible threats of the organization's internal control and risk management systems.
4. The internal audit activity is sufficiently resourced with competent and objective internal audit professionals to carry out the internal audit plan as reviewed and approved by the audit committee.
5. The audit committee should ensure that the internal audit activity is sufficiently empowered to be independent by its appropriate reporting relationships to the executive management and the audit committee.
6. The audit committee should ensure that the audit committee addresses with the HIA/CAE all issues related to internal audit independence and objectivity.
7. The audit committee should ensure that the internal audit activity is quality oriented, and has in place a quality assurance and improvement program.
8. The audit committee should regularly communicate with the HIA/CAE about the performance and improvement of the HIA/CAE and the internal audit activity.
9. The audit committee should ensure that internal audit reports are actionable, and audit recommendations and/or other improvements are satisfactorily implemented by management.
10. The audit committee should meet periodically with the HIA/CAE without the presence of management.

3.8 Authority

Subject to compliance with entity's security policies, internal auditors are authorized to

- Have full, complete, and unrestricted access to all functions, records (whether written or electronic), premises, physical facilities and personnel, and other documentation and information that the HIA considers necessary to enable internal audit to meet its responsibilities.
- Have full and free access to the chief executive officer/board/council, audit committee, and its chairperson, as the case may be. The bottom line here is that the HIA/CAE should have full and free access to the highest decision-making body of the organization.
- Allocate resources, set frequencies, select subjects, determine scopes of work, and apply techniques required to accomplish its work.
- Obtain necessary assistance of personnel in departments of the organization where audits are performed, as well as other specialized services from within or outside the organization.
- Confiscate records if an employee of the organization prohibits access to any records, which are required by internal audit for its activities.

The internal audit must carry out its audit function freely without hindrance, and without interference of officials, in order to do an independent and objective audit of the organization and report to management and the audit committee.

The documents and information handed over or provided to internal auditors during an audit are handled with the same care as would normally be displayed by the employees who are actually responsible for it.

The internal audit is authorized to carry out special investigations, including forensic services; they can also contract special services out to other specialists or consultants after due consultation with the management.

Recommendations by the internal audit are implemented by departments that perform the activities.

3.9 Independence and Objectivity

Independence is essential to the effectiveness of the internal audit function.

According to the IIA (2013), the internal audit activity will remain free from interference by any element in the organization, including matters of audit selection, scope, procedures, frequency, timing, or report content to permit maintenance of a necessary independent and objective mental attitude.

The internal audit function has no direct authority or responsibility for the activities it reviews. It has no responsibility for developing or implementing procedures or systems, and does not prepare records or engage in original line processing functions or activities.

It is important to note that internal audit staff members need to be, and be seen to be, independent in the activities that they check. In order to avoid responsibility of operational systems, the internal audit staff members should have neither direct responsibility for, nor authority over, any of the activities reviewed.

According to the IIA, internal auditors will exhibit the highest level of professional objectivity in gathering, evaluating, and communicating information about the activity or process being examined. Internal auditors will make a balanced assessment of all the relevant circumstances and not be unduly influenced by their own interests or by others in forming judgments.

The CAE will confirm to the board, at least annually, the organizational independence of the internal audit activity.

3.10 Internal Audit Report and Monitoring

A written report will normally be prepared and issued by the CAE or HIA following the conclusion of each internal audit engagement, and distributed appropriately. Internal audit reports will normally explain the scope and objectives of the audit, present findings and conclusions in an objective manner relevant to the specific user's needs, and make recommendations where appropriate.

Before the creation of a draft report, the results of the audit are communicated to the appropriate, designated members of management. The internal audit leader creates written audit reports at the conclusion of the fieldwork. The reports are submitted in draft form, first to the chief executive officer and appropriate management members and the department under review. The internal audit leader will meet with the appropriate individuals to discuss the draft report.

The final draft audit report will be issued, which requests written responses from the auditee or area under review. The written responses shall include corrective action plans intended to address the recommendations in the final audit report. Also, management responses are incorporated in the final audit report, which is distributed according to the policy of the company.

The internal audit activity will be responsible for appropriate follow-up on engagement findings and recommendations. All significant findings will remain in an open issues file until cleared.

3.11 Confidentiality

All records, documentation, and information accessed in the course of undertaking internal audit activities are to be used solely for the conduct of these activities. The HIA and individual internal audit staff are responsible and accountable for maintaining the confidentiality of the information they receive during the course of their work.

Persons performing the internal audit work and those with access to internal audit work papers are expected to maintain the confidentiality of any data that may be considered relevant to the audit assignment. All information relating to internal audits shall be treated in the strictest confidence. For each audit, the following shall have access to records:

- Head of audit department
- Point of contact at the audited entity
- Lead auditor

In addition, lead auditors shall ensure that they minimize the information that they hold by passing as much as possible to the head of the audit department for storage.

Before using the internal audit program within the client's enterprise by any person (whether acting as lead auditor or a member of the audit team), he/she shall be required to sign a confidentiality agreement stating that he/she shall not pass any information to any third party and that he/she shall immediately forward such requests to the head of audit department.

The head of the audit unit shall not pass any information to any organization or individual other than as stated within the client's procedure without the permission of the audited entity concerned. The head of the audit unit and lead auditor shall hold all information relating to internal audits in a secure manner and ensure that access is strictly limited.

3.12 Organization and Resources of Internal Audit Function

The HIA or CAE will report functionally to the board via the audit committee where there is one, and administratively to the chief executive officer. The board will approve all decisions regarding the performance evaluation, appointment, or removal of the CAE as well as the CAE's annual compensation and salary adjustment. The CAE will communicate and interact directly with the board, including in executive sessions and between board meetings as appropriate.

The HIA is accountable to the chief executive or board for the efficient and effective operation of the internal audit function. The HIA has direct access to the chief executive/chair of the board and the chair and other members of the audit committee. Periodic *in camera* meetings will be held between the HIA and the audit committee.

The HIA/CAE will periodically report to senior management and the board on the internal audit activity's purpose, authority, and responsibility, as well as performance relative to its plan. Reporting will also include significant risk exposures and control issues, including fraud risks, governance issues, and other matters needed or requested by senior management and the board.

The HIA/CAE is responsible for the overall operations and the management of the internal audit function and oversight of its efficiency, effectiveness, and economy.

Internal audit staff is expected to abide by the Institute of Internal Auditors Inc.'s Code of Ethics and Rules of Professional Conduct.

The HIA/CAE shall be responsible for the performance of the internal audit function and the performance of staff in accordance with the organization's relevant performance standards or charter establishing it. It should be noted that the provisions of the internal audit opinions and recommendations do not, in any way, diminish the responsibility of other line managers. It is therefore pertinent that in deciding to include any resources (other than available in the internal audit function), the following should be taken into consideration:

- Limitations on the internal auditor's ability to give independent advice on the relevant department's activities or operations
- The availability of skills and knowledge required to effectively perform internal audit work
- The impact of such opinions or recommendations on the core internal audit function

Note that the internal audit function can be staffed by employees of the organization appointed in the internal audit function or by contracting external consultants.

It shall be the responsibility of the HIA/CAE that resources provided are used to ensure that the internal audit function operates efficiently, effectively, and economically.

Where internal audit resources are provided for the purpose of providing certifications or opinions to external organizations, an appropriate fee will be charged for this purpose to the extent that such fee can be fully recovered from the external organization to which the certification or opinion was provided or issued.

3.13 Internal Audit Plan

According to IIA (2013), at least annually, the CAE or HIA is expected to submit to the chief executive and the board an internal audit plan for review and approval, including risk assessment criteria. The internal audit plan will consist of a work schedule as well as the budget and resource requirements for the next fiscal/accounting/calendar year. The CAE is also expected to communicate the impact of resource limitations and significant changes in the course of the year to chief executive officer and the board.

The internal audit plan will be developed on the basis of a prioritization of the global audit requirements using a risk-based methodology, including input of the senior management team and the board. The CAE will then review and adjust the audit plan, as necessary, in response to changes in the organization's business, risks, operations, programs, systems, and controls. Any significant deviation from the approved internal audit plan will be communicated to the chief executive officer and the board through periodic activity reports.

Types of audit services offered by internal audit:

■ Regular audits—these are usually scheduled as part of the annual schedule, but may come up during the year.
■ Follow-up audits—these are usually scheduled as part of the annual schedule. The International Standards for the Professional Practice of Internal Auditing require follow-up work.
■ Consultations reviews—these are requests from interested parties. Requests can be scheduled as part of the annual audit schedule or come up during the year.
■ Special investigations—these come up during the year when interested parties contact the internal auditor where irregularities or inappropriate conduct is identified.
■ Requests for advice—these come up during the year when interested parties contact the internal auditor with questions or for advice.

A risk-based annual audit schedule is created each year, which allows for contingencies that develop during the year. Audit services are coordinated with external auditors and other auditing firms to reduce duplication of audit efforts and increase the audit coverage of the organization.

3.14 Periodic Assessment (Quality Assurance and Improvement Program)

According to the IIA (2013), the internal audit activity will maintain a quality assurance and improvement program that covers all aspects of the internal audit activity. The program will include an evaluation of the internal audit activity's conformance with the definition of internal auditing and the standards and an evaluation of whether internal auditors apply the code of ethics. The quality assurance and improvement program also assesses the efficiency and effectiveness of the internal audit activity and identifies opportunities for improvement.

At least every five years, the CAE is expected to communicate to the chief executive officer and the board the internal audit activity's quality assurance and improvement program, including results of ongoing internal and external assessments conducted.

3.15 Approval and Amendment of the Charter

The CAE has the responsibility to review the internal audit charter regularly in line with the International Professional Practice Framework of internal auditing, and present the same to the audit committee of the organization, council/board, and management who have been delegated the authority to approve and amend the organization's internal audit charter.

Internal Audit Activity Charter

Approved this _____ day of _____, _____.

_____   _____
Chief Audit Executive   Chief Executive Officer

_____   _____
Chairman of the Board of Directors   Chairman of Audit Committee

References

IIA (n.d.). Implementing best practices and high standards. The Audit Committee: Internal Audit Oversight. Retrieved from: https://na.theiia.org/about-ia/PublicDocuments/08775_QUALITY-AC_BROCHURE_1_FINAL.pdf.

IIA (2013). Model internal audit activity charter. Retrieved from: https://global.theiia.org/standards-guidance/Public%20Documents/ModelCharter.pdf.

ROSNEFT (2014). Internal audit department. Investors. 26/1, Sofiyskaya Embankment, 117997, Moscow, Russia. Copyright ROSNEFT 2014. Retrieved November 21, 2015, from: http://www.rosneft.com/Investors/governance/internal_control_and_audit/Internal_Audit/.

University of Swaziland (n.d.). Internal audit charter. Retrieved from: http://www.uniswa.sz/sites/default/files/administration/internalaudit/charter.pdf.

Chapter 4

Managing the Internal Audit Function (IAF)

4.1 Introduction

According to the International Professional Practices Framework (IPPF) Standards 2000—Managing the Internal Audit Activity (as cited in Wasonga, 2013), the chief audit executive (CAE) must effectively manage the internal audit activity to ensure it adds value to the organization.

The internal audit function (IAF) is effectively managed when

- The results of the internal auditor's work achieve the purpose and responsibility included in the internal audit charter.
- The internal auditor conforms with the definition of internal auditing and the standards.
- The individuals who are part of the IAF demonstrate conformance with the code of ethics and the standards.

In this chapter, we shall discuss briefly the IPPF Performance Standards as they affect staffing and managing of the IAF as a component of organizational governance. The main purpose of this chapter is to familiarize interested practitioners and researchers with current knowledge and matters in staffing and managing the IAF. Much of the principles used here are adapted from other disciplines, including the external audit domain. These principles are used as far as useful to this discussion.

The management framework for the chapter is adapted from a widely accepted, fundamental model of management (DuBrin, 1999; Dessler, 2000; Griffen, 2002, as cited in Prawitt, 2003). The major components of that fundamental management model, and of this chapter, are planning, organizing, staffing, leading, and controlling.

At the planning section of this chapter, we shall consider the issues involved in planning at the organizational and individual engagement levels. The organizing section will look at organizing the IAF at a company-wide level and goes further to analyze the use of internal audit teams and the common practice of using the IAF as a management training ground (MTG). In Section 4.5, which is a very critical and significant section, we shall discuss the hiring, training, retention, reward system, and performance measurement of internal auditors, as well as the use of a task structure to make effective staff assignments. Section 4.6 discusses leadership and motivation issues. Finally, Section 4.7 discusses the importance of ensuring the IAF is adding value to the organization (Prawitt, 2003).

In this chapter, we shall also elucidate some of the challenges confronting modern-day IAF and proffer suggestive remedies.

4.2 Policies and Procedures

According IIA Standards, the director of the internal audit should provide written policies and procedures as a guide to the audit staff (Standard 530). The form and content of the written policies and procedures should be suitable to the size and structure of the internal auditing function as well as the complexity of its work.

In a small internal auditing department, formal administrative and technical audit manuals may not be necessary in all the cases and may be managed informally. In this circumstance, its audit staff may be directed and controlled through daily, close supervision and written memoranda.

However, in a large internal auditing department, more formal and comprehensive policies and procedures are required as a guide to the internal audit staff to ensure consistent compliance with the department's standards of performance.

4.3 Planning

According to IPPF Standards 2010—Planning (as cited in Wasonga, 2013), the CAE must establish risk-based plans to determine the priorities of the internal audit activity, consistent with organization's goals.

Planning is performed at two levels: strategic and annual.

4.3.1 Strategic Audit Plan (Internal Audit Planning at the Organizational Level)

This is designed to ensure that no part of the organization is left out from audit attention. This level of audit plan identifies the key strategic, operational and support functions, and process of the organization; the resources required to execute them; and the associated major risks. The internal auditor has a primary interest in critical control systems that treat high inherent risks and areas of high, untreated (residual) risk.

An internal audit strategic plan will identify those areas that organizational management should consider for internal audit activity together with a priority order and reasoning for their identification. The reasoning will be drawn from the risk analysis process (Treasury Act of Australia, April 2007).

Chambers (2014) posits that strategic planning is an exceptional way for IAF to identify, produce, and assess the value it should be delivering to its stakeholders. By taking a systematic and disciplined approach, such as the seven-step process contained in IIA practice guidance, IAF would be moving in the right direction. Those steps include

1. Understand the relevant industry(ies) and the organization's objectives.
2. Consider the IPPF standards and guidance.
3. Understand stakeholder expectations.
4. Update the internal audit vision and mission.
5. Define the critical success factors.
6. Perform a SWOT analysis.
7. Identify key initiatives.

IAF could be performed in-house or outsourced; where it is outsourced, emphasis should be on terms of engagement and monitoring to ensure that the engagement terms are fulfilled. On the other hand, an in-house IAF should develop an understanding of the risks that may prevent the organization from achieving its objectives. On the basis of this understanding, the IAF could then plan its work to help measure and mitigate those risks. As an agent employed to help ensure that the organization accomplishes established objectives, these responsibilities come to IAF as a natural role it plays in the organization.

However, the internal auditor's role is unique in the sense that the internal auditor is an agent that monitors the actions of another agent, the management, both of whom are employed by the same principal (Adams, as cited in Prawitt, 2003).

Traditionally, internal auditors have identified and assessed organizational objectives and risks informally. However, as a result of continuous economic slowdown, the boards and audit committees are focusing to leverage the IAF to mitigate a wide range of risks associated with liquidity, cash management, and market volatility. Hence, auditors today need to vigilantly track the company's debt situation, including debt maturities, access to capital markets, and the impact of the recession on the company's supply chain and distribution channels (MetricStream, 2015). With this emerging trend, for internal auditors to become more deeply and actively involved in organizational risk management, they need to obtain management and board input and feedback.

If, for instance, some auditors conduct one- to two-day seminars together with key management personnel, it is expected that during this session, the participants should attempt to identify key business drivers and objectives, and the possible obstacles that may prevent management from utilizing these drivers and accomplishing their objectives. Equipped with this knowledge, internal audit leaders can establish an internal audit plan that addresses the organization's needs (Homer and Holdren, as cited in Prawitt, 2003). It has been observed that techniques such as seminars, which capture the real-time needs of the organization, help the IAF fulfill its corporate governance responsibilities. In addition to seminars, other techniques such as interviews, surveys, etc., are often conducted on a predetermined time schedule that allows auditors to continuously align the internal audit plan with the organization's objectives (LaTorre, as cited in Prawitt, 2003). On the other hand, other internal auditors may establish risk databases that catalog products or services and processes together with their associated risks, while some IAFs even use more complex algorithms to identify and calculate the organization's level of risk (Leithhead and McNamee, as cited in Prawitt, 2003).

One important area that internal auditors may be called upon to assess and improve is the *tone at the top*. Tone at the top is a basic component of the COSO Internal Control framework, and its importance has been highlighted by recent high-profile business failures and frauds perpetrated by top management. Boards can enlist the help of the IAF to ensure that the tone at the top is appropriate and effectively communicated to all levels of the organization (PricewaterhouseCoopers, as cited in Prawitt, 2003).

Morris (as cited in Prawitt, 2003) posits that once the organization's risks have been identified, the duo of management and internal auditors can also work together to develop, evaluate, and improve internal controls to mitigate exposure to risk. Internal auditors use control self-assessment (CSA) as a tool to include management and other employees in these processes. The use of CSA obliges internal auditors to act as audit facilitators by helping management and other employees identify and monitor control areas that are central in ensuring that business objectives are fulfilled. In addition to the traditional provision of assurance services aimed at mitigating risk, internal auditors have increasingly began to deliver a variety of consulting services that assist clients in developing solutions to mitigate risks. This whole gamut of expectations on internal auditors by the board, audit committee, and management have compelled the internal auditors to broaden their scope in skill acquisition by integrating other related consulting services to meet their expectations.

4.3.2 Annual Internal Audit Plan (Planning Individual Engagements)

Prawitt (2003) states that, in addition to developing an organization-wide audit plan, "internal auditors should also develop and record a plan for each engagement"

(Standard 2200). The IIA's *Standards for the Professional Practice of Internal Auditing* (Standards) also require that auditors consider the objective and scope of each engagement in developing the engagement plan.

The Treasury Act of Australia (2007) posits that this is a work program that sets out how internal audit resources are to be used over a 12-month period or a calendar year. The timing of audit engagements and resource allocations are set out together with the rationale and scope of the proposed audit reviews.

The required resources may include subject-area specialists, and the proposed use of these should be made clear.

On the basis of the resource limitations and the risk profiles of the areas under review, the audit committee and the governing body will decide on the audits to be undertaken, and then endorse the audit plan.

The Institute of Chartered Accountants in England and Wales (ICAEW, 2004) posits that the audit plan should identify how internal audit will

- Obtain assurance on the effectiveness of the governance and risk management processes
- Support the continuous improvement and maintenance of governance and risk management processes
- Review the board's assessment of risk and the controls in place to manage the identified risks
- Evaluate and test the effectiveness of controls in place to manage the identified risks
- Coordinate with other components of assurance (e.g., health and safety, external auditors, etc.)

In developing the engagement plan, internal auditors must certify that the assurance or consulting engagement is designed to meet the objectives of the internal audit plan as aligned with the organization's objectives. Where the internal audit engagement has been properly planned, it will, in turn, contribute to ensuring that the organization's risks were appropriately identified and controlled. The plan for each audit engagement may differ across engagements, but similarities may likely exist between related types of engagements, for example, financial audit engagements, operational audit engagements, compliance engagement, investigation engagement, consulting engagements, etc. (Prawitt, 2003).

The IIA's Performance Standard 2201—Planning Considerations (as cited in ICAEW, 2004), states that internal auditors, in planning their work, should consider the objectives of the activity being reviewed, the risks related to that activity, the adequacy and effectiveness of the activity's risk management and control systems, and the opportunities for making significant improvements to those systems.

When planning internal audits, duplication is to be avoided by organizational internal auditors of the audit work being undertaken, particularly where there is a shared services center.

In setting the audit plan, it is expected that all parties concerned (audit committee, management, internal audit, and external auditors) should put their minds together to ensure that there is adequate assurance from all sources to cover all key business risks. The audit committee should drum to the ears of both internal and external auditors on the need for effective collaboration with each other about how their respective audit plans and objectives will cover these key business risks (ICAEW, 2004).

To enhance the prospect of an effective engagement, internal auditors can obtain management's support early in the planning process by emphasizing that the purpose of their audit is to assist management in adding value to their divisions or departments and by asking the managers to sign off on planning documents before beginning the engagement or service (Hubbard, as cited in Prawitt, 2003). In addition, internal auditors can conduct preliminary engagement planning several months before the commencement of the actual assurance or consulting work.

Each engagement plan should include a budget: an estimate of the cost of the engagement, a detailed schedule of time required to complete the engagement, the number of auditors needed, the skills these auditors should possess, the audit leader, and how the results of the engagement will be reported. In some cases, engagements are designed to provide explicit assurance while others provide implicit assurance.

Another important part of planning an engagement is to assign knowledgeable auditors with relevant experience to each engagement. It has been observed that experienced and knowledgeable auditors are more likely to gain the confidence of the employees whose area they audit. It is equally important that internal audit managers (IAMs) comply with relevant *standards* by assigning auditors who can act independently and objectively in the discharge of their assignment. This attribute of effective staffing for each engagement may require the IAF to outsource personnel from professional services firms who possess the required skills needed to complete an engagement. In addition, the IAF can engage people from within the organization but outside the internal audit department; this practice is known as *insourcing*. Both technique of staffing may be particularly relevant for engagements that require auditors with specialized knowledge and skills or technological know-how and should be planned well in advance (Hubbard, as cited in Prawitt, 2003).

Note that the best IAF understands that both types of planning are necessary. "A risk-based annual plan will guide internal audit activities throughout the year, while a strategic plan will act as a guide beyond the horizon" (Chambers, August 18, 2014).

Finally, according to IPPF Standards 2030—Resource Management (as cited in Wasonga, 2013), the CAE must ensure that internal audit resources are appropriately, sufficiently, and effectively deployed to achieve the approved plan.

4.4 Organizing

Musiri et al. (2014) state that, in the contemporary world, internal audit departments continue to experience challenges related to an expanding audit universe, changes in laws and regulations, greater technology risks, and increased budget pressures. It is expedient that executive management and audit committees should periodically review their company's risk profile to determine if their current internal audit model is optimal for the company and its significant stakeholders. Whether IAF is in-house, outsourced, or co-sourced, the internal audit department model should be based on the defining characteristics of the company as well as the specific applicability and potential benefits, including challenges associated with each operating model.

4.4.1 Internal Audit Operating Models

Increasingly, internal audit departments are being held responsible for implementing enterprise risk management (ERM) programs and coordinating ERM activities together with their primary business functions in the organization. As a result, many internal audit departments are struggling with recruiting the right personnel, training, and retaining talent; maintaining knowledge, skill acquisition and technology; and remaining relevant with a larger global trail in an ever-expanding risk universe. The many challenges IAFs face today, coupled with the administrative costs associated with maintaining an internal audit department, have caused many companies to reevaluate their internal audit operating model. It is believed that with the right model, the IAF can meet the increased expectations, fulfill its audit plan, and ultimately accomplish its mission (Musiri et al., 2014).

4.4.1.1 General Structure

The structure of the internal audit department varies widely in practice. For instance, some IAFs have a CAE or head of internal audit (HIA) who is a member of senior management and participates at the highest level of the organization's hierarchy, while other IAFs are managed as part of the organization's accounting/finance function, but this is not recommended. The HIA should report to the highest decision-making arm of the organization to maintain independence and achieve objectivity. It is morally wrong for internal audit to be subservient to a department or unit whose work it supervises; certainly, there would be compromises. In some cases, the IAF is outsourced, co-sourced, or combined with other assurance functions (e.g., security, quality, compliance; see Roth, as cited in Prawiit, 2003). Combining the IAF with other assurance functions is in consonance with the Standard 2050 directive to "share information and organize activities with other internal and external providers of relevant assurances and consulting services to ensure proper coverage and minimize duplication of efforts." A typical internal audit organogram of an institution is depicted in Figure 4.1.

Musiri et al. (2014) identify that a company's decision to establish and maintain an in-house internal audit department, or enter into a co-sourcing agreement or outright outsourcing relationship, is generally dependent on a number of qualitative factors; however, it is important to note that quantitative factors (such as

Internal Audit Flowchart

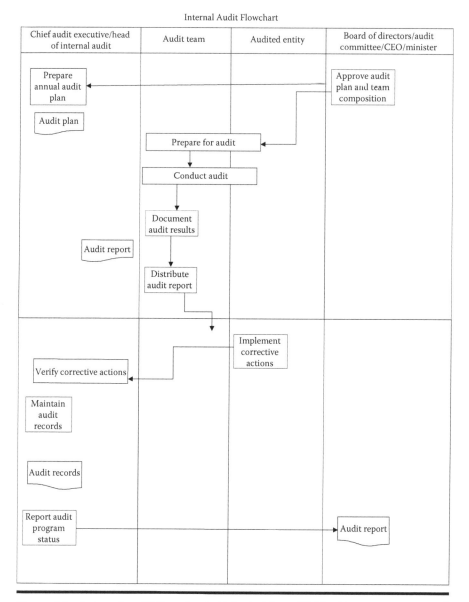

Figure 4.1 Internal audit flowchart. (Adapted from ESCC 11100 (2005). Internal Audit Procedure for the ESCC Issue 1 (PDF P 13). European Space Agency.)

cash constraints, number of staff, number of activities per period, etc.) are equally crucial, as they represent the first visible evidence that the management/board will have to consider before qualitative factors. In Table 4.1 we highlight some of the qualitative and quantitative factors that management and audit committees/board should consider in conjunction with this evaluation.

Table 4.1 Factors to Consider in Chosen Internal Audit Department Model

S/N	Key Characteristics of the Company	In-House	Co-Sourced	Outsourced
1	Is internal audit a core competency for the company?	Yes	Not really	No
2	Is the internal audit department a source of future talent for the company?	Yes	Not really	No
3	How complex are the company's information systems?	Low	Moderate	High
4	How geographically dispersed are the company's locations around the globe?	Fewer locations	Few locations	Many locations
5	How centralized or decentralized is the company's organizational structure?	Centralized	Centralized	Decentralized
6	How complex are the company's business processes?	Simple	Moderate	Complex
7	How regulated is the company's industry?	Low	High	Highly
8	How many acquisitions is the company planning in the near term?	Fewer	Few	Many
9	What is your budget level for running the internal audit department?	Low cash pressure	Moderate cash pressure	High cash pressure

(*Continued*)

Table 4.1 (Continued)   Factors to Consider in Chosen Internal Audit Department Model

S/N	Key Characteristics of the Company	In-House	Co-sourced	Outsourced
10	What is the number of functional departments in your organization?	Fewer functional departments	Few functional departments	Many
11	What is your staff strength?	Small	Large	Larger
12	What is your activity throughput per period?	Fewer	Few	Large

Source: Adapted from *Determining the Right Internal Audit Model for Your Company* (p. 2), by S. Musiri, A. L. Schweik, and W. C. Watts, 2014, Crowe Horwath LLP, Chicago. Copyright 2014 by Horwath LLP.

4.4.1.2 Overview of the Internal Audit Operating Models

Musiri et al. (2014) state that it is important that organizations consider the particular characteristics, specific applicability, and potential benefits and challenges of each of the internal audit operating models as stated above before deciding on the model to adopt. See Table 4.2 (pp. 85–89) for detailed overview of each of the models.

4.4.1.3 Internal Audit Operating Models and Reporting Structures

An IAF structure and its reporting relationships depend on the operating model that management and the audit committee have decided as appropriate for the organization. There is no one size that fits all; and similar organizations can install very different operating models. In addition, the operating model chosen should be flexible to adapt to changes within the organization and its business. Below is an overview of the three most common internal audit operating models and reporting structures.

4.4.1.4 In-House Internal Audit Department

In an in-house internal audit department, the CAE typically reports directly to the audit committee and reports administratively to the chief financial officer (CFO), chief executive officer (CEO), or general counsel. All of the internal auditors are employees of the company (see Figure 4.2, p. 90).

Table 4.2   Comparing and Contrasting the Internal Audit Models

In-House Model	*Co-Source Model*	*Outsource Model*
Overview		
• The internal audit department consists only of company employees. • The internal audit department is responsible for the risk assessment, planning, and execution of the internal audit plan and for reporting the internal audit results. • The company acquires and maintains the methodology, technology, and knowledge infrastructure.	• The internal audit department consists of a combination of company employees and personnel from a third-party provider. • The internal audit department is responsible for risk assessment and planning, and uses people from both groups to execute the internal audit plan and report the internal audit results. • Both the company and the third party supply the methodology, technology, and knowledge infrastructure.	• The internal audit department consists only of employees from a third-party provider, some of whom could be former members of the company's internal audit function. • The third-party provider assists management with developing a risk assessment and audit plan, and is responsible for executing the internal audit plan and reporting the internal audit results. • The third-party provider uses its methodology, technology, and knowledge infrastructure for the company.

(Continued)

Table 4.2 (Continued) Comparing and Contrasting the Internal Audit Models

In-House Model	Co-Source Model	Outsource Model
Characteristics		
Staffing • The internal audit department manages all aspects of recruiting, training, and performance management. **Methodology** • The internal audit department develops and maintains the company's internal audit methodology. **Technology** • The internal audit department develops or purchases, implements, and maintains its technology platform and audit software. **Knowledge Resources** • The internal audit department uses publicly available content, informal networks, or professional organizations to obtain knowledge, benchmarking data, and leading practices.	**Staffing** • The internal staff is supplemented by third-party resources to meet defined resource needs (to fill resource gaps, cover foreign locations, or provide specific skills, for example). **Methodology and Technology** • The internal audit department develops an internal audit methodology and technology platform, or takes advantage of the methodology and technology investments of the third-party provider. **Knowledge Resources** • The third-party provider supplies knowledge of other companies, benchmarking data, and leading practices.	**Staffing** • The third-party provider is responsible for all staffing and personnel matters (such as recruiting, retention, and training). **Methodology, Knowledge, and Technology** • The third-party provider's investments in methodology, knowledge, and technology are available to the company.

(Continued)

Table 4.2 (Continued)   Comparing and Contrasting the Internal Audit Models

In-House Model	Co-Source Model	Outsource Model
Applicability		
• The model is generally driven by corporate culture considerations or a priority placed on using the internal audit department as a source of future talent to the business.	• The model is a solution for elevating the capabilities of the internal audit department. • Internal audit is a variable cost of this moderately flexible staffing model.	• The model is a turnkey solution with full and immediate access to the company's global personnel, subject-matter experts, methodology, and technology. • An internal audit is a variable cost of this fully flexible staffing model. • The model is the quickest route to transformational change.
Potential Benefits		
• Company personnel are generally more receptive to internal auditors who are employees. • The company has a potential source of future management talent. • Institutional knowledge is maintained. • Internal auditors are under direct control and 100% dedicated to the company.	• The model is a moderate route to transformational change. • The staffing model is partially flexible. • The internal audit department is a partially variable cost. • The company has immediate access to the third-party provider's investments in methodology, technology, knowledge, benchmarking data, and best practices.	• The model is the quickest route to transformational change. • The staffing model is fully flexible. • The internal audit department is a variable cost. • The company has immediate access to the third-party provider's investments in methodology, technology, knowledge, benchmarking data, and best practices.

(Continued)

Table 4.2 (Continued)   Comparing and Contrasting the Internal Audit Models

In-House Model	Co-Source Model	Outsource Model
	• The company has immediate access to subject-matter experts or resources in specific geographies. • There is a two-way knowledge transfer between the internal auditors and the third-party provider. • The company continues to have a potential source of future management talent. • Institutional knowledge is maintained. • Travel-related costs are reduced.	• The company has immediate access to subject-matter experts or resources in specific geographies. • The third-party provider is responsible for training, recruiting, and career development. • Travel-related costs are reduced.

(Continued)

Table 4.2 (Continued)   Comparing and Contrasting the Internal Audit Models

In-House Model	Co-Source Model	Outsource Model
Potential Pitfalls		
• The model is the slowest route to transformational change. • The staffing model is the least flexible. • The internal audit department is a fixed cost. • Company access to subject-matter experts is restricted. • Growing costs are associated with investments in methodology, technology, knowledge, and training. • Recruiting and retaining high-quality internal auditors might be difficult. • Travel-related costs are higher.	• Activities between in-house and co-sourced internal auditors require coordination. • The two audit teams require cultural integration. • The model is a cultural change for the company.	• The company no longer has a potential source of future management talent. • There is a potential loss of institutional knowledge. • The internal auditors are not under direct control or 100% dedicated to the company. • Company personnel might consider the internal auditors to be outsiders. • The model is a cultural change for the company.

Source: Adapted from *Determining the Right Internal Audit Model for Your Company* (pp. 2–4), by S. Musiri, CIA, A. L. Schweik, CPA, CGMA, and W. C. Watts, CIA, 2014. Crowe Horwath LLP, Chicago. Copyright (2014) by Horwath LLP.

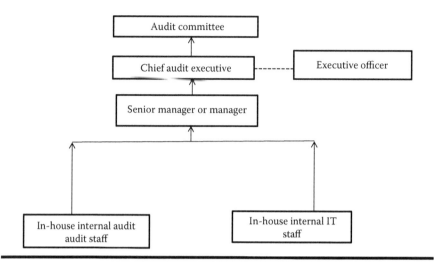

Figure 4.2   Internal audit organizational chart—in-house model.

4.4.1.5 Co-Sourced Internal Audit Department

Typically in a co-sourced internal audit department, the CAE reports directly to the audit committee and administratively to the CEO, CFO, or general counsel, as the case may be. The co-sourced internal audit provider reports directly to the CAE or a person the CAE designates, and the internal auditors are employees of both the company and the co-sourced provider. The in-house and co-sourced internal audit teams can be either integrated or maintained separately. This option is typical when the external provider supplements the IAF with specialist skills that might be too costly to maintain in-house, for example, if the IAF is asked to deal extensively with information systems or other complex areas of the organization. Also, when IAFs face a shortage of qualified auditors, they frequently turn to professional services firms that can place skilled internal auditors on the job site (see Figure 4.3).

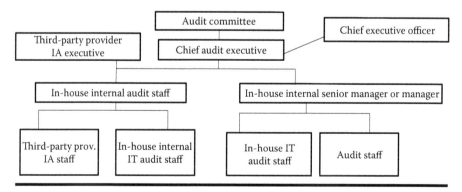

Figure 4.3   Internal audit organizational chart—co-source model.

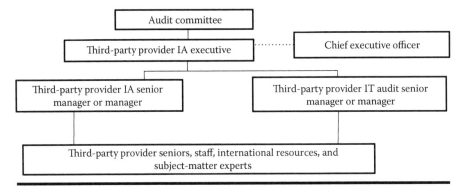

Figure 4.4 Internal audit organizational chart—outsourced model.

4.4.1.6 Outsourced Internal Audit Department

In an outsourced internal audit department, an executive-level resource from the third-party service provider assumes the CAE role. The CAE typically reports directly to the audit committee and administratively to the CFO, CEO, or general counsel. The internal auditors are employees of the third-party service provider. This type of operating model may be cost-effective for smaller organizations or organizations with wide geographical spread or organizations with specific technical expertise (see Figure 4.4).

4.4.1.7 Insourcing the Internal Audit Department

Another option available to the IAF when faced with a shortage of qualified people is called insourcing. This involves bringing in people with specific expertise from other areas within the organization. In many cases, these individuals will not have auditing skills, but the IAF has need for their specialized knowledge and expertise. For example, Exxon used insourcing to help them cope with and learn from the problems stemming from the *Valdez* disaster by bringing in an experienced ship captain to help develop controls and other safety procedures to prevent similar disasters (Anderson, as cited in Prawitt, 2003). This technique can be especially useful in an auditing IT environment by adding to the IAF's available IT expertise.

Standard 1210.A1 specifically allows for these practices and states that, "The chief audit executive should obtain competent advice and assistance if the internal audit staffs lack the knowledge, skills, or other competencies needed to perform all or part of the engagement."

4.4.1.8 Conclusion

In conclusion, it is important that internal auditing continues to monitor industry trends, the current regulatory environment, and their organization's demands for continuous improvement. This will help them properly assess their existing capabilities, predict their future requirements, and adapt the operating model that is appropriate for them.

Cost is usually one of the major issues for an organization attempting to decide whether to completely outsource the IAF or to maintain it in-house. By outsourcing the IAF, an organization essentially converts the costs of maintaining an in-house IAF to the fee it pays the professional services firm to perform its internal audit work. Practitioners and researchers continue to debate whether outsourcing is a better utilization of firm resources.

Once the IAF takes a decision on the operating model, and the extent to which it will partner with other assurance functions within the organization, it must assign responsibility to individuals and groups. As mentioned earlier, some organizations appoint a CAE/IAM to coordinate the work of the IAF and then report administratively to the CEO, general counsel, or CFO; however, Standard 1110 requires that the CAE should report to a level within the organization that allows the internal audit activity to fulfill its responsibilities. It is pertinent note that the organizational level to which the CAE/IAM reports may likely be an indication of whose interests it will ultimately serve. In addition, the IAF must also decide how to assign responsibility within the function. This will include determining the appropriate span of control and the level of centralization in the IAF. Gray and Gray (as cited in Prawitt, 2003) observed that decentralizing decision making within the organization may increase role ambiguity because employees can become confused about their responsibilities in new roles and relationships.

Note: The IIA believes the internal audit activity should never be fully outsourced, but should be managed from within the organization, preferably by a competent CAE.

Finally, the size of the internal audit department heavily influences the operating model to adopt. Large IAFs are more likely to have a hierarchical management structure, with managers exercising control over specified internal auditors and audit teams.

4.4.1.9 Public Sector Structure

In the government circle, the governing body of each ministry, department, and agency is responsible for establishing the audit committee, and the committee is accountable to the governing body. Also, the governing body of each agency is responsible for establishing the IAF and the HIA is primarily accountable to the governing body. The HIA will report to the audit committee on their function, and to the chief executive/minister (or to an officer nominated by the chief executive) for administrative purposes such as for authorization of expenditure and approval of travel and leave.

The auditing guideline stipulates that the governing body is responsible for determining the need for and scope of the internal audit activity. It may delegate this responsibility to the audit committee. The HIA ideally would have no executive or managerial powers, authorities, functions, or duties except those relating to the management of the IAF. The HIA should be responsible to an individual in the organization with sufficient authority to promote independence and to ensure broad audit coverage, adequate consideration of engagement communications, and appropriate action on engagement recommendations.

In deciding whether or not to establish IAF, the governing body should consider the following:

■ Size and scale of the organization
■ Organization's complexity/diversity
■ Organization's overall risk profile
■ History of past issues and incidents
■ Cost–benefit
■ Existence of alternative mechanisms to provide adequate assurance on compliance and the operation of internal controls

If establishing an internal audit department is not necessary, the governing body must take alternative steps to obtain an appropriate level of assurance from an equivalent function. Alternative in-house assurance activities or compliance functions that are sufficiently robust and rigorous may be regarded as an *equivalent function*.

The need for an IAF should be reviewed annually.

Composition

In the case of the internal audit department, the composition depends on the size of the agency/department/ministry but must be headed by a CAE/IAM.

However, internal auditors should possess the knowledge, skills, and other competencies needed to perform their individual responsibilities. There is generally a need for strong financial management and information technology skills.

Internal auditors should have an impartial, unbiased attitude and avoid conflicts of interest. In particular, they should refrain from assessing specific operations for which they were previously responsible.

Internal auditors should enhance their competencies through continuing professional development (Treasury Act of Australia, April 2007). Figure 4.5 is a sample of public sector internal audit structure.

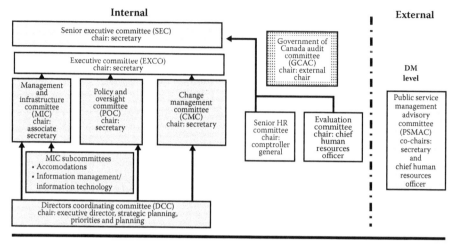

Figure 4.5 Secretariat's governance structure. (Retrieved from Audit of the Treasury Board of Canada Secretariat Governance Framework (October 31, 2009). Treasury Board of Canada Secretariat. Archived March 3, 2010. Copyright by Treasury Board of Canada Secretariat.)

4.4.2 Audit Teams

The business dictionary has defined a team as a group of people with a full set of complementary skills required to complete a task, job, or project.

Ideal team members

1. Operate with a high degree of interdependence
2. Share authority and responsibility for self-management
3. Are accountable for the collective performance
4. Work toward a common goal and shared reward(s)

A team becomes more than just a collection of people when a strong sense of mutual commitment creates synergy, thus generating performance greater than the sum of the performance of its individual members.

It has been observed by Stewart et al. (as cited in Prawitt, 2003) that teams improve productivity and efficiency in some work situations, but not in all. Multidisciplinary, self-directed teams are commonplace in contemporary organizations; a self-directed work team is a team that acts with a relatively high degree of autonomy by exercising control over things like how the work is organized and completed, who performs which roles, and how performance is measured. A self-directed work team also chooses its leaders and sometimes even decides if a leader is necessary.

It is important to note that most times, self-directed teams could lead to role stress and conflict, as the lines of responsibility between managers (leaders) and subordinates, in this case audit staff, could be blurred.

The IAF should form teams that would always improve the quality and efficiency of the audit work, and hence determine which situations and circumstances are appropriate for the use of each team. In many organizations, two types of teams may be identified: (1) teams where individuals are allowed to self-select into them, and (2) teams that are typically assigned by the IAM or by the CAE. These teams can be temporary or relatively permanent, and vary in size depending on the needs of the engagement. Usually, teams are responsible for the majority of the assurance work done in a typical internal audit setting. In most cases, a team is accountable to an audit leader or manager who is accountable to the CAE, and who is responsible for ensuring that the team effectively fulfills its responsibilities.

4.4.3 Making IAF Management Training Ground (MTG)

The use of an IAF as an MTG is a procedure in which individuals are hired into or transferred into internal audit for a short term before being promoted to a management position. The use of an IAF as MTG has become commonplace in recent times. Abbott et al. (as cited in Eller, 2014) note that 65% of their internal auditor respondents from Fortune 1000 firms report that they use the IAF as an MTG. In practice, two variations of MTG could be established: individuals could be hired and initially assigned to internal audit with the promise for promotion to a management position after a stint in internal audit (Goodwin and Yeo, 2001, as cited in Eller, 2014); on the other hand, some companies assign operations managers to internal audit (and often to senior internal audit positions) for a three- to five-year period, after which the individuals return to a higher management position (Chadwick 1995, as cited in Eller, 2014). Where IAF is used as an MTG, it serves management dual functions: providing internal audit services and ground for future recruitment of managers.

The extensive use of IAF as an MTG is a result of derivative benefits associated with the practice. Goodwin and Yeo (2001) and Reeve (1990) (as cited in Eller, 2014) noted that internal audit performs work for various departments within an organization, so future managers can learn how the different departments function. Also, Ridley (2001) and Stewart and Subramaniam (2010) (as cited in Eller, 2014) observed that time spent in internal audit teaches future managers to better understand internal controls. Again, a rotation in internal auditing allows management to evaluate potential talent (Galloway, 1995, as cited in Eller, 2014).

It has been observed that the use of an IAF as an MTG directly influences the kinds of employees recruited into the IAF; it attracts candidates who fit better to the current needs of the organization. It has been observed that they usually possess a broader education as opposed to a strictly accounting/finance education. They have more experience, more confidence, better interviewing and facilitation skills, and better interpersonal relationships (Barrier, 2001, as cited in Prawitt, 2003). In some organizations, MTG is used to improve morale and change the environment of the IAF. For example, at Raychem, the IAF is referred to as the *corporate operations review group*, while the auditors are referred to as business consultants. Raychem's IAF is "seen as a learning and developmental activity rather than as a career" (Stoner and Werner, 1995, as cited in Prawitt, 2003).

It has also been observed that this model can be used to help retain top performers within the organization. This can be achieved by recruiting employees to work in the IAF who agree to stay within the company for a predetermined period of time after leaving the IAF. At Motorola, this approach accounts for 85% of internal audit recruits remaining with the company in other positions after leaving the IAF (Campbell, 2001, as cited in Prawitt, 2003).

Notwithstanding the benefits of using the IAF as an MTG, there are also potential dangers associated with this practice. The primary concern associated with using an IAF as an MTG is centered on its impact on the auditor's objectivity. Chadwick (1995) and Goodwin and Yeo (2001) (as cited in Eller, 2014) observed that internal auditors who are planning a transition to a management position may have little or no drive to improve the long-term objectives of the IAF, and thus may be less willing to take strong positions on matters that arise. Rose et al. (2013) (as cited in Eller, 2014) explicitly tested for this assumption, and found experimental evidence indicating that internal auditors are less objective when being groomed for a management position. Specifically, they found that internal auditors are more likely to agree with a hostile accounting policy promoted by management when the internal auditors are expecting to move into a senior management position. Also, Hoos et al. (2013) (as cited in Eller, 2014), in an experimental examination, found that when the IAF is used as an MTG, internal auditors provide lower risk assessments when reporting to management as against the audit committee and more favorable investment recommendations. These findings represent strong evidence of impaired objectivity stemming from the use of internal audit as an MTG.

It has also been established that the cost of engaging external auditors tends to be higher where management uses IAF as MTG because external auditors perceive internal auditors to be less objective when being groomed for management positions (Messier et al., 2011, as cited in Eller, 2014).

In addition to the above concerns, internal auditors/management trainees may later become managers of departments they have audited, which may raise ethical issues similar to those found in external auditing when clients hire former auditors.

Christ et al. (2013) (as cited in Eller, 2014) found that there is a high correlation between lower financial reporting quality and the use of an IAF as an MTG. It was observed that internal auditors who are being groomed for a management positions face conflicting incentives to protect his future position, particularly where the IAF involves compliance roles. This is contrary to the charge given to internal audit to conduct an objective audit and report all relevant findings.

Another observed demerit of using an IAF as an MTG is a high turnover within the IAF. Some observers have reasoned that the lack of continuity within the internal audit staff may compromise audit quality. As a result, most functions keep a core group of internal auditors within the function to provide a degree of stability. This also is not without its pitfall, as the IAF may face employee morale issues if core auditors are limited in their opportunities for growth while management trainees are consistently promoted to managerial positions.

Finally, "according to *motivated reasoning theory*, a decision maker's judgment can be both knowingly and unknowingly biased when the decision maker is incentivized by personal benefit or avoidance of harm" (Kunda, 1990, as cited in Eller, 2014). In Kunda (as cited in Eller, 2014), it was succinctly stated that, "People are more likely to arrive at those conclusions that they want to arrive at" (p. 495). Thus, in relation to unethical behavior, evidence in psychology on *motivated reasoning* generally finds that unconscious bias toward corruption is the rule, while intentional dishonesty is the exception (Moore et al., 2006, as cited in Eller, 2014). It has been observed that as a result of *motivated reasoning*, with the attendance loss to the internal auditor's objectivity, it can lead to something as grievous as a reduced tendency to report a fraud for which there is fairly strong evidence. This is because in reporting fraud, internal auditors will be potentially exposing the company to reputational and monetary damages and their future position.

4.5 Staffing

Definition: *Staffing* may be defined as the process of hiring (recruitment and selection), positioning (assigning them with specific job functions and charging them with associated responsibilities), and overseeing (assessment, development, training, and compensation) of employees in an organization with the purpose of achieving organizational set goals (Nzechukwu, 2015).

According to the Standards for the Professional Practice of Internal Auditing (IIA), the director of internal auditing should establish a program for selecting and developing the human resources of the internal auditing department (Standard 540). The program should provide for

- Developing written job descriptions for each level of the audit staff
- Selecting qualified and competent individuals
- Training and providing continuing educational opportunities for each internal auditor
- Appraising each internal auditor's performance at least annually
- Providing counsel to internal auditors on their performance and professional development

However, the organization must determine its human capital strategy, which will guide the IAF in all of the staffing decisions it subsequently makes. PricewaterhouseCoopers, LLP, has outlined four basic internal audit human capital models; these models are not necessarily mutually exclusive and can be combined in a number of ways to create a human capital strategy (Anderson, as cited in Prawitt, 2003). These four models are outlined below:

1. **Experienced hire career model:** Where an IAF uses this type of model, it focuses attention on hiring experienced personnel from within or outside the organization. The objective is to ensure that they have auditors with specialized business knowledge and skills. In this case, internal audit activity may be seen as a permanent career destination.
2. **Migration model:** Similarly, this model is designed to ensure that only individuals who possess skills that are proven to make the IAF a successful part of the organization are selected and moved to other functional areas. While this model is not designed to make an IAF *automatically* an MTG, a successful movement of internal auditors into other functional areas of the organization is seen as a positive sign of the IAF's ability to add value to the organization.
3. **Consulting model:** By this model, auditors are recruited into the IAF only to later move them into other functional areas of the organization. Under this model, the IAF consists usually of a group of consultant auditors and another group of core auditors working together to achieve the IAF's objectives. Whereas consultants are internal auditors who are expected to move to other functional areas of the organization upon gaining valuable experience within the IAF, core auditors are those who remain with the IAF for an indefinite period of time as stated earlier. This model uses the IAF as an MTG.
4. **Change agent model:** This type of model views the IAF as an integral part of the organization's human resource strategy. Organizations using this model selectively deploy talent through internal audit into the business units, thereby making the IAF a corporate change agent who continuously refurbishes the business units with talent needs. With this model, the migration of talents to other functional areas of the organization is seen as part of a formal corporate strategy to achieve this objective of corporate staffing; it is also used as a primary performance metric for internal audit.

Finally, the staffing decision of an IAF is dependent on the choice of the human capital strategy it adopts, which may consist of a partial combination of the above component models. For example, an IAF that uses the consulting model will likely attract individuals with more expertise, while an IAF that uses the change agent model will attract individuals with more corporate experiences.

4.5.1 *Hiring*

Definition: According to the *Small Business Encyclopedia, hiring* can be defined as the practice of finding, evaluating, and establishing a working relationship with future employees, interns, contractors, or consultants.

Hiring qualified personnel is an essential part of effectively managing an IAF. However, because of the wide variety of alternative human capital strategies, industry differences, and different knowledge, skills, and experience requirements, the IAF takes different approaches in hiring to meet organizational needs.

Hiring can be in the form taking fresh graduates or hiring experienced business personnel. The latter is based on the assumption that auditors with business experience will add value to the organization and ensure that client needs are met. These experienced business personnel may not necessarily have formal auditing, accounting, or financial skills, but may have knowledge and expertise on other fields, which will add value to the assurance services of the IAF. In addition, the IAF seeks more experienced business personnel because of the candidates' ability to cope and deal with change. It is believed that these new hires are to increase the level of sophistication within the IAF and set an example for other staff members who have difficulties making changes (Gray and Gray, as cited in Prawitt, 2003). Experienced business personnel may come from within or outside the organization. Where they come from within, they may have more knowledge of the organization than outsiders; however, outsiders may bring innovative ideas from other organizations, which may change the mind-set of the insiders on value added.

An effective IAF naturally attempts to hire people who match the culture and needs of the organization. However, in so doing, the IAF must consider several factors, including the type of work it is engaged in (e.g., assurance services or consulting services), the organization's culture, and budget constraints. New hires must possess a reasonable degree of certain skills or at least have the aptitude to learn certain skills in order to be effective in their assignments. This is particularly true in relation to technological skills and ever-increasing enterprise-wide risk management assurance that are becoming increasingly important in an internal audit setting. As the IAF becomes more complex and moves to providing consulting services for the organization, managers must continue to evaluate their human resource needs.

After determining what type of recruits the IAF wants to hire, it is expected that the function must have and implement recruiting practices to attract the required candidates. It has not been determined why some IAFs consistently hire the best available candidates while other IAFs struggle to attract qualified personnel and generally hire mediocre job candidates; however, it should not be unconnected with the fact that while some IAFs may have an attractive organizational culture or implement superior recruiting techniques, others do not.

Finally, the IAF cannot make a decision about adding employees without knowing what it is going to cost to hire them. Salaries and benefits are the obvious costs of having additional employees, and they are the most important ones. But they are hardly the only ones. It also takes money to hire employees, just as it does to compensate them for their work. In addition to the foregoing costs, the IAF will have to budget for some or all of the following one-time hiring costs:

- Paid newspaper classified advertising to attract job applicants
- Own time or staff time to screen, sort, and file incoming resumes and applications
- Time or money (if you use an outside service) to conduct background checks on potential employees
- More of your time and money to conduct interviews
- Money to pay travel expenses for candidates who are located in other towns or states
- Training for new employees to get them up to speed
- Lost productivity resulting from new employees who do not work out
- Fees for executive search consultants or recruiters

All these costs may not be incurred for every employee, but if the IAF is hiring a significant number of new workers, it may likely face all of them sooner or later. Therefore, budgeting for them in advance can help make a realistic assessment of the costs of growth.

4.5.2 Training

Definition: *Training* may be defined generically as teaching or developing, in oneself or others, any skills and knowledge that relate to specific useful competences. In business, we can define training as the process of enhancing the knowledge and skills of the workforce to enable them to perform their job functions efficiently and effectively.

An ineffective audit can mean severe consequences, resulting in process failure, client dissatisfaction, and regular noncompliance. Training serves a vital role in correcting the identified flaws. Therefore, the IIA Standards require auditors to "enhance their knowledge, skills, and other competences through continuing professional development" (Standard 1230). ISO 29990:2010 *Learning services for non-formal education and training—Basic requirements for service providers* stresses the importance of training. This standard tends to improve quality of learning services and facilitate comparison on a worldwide basis.

In developing economies like those of Africa and some Asian countries, personnel training is very poor. Though no research exists to identify remote causes, experience has shown that some of the causes can be related to the following:

- Employer's fear of losing trained employee to another employer.
- In most cases, multinational companies prefer to import expatriates than train local people.

- Lack of legislative backing to compel employers to engage in training their employees; most often, only recommendations are made.
- One of the relative causes is budget constraint.
- In some cases, employees have redeemed the cost of their training by collecting cash for other personal uses.

Riley (2009) has indicated that though training costs can be significant in any business setting, many employers are ready to incur these costs because of the expected benefits accruing to their businesses through employees' development and progress. Training takes place at various points and places in a business life cycle. In most cases, training is required to

- Support new employees (*induction training*)
- Improve productivity
- Increase marketing effectiveness
- Support higher standards of customer/client service and production quality
- Introduce new technology, systems, or other change
- Address changes in policies, procedures, and legislation
- Support employee progression and promotion

It has been observed that effective training has the potential to provide a range of benefits for any business:

- Higher quality
- Better productivity
- Improved profitability
- Improved motivation—through greater empowerment
- More flexibility through better skills
- Less supervision requirement (cost saving in supervision)
- Better recruitment and employee retention
- Easier change implementation in the business

After hiring the appropriate personnel for the IAF, it is important that these personnel undergo proper training to enable them perform their job functions effectively and efficiently. Training is particularly important as organizations implement new programs or new policy directives that are subsequently audited by the IAF. "For example, in the late 1980s, American Standard instituted demand flow manufacturing based on just-in-time production systems. In order to prepare auditors to add value in auditing the organization's various operating functions, auditors received in-depth training in process mapping, quality management tools, business process reengineering, and just-in-time manufacturing principles" (Stoner and Werner, as cited in Prawitt, 2003). The company adjusted training programs to meet organizational changes and needs.

4.5.3 Types of Employee Training Programs

Baumeyer (2003, 2015) posits that most businesses offer their employees some type of training because managers know that the investment in employee training programs in a wide variety of areas is important to the bottom line (net profit or loss of a business income statement). Some of the various types of employee training programs and their benefits include literacy training, interpersonal skills training, technical training, problem-solving training, and diversity or sensitivity training. It is expected that the IAF shall leverage on these training types to function optimally.

Basic literacy training is training for things like reading, writing, and problem-solving skills. Once the employee learned how to read, write, and understand the written word to solve problems, they were better able to communicate with other members of the IAF in particular and the organization as a whole. For example, in a large organization with international locations, the movement of IAF staff from an Anglophone country to a Francophone country requires some basic literacy training. Some of the several benefits of literacy training for employees will include meeting IAF/company goals, ability to perform job tasks, understanding work processes, working in teams, making decisions, learning technology, etc.

Interpersonal skills training is training on how to maintain positive working relationships, maintain a positive mind-set, communicate better, resolve conflicts, and build trust among the workforce. The following are several benefits interpersonal skills training can offer the employee directly and indirectly to the organization: get along with each other, exchange positive communication, minimize conflict, influence others to have a positive mind-set, etc.

Technology training is training on computer software and hardware offered to specific IAF staff members depending on their positions in the department. The overall objective is to enhance their proficiency in technology in order to operate freely on a day-to-day basis and in an emergency situation. Some of the identified benefits include performing at higher standards, having more self-confidence, developing higher skill levels, performing many different tasks, etc.

Problem-solving training is training on how to analyze problems and make decisions, and is mandatory for all audit teams. In this type of training, team members will learn how to identify problems, analyze problems, assess solutions, and recommend solutions and follow-up outcomes. Some of the associated benefits will include offering creative solutions to problems, collaborating on problem solving, and preventing unnecessary risks.

Diversity or sensitivity training is training the IAF staff on cultural mix and how to avoid or manage sensitive discussions. In large organizations, the IAF may comprise people from different cultural backgrounds. This sometimes may elicit arguments among them, which may not be healthy for peaceful coexistence. To maintain civility and avoid mutiny, this type of training forces them to find a way to get along.

4.5.4 Forms or Methods of Training

In addition, there are many methods of training.

1. **In-house training:** In large organizations, auditors participate in formal in-house training programs. These include classroom-based training, distance learning through the Internet and videoconferencing, mentoring, on-the-job training, etc.; furthermore, some organizations cross-train auditors on the job so that they can become familiar with the entire organization.

2. **Outsourced training:** Other companies take a more hands-off approach to training and allow employees to develop their own training programs and to seek training outside the organization, or implement company training programs using outsourced training firms through open/public workshops; this may be typical of smaller IAFs. In addition to using outsourced training programs, IAFs sometimes encourage auditors to seek training from professional organizations like the IIA, the American Institute of Certified Public Accountants (AICPA), Chartered International Investment Analysts (CIIA), or similar bodies. If auditors seek outside training, they are typically encouraged to ensure that the training meets organizational objectives and personal goals.

3. **Mentoring:** Mentoring is another tool that IAFs often use to develop and train employees. Mentoring will often take place on an informal basis as junior auditors seek advice from more experienced personnel. The IAF may consider setting up a formal mentoring program that pairs a junior and senior auditor together. The senior auditor can guide the junior in internal auditing work as well as show his/her the *ropes* of the organization (Ramamoorti et al., as cited in Prawitt, 2003).

4. **Professional certification:** Getting employees ready to pass professional certification examinations is another form of training. This can be done by the IAF itself through in-house training; however, most times, auditors or candidates in this case seek training outside the organization from tutorial houses or learning service providers. Campbell (as cited in Prawitt, 2003) states that many IAFs encourage employees to obtain these certifications and reimburse employees for training and test costs. Candidates or researchers interested in professional certification issues should refer to *The IIA's Annual CIA Survey*, which focuses on such issues as changes in and perceptions of the Certified Internal Auditor (CIA) program, employer support of certification, and demographics of CIAs. Information can be found in the survey report regarding the structure of the CIA certification, how it is administered, the extent and nature of incentives to become a CIA, and other relevant issues relating to fruitful research questions (also see Gramling and Myers, as cited in Prawitt, 2003).

5. **Continuous professional development/education:** As stated earlier, Standard 1230 requires auditors to continually enhance their knowledge, skills, and other competencies through continuing professional development/education/training. Professional bodies like the IIA, CIIA, ICAN, AICPA, etc., continually advertise and encourage their members to refresh and update their knowledge on existing and current issues relating to the profession. IAF, particularly those in large organizations, take advantage of this opportunity to update their knowledge and skills on current events making around the profession.

4.5.5 Become a Professional Internal Auditor (PIA)

To become a PIA, the following steps shall be taken:

a. Step 1: Decide the right certification you want (e.g., CIA, CPA, CPE, etc.); however, since IIA is a globally recognized certifying body, we recommend internal auditors to seek to obtain CIA certification. There are three stages to obtaining CIA certification. The IIA also offers five specialty certifications and qualifications including
   – Certification in Control Self-Assessment (CCSA)
   – Certified Government Auditing Professional (CGAP)
   – Certified Financial Services Auditor (CFSA)
   – Certification in Risk Management Assurance (CRMA)
   – The latest is, Qualification in Internal Audit Leadership (QIAL), launched in July, 2014
   Where an individual could meet with the eligibility requirements of CIA, he/she may wish take one or more of the specialty certifications, which, incidentally, is a one-part examination.
b. Step 2: After making a decision on your preferred certification, you should determine the eligibility requirements to qualify for the exams. If you are seeking for IIA certification, you may wish to do an online self-assessment test on the IIA website to determine your readiness to write proper exams and also know your area weaknesses.
c. Step 3: Register for the exams; The IIA's certification exams are now offered year round using computer-based testing at various centers and affiliates.
d. Step 4: Prepare for the exams by taking a decision on the method to adapt. Some candidates may like independent preparation, whereas others may like using tuition houses or learning service providers. You may also consider using social media like Facebook or LinkedIn to access other candidates taking similar exams and exchange ideas.

e. Step 5: At this step, you are required to take the exams using what is called the Pearson VUE Testing Centre, which is a network of about 500 computer-based testing centers.

f. Step 6: Once you meet the passing requirements through the test, you will be required to log into your candidate record in the Certification Candidate Management System (CCMS) and complete the certificate order form. Thereafter, the certificate would be shipped to you using a standard postal service method at no extra charge.

Finally, besides the formal training programs available to internal auditors, internal auditors also obtain on-the-job-training as they audit other functional areas of the organization and also as a result of clients' continuous demand for more value-added services from the IAF, which is aimed at developing their management and consulting skills. Where there are significant amounts of new hires, the IAF may find it difficult to develop a single training program that meets the needs of all of its employees because of the diverse backgrounds and experiences of many new hires. For instance, a fresh university/college graduate with an accounting degree will have different training needs than an experienced business person; also, an experienced IT audit staff may have a different training need than experienced accounting staff. Understanding how to handle these different needs is the hallmark of an effective IAF.

4.5.6 Analyzing Task Structure

Audit departments must understand the nature of the tasks performed in audit and consulting engagements. A careful analysis of generic tasks performed by internal auditors may help IAMs make effective staff assignments. While little is known about how IAFs deal with these issues, task structure has been researched in several different fields, including our work earlier on this chapter (see Section 4.4.1.3). A general internal audit structure may look as illustrated in Figure 4.6.

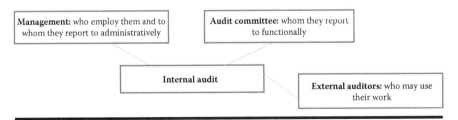

Figure 4.6 Typical internal audit structure.

4.5.7 Necessary Skills

An array of skills and expertise, and continuous professional development are critical to the establishment and maintenance of an effective internal audit activity. The essential components of these varieties include in-depth knowledge of the organization's industry and internal audit standards and best practices; technical understanding and expertise; knowledge on skills for implementing and improving processes in both financial, operational, and compliance areas; strong communication and presentation skills; and professional certification, for example, CIA.

The IIA Standards indicate that "Internal auditors should possess the knowledge, skills, and other competencies needed to perform their individual responsibilities. The internal audit activity collectively should possess or obtain the knowledge, skills, and other competencies needed to perform its responsibilities" (Standard 1210).

In an effort to ensure that internal auditors possess the skills and qualities that enable them to perform their responsibilities, in 1999 the IIA published a set of reports collectively known as the *Competency Framework for Internal Auditing* (*CFIA*) (Birkett et al., as cited in Prawitt, 2003). The *CFIA* was developed through a series of questionnaires sent to internal auditing experts around the world. The result of these questionnaires is a comprehensive listing of competency standards that delineate the "attributes of a competent internal auditing function, in the light of global 'best practice' [and] the capabilities required of key role-takers in a competent internal auditing function."

The competency standards include tasks that must be performed to "meet the functional requirements of the field of practice" (Birkett et al., as cited in Prawitt, 2003). The *CFIA* also discusses the attributes internal auditors must possess in order to make it possible for them to competently perform these tasks. These attributes are separated into two areas: cognitive and behavioral skills, which are each separated into three subcategories. Cognitive skills consist of technical skills, analytic/design skills, and appreciative skills. Behavioral skills consist of personal skills, interpersonal skills, and organizational skills (Table 4.3).

The *CFIA* also presents a comprehensive list of attributes that fall under each category. These attributes are further separated into those that neophyte internal auditors, competent internal auditors, and internal auditing management should possess. Table 4.4 (pp. 108–114) is a reproduction of Table 4.3 included in Birkett et al. (as cited in Prawitt, 2003). This table can be useful for practitioners as they identify qualified recruits, develop training programs, and promote personnel. An understanding of these skills and attributes may also benefit researchers as they study and research related issues.

The *CFIA* provides several skills and attributes that are important for IAMs.

Unlike the general leadership attributes discussed previously, these attributes apply specifically to leaders within the IAF. Please refer to the bolded attributes in Table 4.4 (pp. 108–114).

Table 4.3 Skills Required of Internal Auditors

Category/Subcategory	Description
Cognitive Skills	
Technical skills	Following defined routines with some mastery.
Analytic/design skills	Problem identification or task definition and the structuring of prototype solutions or performances.
Appreciative skills	Making complex and creative judgments, often in situations of ambiguity.
Behavioral Skills	
Personal skills	Handling oneself well in situations of challenge, stress, conflict, time pressure, and change.
Interpersonal skills	Securing outcomes through interpersonal interactions.
Organizational skills	Securing outcomes through the use of organizational networks.

Source: Adapted from Birkett et al., as cited in Prawitt (2003). *Managing the Internal Audit Function* (p. 192). The Institute of Internal Auditors Research Foundation (Research Opportunities in Internal Auditing), Orlando, Florida. Copyright 2003 by The Institute of Internal Auditors.

As the role of the internal auditor shifts from traditional continuous assurance on the effectiveness of control, through regulatory changes or a more volatile economy and stakeholder's expectations on enterprise-wide risk assurances, so, too, do the skills required to do the job well. These expectations have demanded for broader technical skills, yet this alone cannot guarantee the achievement of these expectations. "The evolution of the skills of internal audit professionals is aligning with, or is corresponding to, the evolution of the profession itself," said Richard Chambers, chief executive and president of the Institute of Internal Auditors (Amato, 2013).

Chambers (as cited in Amato, 2013) was the co-author of a recent report, "Succeeding as a 21st century internal auditor: Seven attributes of highly effective internal auditors." He noted that the report, which was produced by the IIA and global staffing firm Robert Half, listed seven traits:

1. **Integrity:** Internal auditors need to be trustworthy but should also have confidence and resilience when faced with complex problems. While this is an important attribute in any business setting, it is especially important in the IAF.

Table 4.4 Individual Attributes Required of Internal Auditors

Technical Skills	Analytic/Design Problem Structuring and Solving Skills	Appreciative Skills Judgment/Synthesis	Personal Skills	Interpersonal Skills	Organizational Skills
* Using information technology - Database systems - Spreadsheets * Communication - Literacy/writing - Structuring reports * Using relevant statistical methods * Understanding of organizational dynamics * Understanding of theories of risk * Understanding of theories of organizational control	* Logical reasoning * Ability to conceptualize * Problem analysis/structuring * Research skills (finding, accessing, and assessing data) * Using data in problem solving * Linking evidence to arguments and conclusions * *Analyzing commercial and financial data* * *Basic analysis of accounts and accounting reports* * *Systems analysis and review*	* *Recognize importance of data* * *Sorting out the relevant (e.g., in data, evidence)* * *Judging whether information is sufficient, supportive of opinions* * *Observant/aware* * *Critical thinking* * *Able to be concise/succinct* * *Accepting of new/other's ideas* * *Strives for continuous improvement in self* * *Finding all that is relevant*	* *Honest* * *With integrity* * *A-political* * *Inquisitive* * *Questioning* * *Balanced (not blinkered) in line of inquiry* * *Not dogmatic* * *Has initiative* * *Self-starter* * *Intelligent* * *Open-minded* * *Flexible* * *Adaptive to circumstances* * *Effecting change in self* * *Creative* * *Objective* * *Has a positive attitude to technology*	* *Communication* - *Aware of audience* - *Listener* - *Oral skills* - *Interpersonal skills* * *Presentation skills* * *Team player* * *Learns from others* * *Handles frustration for self* * *Discrete/tactful* * *Empathic* * *Diplomatic* * *Supportive of others* * *Culturally sensitive* * *Communication* - *Persuasive* - *Influencing, persuading, motivating, changing others*	* *Finding way around organizations* * *Attaining a knowledge of the business (products, strategies, processes, markets, risks)* * *Adapting internal audit work to a wide range of organizational systems, methods, and standards* * *Negotiating the application of professional standards*

Keys: Written in italics, neophyte internal auditor; written in italics bold, competent internal auditor; written in italics underlined, internal auditing management.

(Continued)

Table 4.4 (Continued) Individual Attributes Required of Internal Auditors

Technical Skills	Analytic/Design Problem Structuring and Solving Skills	Appreciative Skills Judgment/ Synthesis	Personal Skills	Interpersonal Skills	Organizational Skills
* Using information technology – Audit software * Apply control system designs and procedures * Documentation of internal audit work * Using/reviewing accounting procedures/ principles * Apply laws and regulations * Apply internal auditing technologies and procedures	* Internal audit requirements analysis/definition * Using sophisticated analytic models in support of internal audit judgment * Using industry-specific databases in the internal audit process * Using comprehensive internal auditing approaches * Using extra-organizational information in the internal audit process	* Sorting out productive, central lines of inquiry * Seeing anomalies and recognizing their implications * Sensing the significance of issues * Seeing the internal audit process as a whole * Locating particular problems or situations in terms of more global contexts/ responsibilities	* Sociable * Confident * Enthusiastic * Accepting of responsibility * Makes things happen * Able to handle pressure * Time management * Decisive * Able to stand ground * Stress management * Patience * Persistence * Dedication * Intuitive/gut-feel	* Leadership (of teams, groups) * Can handle an adversarial role * Can handle multitasking * Able to diffuse conflict, conflict resolution * Able to calm a situation * Can handle frustration for others * Can manage intragroup dynamics * Can define requirements (for team, others) * Can secure control * Can coach/mentor	* Adding commercial value * Making productivity gains * Marketing internal auditing services * Using sophisticated technologies/ approaches in managing internal audit work – TQM – Project management – Time management

(Continued)

Table 4.4 (Continued) Individual Attributes Required of Internal Auditors

Technical Skills	Analytic/Design Problem Structuring and Solving Skills	Appreciative Skills Judgment/Synthesis	Personal Skills	Interpersonal Skills	Organizational Skills
* Using/reviewing accounting principles/ procedures * Master of new information technologies * Understanding key principles of specialty fields, including – Environmental management systems – Quality management systems – Information technology controls	* Using nonfinancial evaluation methods in internal audit work * Designing control systems * Organizational analysis – Strategies – Functions (financing, marketing, production) – Structures – Processes – Risks – Controls * Using models in analysis	* Making associations, thinking outside the square * Comprehending internal audit in the context of business * Discriminating between substance and form * Disciplining imagination * Sensing/serving client needs and expectations * Having a sense of practicability, materiality	* Tenacious * Determined * Handles/welcomes change * Proactive * Assertive * Professional demeanor * Pushing the limits * Incisive * Able to anticipate	* Can develop others * Can manage intergroup dynamics * Can delegate (within teams) * Can conduct meetings * Facilitation * Liaison/negotiation (within team, for team)	– Using performance criteria – Benchmarking – Planning – Scheduling – Coping with international transactions, structures and legal arrangements * Building/using relationships and networks * Adding client value * Building trust * Managing internal audit work

(Continued)

Table 4.4 (Continued)   Individual Attributes Required of Internal Auditors

Technical Skills	Analytic/Design Problem Structuring and Solving Skills	Appreciative Skills Judgment/ Synthesis	Personal Skills	Interpersonal Skills	Organizational Skills
	* Adapting internal audit methodologies for evaluating controls in computer systems * Validating assumptions/ projections underpinning plans and decisions * Developing prototype solutions to problems * Developing technologies for reducing audit risk	* Assessing the risk associated with internal audit assignments * Coping with increasingly complex transactions, regulations, and organizations * Adapting to revised expectations about internal audit processes and outcomes * Risk awareness * Interpreting relevant laws and standards			* Using organizational power sources, and structures * Delegations (within function) * Reading the culture and politics of an organization * Liaison and negotiation (for function) * Leadership (of the function) * Using consulting entrepreneurial approaches in selecting areas of internal audit work

(Continued)

Table 4.4 (Continued) Individual Attributes Required of Internal Auditors

Technical Skills	Analytic/Design Problem Structuring and Solving Skills	Appreciative Skills Judgment/ Synthesis	Personal Skills	Interpersonal Skills	Organizational Skills
	* Designing new internal audit technologies for systems analysis and evaluation * Developing internal audit technologies for assessing business risk * Developing methodologies and databases for establishing performance criteria and measuring performance * Designing risk management systems	* **Applying disciplinary understandings and research findings to internal audit work** * **Extending judgment over time (projection)** * **Knowing what should be there** * **Sensing what is not there** * **Making syntheses from isolated evidence** * **Employing a sense of perspective**			* Expanding internal audit work into new areas (requiring new skills) * Human resource management * Strategy format on (for function) * Structuring change productivity * Championing empowerment

(Continued)

Table 4.4 (Continued) Individual Attributes Required of Internal Auditors

Technical Skills	Analytic/Design Problem Structuring and Solving Skills	Appreciative Skills Judgment/ Synthesis	Personal Skills	Interpersonal Skills	Organizational Skills
		*Taking a strategic view, seeing the macro as well as the micro * Being street wise (applying a sense of commercial reality) * Business acumen * Cope with information overload * Able to see big picture * Expect/cope with the bizarre * Desire for win–win * Making sense of complex situations * Managing complexity*			

(Continued)

Table 4.4 (Continued)   Individual Attributes Required of Internal Auditors

Technical Skills	Analytic/Design Problem Structuring and Solving Skills	Appreciative Skills Judgment/ Synthesis	Personal Skills	Interpersonal Skills	Organizational Skills
		* **Seeks to add value** * **Seeks to instill quality** * **Juggling inconsistent priorities** * **Strives for continuous improvement in others** * *Developing and using criteria to promote consistency in judgment*			
		* *Making complex multivalued judgments in the absence of data and with probabilistic inferences only*			

Source: Adapted from Bi et al., as cited in Prawitt (2003). *Managing the Internal Audit Function* (pp. 193–196). The Institute of Internal Auditors Research Foundation (Research Opportunities in Internal Auditing), Orlando, Florida. Copyright 2003 by The Institute of Internal Auditors.

2. **Relationship building:** Trust and collaboration are more likely when people know each other well. Credibility must be built over time; therefore, it is important that internal auditors familiarize themselves with the auditee well ahead the audit engagement.

3. **Partnering:** The ability to partner enables internal auditors to execute effectively, balancing a customer service orientation with the ability to meet regulatory requirements.

4. **Effective oral and written communication skills:** Concise, compelling reports are part of this skill, as well as the ability to listen and to know the best format in which to present information.

5. **Teamwork:** Working well with others is required in a collaborative environment. According to a report by Karl Erhardt, senior vice president and general auditor at MetLife, "I don't want someone here if they cannot function on a team."

6. **Diversity:** Internal auditors must take on a global mind-set and be cognizant of cultural norms.

7. **Continuous learning:** Nonstop curiosity helps even the most experienced auditors gain new insight. As business needs shift, professionals should be proactive about developing new areas of expertise. "If you want to be successful, you have to be willing to invest in yourself," Chambers said.

Other relevant traits include:

8. **Strong interpersonal skills:** Having positive working relationships, a positive mind-set, and better communication resolve conflicts and build trust among the workforce.

9. **Good coaching and group leadership skills**.

10. **Ability to influence at all levels**.

These attributes mainly fall into the category of soft or technical skills, and more and more those skills are required, not desired, in this 21st century.

"The nontechnical skills—writing skills, solid presentation skills—have really become mandatory," said Paul McDonald, Chambers' co-author and a senior executive director at Robert Half. "As employees advance up the company's org chart, the skills become more critical."

A survey conducted by the IIA in 2012 a round the globe showed that internal audit job postings shop for nontraditional skills to fill vacant positions. In that study, it was discovered that the top five skills of those recruited into IAF were analytical and critical thinking, communication skills, IT general skills, risk management, and business acumen. This amazing discovery showed that the traditionalist skills like accounting did not make it in the top five skill recruitments. This again confirms the growing need for versatile skills in the IAF to be able achieve the objectives of IAF as enshrined in the charter, and adds the desired value to the organization. In a nutshell, it confirms the responsive nature of the internal audit profession where risk profiles drive audit coverage, and audit coverage drives the most pressing skill requirements.

4.5.8 Managing Knowledge and Other Resources in the IAF

Internal audit staff represents the IAF's valuable asset, and their skills must be evaluated and employed optimally. Managing the IAF's intellectual resources does not stop simply at providing internal auditors with training and seeing that they have the necessary skills to complete their work; it involves utilizing auditor skills in the most effective way possible by deploying them in areas and engagements where their skills will meet the needs of their clients (Gibbs, as cited in Prawitt, 2003).

One of the important aspects of managing the IAF's knowledge resources is tracking and appropriately deploying auditor skills. In some large audit functions, databases are used to store employee bio-data or background information including relevant skills, projects completed, acquired training, development needs, and career interests and other relevant information that could best describe the employee. Some companies use a skill matrix that documents the skills possessed by each member of the IAF. The assessments are made by managers and by the staff themselves. The information can then be used to staff engagements with auditors possessing the appropriate skills (Roth, as cited in Prawitt, 2003). In today's world of data mining and analytics, it is easier to sort staff with relevant skills, knowledge, and experience for each audit assignment (Nzechukwu, 2015).

Another important consideration in knowledge management in an IAF is measuring the effectiveness of these staffing procedures. For example, the IAF can attempt to measure effectiveness of staffing practices by tracking employee satisfaction, turnover, average tenure, number of requests for permanent assignments of audit personnel, and number of employee improvement initiatives. To the extent such data are made available for research purposes, researchers could assist in evaluating various approaches to knowledge management within the internal auditing profession.

It is important to note that matching internal audit staff skills to the engagement is not a stand-alone decision by the IAMs but must also consider time and other resource constraints. With the increasing importance of internal auditing's consulting role, audit managers must, at the same time, consider the differences in skill sets required in consulting services as against assurance tasks. Standard 2230 recognizes this potential challenges and requires that, "Staffing should be based on an evaluation of … the available resources."

Finally, the CAE must ensure that internal audit resources are appropriate, sufficient, and effectively deployed to achieve the approved plan (Standard 2030).

4.5.9 *Performance Measurement*

Performance measurement involves evaluating an individual internal auditor's performance in meeting the objectives of each audit engagement, as well as evaluating the IAF in meeting the entire internal audit objectives as stated in the internal audit charter.

Standard 1300—Quality Assurance and Improvement Program (QAIP), stipulates that "the Chief Audit Executive must develop and maintain quality assurance and improvement program that covers all aspect of the internal audit activity." This includes both internal and external assessments and must enable an evaluation of the internal audit activity's conformance with the definition of internal auditing, the international standards for the professional practices of internal auditing (standards), and an evaluation of whether internal auditors apply the code of ethics. The established program should also assess the efficiency and effectiveness of the internal audit activity and identify opportunities for improvement. However, this standard was silent on evaluating the performance of individual auditors, notwithstanding that measuring and assessing the performance of individual internal auditors is imperative in monitoring the effectiveness of recruiting and selection methods, making pay increases and promotion decisions, evaluating training programs, and determining training needs.

Additionally, as IAF leaders assess the performance of individual auditors, they will simultaneously gather important information to help them control the performance of the IAF as a whole. According to Alcantara and Monica (2013), ISO 9001 audits are the most widely used performance measurement method to assess ISO 9001 quality management systems (QMSs). However, in recent years, the effectiveness of ISO 9001 quality auditing has been questioned for the following reasons:

1. Only focuses on compliance
2. Fails to detect problems in products and processes
3. Fails to predict QMS failures
4. Fails to provide added value to organizations

From the foregoing, ISO 9001 is not performance oriented; therefore, it does not promote improvements in business processes and the QMS.

IAFs are primarily evaluated on the basis of the quality of advice and information provided to the audit committee and top management. Because the measures are primarily qualitative in nature, the traditionalists argue that it is difficult to measure. However, the recent adoption of balanced scorecard (BSC) by large organizations, research by performance management experts, and assistance of technology have made it imperative for all factors both quantitative and qualitative to be measurable. The axiom in the BSC framework is that "what can't be measured can't be managed." Some of the typical tools used effectively in measuring the performance of IAF are *customer surveys* sent to key managers after each audit engagement, content report, annual survey to the audit committee, scoring on dimensions such as professionalism, quality of assurance services, timeliness of work product, utility of meetings, and quality of status updates. Understanding the expectations of top management and the audit committee represents an important step in developing a good performance measurement process; also, understanding the metrics that help align the audit function with organizational priorities is key. Sometimes where internal auditors' performance is evaluated partly by post-audit client evaluations of the auditor, technique may introduce a conflict of interest between auditors and auditees. Auditors may alter their recommendations and suggestions in order to receive more favorable post-audit surveys from auditees. This is usually the case if the auditors' performance evaluations or compensation are based on such survey reports. It is therefore expected that at least every five years, the IAF shall be subjected to external appraisal by what is called independent peer reviews as part of the quality assurance process. We shall discuss peer review extensively in Chapter 7.

Performance measurement policies and procedures vary widely among IAFs and industries, and can be designed to meet various needs of the function in particular and the organization as whole. Usually and mostly in large organizations, these policies and procedures, and the performance appraisal results, will be documented to keep track of employee progress. In other smaller organizations, the procedures may be more informal. Where an IAF uses teams, it is expected to maintain performance measurement procedures that allow managers to assess both team and individual performance.

Because performance measures are powerful tools in influencing employee behavior, great care should be taken in developing performance measures that solicit the desired behavior.

Ultimately, performance measures should motivate auditors and audit teams to add value to the organization while maintaining their independence and objectivity.

4.5.10 Compensation

According to Prawitt (2003), compensation is an important motivational tool for improving individual and organizational performance, and for attracting and retaining right and valuable employees. Because of the important role of compensation in organizations, many firms have attempted to create compensation systems that yield a competitive advantage in hiring and retaining human capital. IAFs make use of a variety of compensation schemes, including traditional salary-based systems, pay for skill and pay for performance incentives, and pay for extra performance (overtime) schemes. Unlike external auditors, internal auditors may even participate in company stock-based incentives.

Increasingly, internal audit activities are performed by multidisciplinary teams that include engineers, accountants, management graduates, and even environmental specialists who reflect a broad range of today's assurance needs. Also, information technology audit experts are a core component of modern-day internal audit activities. These types of employees have different backgrounds, experiences, qualifications, skills, expertise, etc. It is therefore expedient that the IAF's compensation plan must take these differences into cognizance, along with related employee motivation and morale issues. The compensation systems of IAFs must also take into account the structural changes occurring in the profession. For instance, the internal auditor's job description is changing and expanding as a result—auditors are performing a wider variety of services for their organizations; they are working together in teams to complete engagements; and the nature of their work is being affected by technology.

4.5.11 Retention

Staff or employee turnover is one of the metrics for determining employee satisfaction or motivation and also one of the key performance indicators (KPIs) for determining an organization's workforce volatility. The turnover an organization experiences to a reasonable extent is determined by its staffing techniques. For example, IAFs that are used as a training ground for management will naturally experience high turnover. Retention goals and objectives will differ significantly among IAFs that are used as an MTG, or that use other human resource strategies. Also, retention rate will vary significantly between IAFs that are used as MTG and those that are not. Even if used as an MTG, retention of the group of core auditors must also be addressed.

To improve retention, many internal auditing functions attempt to provide rich career environments by giving employees challenging assignments with a competitive reward system. They seek to provide auditors with a broad range of experiences by rotating auditors among different assignments, allowing auditors to implement solutions to the problems they find, and giving auditors international work assignments (DeZoort et al., as cited in Prawitt, 2003). Many IAFs attempt to improve job satisfaction and retention by increasingly allowing auditors to exercise their creativity and participate fully in all aspects of assurance and consulting work.

4.6 Leading

4.6.1 Leadership

Leadership can be defined as "the ability to inspire others to follow the one leading and who has a set of goals to accomplish with the followers" (Nzechukwu, 2015). Leadership has been identified as one of the key attributes of contemporary internal auditors. The success of the IAF may depend, to a great extent, on the leadership abilities of internal audit executives and managers. Owing to the unique position of the IAF within the organization, some leadership traits are likely more important than others. The IAF is a *catalyst* that exists to create real value for the parent organization. It is therefore imperative that the IAF leaders must have a vision of the status they want the IAF to achieve within the organization. They must then communicate this vision to other internal auditors, management, and line employees (Griffen, as cited in Prawitt, 2003).

The attributes expected of IAF leaders have been listed above, including integrity and other ethical behaviors as contained in IIA ethical codes. Without integrity, IAF leaders cannot expect their auditors to provide the organization with objective, independent assurance, and consulting services. This quality lends credibility to the internal auditors' work and creates a favorable *tone at the top* for the IAF.

Finally, internal audit leaders must be able to create an organizational culture within the IAF that motivates employees to create real value for the organization. Gray and Gray (as cited in Prawitt, 2003) state that, in some departments, managers allow or even require subordinates to evaluate their performance. These managers were of the opinion that upward reviews allow them to receive useful feedback and communicate their commitment to employees. Additionally, Roth (as cited in Prawitt, 2003) posits that some IAMs involve staff in all meaningful decisions, allow staff to interact with company executives, encourage open communication and creativity, promote core values and ethics, and give recognition and praise for performance.

4.6.2 Communication

Communication is an act of sending and receiving information verbally, in writing, through signs/signals, or any other medium through which parties pass information (Nzechukwu, 2015). According to Standard 2020, the CAE must communicate the internal audit activity's plans and resource requirements, including significant interim changes, to senior management and the board for review and approval. The CAE must also communicate the impact of resource limitations.

Effective communication is key in an IAF; as a catalyst, the IAF acts between other employees and the board or audit committee in discharging its assurance and consulting services. Three reasons give credence to this importance: first, open and detailed communication between the IAF and the board contributes to effective organizational governance. The internal audit standards state, "The chief audit executive should report periodically to the board and senior management on the internal audit activity's purpose, authority, responsibility, and performance relative to its plan" (Standard 2060).

Secondly, effective communication is essential for developing *client* relationships. Whether the IAF is serving the board, management, or some other party, it must clearly define and communicate its activities to these parties. Internal auditors can improve communication with their clients by providing timely feedback, holding pre- and post-engagement meetings to discuss client needs, involving business unit staff to complete various aspects of the engagement, and proactively communicating about problems that arise during the audit (Gray and Gray, as cited in Prawitt, 2003).

Thirdly, internal auditors continuously interact with each other as a team or in teams and other settings.

Therefore, effective communication is sine qua non to coordinate audit work and achieve objectives. Effective communication is particularly imperative as audit managers give feedback to and receive input from subordinates (Griffen, as cited in Prawitt, 2003).

4.7 Controlling

4.7.1 Measuring and Controlling the Performance of the IAF as a Whole

According to Griffen (as cited in Prawitt, 2003), "Control is the regulation of organizational activities so that some targeted element of performance remains within acceptable limits."

Meulder et al. (2012) state that, in the financial sector, the *three lines of defense* model has been adopted, which can also productively be adopted in a wide range of other sectors of the economy. This model is simply a conceptual separation of an organization's internal control levels: first line controls, second line monitoring controls, and third line independent assurance. This model also provides a framework with which the board can understand the role of internal audit in the overall risk management and internal control process of an organization.

The lines of defense can be conceptualized using Figure 4.7.

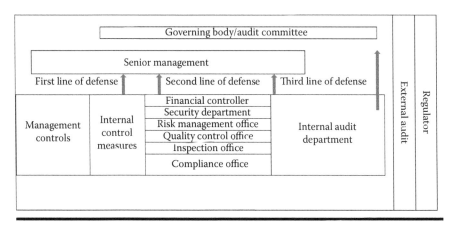

Figure 4.7 Three lines of defense. (Adapted from The European Confederation of Institutes of Internal Auditing (ECIIA), in close cooperation with the European Confederation of Directors' Associations (ecoDa). Making the most of the internal audit function: Recommendations for directors and board committees, 2012.)

Meulder et al. (2012) posit that under the first line of defense, management has rights, responsibility, and accountability for direct assessment, controlling, and mitigation of risks.

The second line of defense consists of line managers or several components of internal governance with activities range of compliance, risk management, quality, and other control departments. This line of defense monitors and expedites the implementation of effective risk management practices by operational management, and assists the risk owners in reporting adequate risk-related information up and down the organization.

On the other hand, a third line of defense forms the IAF, which, through a risk-based approach, provides assurance to the organization's board of directors and senior management on the efficiency and effectiveness of the control system. This assurance will cover how effectively the organization assesses and manages its risks, and will include assurance on the manner in which the first and second lines of defense operate. This assurance covers all elements of the risk management framework, including risk identification, risk assessment, response to risk and effectiveness, and efficiency of lines of communicating risk-related information. This assurance also comprises all categories of organizational objectives: strategic, operational, reporting, and compliance. From Figure 4.7, it can be deduced that the IAF is uniquely positioned within an organization to provide global assurance to the board and senior management on the effectiveness of internal governance and risk processes. The IAF is also well placed to fulfill an advisory role in respect of effective ways of improving existing processes and assisting management through its recommendations for improvement (Meulder et al., 2012).

Prawitt (2003) posits that though the IAF is part of the organization's control framework, it is pertinent that it establishes its own control framework to monitor compliance with its role and with other important goals and objectives it sets to achieve. The IIA Standards stipulate that the HIA/CAE should develop and maintain a quality assurance and improvement program that would cover all aspects of the internal audit tasks and continuously monitor its effectiveness (Standard 1300). The standards went further to state that the quality assurance program must monitor the IAF in two fundamental ways: first, the program should help the IAF add value to and improve the organization's operations; secondly, the quality assurance program should be of tremendous help to the IAF to comply with the standards.

One of the key ways that the IAF can add value to and improve the organization's operations and its governance is to successfully fulfill its role, as defined and contained in the internal audit charter. The IAF should develop methods to track its progress in fulfilling the goals and objectives established in its role as contained in the charter. One of the best methods of tracking progress is to use measurable KPIs to measure its assurance services; examples of measurable KPIs include the number of reports issued, percentage of the work plan completed, percentage over/under budget, etc. These performance measures must be carefully selected and designed in order to communicate true information that is supportive to the

IAF's role and strategy. To achieve this objective, some IAFs have begun to initiate BSCs that attempt to capture and measure the key drivers of internal audit success (Wong, as cited in Prawitt, 2003). This position is premised on the axiom "what's gets measured and rewarded, gets done," or "what can't be measured, can't be managed."

Besides the numerical measures, some IAFs sometimes send post-audit surveys to staff and managers of the business units. Some IAFs even conduct post-audit interviews with clients to help ensure that they are providing valuable services that meet organizational objectives (Roth, as cited in Prawitt, 2003).

4.8 Internal Audit Management Challenges

Wasonga (2013) states that, as a result of the demands of the current business environment, which has turned the spotlight on the role that a robust internal audit system must play within the larger drive toward effective governance, risk management, compliance, and quality assurance, an internal auditor has to work as a knowledgeable in-house cop who not only reports problems but also gives constructive suggestions to line managers about how to improve the performance of the business. As a result, the internal auditing and corporate control environments are receiving increased attention and resources, necessary to comply with the regulations.

Despite the increased exposure and buy-in from executive management, internal audit departments face many challenges. The challenges include

- Immature implementation of risk strategies
- Top–down view
- Complex financial disclosures
- Complex business models
- Growing regulatory guidelines and compliance
- Risk quantification
- Governance
- Tone at the top
- Monitoring and oversight
- Information sharing and communication

1. **Immature implementation of risk strategies**

    MetricStream (2015) reports that in a survey of audit committee members attending the Fourth Annual Audit Committee Issues Conference, 44% of conference attendees said that their company's processes to identify significant business risks need improvement, and 18% said the risk reports that management provides to the audit committee are not meaningful/useful. "Audit committees are taking a hard look at risk management processes, with a particular focus on the quality of risk inventories and assessments, as well as the usefulness of management's risk reports," said one of the directors at the conference. He said, "Key challenges include identifying risks early-on, and maintaining a 'big picture' view of the risks facing the business." From the foregoing, the audit committee is suggesting a need to focus on risk management processes, the quality of risk inventories and their assessment, as well as quality of risk management reports submitted by management.

2. **Top–down view**

    According to MetricStream (2015), a careful analysis of frauds, which led to the beginning of the SOX legislation, exposed major weaknesses in the top management and the control environment. This puts the spotlight on internal auditors to view the business from the top down, and increases the scope of reviews at corporate offices. The scope should not only include day-to-day transactions, but specific monthly, quarterly, and yearly management processes that strongly influence the financial statements.

3. **Complex financial disclosures**

    Wasonga (2013) identifies that the "board shoulders the ultimate responsibility for the integrity of the corporation's financial disclosure." Management is responsible for a fair presentation of the financial statements but the internal audit department must ensure that the financial statements do pass the litmus test. Accordingly, the challenge for internal auditors is to identify if there are discrepancies in the company's financial statements, confirm whether they are abiding by the financial reporting standards, verify whether sufficient controls are in place, and affirm whether shareholders or potential investors or lenders have sufficient information to make informed decisions.

4. **Complex business models**

    The board and management are responsible for ensuring the integrity of the business.

    The internal auditor is responsible for validating, directly or indirectly, whether the company's business model is sound. Internal audits confront issues like, "Will the company be able to survive, or compete in the market?" "Does it adhere to sound business practices?" "Does it have appropriate place for risk management and corporate governance programs in the organization?" Moreover, with communication making the world a global village, and global economies growing ever more complicatedly connected, organizations operate in a far more complex fashion than before. This increases the potentials for negative circumstances like inconsistency in enforcing audit processes across business units, erroneous data collection, and various gaps that result from isolated silos of information. It is difficult to gain the comprehensive visual map of the entire business, essential to effective management of risk, governance, compliance, and quality issues. The audit life cycle can often meet a variety of roadblocks that drag deadlines and jeopardize the quality and legal safeguards (MetricStream, 2015).

5. **Growing regulatory guidelines and compliance demands**

    The global regulatory environment is in an arena of constant change. Stipulations and guidelines are regularly reviewed and refined to retain their effectiveness. Very often, different countries may have distinct recommendations or legal expectations that can complicate the role and consistency of the internal audit process across a geographically spread enterprise. Whether it is ISO, SEC, IIA, or SOX guidelines, companies are now expected to proactively initiate internal, IT-enabled enterprisewide audit solutions that ensure compliance (MetricStream, 2013).

6. **Risk quantification**

    Risk is an integral part of any endeavor. In large organizations, the risk management unit and the risk management committee are responsible for risk management; however, it is the internal auditor's task to ensure that the risk management program works. An effective internal audit management system depends on the ability to build process cycles against an accurate matrix of assessed risk. However, given the dynamic regulatory environment and the complex interconnectedness of business functionalities, it is often extremely difficult to assess the multifaceted nature of business risk (Wasonga, 2013).

7. **Information sharing and communication**

    Organizations assist each other by sharing experiences and lessons. It would also be advantageous for boards and executive management to drive the implementation of such a model throughout the business. This should provide those who lag behind with a better perspective on risks and controls and what areas need to be considered in the everyday conduct of business to allow employees to take a proactive approach in enhancing the control environment.

    Progressive companies are increasingly seeing the answer to these challenges in a unified approach that integrates the audit cycle within closed-loop systems and affords end-to-end functionality across the board (MetricStream, 2015).

8. **Monitoring and oversight**

    Wasonga (2013) noted that most organizations expect internal audit departments to provide additional input to management, the board of directors, and the audit committee in the form of monitoring and oversight function, ensuring compliance monitoring and implementation of essential requirements.

    To address the issue of weaknesses in oversight programs, the department needs to establish the minimum standards for monitoring compliance and risk management programs. These standards should address compliance monitoring activities; technical assistance; enforcement; and documentation, analysis, and reporting of results.

Stiff penalties for noncompliance have prompted employers and employees to take a proactive approach to reduce the risks of fraud within their organizations.

However, with an increase in awareness and interest in corporate governance, the audit function faces an upsurge in the number of special requests.

This increase in demand for services, implementing a system to evaluate and prioritize the nature and timing of reviews, will no doubt provide an additional challenge for businesses and their audit function.

9. **Governance**

Wasonga (2013) is of the opinion that an ideal corporate governance framework consists of seven knotted elements, which include the board and its committees, legal and regulatory concerns, business practices and ethics, disclosure and transparency, ERM, monitoring, and communication.

It is the task of internal auditors to review each of these elements, and report their findings on a scorecard, rating their developmental stage along a scale as *compliant*, *developed*, or *advanced*.

From the beginning, the CAEs should review key organizational documents such as articles of incorporation, board and committee minutes, the annual report, investor relations policy, code of conduct and ethics, shareholder rights, and board calendar of events.

10. **Tone at the top**

According to MetricStream (2015), the IAF can only achieve top–down *buy-in* when the leadership of the organization is sensitized to and convinced of the vital impacts it has on compliance, quality, business continuity, and operational profitability.

Internal auditors naturally should work closely with the audit committee to establish the audit department's responsibilities, and the board and management should support those duties by creating the enabling environment. However, it has been observed that internal audit processes can sometimes be ignored by top management, who may choose to focus time and resources on areas they deem to be more pressing to bottom lines.

4.9 Overcoming the Challenges

Finally, in this chapter, we shall attempt to review the identified and suggested solutions to the above identified internal audit management challenges. Wasonga (2013), in their annual internal audit conference, ICPAK, held in Sai Eden Roc

Hotel, Malindi, observed that in order to address the rising expectations of chief stakeholders in any organization, internal audit needs to find new ways of deploying its risk- and control-based skills to help the organization achieve its strategic objectives and enable value creation. In a more elaborate contribution, MetricStream (2015) also explained some steps needed to ameliorate the identified challenges. Their contributions are as stated below:

1. **Risk identification and assessment**

   The internal audit should examine whether the risk assessment process synchronizes with the latest changes in the organization, addresses all activities conducted by the company, and includes all applicable regulatory requirements, and should also document the methodology used to conduct the risk assessment.

2. **Self-Monitoring and Remediation**

   The internal auditor's evaluation of a company's self-monitoring and remediation activities should begin with verifying that the monitoring program incorporates requirements specifically mandated by laws or regulations, and that it is appropriately aligned with compliance risk assessment.

3. **Internal controls**

   Internal audit should consider whether or not there is a system of adequate internal controls. The considerations are much the same as they would be in any other auditable area: separation of duties, access limitations, second-person review processes and proper documentation of reviews and approvals, etc. Another consideration would be whether the controls are manual or automated. Where internal controls are manual, internal auditors need to inspect whether the controls are addressing the requirements of the organization and possible review requirement. On the other hand, where they are automated, the internal auditors need to confirm that the workforce understands the technology and is working as intended.

4. **Role accountability and responsibility**

   During this part of the evaluation, it is important to consider the credibility, qualifications, and experience of key personnel who have been assigned the critical tasks. Internal auditors are charged with the responsibility of assuring the board of directors or the audit committee that management, financial systems, and processes are working effectively. In all other matters, the CEO represents management at the board of directors level. However, in this case, the CEO belongs to the group that is being audited, so it is important for the internal auditors to have direct reporting channels to the board or through the audit committee.

   The internal audit should examine the plan these individuals have developed for directing the company's compliance effort. This plan should be updated on a regular basis, and should set forth the compliance goals and the tactics (monitoring, training, policy and procedure review, and updating) for realizing these goals.

5. **Policies and procedures**

The internal auditor should focus its assessment on the company's process for ensuring that policies and procedures are comprehensive, reviewed, and updated on a periodic and reasonably frequent basis, as well as accessible and understandable. This should also verify that the company has a process in place for communicating important changes between periodic updates. In developing this assessment, internal auditors can test the process by selecting a significant and relatively new regulatory requirement and determining how effectively and efficiently the requirement has been incorporated into policies and procedures, and communicated to affected personnel.

6. **Board of directors and senior management oversight**

The assessment by the internal auditor of the role of the top management in overseeing a company's affairs should be considered from the point of view of the objective it tends to achieve, such as

- Whether the necessary resources (people and otherwise) and tools have been dedicated to the compliance and risk management effort
- Whether the tone at the top is inclined toward having tighter internal controls
- Whether the board of directors and senior management, through their words and actions, are communicating the importance of risk awareness across the company

This also includes instituting communication channels, including a whistleblower hotline to encourage reporting of compliance issues and risk concerns.

Here, the internal audit department should evaluate the processes put in place by management to establish and enforce accountability for compliance deficiencies. If evidence suggests that there are discrepancies in internal controls and risk management structure, this should be a cause for concern.

7. **Reporting and record keeping**

The internal auditor should also review how the organization manages the innumerable number of reporting and record-keeping requirements, as in the case of financial services companies. This requires validating that all such applicable requirements have been identified, responsibilities are assigned, and controls are put into place to ensure the required information is retained and retrievable for prescribed periods.

It is important to note that the *need of the hour* is an internal audit framework that provides a strategic model, for internal auditors and stakeholders, to understand the elements necessary to achieve a high-quality and effective IAF. Research effort in this area is open to the academia.

References

Alcantara, G., and Monica, F. (2013). Building a performance measurement internal auditing framework for the ISO 9001 quality management system. Faculty of Social Sciences, Law and Education. Nottingham University Business School. Modified November 18, 2014. Retrieved December 10, 2015, from URI: http://eprints .nottingham.ac.uk/id/eprint/13353.

Amato, N. (2013). The effective internal auditor: 7 key attributes. *CGMA Magazine.* American Institute of CPAs and Chartered Institute of Management Accountants. Copyright 2011–2015. Retrieved December 3, 2015, from: http://www.cgma.org /Magazine/News/pages/20137573.aspx.

Baumeyer, K. K. (2003, 2015). Types of employee training program. Study.com. Copyright 2003–2015 Study.com. Retrieved December 2, 2015, from: http://study.com/academy /lesson/types-of-employee-training-programs.html.

Chambers, R. (2014). From good to great: Strategic planning can define an internal audit function. Retrieved November 20, 2015, from: https://iaonline.theiia.org/from-good -to-great-strategic-planning-can-define-an-internal-audit-function.

Eller, C. K. (2014). Can using the internal audit function as a training ground for management deter internal auditor fraud reporting? Virginia Commonwealth University. Copyright the Author. Retrieved November 23, 2015, from: http://scholarscompass .vcu.edu/cgi/viewcontent.cgi?article=4591&context=etd.

ICAEW. (2004). Guidance for audit committees: The internal audit function. Retrieved November 20, 2015, from: http://www.icaew.com/~/media/corporate/files/technical /audit%20and%20assurance/audit/guidance%20for%20audit%20committees /the%20internal%20audit%20function.ashx.

Meulder, R. D., Barker, R., Vaurs, L., Wéry, P. F., Berliner, L., Nedervelde, C. V., Richez-Baum, B., Vandenbussche, P., Dittmeier, C. (2012). Making the most of the internal audit function: Recommendations for directors and board committees. ECIIA, Koningsstraat 109-111 bus 5, 1000 Brussels. ecoDA, 42, rue de la Loi, 1040 Brussels, Belgium. Retrieved November 14, 2015, from: http://www.ferma.eu/app /uploads/2012/12/2012-12-03-ecoda-eciia-audit-reform-guidance.pdf.

MetricStream. (2015). Effective internal audit management. MetricStream Inc. Retrieved November 18, 2015, from: http://www.metricstream.com/solution_briefs/Internal _Audit.htm.

Musiri, S., Schweik, A. L., and Watts, W. C. (2014). *Determining the Right Internal Audit Model for Your Company.* Crowe Horwath LLP, Chicago. Copyright (2014) by Horwath LLP. Retrieved November 21, 2015, from: http://bleu-azur-consulting.eu /fr/system/files/sites/bleu-azur-consulting.eu/files/bacprive/determiningrightinterna lauditmodel_risk14937.pdf.

Nzechukwu, O. P. (2015). *Staffing; Internal Audit Practice, from A to Z; How It Works.*

Prawitt, D. F. (2003). Managing the internal audit function. The Institute of Internal Audit Research Foundation. The Institute of Internal Auditors, 247 Maitland Avenue, Altamonte Springs, Florida. Retrieved October 28, 2012: https://na.theiia.org/iiarf /Public%20Documents/Chapter%206%20Managing%20the%20Internal%20Audit %20Function.pdf.

Riley, J. (2009). Business blog: Q&A—What is training? tutor2u. Copyright 2015, tutor2u.

Treasury Act of Australia. (2007). Internal audit framework. Retrieved from: http://apps
.treasury.act.gov.au/__data/assets/pdf_file/0007/617920/Internal-Audit-Framework
-April-2007.pdf.

Treasury Board of Canada Secretariat. (2009). Audit of the Treasury Board of Canada
Secretariat Governance Framework. Archived March 3, 2010. Copyright by: Treasury
Board of Canada Secretariat. Retrieved November 22, 2015, from: https://www.tbs
-sct.gc.ca/report/orp/2010/agf-acg01-eng.asp.

Wasonga, J. K. (2013). Managing the internal audit function; The annual internal audit
conference. Retrieved November 2015, from: http://www.icpak.com/wp-content
/uploads/2015/09/Managing-the-Internal-Audit-Function.pdf.

Chapter 5

Internal Audit Practice Layout

5.1 Introduction

Although every audit project is unique, the audit process is similar for most engagements and normally consists of four stages: planning (sometimes called survey or preliminary review), fieldwork, audit report, and follow-up review. Through these stages, the internal audit will determine ways to minimize risks and increase efficiencies within the area. Client involvement is critical at each stage of the audit process. As in any special project, an audit results in a certain amount of time being diverted from the auditee's/client's usual routine. One of the key objectives is to minimize this time and avoid disrupting ongoing activities (AuditNet LLC, 2014, p. 1).

5.2 Internal Audit Planning

5.2.1 Developing a Risk-Based Internal Audit Plan

It is said that "every successful audit is based on sound planning." The auditor should plan the audit in a manner that ensures that the audit is carried out in an economic, efficient, and effective way, and in a timely manner (Blume, 2014a).

The planning process must include the development of an in-depth, well-conceived, overall strategic plan that clearly defines the desired future state of the internal audit function. In addition, it is essential to create detailed tactical plans that support the overarching strategy, and to clearly describe the specific initiatives required to achieve the transformation. Too often, we see internal audit functions diving straight into tactical planning—especially regarding the deployment of technology—without first comprehending how their overall strategic plans and tactical plans fit together.

The following need to be considered while preparing the audit plan:

- Nature, size, and operation of the office, entity, or business
- Previous audit paragraphs and observations
- Availability and competence of audit staff
- Audit methodology most suited to the operations to be audited
- Format and general content of the report to be prepared

Performance Standard 2010 of the Institute of Internal Auditors (IIA) requires the "chief audit executive to establish risk-based audit plans to determine the priorities of the internal audit activity, consistent with the organization's goals."

The IIA defines risk-based internal auditing (RBIA) as a methodology that links internal auditing to an organization's overall risk management framework. RBIA allows internal audit to provide assurance to the board that risk management processes are managing risks effectively, in relation to the risk appetite. According to Griffiths, RBIA is a process, an approach, a methodology, and an attitude of mind rolled into one. The simplest way to think about risk-based auditing theoretically is to audit the things that really matter to your organization. To fully engage management and demonstrate your eagle-like qualities, you need to talk to them about something that is important to them. If you start by discussing their objectives, what they need to achieve, and how this is measured, you will attract their attention. Having created the common ground, you can now go on to discuss the threats to the achievement of those objectives, the barriers to success; these are, of course, the risks.

The kernel of a risk-based audit is therefore customer focused, starting with the objectives of the activity being audited, then moving on to the threats (or risks) to achievement of those goals, and then to the procedures and processes to mitigate the risks. Risk-based audits are therefore an evolution rather than a revolution, although the results obtained can be revolutionary in their magnitude (Griffiths).

The key points of using a risk-based approach to internal audit plans include the following:

- It helps focus the audit effort on areas that matter most (i.e., risky areas of the organization), hence economic use of audit resources.
- It improves the ability to influence and improve the organization by targeting the areas that erode value.
- It generates credibility from management.

5.3 Risk Management Process

As cited in Blume (2014b), risk is the uncertainty/possibility of an event occurring that will have an impact on the achievement of objectives. Risk is measured in terms of impact and likelihood (IIA). ISO/IEC 73 discusses the effect of uncertainty on objectives. Note that an effect may be positive, negative, or a deviation from the expected. Risk is combination of the probability of an event and its consequence. Consequences can range from positive to negative (Institute of Risk Management).

The following key points can be deduced from the above definitions:

■ Risk is a consequence of pursuing an OBJECTIVE.
■ Risk is something (event, situation, circumstances) that is UNCERTAIN.
■ Risk has an IMPACT on the objective, and a LIKELIHOOD of occurring.

Note: A distinction must be made between a *risk* and a *problem*. Whereas risk is the possibility of future events, which may happen or not (UNCERTAIN), a problem is an event that is CERTAIN (i.e., has or is happening or is known for sure to happen; hence, one does not need to prepare for it but to solve it).

5.3.1 Types and Categories of Risks

According to Blume (2014b), risks can be grouped into different categories according to their nature and effect; the underlisted are the most common types and categories of risks (Table 5.1):

i. Strategic risks: risks to the entity's direction, external environment, and to the achievement of its plans, for example, changes in government policies, political changes, etc.
ii. Compliance/commercial/legal risks: risks of commercial relationships/meeting regulatory obligations, such as breach of contract, noncompliance with accounting standards, or environmental regulations
iii. Operational risks: operational activities such as inadequate human resources, poor service levels, physical damage to assets, or threats to physical safety
iv. Technical risks: risks of managing assets such as equipment failure, IT risks like virus incidents, computer crash, etc.
v. Financial and systems risks: risks in financial controls and systems, such as fraud, theft or misappropriation of funds, inadequate funding, delayed procurement, delayed reports, risk of material misstatement, etc.

Risk management is a process for identifying, assessing, managing, and controlling potential events or situations to provide reasonable assurance regarding the achievement of the organization's objectives (IIA). Risk management involves an iterative process consisting of well-defined steps that, when taken in sequence, support better decision making by contributing a greater insight into risk and their impact. Risk management can be applied to any situation where an underdesired or unexpected outcome could be significant or where an opportunity can be identified. Decision makers need to know about possible outcomes and take steps to control their impact.

Table 5.1 Examples of Risks in Different Categories (Risk Management Guideline, 2012)

Strategic	Financial	Operational	Knowledge and System
Loss of customers to competitors	Incorrect valuation of capital assets	Absenteeism	Inadequate system security/ confidential information not adequately protected
Change of political power	Capital assets not maintained/ deterioration	Inability to attract and retain staff/staff turnover	IT systems not integrated
Inaccurate forecasting	Equipment obsolescence	Poor service provided by staff	Network failure/ network unavailability
Unethical business practices	Customer revenue/ collections targets not met	Strikes and workplace unrest	Unauthorized system access/IT security breach or failure
Strategic plan not implemented	Unauthorized and irregular expenditure	Wrongful termination	IT system/ software obsolescence
Business continuity planning inadequate/or not developed	Wasteful or unproductive expenditure	Uncompetitive remuneration	Ineffective disaster recovery plan
Poor customer relationships	Changes in funding allocations	Job roles/ accountabilities unclear	Poor choice of software/IT solution/IT solution does not support business requirements

(Continued)

Table 5.1 (Continued) Examples of Risks in Different Categories (Risk Management Guideline, 2012)

Strategic	Financial	Operational	Knowledge and System
Negative/hostile/ inaccurate press coverage	Over-/ underspending budget allocations	Workplace injury: burns, falls, food poisoning, car accident, etc.	System not scalable/cannot meet increased capacity requirements
Ineffective communication strategy/plans	Inaccurate revenue forecasting	Pandemic and infectious disease outbreak	Loss of data/ information
Failure to meet sustainability targets	Inaccurate expenditure forecasting	Failure of/no fire suppression system	
Shortfall in project specifications	Financial reporting requirements not understood	Sexual harassment/ violence	
Late completion of project	Reporting deadlines not met	Equipment obsolescence	
	Errors/omissions in financial statements	Failure to maintain/repair assets	
Damage to/ development of protected sensitive natural habitats	Reporting not in correct format	Unauthorized use/misuse of fleet vehicles	
Air or water pollution	Fraud	Failure to maintain assets/ equipment	
		Theft	

Source: Adapted from Blume, A. (2014b). *Risk Management. Participants' Handbook.* Support to Local Governance Processes (SULGO) in Tanzania. Project: Strengthening internal controls at sub-national level.

Risk management is recognized as an integral part of good management practice and should become part of organization's culture for effectiveness. When this is achieved, risk management becomes the business of everyone in the organization.

Risk management is the term applied to a logical and systematic method of establishing the context, identifying, analyzing, evaluating, treating, monitoring, and communicating risk associated with any activity, function, or process in a way that enables organizations to minimize losses and maximize opportunities. It should be noted that there is no single international standard on risk management. This chapter will present two of the most common risk management standards/models (i.e., the ISO 31000 of 2009 and the COSO of 2004). It is also important to apply the risk management process from the beginning to achieve maximum benefits. According to ISO 31000:2009 as cited in Blume (2014b), the main elements of the risk management process are described as hereunder:

1. **Establish the context:** Establish the strategic, organizational, and risk management environment in which the rest of the process will take place. The criteria against which risk will be evaluated should be established and the structure of the analysis defined. The context could be viewed in terms of external (political, legal, technological, economic, social, and environmental) and in terms of the internal environment of the organization.
2. **Identify risks:** Identify what, why, and how events arise as a basis for further analysis.
3. **Analyze risks:** Determine the existing controls and analyze risk in terms of likelihood and consequences in the context of those controls. The analysis should consider the range of potential consequences and how likely those consequences are to occur. Consequences and likelihood may be combined to produce an estimated level of risk.
4. **Evaluate risks:** Compare estimated levels of risks against the preestablished criteria. This enables risk to be ranked so as to determine management priorities; if the levels risks established are low, then the risk may fall into an acceptable category and treatment may not be required.
5. **Treat risks:** Accept and monitor low-priority risks; develop and implement a specific management plan that includes consideration of funding.
6. **Monitor and review:** Monitor and review the performance of risk management system and changes that might affect it.
7. **Communicate and consult:** Communicate and consult with internal and external stakeholders at the appropriate stage of the risk management process and concerning the process as a whole.

Risk management can be applied at many levels of the organization, including the strategic and operational levels. It may be applied to specific projects, to assist with a specific decision, or to manage specific recognized risk areas (Zarkasyi, 2006).

On the other hand, according to the COSO (2004) model, as cited in Blume (2014b), risk management is geared to achieving an entity's objectives based on four categories:

- **Strategic**—high-level goals, aligned with and supporting its mission
- **Operations**—effective and efficient use of its resources
- **Reporting**—reliability of reporting
- **Compliance**—compliance with applicable laws and regulations

This categorization of entity objectives allows focusing on separate aspects of risk management. Similar to the ISO 31000, COSO views risk management as a process consisting of eight interrelated components:

1. Internal environment—The internal environment encompasses the tone of an organization, and sets the basis for how risk is viewed and addressed by an entity's employees.
2. Objective setting—Objectives must exist before management can identify potential events affecting their achievement.
3. Event identification—Internal and external events affecting the achievement of the organization's objectives must be identified, distinguishing between risks and opportunities.
4. Risk assessment—Risks are analyzed, considering likelihood and impact, as a basis for determining how they should be managed.
5. Risk response—Management selects risk responses (avoiding, accepting, reducing, or sharing risk), developing a set of actions to align risks with the organization's risk tolerances and risk appetite.
6. Control activities—Policies and procedures are established and implemented to help ensure the risk responses are effectively carried out.
7. Information and communication—Relevant information is identified, captured, and communicated in a form and time frame that enable people to carry out their responsibilities.
8. Monitoring—The entire enterprise risk management is monitored and modifications are made as necessary.

5.3.2 Principles of Risk Management

The International Organization for Standardization (ISO) identifies the following principles of risk management. According to Standard 31000, risk management should

- Create value—Resources expended to mitigate risk should be less than the consequence of inaction, or (as in value engineering) the gain should exceed the pain.
- Be an integral part of organizational processes.
- Be part of the decision-making process.

- Explicitly address uncertainty and assumptions.
- Be a systematic and structured process.
- Be based on the best available information.
- Be tailorable.
- Take human factors into account.
- Be transparent and inclusive.
- Be dynamic, iterative, and responsive to change.
- Be capable of continual improvement and enhancement.
- Be continually or periodically reassessed.

5.3.3 Risk Assessment Process to Facilitate Audit Planning

"Risk assessment is a systematic process for identifying and evaluating events (i.e., possible risks and opportunities) that could affect the achievement of objectives, positively or negatively" (PriceWaterHouseCoopers, 2008, as cited in Blume, 2014b).

Risk assessment is a key step/phase in the implementation of the organization's risk management process. According to ISO 31000:2009 as cited in Blume (2014b), risk assessment involves three levels of the risk management process:

- **Risk identification:** What events or circumstances may occur to affect the objective?
- **Risk analysis:** What is the impact and likelihood of the risk happening?
- **Risk evaluation:** What controls exist against the risks?

5.3.4 Risk Identification

According to ISO 31000:2009, "Risk identification is the process of finding, recognizing, and recording risks."

Several methods could be applied in identifying risks, including but not limited to (Table 5.2)

- **Systematic team approach:** A team of experts follows a systematic process to identify risks by means of a structured set of prompts or questions.
- **Brainstorming session:** In this case, members of the staff are grouped in terms of their department, division, sector, or relationship with the objective/target, and engage in brainstorming all possible events that might occur in the context of the objective/target.

Whichever method of risk identification was selected, the following should be considered:

- Risks should be identified on the basis of preidentified organizational objectives (strategic or operational/functional).
- Both external and internal categories of risks need to be considered.

Table 5.2 Sources of Risk

External Sources	Internal Sources
• Outsourcing to external service providers • Commercial/legal changes • Changes in the economic conditions • Political environment: socio-political changes, like elections • National and international events • Behavior of contractors/private suppliers • Financial/market conditions • Natural events • Misinformation • Public image • Regulatory guidelines • Financial markets	• New activities • Disposal or cessation of current activities • Personnel/human behavior • Management activities and controls/executive assessment • Operational (the activity itself) changes/process liquidity • Department interruption • Occupational health and safety • Technology/technical changes, i.e., new hardware and software implementations • Asset liquidity • Security (including theft and fraud) • Public/professional/product liability • Budget deviations • Process stability • Recent audit history • Financial value

Source: Adapted from Blume, A. (2014b). *Risk Management. Participants' Handbook.* Support to Local Governance Processes (SULGO) in Tanzania. Project: Strengthening internal controls at sub-national level.

■ Knowledgeable stakeholders (especially members of staff with experience or training that matches the objectives under discussion) and staff who actually work in the specific operations should be included.
■ Risk identification should be a continuous process and an integral part to the organizational processes.
■ Once identified, risks (along with their sources) should be clearly described and documented in a specialized risk identification form.

5.3.5 Risk Analysis

This analyzes the causes and consequences of risks. When analyzing the risks in each objective, the team should view the risk in terms of its causes and consequences, that is, situations that may cause the risk to happen and their ultimate effect on the objective/organization (Table 5.3).

Table 5.3 Example of Risk Identification by Considering the Causes and Consequences

Example 1	
Risk:	High employee turnover
Causes:	• Job dissatisfaction • Uncompetitive remuneration
Consequences:	• Loss of corporate knowledge • Delay in delivery of business objectives
Objective:	Improved human resources management
Example 2	
Risk:	IT failure
Causes:	• Power outage • Software failure
Consequences:	• Loss of data • Delay or failure in delivery of business objectives
Objective:	Enhanced information, communication, and technology capacity service

Source: Adapted from Blume, A. (2014b). *Risk Management. Participants' Handbook.* Support to Local Governance Processes (SULGO) in Tanzania. Project: Strengthening internal controls at sub-national level.

5.3.6 Internal Audit Risk Evaluation

The purpose of risk evaluation is to identify the *inherent risk* of performing various business functions. Audit resources will be allocated to the functions with the highest risk. Risk evaluation will directly affect the nature, timing, and extent of the audit resources allocated.

The two fundamental questions to consider when evaluating the risk inherent in a business function are as follows:

1. What is the probability that things can go wrong? (The *probability* of one event.)
2. What is the cost if what can go wrong does go wrong? (The *exposure* of one event.)

Risk is evaluated by answering the above questions for various risk factors and assessing the probability of failure and the impact of exposure for each risk factor.

Risk is the probability times the exposure ($R = P \times E$).

The *risk factors* inherent in business include the following:

* Access risk	* Business disruption risk
* Credit risk	* Customer service risk
* Data integrity risk	* Financial/external report misstatement risk
* Float risk	* Fraud risk
* Legal and regulatory risk	* Physical harm risk

These risk factors cause potential exposures. The potential exposures include (but are not limited to)

- Financial loss
- Legal and regulatory violations/censorship
- Negative customer impact
- Loss of business opportunities
- Public embarrassment
- Inefficiencies in the business process

The evaluation should *not* consider the effectiveness of the current internal control environment. The evaluation should focus on the risks and exposures inherent to the function being evaluated. However, while performing the risk evaluation, the auditor should consider what controls are needed in order to minimize, if not eliminate, the risks and exposures. See Chapter 6 (Figure 6.11: Risk Evaluation Form).

After the inherent risk rating, it becomes obvious that some of the risks will fall in the red, others in light brown, yellow, or green colors.

The internal audit team will now need to evaluate how the auditee is controlling each of the risks, that is, by assessing the *existing controls* (and their weakness) in order to determine the *residual risk*; that is

- The risk remaining even after being controlled
- The remaining risk owing to some existing weaknesses in the controls

Questions to be addressed when assessing the current controls against each risk include

- What are the existing controls for a particular risk?
- Are those controls capable of adequately treating the risk so that it is controlled to a level that is tolerable?
- In practice, are the controls operating in the manner intended, and can they be demonstrated to be effective when required?

The residual risk needs to be reassessed to see whether it is within the organization's *tolerable level*. The tolerable level of the risk is the extent to which the organization is ready to bear the risk after it has been treated in order to achieve organization objectives. The tolerable level of risk is determined by the management and may be stipulated in the risk policy. Again, as in inherent risk assessment, the risk will be rated in terms of *likelihood* (of happening) and *impact* (to the objective) given the current controls.

Note: It is expected that the residual risk will be lower than the inherent risks; this will happen if the existing controls are effective. If the residual risk remains above the organization's acceptable level, more mitigation controls need to be taken to reduce the risks.

Risks are not always evident; therefore, key risks can be identified by creating awareness, through relationships, research, and business acumen.

For future risks, consider strategic and reputation risks equally or with greater emphasis than operational and compliance risks.

Be careful of people who share information about *all* other areas than the one where they have responsibility; they are called *business sharks* (Flora and FloBiz & Associates, 2012).

5.3.7 Rating of Risks

Risks are rated using various classification band levels:

- Five-band level: very high = 5, high = 4, medium = 3, low = 2, very low = 1
- Four-band level: very high = 4, high = 3, medium = 2, low = 1
- Three-band level: high = 3, medium = 2, low = 1

In this chapter, a five-band level for both likelihood and impact is presented, as this scheme has been adopted in a Government's Risk Management Guideline (see Table 5.4).

Table 5.4   Meaning of Rates on Impact and Likelihood of Risks

S/N	Impact	Likelihood
5	Very high (VH), also catastrophic	Very high (VH), also almost certain
4	High (H), also major	High (H), also likely
3	Medium (M), also moderate	Medium (M), also possible
2	Low (L), also minor	Low (L), also unlikely
1	Very low (VL), also insignificant	Very low (VL), also rare

Source: Adapted from Blume, A. (2014b). *Risk Management. Participants' Handbook.* Support to Local Governance Processes (SULGO) in Tanzania. Project: Strengthening internal controls at sub-national level.

Then, rating is made by multiplying the likelihood and impact: the highest level of a risk is the one with a product of 25 (i.e., 5 × 5); the lowest level is 1 (i.e., 1 × 1).

Note: The result (product) is called the total risk. The total risk assists in indicating the priority of the risk as especially very high risks have to be dealt with.

Note also that, like objectives, risk falls under different areas of responsibilities. The internal audit should give assurance that responsible officials under whom the risk functionally falls (department or unit) are taking responsibility for the risk treatment. Naturally, the risk owner is assigned responsibility for the risk by the executive director. A risk owner should be a person who has the ability to carry out the proposed treatment options. He/she is responsible and accountable for the risk (see Tables 5.5 and 5.6).

Table 5.5 Risk Ratings, Color Expression, and Responses (Risk Management Guideline, 2012)

Total Risk/Risk Status (Impact × Likelihood)	Description	Expression in Color	Meaning and Responses
13–16	Extreme or severe	Red	Very serious concern; highest priority. Take immediate action and review regularly.
9–12	High	Light brown	Serious concern; higher priority. Take immediate action and review at least three times a year.
5–8	Moderate	Yellow	Moderate concern; steady improvement needed. Possibly review biannually.
1–4	Low	Green	Low concern; occasional monitoring. Tolerate/accept. Continue with existing measures and review annually.

Source: Adapted from Blume, A. (2014b). *Risk Management. Participants' Handbook.* Support to Local Governance Processes (SULGO) in Tanzania. Project: Strengthening internal controls at sub-national level.

Note: Darkest grey: Red; Darker grey: Light brown; Dark grey: Green; Light grey: Yellow.

Table 5.6 Illustration of Risk Assessment Based on Risk Matrix of Auditable Entities

S/N	Auditable Entity	Score
1	Sales department	19
2	Procurement process	20
3	Human resources department	10
4	Revenue collection unit	18
5	Payroll unit	9
6	Travel expenses	4
7	Stores	17
8	Etc.	

Source: Adapted from Blume, A. (2014a). *Internal Audit Techniques. Participants' Handbook.* Support to Local Governance Processes (SULGO) in Tanzania. Project: Strengthening internal controls at sub-national level.

The most significant auditable entities are those in the red zone; that is, rows 1, 2, 4, and 7. Next in the critical level are those in light brown (e.g., row 3); of moderate concern are those in yellow color (e.g., row 5); while row 6 in green color represents those in comfort zone with acceptable level of risk (Tables 5.6 and 5.7).

Table 5.7 Illustration of Risk Assessment Based on Common Risk Factors

S/N	Auditable Entity	Risk Factors				Probability	Score
		Materiality	*Impact*	*Sensitivity*	*Average*		
1	Sales department	3	3	2	2.67	3	8
2	Procurement process	3	3	3	3	3	9
3	Human resources	2	2	2	2	1	2
4	Revenue collection unit	3	3	2	2.67	2	5.33
5	Payroll unit	3	2	2	2.33	2	4.67
6	Travel expenses	2	2	1	1.67	1	1.67
7	Stores	3	3	2.5	2.83	3	8.5
8							

Source: Adapted from Blume, A. (2014a). *Internal Audit Techniques. Participants' Handbook. Support to Local Governance Processes (SULGO) in Tanzania. Project: Strengthening internal controls at sub-national level.*

5.3.8 Approach to Conduct the Risk Assessment Exercise

There are several approaches or methods used in conducting the risk assessment exercise, including but not limited to

- Desktop review of documentation
- Survey using a specific questionnaire
- One-to-one interviews with employees in the organization
- Group interviews (e.g., in a group of three staff members)
- A workshop approach

Potential Risk Treatments

According to Flora and FloBiz & Associates (2012), potential risk treatment has the following attributes:

- **Risk avoidance** —This involves not performing an activity that could carry risk.
- **Risk mitigation/reduction**—This involves methods that reduce the severity of the loss.
- **Risk acceptance/retention**—This involves accepting the loss when it occurs.
- **Risk transfer**—This means causing another party to accept the risk, typically by contract or by hedging.

5.4 Integrating Risk Management Activities in the Organization Planning Process

Most organizations in both the public and private sectors have experienced problems in linking their risk management activities with other activities, especially when implementing their strategic plans. This problem usually originates from the lack of connection between the organization planning and budgeting process with the risk management process, hence leading to limited attention and no resources committed to risk treatments.

Figure 5.1 Linking risk management with the planning process. (Adapted from Blume, A. (2014b). *Risk Management. Participants' Handbook.* Support to Local Governance Processes (SULGO) in Tanzania. Project: Strengthening internal controls at sub-national level.)

The linking of risk management with the planning process and ensuring that risk management activities are implemented along other activities within the organization can be demonstrated using the approach in Figure 5.1.

- The organization sets strategic and operational objectives and their respective implementing activities.
- The assessment of risks against those strategic objectives or targets is conducted and leads to the preparation of a risk register.
- Risk treatment plans/controls are formulated and incorporated in activities in the strategic plan according to their respective strategic objectives.
- In a final step, the budget is prepared to include both the activities for implementing the strategic objectives and risk treatment actions.

5.4.1 Determining the Audit Universe

Blume (2014a) posits that the first step in audit planning is for internal auditors to define their audit universe, which is the aggregate of all areas that are available to be audited within the organization. The primary objective of determining an audit universe is to define the scope of the internal audit's planned activities by segmenting its operations into individual *audit entities* that may be subjected to audit.

5.4.1.1 Methods of Determining the Audit Universe

According to GAIN, as cited in Blume (2014a), a survey report concluded that internal auditors across the globe used different methods in listing their audit universe (see Table 5.8).

Table 5.8   Audit Universe Distribution Table

Respondent	Graph	Frequency (%)
Department	....	71.3
Function	....	68.7
Risk management	....	58.2
Senior executive	.....	15.4
Middle level managers	....	31.1

Source: Adapted from GAIN Flash Report 2009, as cited in Blume, A. (2014a). *Internal Audit Techniques. Participants' Handbook.* Deutsche Gesellschaft für Internationale Zusammenarbeit (GIZ) GmbH; Dar es Salaam, Tanzania, April 2014.

From Table 5.8, the majority of internal auditors base their audit universe on the company's departments and functions; there is also high concentration on risk management in their organization.

The major use of this tool is to understand the structure of the organization or use the organization structure to list the departments and functions/processes within the departments.

Some examples of auditable activities within the audit universe may include

- Functions such as purchasing, accounting, finance, marketing and sales, etc.
- Operations and activities within the organization
- Information systems on infrastructure and specific application levels of accounting or administrative processes
- Major contracts or product lines

The audit universe should be a full list of all possible audits even if there is no intention currently (or insufficient resources) to audit them all. This should be listed on a table or spreadsheet (e.g., an Excel spreadsheet).

5.4.1.2 Considerations in Defining the Audit Universe

The selections of the auditable entities to be included in the audit universe should consider, but should not be limited to, the following:

- The risk profile of the auditee (the more risky areas will be given more attention than others)
- Availability of human resources and competency of internal audit staff (areas that internal audit is not competent with will likely be missed out, but the internal audit function should consider seeking an expert to join the internal audit team)
- Discussions with the audit committee and management requests (management may request the internal auditor to include other audit projects)
- Personal intuition of internal auditors (the internal audit function may come up with audit projects that do not fall in any of the auditable areas of the organization, but they feel should be included in the audit universe)

5.5 Types and Levels of Internal Audit Plans

Internal auditors usually prepare three levels (types) of audit plans (Figure 5.2):

i. Strategic audit plans—covering a period of three to five years
ii. Annual audit plans—covering one year/annual plans, broken into quarterly plans
iii. Engagement audit plans—covering a specific audit project (e.g., audit of payroll)

Strategic plan

Annual plan

Engagement plan

Figure 5.2 Levels of internal audit plan. (Adapted from Blume, A. (2014a). *Internal Audit Techniques. Participants' Handbook.* **Deutsche Gesellschaft für Internationale Zusammenarbeit (GIZ) GmbH; Dar es Salaam, Tanzania.)**

Note that these plans are dependent on one another, such that a strategic plan will be a source of an annual planning process, while an annual plan will lead to individual engagement plans.

5.5.1 Formulating a Strategic Audit Plan

Depending on the amount of auditable entities in the audit universe, the audit coverage may be spread to cover three to five years (Table 5.9).

On the basis of the scoring from the risk assessment, the auditable entities are ranked to determine priority, such that

- Higher-risk audit entities would be audited more frequently, or some may have continuous audits scheduled in intervening years.
- Medium-ranked audit entities would be audited at least once in a three-year audit cycle.
- Low-risk audit entities would not be audited but would be continued to be assessed for higher risk and hence the necessity for audit.

Table 5.9 Illustration of a Three-Year Audit Schedule

S/N	Auditable Entity	Score in Risk Assessment	Year 1	Year 2	Year 3
1	Sales department	8	×	×	×
2	Procurement process	9	×	×	×
3	Human resources	2			
4	Revenue collection unit	5.33	×		
5	Payroll unit	4.67		×	
6	Travel expenses	1.67			
7	Stores	8.5	×	×	×
8					

Source: Adapted from Blume, A. (2014a). *Internal Audit Techniques. Participants' Handbook.* Support to Local Governance Processes (SULGO) in Tanzania. Project: Strengthening internal controls at sub-national level.

5.5.2 *Formulating an Annual Audit Plan*

According to Blume (2014a), the annual plan will assume the list of auditable entities from the current year of the strategic plan; it will now list those high-risk areas that are targeted for audit cover during the next 12 months. The formulation of the annual audit plan is not different from that of the strategic plan since the risk assessment approach is still the same. Once there is a strategic plan as in the above example, then the annual plan of auditable entities is to be drawn from one of the years in the three-year plan, and then broken down into quarterly or monthly audit schedules.

According to Nzechukwu (2015), before the start of each accounting year, the chief audit executive (CAE) shall prepare an internal audit program for the following year for approval by the board or audit committee or chief executive officer (CEO), as the case may be. The audit plan shall contain a schedule of all audits planned for the year under focus. Each audit plan shall identify

1. The purpose and scope of the audit program as it relates to organization's objectives for the year
2. The program stating the month for which each audit is planned
3. The activities of the entity/entities to be audited, distinguishing between horizontal and vertical audits
4. List of audit team leaders and auditors, including the proposed composition for each audit
5. The estimated total resources required for the audits

The overall objective of the audit plan shall be to ensure that each part of the client's organization shall be subject to an internal audit at least once in any 24-month period, or as the organization may deem fit.

Changes with respect to the audit plan with the associated reasons or causes shall be reported to the board.

Before the beginning of the accounting year, the audit plan shall be distributed to the managers of the entities to be audited; also, the audit assignments shall be distributed to the planned audit leaders and auditors.

In the event of changes to the annual audit plan, the reasons or causes for the changes shall be communicated to the approving authority.

Sometimes, we could have unplanned audits, for example, a complaint or special request from a department; preparation for the audit shall involve the same activities according to the schedule agreed with the head of the audit department.

Preparation for audits, as shown in the annual audit plan above, shall be conducted as described below.

For each audit, the head of the audit unit shall verify the availability of the audit leader and audit team identified in the plan.

According to ESCC 11100 (2005), at least one month before the intended audit, the designated audit leader shall

1. Review the intended scope of the audit with the head of the audit unit to ensure its consistency with the objectives of the audit program.
2. Review with the audit team the audit reference/baseline point and scope, and identify all activities needed to sufficiently prepare for the audit; this is necessary to increase the plan quality input and promote buy-in.
3. Review and address the top areas in the audit universe.
4. Prepare or review checklists for the intended audit.
5. Review and agree on the date of the audit with the manager of the entity to be audited.
6. Review and agree with the manager of the entity to be audited on the scope of the audit, the planned activities, and the amount of support required.

On other hand, the manager responsible for the entity to be audited shall

1. Agree on the audit schedule and scope with the audit leader
2. Provide access and support to the auditors
3. Inform involved staff of the audit schedule and objectives
4. Authorize corrective actions with no cost impact
5. Agree on corrective/preventive actions with the audit leader, and refer actions with cost impacts to the relevant budget authority
6. Implement the agreed on corrective/preventive actions

Example

From the three-year plan as shown above, we take year 1, for example, 2016, and break it into quarterly schedules as shown in Table 5.10.

Table 5.10 Illustration of an Annual Internal Audit Schedule Broken into Quarterly Plans

S/N	Auditable Entity	Score in Risk Assessment	Estimated Audit Days	Year 1 (e.g., 1916)			
				Quarter 1	*Quarter 2*	*Quarter 3*	*Quarter 4*
1	Sales department	8	10	×	×	×	×
2	Procurement process	9	10	×	×	×	×
3	Human resources	2					
4	Revenue collection unit	5.33	5		×		×
5	Payroll unit	4.67	5		×		×
6	Travel expenses	1.67					
7	Stores	8.5	10	×	×		×
8	Etc.						

Source: Adapted from Blume, A. (2014a). *Internal Audit Techniques. Participants' Handbook. Support to Local Governance Processes* (SULGO) in Tanzania. Project: Strengthening internal controls at sub-national level.

5.5.3 Estimating the Audit Resources

The most appropriate starting point for resourcing the internal audit plan is the estimation of available audit days to cover the planned audit projects in a financial year.

Consideration should be made on the number of auditors and the scope of coverage as shown below:

   i. Start with the available number of internal audit staff.
  ii. Multiply that number by the available workdays in the year.
 iii. Reduce these days with allowance for vacation, sick leave, employee training, staff meeting, etc.
  iv. The remaining is the available audit days, which are allotted to specific auditable entities according to the internal auditor's judgment and past experience.

Note: It is important that audit plans are reviewed by the management so as to get their inputs and approval. This will definitely get management commitment in the development of audit plans and, hence, include their area of priority while at the same time understanding the resources needed by the internal audit unit.

5.5.4 Planning Internal Audit Engagement

"Internal auditors must develop and document a plan for each engagement, including the scope, objectives, and timing and resource allocations" (Performance Standard 2200).

Without adequate planning, there may be a likelihood of missing relevant control weaknesses or creating engagement-related problems. See Chapter 6 (Table 6.6: Planning Memorandum Form and Figure 6.5: Audit Assignment Form [Format B]) for templates.

5.5.4.1 Important Definitions

Audit objective: This represents the high-level goals and anticipated accomplishments of the audit assignment/review, and addresses the controls and risks associated with the client's activity.

Audit program: This is a document that comprises a detailed plan of the work to be performed and includes the step-by-step approach required to achieve audit objectives.

5.5.4.2 Purpose of Planning the Audit Engagement

According to Blume (2014a), planning the audit engagement is essential to providing a means for understanding

- The objectives of the auditee unit
- The methods used to achieve those objectives
- The risks associated with those methods
- The controls implemented by management to mitigate those risks and provide assurance of achieving the desired objectives

Understanding the auditee's unit enables the auditor to

- Identify/formulate significant audit objectives
- Prepare an audit program that tests significant controls and operations

5.5.4.3 Team Appointment

Sawyer (2012), as cited in Blume (2014a), explains that the most important resource for a successful audit engagement is the knowledge, skills, and experience of the audit team. It is therefore important that care is taken in selecting internal auditors to be assigned to the engagement. In appointing the audit team, the head of audit should consider the nature and complexity of the engagement; however, a balance should be obtained to create a learning opportunity for new and inexperienced auditors.

Outsourcing or hiring of experts or guest auditors should be considered where the internal audit unit is faced with an assignment that is beyond its current expertise.

5.5.4.4 Preliminary Team Meeting and In-Office Review

At the request of the lead auditor, the internal auditing staff assigned to the engagement should meet to discuss the preliminary objectives or information regarding the activity to be audited, particularly where the activity has not been audited before. Where necessary, the CAE should attend the preliminary meeting.

At this meeting, the team will discuss a number of issues relating to the assignment including

- The unit to be audited, its objectives, and potential issues/risks
- Policies, laws, and any criteria existing for the unit
- Past audit reports and issues from the CAE reports
- Setting tentative audit objectives

At this point, the audit team will also need to review a number of documents from previous audit files (if any), or search for any literature related to the audit engagement.

5.5.4.5 Engagement/Announcement/Notification Letter

The client is informed of the audit schedule through an announcement or engagement letter from the internal audit director or CAE. This letter communicates the purpose of the audit, date of the entrance conference, scope and objectives of the audit, auditors assigned to the project, type of information/documents that they should prepare (if known), and other relevant information. See Chapter 6 (Table 6.4: Information Request List and Figures 6.3 and 6.4: Engagement Letter) for templates.

Note: Auditees of certain engagements, such as surprise cash counts and investigations, are not sent notifications.

5.5.4.6 Internal Audit Opening/Initial/Entrance Conference

According to Blume (2014a), entrance conferences are conducted with the internal auditing staff and management of the activity being audited in order to discuss the audit process and to obtain information from the management of the activity. During this opening conference meeting, the auditee/client describes the unit or system to be reviewed, the organization, available resources (personnel, facilities, equipment, funds, etc.), and other relevant information. The internal auditor meets with the senior officer directly responsible for the unit under review and any staff members he/she wishes to include. It is important that the client identify issues or areas of special concern that should be addressed.

Note: Auditees of certain engagements, such as surprise cash counts and investigations, are not sent notifications.

Outlined below are standard agenda items that are discussed at entrance conferences:

- Planned engagement objectives and scope of work
- Timing of engagement work
- Internal auditors assigned to the engagement
- Process of communicating throughout the engagement, including the methods, time frames, and individuals who will be responsible
- Conditions and operations of the activity being reviewed, including recent changes in management or major systems
- Concerns or any requests of management
- Matters of particular interest or concern to the internal auditor
- Description of the internal auditing activity, reporting procedures, and follow-up process

Note: It is important that a rapport is created for a participative audit. The auditee staff should be made to feel that the auditors are there to provide them with assurance on the achievement of their unit's objectives, as opposed to the idea of identifying their mistakes. Also, auditees should be given the opportunity to make their inputs on what they think are key areas that the auditors should give more attention to. They should also be informed that their audit reports will not be issued before they give their comments. See Chapter 6 (Table 6.7: Entrance Conference Form) for template.

5.5.4.7 Internal Audit Preliminary Survey

In this phase, the auditor gathers relevant information about the unit to be audited, including an understanding of the activity to be audited, and identifies risks associated with the activity in order to obtain a general overview of operations. The auditor talks with key personnel and reviews reports, files, and other sources of information.

Where the auditee has a comprehensive risk register, the audit staff may use it as a source to identify risks that are related to the audited activity.

During the survey, the auditors should find out

- Who does what, why it is done, where it is done, how it is done?
- How is it administered?
- How much does it cost?
- What are its objectives, goals, and standards?
- What are the risks to the operation/activity?
- What controls have been devised to see that objectives are met and risks are minimized?

The auditors may conduct the preliminary survey by

- Conducting a physical tour of the offices with the auditee manager (if it is out of their normal area of work)
- Reviewing legally required documents (e.g., law and regulations, policies etc.)
- Studying the financial profile of the activity
- Performing interviews on operating instructions
- Assessing problem areas and risks (use a risk register if any)

According to Blume (2014a), the auditor may also structure their preliminary survey using COSO (2013)—Integrated Internal Control Framework. Where this applies, information may be gathered using components of internal control as follows:

- i. Control environment
    - Includes the volume of activity, objectives, organization, locations, and processes to be reviewed, for the period to be covered by the planned audit

- Policies, plans, procedures, laws, regulations, and contracts, which could have a significant impact on operations and reports of the unit to be audited
- Managerial tone and operating style and assignments of responsibility

ii. Risk assessment

- The risks that the unit is exposed to and are being managed by the unit, location, or process, and the results of any recent risk and control self-assessments. The focus should be on the *inherent risks*, not residual risks.
- The risk register, if present, will be a valuable source of these risks. However, internal auditors must judge whether this register is comprehensive enough for their purpose.

iii. Control activities

- The overall system of internal controls governing the unit, location, or process (though not at a detailed level; this will be examined during the fieldwork/audit)

iv. Monitoring

- The results of past internal and external audits, or internal reviews carried out
- The results (current, recent trends) of performance indicators, where available, for the unit, location, or process, or particular problems or events that indicate vulnerabilities in the policies, processes, or systems to be audited

v. Information and communications

- The information systems being used to support the unit, location, or process, and whether it would be appropriate to include the use of computer-assisted audit tools and other data analysis techniques
- Reports and communication on the unit, location, or process to be audited

5.5.5 Setting Audit Objectives

As defined above, audit objectives are specific statements about what the audit engagement wants to achieve. The audit objectives must be clearly stated, specific, capable of being evaluated with the available audit evidence, sufficient to render an audit opinion, and likely to result in a useful audit report.

Note that the overall objective of an internal audit is to obtain sufficient, competent, relevant, and useful information to provide a sound basis for audit findings and recommendations.

Audit objectives should reflect the results of a preliminary survey (Performance Standard 2210).

Precisely, the following key issues should guide in the formulation of audit objectives:

- Objectives and goals of the unit to be audited
- Risks of the activity
- Possible errors, fraud, noncompliance issues, and other exposures facing the unit to be audited

Example

In a procurement audit engagement, the engagement objective may be to ascertain whether

    i. Comprehensive policies and procedures addressing procurement activities have been developed and documented.
    ii. The auditee is in compliance with established policies, procedures, and regulatory requirements for procurement and relevant taxations.
    iii. Access to procurement records is limited to authorized personnel.
    iv. Bills payable and relevant taxes (value-added tax and withholding tax) are authorized and accurately recorded.
    v. Procurement requests and orders are properly prepared, approved, and recorded.
    vi. Recorded balances are regularly substantiated and reviewed.

Note that most of the clues on how to set audit objectives are obtained during the in-office review and preliminary survey.

In these stages, internal auditors may likely ask these questions:

- What are the operating objectives of this activity?
- What are the policies, laws, and regulations that should be applied here? Are they complied with?
- What are the risks relating to noncompliance, fraud, errors, reporting, injury, etc.? And what are the mitigating controls against those risks?
- Are these controls effective?

See Chapter 6 (Figure 6.6: Individual Interview Form, Figure 6.7: Self-Assessment Questionnaire [Format A—Corporate], and Figure 6.8: Self-Audit Questionnaire [Format B—Institutions/MDAs]) for templates.

5.5.6 *Internal Control Review*

The auditor will review the unit's internal control structure; this process usually consumes time. In doing this, the auditor uses a variety of tools and techniques to gather and analyze information about the operation of the unit or enterprise to be audited. The review of internal controls helps the auditor determine the areas of highest risk and design tests to be performed in the fieldwork section. See Chapter 6 (Figure 6.9: Internal Control Questionnaire Form and Figure 6.10: Internal Control Review Checklist).

5.5.7 Unplanned Audits

The head of the internal audit unit shall authorize unplanned audits in the following cases:

- Where a complaint or appeal requires an audit to be performed
- Where a trend in nonconformances has been identified that warrants an audit across the organization with respect to a specific procedure or process
- Where the board requires an investigation into a failure or specific event

In all cases, the audit shall be conducted in accordance with this procedure and the result reported as below.

5.6 Preparing the Internal Audit Engagement Work Program

As stated above, the audit program consists of a detailed plan of the work to be performed and includes the steps required to achieve the audit objectives. Preparation of the internal audit program concludes the preliminary review phase. The audit program outlines the fieldwork necessary to achieve the audit objectives. The purpose of an audit program is to show the procedures to follow during the audit, so that the audit can reach its specific objectives. After the conclusion of the preliminary survey, the auditor has a fair idea of the audit objectives and the control systems. At this stage, the audit program should be made providing the proposed procedures, budgeting, and basis for controlling the audit. The audit program will prevent the auditor from going off the scope pursuing irrelevant items and help in completing the audit project in an efficient manner.

This program outlines the fieldwork necessary to achieve the audit objectives.

5.6.1 Things to Consider while Preparing the Audit Program

- Needs of potential users of the audit report.
- Legal and regulatory requirements.
- Management controls.
- Significant findings and recommendations from previous audits that could affect the current audit objectives. Also, whether corrective action has been taken and earlier recommendations were implemented should be determined.
- Potential sources of data that could be used as audit evidence; consider the validity and reliability of these data.
- Consider whether the work of other auditors and experts may be used to satisfy some of the audit objectives.

- Provide sufficient staff and other resources to do the audit.
- Criteria for evaluating areas under audit.

5.6.2 Framing the Program

- Review the results of the preliminary survey with the audit supervisor.
- The audit team holds a meeting with the audit supervisor to decide on the priority/high-risk areas and tests to be conducted.
- Identify, review, and summarize primary organizational information:
  - Corporate policies/procedures
  - Status reporting
  - Performance measures
  - Strategic planning information
  - Insurance policies/coverage
  - Human resource policies
  - Health and safety information
  - Training and awareness information
  - Information security
  - Privacy
  - Communication/reputation
  - Others
- Provide a general overview of the auditee's operations. Include in the narrative statistical and monetary information, locations, authority, staffing, and main duties and responsibilities.
- Identify who to interview and who to survey.
- Potential interview/survey questions:
  - What do you see as the top (two to five) organizational risks over the next one to three years?
  - Identify the primary (two to five) risk management activities you see occurring.
  - What are the strengths related to risk management?
  - What are the opportunities for improvement?
  - How is risk management success measured within the organization?
- The program should consist of detailed directions for carrying out the assignment.
- Prepare draft audit program and document transaction flows.
- Audit programs should be consistent. Some organizations may have standardized audit programs.
- It should contain an estimate of the time necessary to complete the project.
- Number the audit program steps consecutively.
- Have the final program reviewed by the audit supervisor and audit manager.
- All major changes must be documented in writing and the reason documented.

- The audit program should contain a statement of the objectives of the area being reviewed. These objectives would be achieved through the detailed audit program procedure. Objectives should fit within the overall scope of the audit.
- Every audit procedure should help answer one of the objectives, and every objective should be addressed in the procedures or steps.
- The tests have to be designed in such a manner that they achieve their objectives. Use imagination, ingenuity, and intelligence in creating audit steps responsive to objectives.
- The goals should be made amply clear by prefacing major steps with "to test whether" or "to determine that."

See Chapter 6 (Table 6.3: Internal Audit Program).

5.6.3 Advantages of a Well-Prepared Audit Program

According to Blume (2014a), a well-structured audit program has the following advantages:

- Provides an outline of the work to be performed and encourages a thorough understanding of the audited unit
- Furnishes evidence that the work is adequately planned
- Assists in controlling work and assigning responsibility to audit staff in the team
- Aids in reviewing the progress and quality of the audit
- Provides a record that can be reviewed and approved by the head of the internal audit unit before performance of work, thereby contributing to assignment supervision
- Provides assurances that all appropriate risk areas have received adequate consideration and that important aspects of the audit have not been omitted

5.6.4 Terminologies Used in Audit Programs

An audit program is usually written in an instructive language with common terms. For convenience sake, we shall, in this section, identify some of the common terms with their meaning as shown in Table 5.11.

Table 5.11   Terms Used in Audit Programs and Their Meaning

Audit Program Terms	Meaning of the Procedure
Analysis	Analysis is the separation of an entity for the purpose of studying the individual parts of data. The elements of the entity can be isolated, identified, quantified, and measured. The quantification may require the auditor to perform detailed calculations and computations. Furthermore, the auditor can document ratios and trends, make comparisons and isolate unusual transactions or conditions.
Compare	Identify similar or different characteristics of information from two or more sources. Types of comparisons include comparison of current operations with past or similar operations, with written policies and procedures, with laws or regulations, or with other reasonable criteria.
Confirm	Obtain information from an independent source (third party; i.e., bank statements) for the purpose of verifying information.
Examine	To look over something very carefully, such as a document, in order to detect errors or irregularities. Example: Examine a document to verify that it has been executed by authorized persons.
Inquiry	Auditors perform interviews with the auditee and related parties throughout the audit. Good oral communication skills and listening ability on the part of the auditor assist in getting accurate and meaningful information from the interviewee. Auditors should use open-ended questions when possible. Depending on the type of information received in an interview, it may need to be confirmed through documentation communication.
Observation	Observation is auditors seeing with a purpose, making mental notes, and using judgment to measure what they see against standards in their minds.
Recompute	To check mathematical computations performed by others.

(Continued)

Table 5.11 (Continued)   Instructions Used in Audit Programs and Their Meaning

Audit Program Instruction	Meaning of the Procedure
Reconcile	This is the process of matching two independent sets of records in order to show mathematically, with the use of supporting documentation, that the difference between the two records is justified. For example, the reconciliation of a bank statement's balance at the end of the month with the book balance, or the reconciliation of the supplier's debtor statement with the book balances.
Trace	Tracing procedures begin with the original documents and are followed through the processing cycles into summary accounting records. In tracing, the direction of testing is from supporting documentation to the recorded item. The purpose of tracing is to verify that all actual transactions have been recorded.
Verification	Verification is the confirmation of things, such as records, statements, and documents; compliance with laws and regulations; effectiveness of internal controls. The purpose of verification is to establish the accuracy, reliability, or validity of something.
Vouch	Verify recorded transactions or amounts by examining supporting documents. In vouching, the direction of testing is from the recorded item to supporting documentation. The purpose for vouching is to verify that recorded transactions represent actual transactions.

Source: Adapted from Blume, A. (2014a). *Internal Audit Techniques. Participants' Handbook.* Deutsche Gesellschaft für Internationale Zusammenarbeit (GIZ) GmbH; Dar es Salaam, Tanzania.

5.6.5 *Linking Audit Objectives to Audit Procedures*

While preparing for an audit program, it is important to focus on steps (audit procedures) that will lead to the accomplishment of the audit objectives. This is only possible if each audit objective is thought out separately and specific procedures are developed in that regard. An example is shown in Table 5.12.

Table 5.12 Extract of a Payroll Audit Program Linking Audit Objective and Audit Procedures

Audit objective:	To ensure all new recruits/hires were legitimate, properly authorized and accurately recorded in a timely manner.		
S/N	*Audit Procedure*	*W/P Ref.*	*Initials*
1	Review new recruit report and randomly select 10 new recruits.		
2	Note important information on a spreadsheet (i.e., name, qualification, experience, employee no., pay rate).		
3	Trace information to supporting documentation in the employee files and online system to ensure accuracy.		

4	Test the following attributes:
	  i. New recruit is actually an employee (should exist in organization directory, e-mail system, etc.). Not ghost worker.
	  ii. Possess relevant qualification and experience.
	  iii. Payroll added new hire to payroll register in a timely manner.
	  iv. New hire transferred to relevant department.
	  v. Pay rate information is consistent with supporting documentation.
	  vi. Employee attended orientation in a timely manner.
	  vii. Senior payroll/HR lead initialed form indicating review of entry.
	  viii. A complete background check was performed on the employee.
	  ix. Employee signed the security policy acknowledgment form.		

5	Etc.		

Source: Adapted from Blume, A. (2014a). *Internal Audit Techniques. Participants' Handbook.* Deutsche Gesellschaft für Internationale Zusammenarbeit (GIZ) GmbH; Dar es Salaam, Tanzania.

5.6.6 Internal Audit Time Budget

At the planning phase, an estimated time budget should be prepared to control the audit and complete it efficiently. The detailed project time budget should be computed at the conclusion of the preliminary review. The time budget should be approved by the audit manager and audit administration. This budget will include all the time necessary to complete the audit, from assignment through issuance of the final report.

5.7 Internal Audit Fieldwork

According to Nzechukwu (2016), fieldwork involves the process of implementing the audit program, and it includes all efforts to collect or accumulate, analyze, classify, appraise, interpret, and document information so that we can express an opinion and provide recommendations for improvement.

5.7.1 Important Definitions

Audit evidence: Audit evidence refers to all the information used by the auditor in arriving at the audit opinions, conclusions, and recommendations.

Working papers: Audit working papers are the records kept by the auditor of the audit procedures applied, the tests performed, the information obtained, and the relevant conclusions reached in the audit engagement.

5.7.2 Qualities of Good Audit Evidence

According to Blume (2014a), Performance Standard 2300 requires internal auditors to identify, analyze, evaluate, and document sufficient information to achieve the engagement's objectives. Evidence may be categorized as physical, documentary, testimonial, and analytical.

To qualify to be used as audit evidence, the information collected by internal auditors should have the following qualities:

i. Sufficient
   - Sufficient information is factual, adequate, and convincing so that a prudent, informed person would reach the same conclusions as the auditor.
   - There should be enough of it to support the auditor's findings.
   - In determining the sufficiency of evidence, it may be helpful to ask such questions as
     • Is there enough evidence to persuade a reasonable person of the validity of the findings?
     • When should appropriate statistical sampling methods be used to establish sufficiency?

ii. Competent
- Competent information is reliable and the best attainable through the use of appropriate engagement techniques such as statistical sampling and analytical audit procedures.
- Information is more competent if it is
  - Obtained from an independent source
  - Corroborated by other information
  - Obtained directly by the auditor, such as through personal observation
  - Documented
  - Original document rather than a copy
iii. Relevant
- Relevant information supports engagement observations and recommendations, and is consistent with the objectives for the engagement.
- Relevant information should have a logical, sensible relationship with the associated audit finding.
iv. Useful
- Useful information helps the LGA meet its goals.

Evidence collected by the internal auditor should possess all of these qualities.
For example:

- It is not enough to merely interview staff members without corroborating the information obtained with that from other sources.
- Sample sizes should be representative so that conclusions reached may be validly extended to the rest of the population.

5.7.3 Testing Procedures, Strategies, and Techniques

Fieldwork implies measurement and evaluation of the existence or development of standards. Fieldwork can be performed through survey or detailed tests; the techniques used will depend on the particular situation but may include observing, questioning, analyzing, comparing, investigating, and evaluating.

Fieldwork will usually include some form of testing, which includes

1. Determining standards
2. Defining population
3. Selecting a sample
4. Examining selected information

Testing is the art of securing suitable evidence to support an audit. The next discussion is based on Pickett's (2005, as cited in Blume, 2014a) presentation of testing process, testing strategies, and techniques.

5.7.3.1 Testing Process

The testing process may be demonstrated in the following series of events:

    i. An auditor defines the test objective (as in audit objective setting and audit program).

    ii. Then, he/she defines the testing strategies (as shown in Section 5.7.3.2).

    iii. The auditor formulates a series of audit testing programs (as in audit/engagement work program).

    iv. The auditor then performs the tests (see Section 5.7.3.3).

    v. The auditor documents the evidence and interprets the results.

5.7.3.2 Testing Strategies

There are three types of tests (walkthrough, compliance, and substantive):

    i. Walkthrough test: see Chapter 6 (Figure 6.14: Interview Summary Form)
- This involves taking a small sample of items that are traced throughout the system (audit trail) to make sure that the auditor understands the system.
- Usually, this is used by the auditors when ascertaining the system; hence, it may lead to further tests.

    ii. Compliance test: see Chapter 6 (Figure 6.13: Compliance Test Form)
- These are tests done when auditors want to establish whether key controls are being adhered to.
- It uncovers noncompliance, or if controls are not implemented as intended.

    iii. Substantive: see Chapter 6 (Figure 6.9: Internal Control Questionnaire Form)
- These are tests to determine whether control objectives are being achieved.
- They are usually done after compliance tests—to determine the effect of noncompliance.

5.7.3.3 Testing Techniques

After the preliminary review is completed, the auditor performs the procedures adopted in the audit program. These procedures usually test the major internal controls and the accuracy and propriety of the transactions. Various techniques, including sampling, are used during this phase of the audit.

Testing techniques are ways in which auditors gather evidence to support testing objectives. There is no restriction to such testing as long as it makes sense and leads to desired results; examples of some of the techniques include, but are not limited to, the following:

i. Observation: (see Chapter 6, Table 6.11: Project Observation Form)

This is when an audit uses the senses to assess certain activities; for example, observing inventory stock taking to assess whether employees are doing the right thing.

ii. Confirmation

This involves receipt of a written or oral response from an independent third party, for example, confirmations of bank balances.

iii. Inquiries

Inquiries of client/auditee could be written on the basis of oral information from the client/auditee. Examples of this technique include internal control questionnaires or asking employees if certain procedures are being followed.

iv. Reperformance

Reperformance or mechanical accuracy involves rechecking computations for arithmetic accuracy or reperforming accounting routines.

v. Vouching

Vouching involves agreeing amounts of two or more different documents, for example, agreeing amounts on purchase orders to supplier invoices and receiving reports.

vi. Physical examination

This is an inspection or counting by the auditor of tangible assets; for example, cash, inventory, etc.

vii. Scrutiny or scanning

Scrutiny is a searching review of data in order to locate significant items that require further investigation, for example, scrutiny of the general ledger for unusual or unexpectedly high or low values, etc.

viii. Inspection

Inspection is the examination of documents other than source documents for a transaction, for example, inspection of lease agreements, or legal advisor's letter reporting on a land purchase.

As pointed out above, the choice and type of testing techniques are limitless. There are other techniques that an auditor can use to establish audit evidence and come up with relevant findings that meet audit objectives that are not listed in this section. Some of these techniques are mentioned in Chapter 2 of this book. However, auditors are required to be both innovative and adoptive to the circumstances surrounding the engagement and the achievement of the audit objectives.

We should review fieldwork work papers to be sure that the work was performed in a professional and thorough manner, and work and work papers adequately support findings and recommendations.

The fieldwork concentrates on transaction testing and informal communications. It is during this phase that the auditor determines whether the controls identified during the preliminary review are operating properly and in the manner described by the client. The fieldwork stage concludes with a list of significant findings from which the auditor will prepare a draft of the audit report (AuditNet LLC, 2014, p. 2).

5.7.3.4 Recognizing and Recording of Audit Finding

Audit findings or observations are those errors or situations that are not matching the required or expected standards or criteria discovered during the testing procedure or when gathering audit evidence. All significant audit findings should be reported to management for corrective action.

Audit finding is a significant and reportable condition if it

■ Warrants the attention of management
■ Is documented by facts, not opinions, and by evidence that is sufficient, competent, and relevant
■ Is objectively developed without bias or preconceived ideas
■ Is relevant to the issue involved
■ Is convincing enough to compel action to correct the defective condition

5.7.3.5 Attributes of Audit Finding

Audit findings should contain the following five attributes/elements: criteria, condition, cause, effect, and recommendation, as given in Figure 5.3 and explained thereafter.

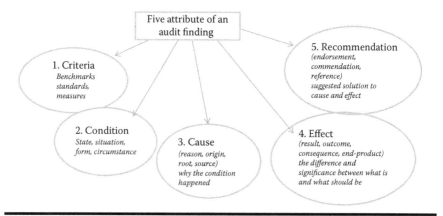

Figure 5.3 Five attributes of audit finding. (Adapted from Blume, A. (2014a). *Internal Audit Techniques. Participants' Handbook.* Deutsche Gesellschaft für Internationale Zusammenarbeit (GIZ) GmbH; Dar es Salaam, Tanzania.)

i. Criteria
   ■ The standards, measures, or expectations used in making an evaluation or verification.
   ■ What should exist?
   ■ Written requirements (laws, regulations, instructions, manuals, directives, etc.).
   ■ Overall objectives of the organization.
   ■ Auditor's experience.
   ■ Common-sense, prudent business practice.
   ■ Independent opinion of experts.
   ■ Generally accepted standards.
   ■ The criteria is usually established during the preliminary survey or planning stage of an audit.
ii. Condition
   ■ The factual evidence that the auditor found during the audit, which shows what actually exists.
   ■ What does exist?
   ■ What is defective?
   ■ What is deficient?
   ■ Uneconomical or inefficient use of resources.
   ■ What is in error?
   ■ Is it isolated or widespread?
   ■ Violation of law.
   ■ Ineffectiveness (job not being done as well as it could be).
   ■ Funds improperly spent.
   ■ Job not being done properly.
   ■ This is usually the difference (a deviation) between the criteria and the actual situation that the auditor finds.
iii. Effect/impact/risk
   ■ The risk or exposure to the organization being audited because the condition is not the same as the criteria.
   ■ Difference between criteria and condition.
   ■ Financial loss.
   ■ Increase in cost.
   ■ Loss of potential income.
   ■ Loss of potential customer.
   ■ Imposition of fine as result of violation of law.
   ■ Funds restriction as a result of impropriety spending.
   ■ Information, records, or reports are not useful, meaningful, or accurate.
   ■ Inadequate control or loss of control over resources.
   ■ Lowered morale.

    iv. Cause

- The reason for the difference between the criteria and condition. (Why does the difference exist?)
- Lack of qualifications to do the job.
- Management not doing its job.
- Lack of training.
- Lack of communication.
- Negligence or carelessness.
- Instructions are faulty.
- Lack of resources.
- Dishonesty.
- Insufficient effort or interest.
- Unwillingness to change.
- Faulty or ineffective organizational arrangement.
- It is important for auditors to investigate the cause of deviations. This is because recommendations for corrective efforts are addressed on the cause of the problem.

    v. Recommendation

- The action necessary to bring the condition in line with the criteria
- Should focus to correct the *cause* of the deviation
- Should be specific and helpful
- Should pinpoint accountability and responsibility
- Should not supersede management's responsibility to manage, and addressed to officials with power to make a change

It has been observed that many internal auditor reports omit *cause and effect*, the two most critical components of audit finding and which render the report unconvincing with poor recommendation.

As a result, auditors make use of a special form called the Findings Report Form, which captures the five attributes of the finding. See Chapter 6, Table 6.12: Internal Audit Finding Report (Format A), Figure 6.15: Internal Audit Finding Report (Format B), and Figure 6.16: Developing a Finding (Format C).

5.7.4 Advice and Informal Communications

As the fieldwork progresses, the auditor discusses any significant findings with the client, with the expectation that the client can offer insights and work to determine the best method of resolving the finding. Usually, these communications are oral. However, in more complex situations, memos or e-mails are written in order to ensure full understanding by the client and the auditor. Our goal: No surprises!

5.7.5 Internal Audit Summary

After completing the fieldwork, the auditor summarizes the audit findings, conclusions, and recommendations necessary for the audit draft report discussion.

5.7.6 Internal Audit Working Papers

Audit working papers are a vital tool in the audit profession. They are the support document of the audit opinion. They link the client's accounting records and financials to the auditor's opinion. They are usually comprehensive and serve various functions.

5.8 Internal Audit Report

The principal product of internal auditing is the final report in which the auditor expresses opinions, presents the audit findings, and discusses recommendations for improvements. To facilitate communication and ensure that the recommendations presented in the final report are realistic, internal audit discusses the draft report with the client before issuing the final report. For an internal audit report template including an executive summary, go to Chapter 6.

5.8.1 Discussion Draft

At the conclusion of fieldwork, the auditor drafts a report. The audit management thoroughly reviews the audit working papers and the discussion draft or draft report before it is presented to the client/auditee for comment. This discussion draft is prepared for the unit's operating management and is submitted for the client's/auditee's review before the exit conference.

5.8.2 Exit Conference

When audit management has approved the discussion draft, the internal auditor meets with the unit's management team to discuss the findings, recommendations, and text of the draft. At this meeting, the client comments on the draft and the group work to reach an agreement on the audit findings. See Chapter 6 for the exit conference template.

5.8.3 Formal Draft

The internal auditor then prepares a formal draft, taking into account any revisions resulting from the exit conference and other discussions. When the changes have been reviewed by the auditor, management, and the client/auditee, the final report is prepared and issued.

5.8.4 Client Response

The client has the opportunity to respond to the audit findings before issuance of the final report, which can be included or attached to the final report. However, if the client decides to respond after issuing the final report, the first page of the final report should contain a letter requesting the client's/auditee's written response to the report recommendations.

In the response, the client/auditee should explain how report findings will be resolved and include an implementation timetable. In some cases, managers may choose to respond with a decision not to implement audit recommendations and to accept the risks associated with the audit findings. The client/auditee should copy the response to all recipients of the final report where he/she decides not to have their response included/attached to the internal audit's final report.

5.8.5 Final Report

Internal audit prints and distributes the final report to the unit's operating management, the unit's reporting supervisor, the CEO, the chief finance officer, and other appropriate members of senior management. This report is primarily for internal management use and must require the approval of CEO for any external use.

5.8.6 Internal Audit Annual Report to the Board

In addition to the distribution discussed earlier, the contents of the audit report, client response, and follow-up report shall also be communicated to the audit committee or the board of directors as part of the internal audit annual report. The CAE traditionally reports the most critical issues to the audit committee quarterly, along with management's progress toward resolving them. Critical issues usually have a potential of causing substantial financial or reputational damage to the organization. For such complex issues, the responsible manager may participate in the discussion. Such reporting is critical to ensure the internal audit function is respected, and also that the proper *tone at the top* exists in the organization, and to expedite resolution of such issues. The judgmental tasks of selecting appropriate issues for the audit committee's or board's attention and to describe them in the proper context are significant, and this is where the competency of the CAE is tested.

5.8.7 Client Comments

Finally, as part of internal audit's self-evaluation program, the internal auditor should usually ask clients to comment on the internal audit's performance. This feedback has proven to be very beneficial to the internal audit, and has made changes in audit procedures as a result of clients' suggestions.

5.9 Audit Follow-Up

Within approximately one year or less of the final report, depending on the nature of the findings, the internal auditor will perform a follow-up review to verify the resolution of the report findings.

5.9.1 Follow-Up Review

The client/auditee response letter is reviewed and the actions taken to resolve the audit report findings may be tested to ensure that the desired results were achieved. All unresolved findings will be discussed in the follow-up report.

5.9.2 Follow-Up Report

The review will conclude with a follow-up report that lists the actions taken by the client/auditee to resolve the original report findings. Unresolved findings will also appear in the follow-up report and will include a brief description of the finding, the original audit recommendation, the client response, the current condition, and the continued exposure to the client's enterprise. A discussion draft of each report with unresolved findings is circulated to the client/auditee before the report is issued. The follow-up review results will be circulated to the original report recipients and other senior officials as deemed appropriate.

See Chapter 6 for the internal audit follow-up template.

5.9.3 Internal Audit Follow-Up Policy

5.9.3.1 Purpose

The purpose of the internal audit follow-up policy is to outline the policy and procedure for follow-up of recommendations in audit reports issued by the internal audit department and management letters issued by external auditors.

5.9.3.2 Policy and Procedure

It is recommended that NOT more than 90 days after a final report is issued, a Recommendation Implementation Status Summary (RISS) be sent to the individuals whose responses are reflected in the final report. Each addressee will be asked to indicate the status of the recommendations listed on the RISS and return it to the internal audit department. For any recommendation not implemented, the auditee will be asked to provide the targeted implementation date, and if not implemented, the reason and a description of any alternate solutions implemented or planned.

After the completed RISS is received, the internal audit department will verify the implementation status of recommendations related to significant findings.

For any unimplemented recommendations relating to significant findings, the internal audit department will continue following-up quarterly with the appropriate individuals (Washington University in St. Louis, 2000–2004).

References

AuditNet LLC. (2014). The-internal-audit-process-from-a-to-z-how-it-works. Retrieved July 1, 2014, from: http://www.auditnet.org/audit-library/the-internal-audit-process-from-a-to-z-how-it-works.

Blume, A. (2014a). *Internal Audit Techniques. Participants' Handbook.* Deutsche Gesellschaft für Internationale Zusammenarbeit (GIZ) GmbH; Dar es Salaam, Tanzania, April 2014. Retrieved December 15, 2015, from: http://www.sulgo.or.tz/uploads/media/Internal_Audit_Participants_3.pdf.

Blume, A. (2014b). *Risk Management. Participants' Handbook.* Support to Local Governance Processes (SULGO) in Tanzania. Project: Strengthening internal controls at sub-national level. Deutsche Gesellschaft für; Internationale Zusammenarbeit (GIZ) GmbH. Retrieved December 15, 2015, from: http://www.sulgo.or.tz/uploads/media/Risk_Participants_Down_3.pdf.

Flora, P. E., and FloBiz & Associates (2012). *Developing a Risk-Based Audit Plan.* ISACA. Flora and FloBiz & Associates, LLC.

Nzechukwu, P. O. (2015). Internal Audit Practice, how it works from A to Z, p. 148.

Zarkasyi, W. S. (2006). Internal audit techniques, traditional vs progressive approach. *Jurnal Ekonomi dan Bisnis Terapan*, vol. 2, no. 1, February 2006.

Chapter 6

Internal Audit Documentation and Reporting

6.1 Introduction

Audit documentation is the principal record of auditing procedures applied, evidence obtained, and conclusions reached by the auditor in the engagement. The quantity, type, and content of audit documentation are matters of the auditor's professional judgment.

According to AICPA (2006), AU Section 339 (as cited in SAS No. 103), the auditor must prepare audit documentation in connection with each engagement in sufficient detail to provide a clear understanding of the work performed (including the nature, timing, extent, and results of audit procedures performed), the audit evidence obtained and its source, and the conclusions reached. Audit documentation

a. Provides the principal support for the representation in the auditor's report that the auditor performed the audit in accordance with generally accepted auditing standards
b. Provides the principal support for the opinion expressed regarding the financial information or the assertion to the effect that an opinion cannot be expressed

The American Institute of Certified Public Accountants (AICPA) standards and Generally Accepted Government Auditing Standards (GAGAS) require the following:

■ A record of the auditors' work should be retained in the form of working papers.
■ The additional working paper standard for financial statement audits is that working papers should contain sufficient information to enable an experienced auditor having no previous connection with the audit to ascertain from them the evidence that supports the auditors' significant conclusions and judgments.

In a related development, Code of Ethics, under the Confidentiality Principle, states that "internal auditors respect the value and ownership of information they receive and do not disclose information without appropriate authority unless there is a legal or professional obligation to do so." In addition, the Government Internal Audit Standards state that the HIA/CAE "must develop retention requirements consistent with the organization's guidelines and any pertinent regulatory or other requirements" (2330.A2).

According to IIA 2330, internal auditors must document relevant information to support the conclusions and engagement results.

Standard 2330.A1 of IIA—The chief audit executive must control access to engagement records. The chief audit executive must obtain the approval of senior management and/or legal counsel prior to releasing such records to external parties, as appropriate.

In this chapter, we shall provide internal auditors around the world the opportunity to share what may be considered a Project Standard Audit Work Paper.

6.2 Internal Audit Record Retention and Disposal

6.2.1 Records

According to HM Treasury (2011), a record is information created, received, and maintained by an organization or a person in the transaction of business, or in the maintenance of legal obligations, regardless of the medium. In the case of internal auditing, records are gathered and created as part of individual audit engagements, including the planning, direction, and control of internal audit work at all levels. For any internal audit to function effectively, it not only must have good records but also must manage its records effectively, without which the wider organization may be rendered vulnerable to breaching of appropriate regulations. Also, internal audit services themselves are auditable, and good record management demonstrates compliance with the relevant standards.

Internal auditors record relevant information to support conclusions and engagement results in order to

- Aid planning, performance, and review of engagements
- Document the extent to which engagement objectives were achieved
- Facilitate third-party reviews
- Provide a basis for assuring the quality of audits
- Demonstrate compliance with standards for the professional practice of internal auditing and with relevant legislation and regulations

According to the archives and records management of Vigilate (Government of the Virgin Islands 2005), internal audit records include

- Reports
- Terms of reference
- Programs/plans
- Correspondence, including management letter, advice, and consultancy
- Minutes of meetings, etc.
- Working papers

6.2.2 Record Retention

According to Public Sector Internal Audit Standards (PSIAS, 2012; 2330.A2), the head of internal audit/chief audit executive (HIA/CAE) must develop retention requirements for engagement records, regardless of the medium in which each record is stored. These retention requirements must be consistent with the organization's guidelines and any pertinent regulatory or other requirements.

Also, the HIA/CAE must develop policies governing the custody and retention of consulting engagement records, as well as their release to internal and external parties. These must be consistent with the organization's guidelines and any pertinent regulatory or other requirements (2330.C1).

In his article "Sarbanes-Oxley document retention and best practices," Balovich (2007) stated that Sections 103, 801(a), and 802 are the core of the Sarbanes-Oxley (SOX) record retention rules. Sections 103(a) and 801(a) require public companies and registered public accounting firms to maintain audit work papers, documents that form the basis of an audit or review, and all information supporting conclusions for at least seven years. According to Balovich (2007), Section 802 addresses the retention and destruction of records, with implied penalties. Under Section 802, it is a crime for anyone to intentionally destroy, alter, mutilate, conceal, cover up, or falsify any records, documents, or tangible objects that are—or could be—involved in a U.S. government investigation or prosecution of any matter, or in a Chapter 11 bankruptcy filing. This section also stresses the importance of record retention and destruction policies that affect all of a company's e-mail, e-mail attachments, and documents retained on computers, servers, auxiliary drives, e-data, websites, and hard copies of all company records. The rules state that any employee who knows their company is under investigation, or suspects that it might be, must stop all document destruction and alteration immediately. Moreover, the employee must create a company record showing that a halt had been ordered to all automatic e-data destruction practices.

Private companies are also expected to comply with SOX Section 802. Private companies now face fines plus up to 20 years imprisonment for knowingly destroying, altering, or falsifying records with the intent to impede or influence a federal investigation.

Balovich (2007) states that there are four key components to ensure compliance under SOX. E-mail must be tamper-proof. It must be password-protected, read-only, and nondeletable; encrypted, and digitally signed. It must exist in a closed system both online and offline. E-mail must follow the defined policies of the business. Policies include what e-mail is archived, the retention period, and how e-mail is protected. E-mail must have full audit ability of access and movement. It must have the ability to be audited by a third party. And finally, e-mail must be fully indexed and provide full search capability. Specifically, e-mail archiving must be index based in capturing standard RFC-822 header information.

According to HM Treasury (2011), records should not be kept after they have ceased to be of use, unless they are known to be the subject of litigation or a request for information. If so, destruction should be delayed until the litigation is complete or, in the case of an information request, all relevant complaint and appeal provisions have been exhausted. In such cases, a disposal *hold* should be applied to the records that must only be placed or removed by authorized users. By placing a hold on a folder, any disposal actions are paused and cannot be executed until the hold is removed. The records management system must suspend the execution of any disposal action while the disposal hold is in place.

It is very important to keep a record of information sent for destruction (the disposal schedule). This record acts as proof that disposal of information is taking place in a controlled manner. It is advisable that whoever is designated to control the disposal process signs off and dates the disposal schedule as proof that the information has been archived or destroyed.

6.2.3 External Service Providers/Shared Services/ Third-Party Assurance

Where internal audit services, or part thereof, are supplied by external parties, contracts with those parties should make it clear that any information they collect or generate as part of any review undertaken is the property of the organization that appointed them, must be accessible as required and handed over at an appropriately agreed point, as well as retained in accordance with the policy for the management of information. Similarly, any papers generated by the audit process must be made available for quality review purposes.

Where internal audit services are supplied by shared service arrangements, the HIA/CAE must ensure that the obligations and guidelines for each of the organizations involved are met.

Where HIA/CAE seek assurance from other assurance providers in their organizations (e.g., health and safety experts, antifraud experts, etc.), then they will have to ensure that all information created by these other bodies that support any assurance given by the internal audit service is clearly identifiable, can be located easily and quickly, and is kept for whatever period that the internal audit service requires (HM Treasury, 2011).

6.2.4 Reasons for Record Retention

The main reasons information is preserved are to provide evidence supporting audit findings and recommendations, and to demonstrate that audit was carried out to acceptable standards. It is recommended that those working papers that support audit findings should be kept at least until all accepted recommendations have been implemented. Other reasons for keeping audit working papers for longer include

- To comply with legislation or organizational policies.
- To meet the needs of audit committees. It is important that sufficient internal audit records supporting the audit opinion are kept, at least until after an annual meeting of the audit committee has taken place and the accounts have been laid.
- To provide external auditors with information to support their work. Internal audit should provide the external auditors with their annual audit program together with those records relating to the reviews that the external auditors are interested in seeing, and dispose them after they have seen them.
- To provide information for quality reviewers. Government Internal Audit Standard (GIAS) no. 1310 on external assessments states that "the chief audit executive must develop and maintain a quality assurance and improvement program that covers all aspects of internal audit activity." When quality reviews have been completed; there is no need to retain records unless there is a good reason for doing so. There is no need to retain all evidence supporting all audits until a quality review is completed, however, those evidence supporting audits that are under way at the time of the quality review should be sufficient for this purpose.
- Historic purposes. Some internal audit records are regarded as permanent audit files; these records will be selected for permanent preservation. The criteria for selecting records for historical purposes can be found in the publication *Acquisition and Disposition Policies* (PRO 2000), and in more detailed operational selection policies. No records should be destroyed without reference to

those documents, and all internal audit records no longer required for business purposes should be subject to the formal appraisal process to determine whether they fall within the criteria of selection for permanent preservation.

6.2.5 Retention Schedule

The retention of internal audit information should be considered in the light of both business (e.g., internal audit quality review purposes) and legislative requirements, taking into account the cost of retention and the use to which the records might be put in the future.

In this chapter, we shall consider the record retention schedule enunciated by GIAS and by SOX.

The following schedule by GIAS gives an indication of the minimum retention periods for internal audit records after which they should be reviewed to determine whether they should be kept for longer, destroyed, or sent to an archive for permanent preservation. The retention period starts after audits are completed (i.e., when all accepted recommendations have been implemented by management) (Table 6.1).

Table 6.1 Record Retention Schedule by HM Treasury

Item	Description	Minimum Retention Period	Maximum Retention Period
Reports			
1	Audit reports (including interim) where these have included the examination of long-term contracts	1 year	6 years
2	Report papers used in the course of a fraud investigation	1 year after legal proceedings have been completed	6 years after legal proceedings have been completed
3	Annual reports and information supporting the SIC/governance statement	1 year	1 year
4	Other audit reports (including interim)		

(Continued)

Table 6.1 (Continued)   Record Retention Schedule by HM Treasury

Item	Description	Minimum Retention Period	Maximum Retention Period
Undertakings			
5	Terms of reference	On completion of reviews (i.e., when all agreed actions have been implemented by management)	3 years
6	Programs/plans/ strategies	As soon as they have been replaced by a new program/ plan/strategy	1 year after the last date of the plan
7	Correspondence	Correspondence relating to reviews should be reviewed at the same time as other working papers (see below). Other correspondence should be reviewed after 6 months.	3 years
8	Minutes of meetings and related papers	1 year	3 years
9	Working papers	On completion of reviews (i.e., when all agreed actions have been implemented by management)	3 years
Other Information			
10	Internal audit guides	When superseded	When superseded
11	Manuals and guides relating to departmental procedures	When superseded	When superseded
12	Local auditing standards	When superseded	When superseded

Source: Adapted from HM Treasury (2011). Internal Audit Records Management. Copyright 2011 Crown. ISBN 978-1-84532-889-4 PU1194.

Table 6.2   Record Retention Schedule by SOX

Document Type	Retention Period
Accounts payable ledger	7 years
Accounts receivable ledger	7 years
Bank statements	Permanent
Charts of account	Permanent
Contracts and leases	Permanent
Correspondence (legal)	Permanent
Employee payroll records	Permanent
Employment applications	3 years
Inventories of products	7 years
Invoices to customers	5 years
Invoices from vendors	5 years
Payroll records and tax returns	7 years
Purchase orders	5 years
Time cards and daily reports	7 years
Training manuals	Permanent
Union agreements	Permanent

Source: Balovich, D. (2007). Sarbanes-Oxley document retention and best practices. Creditworthy News.

In a similar publication, Balovich (2007) showed a record retention schedule generally accepted under SOX (Table 6.2).

6.3 Working Papers

Audit working papers are the records kept by the auditor showing the audit procedures applied, the tests performed, the information obtained, and the reasonable conclusions reached in the audit engagement. Ostensibly, audit working papers contain the *second level* audit evidence or audit evidence obtained by the auditor himself/herself.

Internal auditors are required to keep audit working papers that contain all information of the work done and that support the audit report generated.

6.3.1 Objectives of Audit Working Papers

According to Blume (2014), audit working papers serve the following objectives:

- Provide a historical record of the information collected during the conduct of audits
- Provide a record of the audit tasks performed
- Identify audit objectives and methods chosen as a basis for planning future audits and for review purposes
- Allow a lead auditor or supervisor/manager to make an interim review of what has been done during the audit to date
- Allow an audit supervisor or manager to carry out final assessment of the validity of draft audit conclusions before they are expressed as audit findings
- Provide support for audit findings and evidence of compliance with the internal audit standards
- Establish a record for the purposes of peer review
- Provide a framework for further review in cases where management disagrees with audit findings and the audit methods and conclusions have to be reassessed
- Provide a framework of control whereby delegated work is monitored

6.3.2 Principles of Maintaining Audit Working Papers

To prepare and maintain audit working papers of good quality, internal auditors should observe the following principles:

i. **Consistency and standardization**

   When carrying out audits, internal auditors should use consistent writing or reporting methods.

   Consistency is achieved by using the standard formats as shown in an internal audit manual. Completing the recommended formats will make documentation easier to understand and review. Where an auditor takes over a work that has been started by another auditor, the use of standardized formats will promote continuity. Though standard formats could be amended to reflect changes in style, the auditor could also introduce additional formats as necessary.

ii. **Accuracy and timeliness**

   Documentation should accurately reflect the tests planned, the tests carried out, and the result of these tests. There should also be documents that show the timing of the work carried out.

iii. **Clarity and conciseness**

   The primary objective is to provide working papers that will make it easy to understand the way the audit was carried out. In this regard, the working papers should be well organized and cross-referenced with clear and concise language and structure.

Also, the information recorded should be sufficient for the purposes of subsequent review by another auditor, where necessary.

iv. **Completeness**

The audit working papers should be complete in the sense of covering the whole audit, for example, the tests carried out, meetings held, queries raised, management responses, and draft conclusions reached.

v. **Authorship and review**

Audit working papers should reveal who carried out each piece of work. In addition to that, working papers should be reviewed by the chief audit executive or head of internal audit or auditor in charge. Also, information regarding the identity of reviewers and their instructions or advice should be documented.

vi. **Confidentiality**

Audit working papers are, in principle, confidential. The chief audit executive or head of the internal audit unit may decide to share audit working papers, only for reason of utmost interest.

6.3.3 Preparation of Working Papers

Audit working papers are prepared throughout the audit process, that is, from planning to fieldwork and reports. At each stage of the audit, each working paper should be properly identified with such information as

1. The name of the entity or unit being audited.
2. The title or description of the content or purpose of the working paper.
3. The period covered by the audit.
4. The preparer and reviewer with respective dates of preparation and review.
5. The index and code (as can be shown in an internal audit manual for indexing and codes).
6. Each working paper should be signed (or initialed) by the preparer and the reviewer.
7. Each working paper should be properly indexed and cross-referenced to aid in organizing and filing.
8. Indexing is done at the front of each paper using combinations of letters.

Below are examples of internal audit working papers for planning, fieldwork, and report generation.

6.3.4 Internal Audit Program (Table 6.3)

As pointed earlier in Chapter 5, the preparation of the internal audit program concludes the preliminary review phase. The audit program outlines the fieldwork necessary to achieve the audit objectives. The purpose of an audit program is to show the

Table 6.3   Internal Audit Program

<table>
<tr>
<td colspan="3">

PATRICKONSULT LTD
OFFICE OF INTERNAL AUDIT
(Insert Street)
(Insert Zip Code)

(Audit period)
AUDIT PROGRAM
(Area audited)
(Audit Project Title and No.)

Reviewer: _____   Date: _____   Initials: _____   Date: _____
</td>
</tr>
<tr>
<td>Audit Procedure</td>
<td>W/P Ref.</td>
<td>Initials Date</td>
</tr>
<tr>
<td>A. Planning and Preliminary Survey
Following steps listed in the Planning and Preliminary Survey Checklist, analyze background information about an area to be audited. On the basis of these analyses and reviews, select relevant objectives for the audit. Objectives should be based on the major functions of the area to be audited and, whenever possible, should include management's suggestions for items to be addressed in the audit.</td>
<td></td>
<td></td>
</tr>
<tr>
<td>a. Section related to first audit objective—A general statement of the purpose of the tests should follow the title.
1.</td>
<td></td>
<td></td>
</tr>
<tr>
<td>2nd Objective</td>
<td></td>
<td></td>
</tr>
<tr>
<td>3rd Objective</td>
<td></td>
<td></td>
</tr>
<tr>
<td>4th Objective</td>
<td></td>
<td></td>
</tr>
<tr>
<td>5th Objective</td>
<td></td>
<td></td>
</tr>
<tr>
<td>b. Analysis of internal controls
Following steps in the Internal Control Review Checklist, assess the adequacy of the systems of internal control relating to each audit objective.</td>
<td></td>
<td></td>
</tr>
</table>

(*Continued*)

Table 6.3 (Continued)   Internal Audit Program

Audit Procedure	W/P Ref.	Initials Date
B. Audit Program Develop an audit program with tests designed to determine whether control strengths identified during the analysis of internal controls are appropriate. If appropriate, tests to investigate the effect of serious weaknesses may also need to be included.		
C. Fieldwork **i. Point sheet analysis** Prepare point sheet describing audit findings and recommendations. Discuss issues with management and summarize their responses on the point sheet form. Complete point sheet index, indicate which point sheets will be included in the audit report, and reference these point sheets to the related finding in the audit report. **ii. Audit administration** Follow steps in Administrative Documentation Index. Prepare time summary of total hours charged to the audit; if hours vary from approved budget by ±10%, provide explanation of cause of variance. Complete Revised Risk Assessment Score Sheet using information obtained and conclusions reached during the audit.		
D. Communicating Results Follow steps described in the Communicating Results Checklist to inform auditees about the status and results of the audit.		
Approval of Audit Program Signature _____ Date _____		

procedures to follow during the audit, so that the audit can reach its specific objectives. After the conclusion of preliminary survey, the auditor has a fair idea of the audit objectives and the control systems. At this stage, the audit program should be made providing the proposed procedures, budgeting, and basis for controlling the audit. The audit program will prevent the auditor from going off the scope pursuing irrelevant items and help in completing the audit project in an efficient manner.

6.3.5 Planning and Preliminary Survey (Appendix A)

Audit planning (sometimes called Survey or Preliminary) involves the development of an in-depth, well-conceived, overall strategic plan that clearly defines the desired future state of the internal audit function (Review). Audit planning also involves the development of annual plan for each auditable entity from the strategic plan for each year under consideration. Similarly, planning involves the development and documentation of a plan for each engagement, including the scope, objectives, and timing and resource allocations (Performance standard 2200).

According to Blume (2014), the auditor should plan the audit in a manner that ensures that the audit is carried out in an economic, efficient, and effective way and in a timely manner.

Below are the various forms for Internal Auditing Planning or Preliminary Survey forms; these are captured as Appendix A.

6.3.5.1 Planning and Preliminary Survey Checklist/Template (Figure 6.1)

6.3.5.2 Work Paper Cover Template (Figure 6.2)

6.3.5.3 Information Request List (Table 6.4)

6.3.5.4 Request for Management Input (Table 6.5)

6.3.5.5 Internal Audit Engagement Letter (Figures 6.3 [Format A] and 6.4 [Format B])

6.3.5.6 Planning Memorandum Form (Format A) (Table 6.6)

6.3.5.7 Audit Assignment Form (Format B) (Figure 6.5)

6.3.5.8 Entrance Conference Form (Format A) (Table 6.7)

PATRICKONSULT LTD

OFFICE OF INTERNAL AUDIT
(Insert Street),
(Insert Zip Code)

(Area audited)
(Audit period)
(Audit Project Title and No.)

PLANNING AND PRELIMINARY SURVEY CHECKLIST/TEMPLATE

Initials		**Date**
Reviewer		**Date**

Audit Procedures	W/P Ref.	Auditor/Date

1. Contact auditee to notify them of upcoming audit and arrange for entrance meeting. When making arrangements, identify document(s) or information that will be needed early in the audit process. Ask management or auditee to consider items that they would like to be included in audit.

2. Confirm discussion with a written memorandum that identifies the
(a) Audit period
(b) Estimated start date and duration of the audit
(c) Staff assigned
(d) Physical facilities required

3. Hold entrance conference; document results using Entrance Conference Form. At the opening meeting:
- Explain the role of internal audit (only if it is the first time an audit has been done in the organization), and emphasize that the main objective is to provide constructive help and advice to the management.
- Discuss and agree on the scope and objectives of the audit—making it clear that you welcome any questions and also the views and suggestions of management.
- Ask for the views of management on any problems that may exist, activities that fall within the scope of the audit. This helps demonstrate that you welcome their input and that you are not just looking to be critical of what they are doing.
- Discuss the timing of the audit—and any difficulties which could arise from it (e.g., the absence of key personnel, new systems development etc.). You need to beware of the danger of management raising timing difficulties as a way of having the audit postponed.

Figure 6.1   Planning and Preliminary Survey Checklist/Template.   (*Continued*)

- Establish who are the main people you need to see at the start of the audit. It is also important to agree with management that you can make direct contact with staff, rather than clearing all meetings, etc. with the line manager.
- Set out the procedures that will be adopted for
  - Confirming audit findings
  - Discussing the draft report
  - Issuing the previous and the final report
- Explain that all information will be treated in confidence.
- Establish the normal working hours of staff in the department, where they are located (particularly if some work is done outside of the organization's offices) and any other office routines—to make it easier to arrange meetings, locate people, etc.
- Make it clear that you will need access to all relevant files and documents.
- Ask for the use of an office/desk during the course of the audit—if necessary.

4. Become familiar with area being audited by reviewing various types of information. Summarize results of reviews, highlighting key points, patterns, and trends. Draw conclusions about possible audit objectives suggested by

(a) Information about structure and activities of area audited such as

(i) Organization chart

(ii) Key personnel and their major areas of responsibility

(iii) Approximate number of employees and, for academic departments, students

(iv) Mission statement and any goals and objectives

(b) Financial information to identify

(i) Source of funding

(ii) Types and amount of revenue

(iii) Nature and amount of expenditures

(iv) Amount/location of any petty cash or change funds, or other liquid assets

(c) Department files and prior working papers and reports for information about area's past activities, results of past audits, problems noted related areas, etc.

(d) Audit library materials to identify laws, regulations, policies, procedures, or recent developments related to area

(e) Information about nature and purpose of any separate EDP systems used in the area

5. Review any departmental policies and procedures manuals, flowcharts, or control narratives that may exist.

6. Review reports or management letters issued by State Auditor's Office or other auditors, consultants, or program review groups to identify possibilities to coordinate work or problem areas that may need to be included in the audit. If work performed by other auditors will be relied on, make arrangements to review the supporting work papers.

Figure 6.1 (Continued)   Planning and Preliminary Survey Checklist/Template.
(Continued)

7. Select final audit objectives based on issues identified during the preliminary survey. Preference should be given to management's requests for items to be included in audit (to the extent possible), activities, or functions that relate to the area's mission, and any patterns identified during review of background information.

8. Prepare and obtain approval of a Planning Memorandum which documents
      (a) Planned scope, objectives, and audit period
      (b) Audit areas that will be excluded from the audit and reasons these will not be reviewed
      (c) Resources necessary to complete audit
      (d) Target completion dates

9. Prepare an engagement memorandum for auditee that communicates final objectives and any changes to planned completion of audit.

Approval of Adequate Completion of Preliminary Survey Procedures:

Name and Date_____

Figure 6.1 (Continued)   Planning and Preliminary Survey Checklist/Template. (Adapted from UNC Internal Audit: Sample Standard Forms. http://www.unc .edu/depts/intaudit/PDF/Sample%20Standard%20Forms.pdf.)

PATRICKONSULT LTD

OFFICE OF INTERNAL AUDIT
(Insert Street),
(Insert City or State),
(Insert Zip Code)

WORKPAPER COVER TEMPLATE

ORGANIZATION /AUDITEE NAME

PROJECT TITLE:
(e.g., INTERNAL CONTROLS
FOR REVENUE/CASH RECEIPTS)

AUDIT PROJECT NO.---------------

PERIOD COVERED

PLANNING PHASE (INSERT GRAPHIC)

wpcover.pln

Figure 6.2   Work Paper Cover Template.

Table 6.4   Information Request List for the Fiscal Year 20XX Audit Plan

<table>
<tr><td colspan="5" align="center">**PATRICKONSULT LTD**
OFFICE OF INTERNAL AUDIT
INFORMATION REQUEST LIST FOR THE FISCAL YEAR 20XX AUDIT PLAN
<Insert date>
<Insert position>
<Insert department>
<Insert street address>
<Insert city, state, zip>
(Area audited)
(Audit period)
(Audit Project Title and No.)</td></tr>
<tr><td>*S/N*</td><td>*Scope Area*</td><td>*Document Required*</td><td>*Due Date*</td><td>*Date Received*</td></tr>
<tr><td colspan="5">**Operations**</td></tr>
<tr><td>1</td><td>Organization/ operational</td><td>Departmental organizational chart(s) including roles and responsibilities.
Please identify process owners and name and contact person in each organization for IT areas.</td><td></td><td></td></tr>
<tr><td>2</td><td>Organization/ operational</td><td>List of personnel within each unit</td><td></td><td></td></tr>
<tr><td>3</td><td>Organization/ operational</td><td>Strategic/business plan for the S/C/D</td><td></td><td></td></tr>
<tr><td>4</td><td>Operational</td><td>FY20XX approved budgets</td><td></td><td></td></tr>
<tr><td>5</td><td>Operational</td><td>List of all accounts (numbers and account titles) maintained by your unit</td><td></td><td></td></tr>
<tr><td>6</td><td>Operational</td><td>Operating or comparative analysis reports prepared or issued by your department on an annual basis</td><td></td><td></td></tr>
<tr><td>7</td><td>Operational</td><td>Description of significant departmental processes (include flowcharts if available)</td><td></td><td></td></tr>
<tr><td>8</td><td>Operational</td><td>Internal policies and procedures manual</td><td></td><td></td></tr>
</table>

(Continued)

Table 6.4 (Continued) Information Request List for the Fiscal Year 20XX Audit Plan

S/N	Scope Area	Document Required	Due Date	Date Received
9	Operational	Proposed or pending changes in policies and procedures		
10	Operational	Copies of external regulations applicable to the department		
11	Operational	List of key personnel contacts *(including any significant upcoming leaves)*		
Information Technology				
12	Control environment	A list of any known deficiencies or deviations as defined in the organization or IT policy manual		
13	Control environment	An application inventory for the S/C/D		
14	Infrastructure controls	Overview of the hardware and software platforms (servers inventory, operating system, database management system, authentication software, server type and IP addresses, patch status and virus DAT file level)		
15	Infrastructure controls	Overview documentation for S/C/D IT strategy		
16	Infrastructure controls	WAN diagram of network infrastructure supporting the S/C/D		
17	Disaster recovery	High-level summary of business continuity and disaster recovery plan for recovery procedures from the loss of applications, hardware, and infrastructure. Information on application-specific backup procedures is recommended		

(Continued)

Table 6.4 (Continued)   Information Request List for the Fiscal Year 20XX Audit Plan

S/N	Scope Area	Document Required	Due Date	Date Received
18	Other	List of major IT supplier contracts and agreements		
19	Other	Reports of unusual events since the last audit (e.g., security breaches, failed access attempt reports, and improper practices)		

Source: Adapted from Office of Internal Audit. Wayne State University, http://internal audit.wayne.edu/pdf/information_request.pdf.

Note: Any documentation listed above may be sent electronically to the in-charge auditor for the engagement. Thank you for your attention and cooperation.

Table 6.5   Request for Management Input for the Fiscal Year 20XX Audit Plan

<table>
<tr><td colspan="4">

PATRICKONSULT LTD
OFFICE OF INTERNAL AUDIT
REQUEST FOR MANAGEMENT INPUT FOR THE FISCAL YEAR 20XX AUDIT PLAN
<Insert department>
<Insert street address>
<Insert city, state, zip>
(Area audited)
(Audit period)
(Audit Project Title and No.)
* Required Information

</td></tr>
<tr><td colspan="4">*Area(s) of Concern or Interest*</td></tr>
<tr>
<td>School/College/ Division</td>
<td>Department/ Unit</td>
<td>Reason Requested*</td>
<td>Timing Convenient for Unit (Please Provide Month/Year)</td>
</tr>
<tr><td></td><td></td><td></td><td></td></tr>
<tr><td></td><td></td><td></td><td></td></tr>
<tr><td></td><td></td><td></td><td></td></tr>
<tr><td colspan="4">Signature and Title: _____ Date:_____</td></tr>
</table>

Source: Adapted from Office of Internal Audit. Wayne State University. http://internal audit.wayne.edu/pdf/request_for_management_input_form.pdf.

CONTEC Global Ltd
7A Ruxton Road, Lagos

INTERNAL AUDIT OFFICE

<insert date>

The Director or Program Manager
Procurement Dept.
<insert building>
<insert street address>
<insert city, state, zip>
(Audit Project Title and No.)

Attention: <Name>

Dear Sir:

I have scheduled an audit of the CONTEC Global Ltd <insert audit area>. These audits are being conducted in accordance with Regulation <insert regulation or authority if any>. <insert detail> I included these audits in the FY2011 Internal Audit Plan approved by the Managing Director/Chief Executive Officer.

The purpose of this audit is to verify that:

Insert objectives:

As part of this audit I will also <include additional areas>. These audits are part of the Internal Audit Work plan and should not be considered an indication of a problem. I will keep you informed of the progress with periodic discussions throughout the audit as deemed necessary. My report will provide the status of <audit area>, noncompliance comments and recommendations for improvement. Should you have any questions, do not hesitate to call me at +234-080xxxxxxxx.

Sincerely,

Patrick Onwura (Odunze) Nzechukwu
(Internal Auditor)

Accepted by: Date:

Cc:

Figure 6.3   Internal Audit Engagement Letter (Format A).

PATRICKONSULT LTD

Ndionyemobi, Oguta,
Imo State
(Area audited)
(Audit period)
(Audit Project Title and No.)

INTERNAL AUDIT OFFICE
MEMORANDUM

TO: Name, Director Department   **DATE:**

FROM: Director
Internal Audit Office

SUBJECT: Audit of (insert area)

Internal Audit will be performing an audit of (function/department), which is scheduled to begin on (date). We tentatively plan to complete our fieldwork by (date). Our audit scope will cover the period (date) to (date), and may be changed after the survey is completed. The general objectives of this audit will be to evaluate compliance with organization policies and procedures; laws, regulations or guidelines. We will also evaluate internal controls. This audit will focus on applicable financial and performance issues.

To assist us with this audit, we would like to obtain some documentation prior to the start of fieldwork. Please provide the following documentation:

- All applicable laws, regulations, and guidelines
- Any policy memorandums or directives
- A copy of your operating procedures manual (if available)
- Current organizational chart
- Applicable budget goals and objectives

Please feel free to designate a key member of your staff whom the auditors may contact when requesting data. In addition, please arrange a workspace for the auditor(s).

Rest assured that inclusion of your department for audit on the Long-Range Audit Plan does not mean that something is wrong. Our office is responsible for examining and evaluating the adequacy and effectiveness of the organization's systems of internal controls and the quality of performance by county departments.

I have assigned the following audit staff to this project:

	Name	**Phone #**
Supervisor:	_____	_____
Auditor in Charge:	_____	_____
Staff Auditors:	_____	_____
	_____	_____

I have enclosed a brochure describing our audit process for your information. (Name of Auditor-in-Charge [AIC]) will be contacting you to arrange a convenient time for the Entrance Conference meeting. Should you have any questions before we meet, do not hesitate to call me at (insert contact information).

Figure 6.4   Internal Audit Engagement Letter (Format B).

Table 6.6   Planning Memorandum Form (Format A)

PATRICKONSULT LTD Office of Internal Audit (Area audited) (Audit period) (Audit Project Title and No.) PLANNING MEMORANDUM FORM	
Initials	**Date**
Area audited:	Reports to:
Contact person:	Location:

Audit staff assigned:
Hours budgeted:
	Target dates:
	    Start
	    Preliminary
	    Internal control review
	    Fieldwork
	    Initial report
	    Issue draft report
	    Issue final

Assignment overview:	
Potential objectives:	
Other:	

PATRICKONSULT LTD
Office of Internal Audit
(Area audited)
(Audit period)
(Audit Project Title and No.)

AUDIT ASSIGNMENT FORM

INTERNAL AUDIT
AUDIT ASSIGNMENT FORM

Prepared by: —————————

Date: —————————

Project Title: ————————————————————

Project Number: ————————————————

Auditor in Charge: ——————————————————————————

Audit Team:

Supervisor: ————————————————————

Assignment Source:

Audit Type:

Audit Scope:

Audit Objectives:

Special Instructions:

Start Date:—————————————————————————

Estimated Planning Completion Date: ——————————————————

Figure 6.5   Audit Assignment Form (Format B).

Table 6.7   Entrance Conference Form

PATRICKONSULT LTD **Office of Internal Audit** **(Area audited)** **(Audit period)** **(Audit Project Title and No.)** **ENTRANCE CONFERENCE FORM**	
Date:	
Attendees:	
Audit Objectives Discussed:	
Potential Objectives/Concerns Identified by Management:	
Other Items Discussed with Management (time frame, audit process, major functions of audit area, etc.)	

Other forms/templates for Appendix A includes but not limited to:

6.3.5.9 Analysis of Internal Controls

6.3.5.9.1 Individual Interview Form (Figure 6.6)

6.3.5.9.2 Self-Assessment Questionnaire—Preliminary Survey (Format A—Corporate) (Figure 6.7)

6.3.5.9.3 Self-Audit Questionnaire (Format B—Institutions/MDAs) (Figure 6.8)

6.3.5.9.4 Internal Control Questionnaire Form (Figure 6.9)

6.3.5.9.5 Internal Control Review Checklist (Figure 6.10)

6.3.5.10 Risk Evaluation Form (Figure 6.11)

6.3.5.11 Planning Paperwork Index Template W/P Reference (Table 6.8)

6.3.5.12 Auditor Assignment and Independence Statement Form (Figure 6.12)

6.3.5.13 Quality Control Checklist—Survey Phase (Table 6.9)

PATRICKONSULT LTD
Office of Internal Audit
(Area audited)
(Audit period)

(Audit Project Title and No.)

INDIVIDUAL INTERVIEW FORM

Title: ————————————————

Agency/Division: ————————————————————

Time/Date of Interview: ————————————————————

Auditor: ————————————————————

Others Present at interview:

Name: ————————————————————

Title: ————————————————

Name: ————————————————

Title: ————————————————————

Summary of Discussion:
_____

Figure 6.6 Individual Interview Form.

PATRICKONSULT LTD
Office of Internal Audit
(Area audited)
(Audit period)

Self-Assessment Questionnaire—PRELIMINARY SURVEY

Purpose: As a management team member of (organization name), it is your responsibility to design, adhere to and monitor the significant operating and financial controls of your organization. This short self-assessment has been designed to obtain input from you so that Internal Audit can effectively determine the correct level and areas of focus of their activity in the upcoming review of your area. Your input is important and appreciated. It should take approximately 20 minutes to complete this form.

Area/Department: _____

Responsible Party: _____

Please describe **the key business objectives** of your area. (i.e. What is the mission of your area?)

Are the *Policies and Procedures* in your area *documented*? (circle one)
          Yes   No
Comments:

Are the *Policies and Procedures* in your area *up-to-date*? (circle one)
      Yes   No
Comments:

Please describe the *key business processes* that occur in your area (i.e., What are the activities which are completed in your area?)

Please describe the *key internal controls* that you believe exist in your area (i.e., How do you control the major activities, output, etc., in your area?)

What are the *key information systems utilized* in your area?

Figure 6.7 **Self-Assessment Questionnaire—Preliminary Survey (Format A—Corporate).** *(Continued)*

Please describe *the key performance measures* you obtain and utilize to monitor the effectiveness/efficiency of your business processes.

Please describe *the key means of communication* you utilize to inform other departments of activities/issues occurring in your area.

Which departments would benefit from communication with your department?

Which departments do you currently communicate with?

Are there any areas that you would like Internal Audit to specifically review (i.e. areas of immediate control concern or inefficient process)?

Overall, how would you rate the following in your area?	Poor	Average	World Class
The effectiveness of your internal controls	1–2	3–4	5
The quality of your output	1–2	3–4	5
The efficiency of your business processes	1–2	3–4	5

NB: If there is any additional information you feel we should have prior to our review (such as organization charts, policies, reports, etc.), please attach it to this questionnaire. Please return this questionnaire and any attachments to:

(name)   by   (insert date).

Figure 6.7 (Continued)   Self-Assessment Questionnaire—Preliminary Survey (Format A—Corporate).

PATRICKONSULT LTD
Office of Internal Audit
(Area audited)
(Audit period)

Self-Audit Questionnaire

TO: Name, Director Department   **DATE:**

FROM: Director
           Internal Audit Office

SUBJECT: Audit of (insert area)

1. Notification and Overview

A Self-Audit of your unit is included in the Internal Audit Plan for the current year. A Self-Audit Questionnaire is a checklist used as the primary tool for performing a self-audit to assess your internal control environment. This questionnaire was developed in a Yes/No/Not Applicable format, which also requests short answers in some cases. It will request department personnel to respond to a number of questions designed to identify areas of audit risk, the presence of internal controls to mitigate the occurrence of risks, fraud awareness, management oversight, and assess the strength of your unit's overall internal control structure. Upon receipt of the completed Self-Audit Questionnaire, we will review and evaluate the answers provided. Based on the results of the questionnaire, the performance of additional, more comprehensive procedures may be deemed necessary.

These procedures may include a planned full scope audit of a Specific Procedures Review in which a particular aspect of your operations is reviewed in detail. In most cases, however, Internal Audit will provide suggestions for improvement of your unit. If a Specific Procedures Review or full scope audit were deemed necessary, we would notify you and request a convenient time to continue with these activities at a later date. We have tentatively scheduled the self-audit to be performed during the following time period: December 15, 20xx to December 20, 20xx.

We estimate that it should take approximately 15 hours to fully and adequately complete the questionnaire. As we are not necessarily aware of all time constraints you may have during this period, we would appreciate your comments regarding the feasibility of performing this self-audit during the identified time period. If an alternative time period is necessary, please indicate the reason(s) along with your specific suggestion for a more suitable time period.

In order to allow adequate time to reschedule any audits, we would appreciate your response regarding the timing of the audit by December 27, 20xx.

Figure 6.8   Self-Audit Questionnaire (Format B—Institutions/MDAs).   (*Continued*)

For your convenience, your Business Manager will receive a survey link by e-mail to complete the Self-Audit Questionnaire via Survey Monkey. We will also e-mail the questionnaire as a PDF document to you and your Business Manager to provide you the opportunity to print and review the survey prior to completing it online. You may also use the PDF document to review with other individuals, within your unit, who can answer questions regarding areas with which you are unfamiliar. Please note that if you are unable to complete the survey in one sitting, Survey Monkey allows you to go back and continue to complete the questionnaire. However, only click "Submit" when you have fully completed the survey and no other changes need to be made.

If you have any questions or concerns, please call Henry Odunze, Interim Audit Manager at Mobile No. 080xxxxxxxx.

We look forward to working with you in the near future.

Patrick Nzechukwu, CAE
Office of Internal Audit

SURVEY QUESTIONNAIRE

2. General Information

*1. **Please complete the following:**

Date:

School/Department/Program:

Individual Supplying Information:

Position/Title:

Phone:

Email:

3. Background Information

* 1. **Please provide a brief description of the unit's operations. This description should include a discussion of your unit's significant operational processes, product(s), and customer(s):**

Please attach a list of all accounts (numbers and account titles) maintained by your unit.

Figure 6.8 (Continued) **Self-Audit Questionnaire (Format B—Institutions/MDAs).**
(Continued)

*2. What was the unit's original general fund budget at the beginning of the current fiscal year?

Non Personnel:

Personnel:

*3. Does your section/unit/department maintain a list of individuals authorized to sign personnel actions, payroll documents, budget changes, institution review board (IRB), etc.?

If your answer is yes, please provide a copy of the list.

  ○ Yes

  ○ No

* 4. Do you have any supplementary internal operating procedures for the control of your unit?

  ○ Yes

  ○ No

*5. If you answered yes to the previous question, are they documented in written form? Please provide a copy if applicable.

  ○ Yes

  ○ No

  ○ N/A

*6. Are internal policies and procedures reviewed and revised to reflect current practice?

  ○ Yes

  ○ No

4. Operations and Activities

*1. Please rate the frequency at which your unit interacts with the public (i.e., granting institutions, donors, outreach activities, etc.)

  ○ Low   ○ High

  ○ Medium   ○ N/A

Please describe if rated medium or high:

*2. Do your unit's operations routinely include the handling of significant amounts of confidential information?

  ○ Yes

  ○ No

If yes, please describe:

Figure 6.8 (Continued)   **Self-Audit Questionnaire (Format B—Institutions/MDAs).**
(*Continued*)

3. Do your unit's operations include monitoring responsibility, i.e., responsibility for ensuring that other units comply with internal/external policies and procedures, meet specified goals, maintain adequate documentation and/or submit reports on a timely basis?

○ Yes

○ No

If yes, please describe:

---

*4. Are any aspects of your unit's operations subject to external reporting requirements or regulations, i.e., federal or state agency regulation, professional society procedural or ethical regulations, etc.?

○ Yes

○ No

If yes, please describe:

---

*5. Have any aspects of your unit's operations been audited or reviewed by the University's external auditors (currently Plante & Moran) within the past five years?

○ Yes

○ No

If yes, please describe:

---

5. Financial Activity and Personnel Composition

*1. What are your unit's top five revenue sources and expenditures (excluding payroll expenditures) based on dollars received and spent?

1a. Revenue Sources:
1b. Expenditures
2a. Revenue Sources:
2b. Expenditures:
3a. Revenue Sources:
3b. Expenditures:
4a. Revenue Sources:
4b. Expenditures:
5a. Revenue Sources:
5b. Expenditures

*2. Does your unit issue invoices for sales or services?

○ Yes

○ No

If yes, please describe activities that generate invoices and how much revenue has been generated this fiscal year

---

*3. Does your unit receive cash receipts (i.e., cash, check, money order, etc)? (If not, please skip to question #7)

○ Yes

○ No

If yes, what type(s) do you receive?

Figure 6.8 (Continued)   Self-Audit Questionnaire (Format B—Institutions/MDAs).
(Continued)

4. Please indicate the average cash receipts (C/R) received per fiscal year within your unit and describe the source of these:

Average C/R Revenue:

Source:

5. What internal records does your unit maintain on cash amounts received?

6. Please answer the following:
Does your unit use prenumbered receipts to record checks or cash received?

- ○ **Yes**
- ○ **No**

Does your unit maintain a record of checks and/or cash received?

- ○ **Yes**
- ○ **No**

Does your unit promptly deliver all funds to the Cashier's Office as required by University policy?

- ○ **Yes**
- ○ **No**

Does your unit have a secure place for storing funds? (If yes, please describe below.)

- ○ **Yes**
- ○ **No**

Does your unit restrictively endorse checks/cheques as soon as practicable after receipt?

- ○ **Yes**
- ○ **No**

Are cash deposits reconciled to University financial accounting records?

- ○ **Yes**
- ○ **No**

Is there adequate segregation of duties between the individuals responsible for receiving cash, individual(s) responsible for processing the deposit and the individual(s) responsible for reconciling internal deposit records to University records?

- ○ **Yes**
- ○ **No**

If you answered yes to "Do you have a secure place for storing funds?," please describe the location:

Figure 6.8 (Continued)   Self-Audit Questionnaire (Format B—Institutions/MDAs).
(Continued)

7. Does your unit have a petty cash fund? (If no, please skip to question #16.)

    ○ Yes

    ○ No

8. Is the custodian knowledgeable of the University's/MDA's petty cash policies and procedures?

    ○ Yes

    ○ No

9. Is the fund kept in a secure location?

    ○ Yes

    ○ No

10. Does an individual other than the petty cash custodian balance each fund on a monthly basis to see that cash on hand and un reimbursed vouchers equal the fund?

    ○ Yes

    ○ No

11. Do you limit access to petty cash funds to the custodian?

    ○ Yes

    ○ No

12. If you answered "no" to the previous question, please indicate who has access to petty cash funds:

_____

13. Who reimburses the custodian for petty cash transactions? (Please include name and title.)

_____

14. Do you prohibit the use of petty cash for personal services, meals, travel, employee loans, IOUs, or post dated checks/cheques?

    ○ Yes

    ○ No

15. Do you limit petty cash purchases to amounts specified by University/MDA policies and procedures, i.e., $x reimbursement limit and $x single transaction limit?

    ○ Yes

    ○ No

Figure 6.8 (Continued)   Self-Audit Questionnaire (Format B—Institutions/MDAs).
(*Continued*)

16. Please list all reports specifically designed for your department that you receive from University/MDA administrative departments or other sources and depend on to perform routine activities:

17. Please answer the following:
Do you find these various reports to be adequate to meet your unit's operating needs?

○ **Yes**

○ **No**

Do you or someone within your unit review these various reports at least monthly?

○ **Yes**

○ **No**

Are these reports received timely?

○ **Yes**

○ **No**

Upon review, does your unit initiate action to facilitate correction of any errors that are found?

○ **Yes**

○ **No**

18. Is a monthly reconciliation of internal records to recorded activity utilizing these reports or other online reports and data, i.e., revenue and expenditure activity, performed?

○ **Yes**

○ **No**

If yes, who is responsible for this activity?

19. Are unreconciled items investigated? If so, please explain the process and who is responsible for this process:

20. Is the reconciliation documented?

○ **Yes**

○ **No**

21. Who reviews and approves the reconciliation? (Please provide name and title)

22. Are there reports that you do not currently receive which you require?

○ **Yes**

○ **No**

If yes, please elaborate:

Figure 6.8 Self-Audit Questionnaire (Format B—Institutions/MDAs). (*Continued*)

23. Has your unit issued any personal service contracts during the last five years?

    ○   Yes

    ○   No

If yes, please describe and indicate the total number of personal service contracts issued:

24. Please provide the total number of employees within your unit as follows:

Number of nonacademic full-time personnel: ————————————————

Number of nonacademic part-time personnel: ————————————————

Number of academic full-time personnel: ————————————————

Number of academic part-time personnel: ————————————————

Number of graduate assistants: ————————————————

Number of student personnel (student assistants, interns, College Work Study, etc.):

Other (please describe): ————————————————

Total number of personnel: ————————————————

25. Please answer the following:

Are bi-weekly payroll documents properly approved and submitted via Web Time Entry (WTE) in a timely manner to the Payroll Office?

    ○   Yes

    ○   No

    ○   N/A

Does the person approving Time and Exception document have first-hand knowledge that the hours shown have actually been worked?

    ○   Yes

    ○   No

    ○   N/A

Do departmental policies prohibit the signing of blank time documents, i.e., before "hours worked" have been entered?

    ○   Yes

    ○   No

    ○   N/A

Figure 6.8 (Continued) Self-Audit Questionnaire (Format B—Institutions/MDAs).
(Continued)

Do departmental policies prohibit the projection of time worked, i.e., entering data on time cards before the hours are actually worked?

- ○ **Yes**
- ○ **No**
- ○ **N/A**

Are all time documents authorized by someone other than the employee?

- ○ **Yes**
- ○ **No**
- ○ **N/A**

Are student assistants' sign in/out sheets maintained for three years in compliance with the On-Campus Employment Guide?

- ○ **Yes**
- ○ **No**
- ○ **N/A**

Are any of your employees paid overtime?

- ○ **Yes**
- ○ **No**
- ○ **N/A**

Does your unit have any employees who are supervised by a relative?

- ○ **Yes**
- ○ **No**
- ○ **N/A**

Have employees who sign for/pick up payroll checks at the Cashier's Office been approved for this function?

- ○ **Yes**
- ○ **No**
- ○ **N/A**

Does your unit have procedures in place to ensure that payroll checks are distributed only to named payees?

- ○ **Yes**
- ○ **No**
- ○ **N/A**

Do you or your unit currently have any checks on hand that have not been distributed?

- ○ **Yes**
- ○ **No**
- ○ **N/A**

Do you or your unit maintain internal departmental vacation and sick leave records on all employees within your department?

- ○ **Yes**
- ○ **No**
- ○ **N/A**

Figure 6.8 (Continued)   Self-Audit Questionnaire (Format B—Institutions/MDAs).
(Continued)

26. Please list all individuals authorized to pick up payroll checks from the Cashier's Office (if applicable):

_____

_____

_____

27. What procedures does your unit perform for undistributed payroll checks?

_____

_____

28. With respect to vacation and sick leave records, does your unit:
Report vacation and sick leave bi-weekly to Payroll via the WTE time and exception report?

    ○ Yes

    ○ No

Regularly reconcile payroll records with your internal records?

    ○ Yes

    ○ No

Confirm periodically with employees that leave records are correct?

    ○ Yes

    ○ No

29. Have you employed any consultants during the year? (If no, skip to question #31.)

    ○ Yes

    ○ No

30. If you answered yes to the above question, did you obtain the required professional service contract?

    ○ Yes

    ○ No

31. Please answer the following:

Is your unit currently operating within the approved total for your current fiscal year budget?

    ○ Yes

    ○ No

    ○ N/A

Does your unit anticipate any problems in staying within your budget for the current fiscal year?

    ○ Yes

    ○ No

    ○ N/A

Figure 6.8 (Continued)   **Self-Audit Questionnaire (Format B—Institutions/MDAs).**
(Continued)

Does your unit maintain separate internal records for controlling your budget and expenditures?

- ○ **Yes**
- ○ **No**
- ○ **N/A**

Does your unit monitor budget versus actual financial activity?

- ○ **Yes**
- ○ **No**
- ○ **N/A**

Are discrepancies between actual and budgeted financial activity investigated and/or corrected timely?

- ○ **Yes**
- ○ **No**
- ○ **N/A**

32. Other than normal supply inventories, does your unit have inventories for resale for departmental/campus usage? (If no, please skip to question #34.)

- ○ **Yes**
- ○ **No**

If yes, please list the types of inventory and balances at the end of the past fiscal year:

33. Please answer the following:

Are inventories recorded on the University's general ledger?

- ○ **Yes**
- ○ **No**

Does your unit take periodic physical inventories for the purpose of adjusting inventory records?

- ○ **Yes**
- ○ **No**

Have your unit's inventory records been adjusted to the last physical count?

- ○ **Yes**
- ○ **No**

Does your unit maintain perpetual inventory records?

- ○ **Yes**
- ○ **No**

Does your unit have a specific person designated as being in charge of inventory control?

- ○ **Yes**
- ○ **No**

Is your unit's inventory properly safeguarded against theft and pilferage?

- ○ **Yes**
- ○ **No**

Figure 6.8 (Continued)   Self-Audit Questionnaire (Format B—Institutions/MDAs).
(Continued)

34. What is the value of your unit's equipment purchases (current fiscal year-to-date) per the financial accounting records?

35. Does your unit have a person who has been assigned the full responsibility for asset control and record maintenance?

○ Yes

○ No

If so, who?

36. Does your unit perform an inventory of equipment?

○ Yes

○ No

○ N/A

If so, when was the last inventory performed? _____

37. Does your unit investigate any differences between equipment records and equipment actually on hand?

○ Yes

○ No

38. Do you have University equipment that is maintained off site, i.e., not on University premises?

○ Yes

○ No

If so, please describe equipment and location: _____

_____

39. Does your unit record and control all equipment not located within your specific area?

○ Yes

○ No

If so, please describe the method(s) utilized: _____

40. Does your unit have restrictions on the use of equipment for personal use?

○ Yes

○ No

If yes, please describe: _____

41. Does your unit promptly report stolen equipment to the appropriate authority?

○ Yes

○ No

Figure 6.8 (Continued) Self-Audit Questionnaire (Format B—Institutions/MDAs).
(Continued)

42. Does your unit promptly submit the certification on Federal property?
- ○ Yes
- ○ No
- ○ N/A

43. Does your unit review and approve travel expense reports (TERs) before they are submitted for reimbursement?
- ○ Yes
- ○ No

44. Are TERs submitted promptly for reimbursement in accordance with University policy and procedure?
- ○ Yes
- ○ No

45. Who approves TERs? _____

46. Does the person approving the TERs ensure that requests conform to regulations and all necessary information and receipts have been included?
- ○ Yes
- ○ No

47. Does the traveller sign and date each TER?
- ○ Yes
- ○ No

48. Please answer the following:
Is the telecommunication bill analyzed monthly for improper charges?
- ○ Yes
- ○ No

Are telephones and telephone jacks protected against improper usage for long distance calls?
- ○ Yes
- ○ No

Does your unit review departmental monthly telephone bills for improper use of regular long distance?
- ○ Yes
- ○ No

Does your unit review departmental telephone bills for personal charges?
- ○ Yes
- ○ No

Are employees required to reimburse the department if personal long distance charges are noted?
- ○ Yes
- ○ No

Figure 6.8 (Continued)   Self-Audit Questionnaire (Format B—Institutions/MDAs).
(*Continued*)

Within your department, does your unit enforce University restrictions on the use of institutional funds for the purchase of beverages and food items?

○ **Yes**

○ **No**

Within your department, do you enforce University restrictions on the use of institutional funds for the payment of entertainment costs?

○ **Yes**

○ **No**

Do you prohibit employees to use University funds for the purchase of personal goods or services?

○ **Yes**

○ **No**

Does your unit have any contracts for maintenance or services?

○ **Yes**

○ **No**

6. Human Resources

1. Please answer the following in regards to Human Resources activities within your department:

Are roster reconciliations performed and submitted to the Budget Office throughout the fiscal year?

○ **Yes**

○ **No**

○ **N/A**

How does your unit ensure that reconciliations are completed accurately?

○ **Yes**

○ **No**

○ **N/A**

Are payroll reports reviewed bi-weekly to ensure that only eligible individuals are paid and are paid accurately?

○ **Yes**

○ **No**

○ **N/A**

Are employee background and/or reference checks performed for prospective employees?

○ **Yes**

○ **No**

○ **N/A**

Are job duties periodically reviewed to ensure that the right person is performing the job?

○ **Yes**

○ **No**

○ **N/A**

Are annual employee evaluations performed?

○ **Yes**

○ **No**

○ **N/A**

Are job descriptions periodically reviewed to ensure that they correlate with what the employee's actual duties are?

○ **Yes**

○ **No**

○ **N/A**

Figure 6.8 (Continued)   Self-Audit Questionnaire (Format B—Institutions/MDAs).
(*Continued*)

2. If you answered "yes" to the question "are employee background and/or reference checks performed for prospective employees," please give the name and position of the person who performs such checks:

3. How does your unit ensure that you have qualified people conducting interviews of prospective employees?

4. How does your unit ensure that individuals conducting interviews are aware of questions that legally can or cannot be asked?

5. Are duties related to HR personnel transactions separated (i.e., one individual completes the paperwork or enters transaction into electronic personnel action form (EPAF) and another approves the transaction)?

○ **Yes**

○ **No**

If you chose no, please explain why: _____

_____

6. Are EPAF exception reports run to verify that the only authorized individuals have approved personnel transactions?

○ **Yes**

○ **No**

7. Are employees' roles and responsibilities communicated to them?

○ **Yes**

○ **No**

If you chose yes, please explain how and by whom: _____

_____

8. How do you ensure that employees' goals are aligned with the University's strategic goals?

9. How do you ensure that employees are complying with University/Ministry's/Agency's/Dept's policies, as it is related to Human Resources (e.g., employee relationship, attendance, etc.)?

Figure 6.8 (Continued) Self-Audit Questionnaire (Format B—Institutions/MDAs).
(Continued)

10. In instances when employees are not complying with University policies, how are such issues addressed?

_____

_____

7. Grant and Contract Activity

If your department has no grant and/or contract activity, please skip this section

1. Please answer the following:

Do your unit's operations include the utilization of animal subjects?

○ **Yes**

○ **No**

Do your unit's operations include the utilization of human subjects?

○ **Yes**

○ **No**

Are those responsible for classifying expenditures knowledgeable of Federal guidelines regarding Unallowable Expenses and specific expense restrictions included in particular grant/contract agreements?

○ **Yes**

○ **No**

Are those individuals who prepare grant and contract proposals knowledgeable of the University's indirect cost and fringe benefit rates?

○ **Yes**

○ **No**

Are those who are involved with sponsored programs knowledgeable of the University's cost transfer policies and procedures?

○ **Yes**

○ **No**

Are accounts reviewed/reconciled at least monthly to identify any corrections or items that should be cost transferred?

○ **Yes**

○ **No**

Are cost transfers (including personnel costs) submitted timely and with complete Supporting documentation?

○ **Yes**

○ **No**

Are procedures in place to ensure that sponsored projects are ready for financial close out within 60 days after termination (or as otherwise specified)?

○ **Yes**

○ **No**

Are University accounts in your department monitored to ensure that budgets are properly maintained in accordance with University and grant/contract specifications?

○ **Yes**

○ **No**

Figure 6.8 (Continued)   Self-Audit Questionnaire (Format B—Institutions/MDAs).
(Continued)

Are sponsored accounts within your department operated within their approved budget and the terms/conditions of the agreement?

○ **Yes**

○ **No**

Are all outstanding obligations cleared within a reasonable time in order to permit financial close-out of sponsored projects within sponsor and University guidelines?

○ **Yes**

○ **No**

Is appropriate documentation included with travel requests to support costs applicable to sponsored awards?

○ **Yes**

○ **No**

8. Interactions with Students

1. Please describe your unit's interaction with students or services provided to students:

_____

_____

2. Please indicate the number and value of scholarships, loans, and/or prizes awarded per fiscal year:

Number of Awards per Fiscal Year: _____

Value of Total Awards per Fiscal Year: _____

3. Do your unit's operations include generating or releasing holds (transcripts, registration, financial, etc.)?

○ **Yes**

○ **No**

If yes, please describe what type of holds are released (i.e., academic or financial) and the procedures performed to release holds including personnel responsible for performing procedures:

_____

_____

9. Use of Information Technology
1. Does your unit have its own IT support team/group? (If not, please skip question #2.)

○ **Yes**

○ **No**

2. Please answer the following if you answered yes to question #1:

Do you have system support, a technical support team, or system administrator for your S/C/D's computer system?

○ **Yes**

○ **No**

○ **N/A**

○ **Don't Know**

Figure 6.8 (Continued)   Self-Audit Questionnaire (Format B—Institutions/MDAs).
(Continued)

For each computing system, does your department limit physical access to only those system administration personnel necessary to administer and maintain the system?

- ○ **Yes**
- ○ **No**
- ○ **N/A**
- ○ **Don't Know**

For each computing system, does your unit have an access control policy?

- ○ **Yes**
- ○ **No**
- ○ **N/A**
- ○ **Don't Know**

Are there any shared IDs?

- ○ **Yes**
- ○ **No**
- ○ **N/A**
- ○ **Don't Know**

Are there any shared passwords?

- ○ **Yes**
- ○ **No**
- ○ **N/A**
- ○ **Don't Know**

For each computing system, does your unit maintain and monitor logs for access control violations?

- ○ **Yes**
- ○ **No**
- ○ **N/A**
- ○ **Don't Know**

Do employees have desktop PCs or laptops?

- ○ **Yes**
- ○ **No**
- ○ **N/A**
- ○ **Don't Know**

If employees have desktop PCs or laptops, are they backed up?

- ○ **Yes**
- ○ **No**
- ○ **N/A**
- ○ **Don't Know**

Are regular disk backups performed?

- ○ **Yes**
- ○ **No**
- ○ **N/A**
- ○ **Don't Know**

Figure 6.8 (Continued) Self-Audit Questionnaire (Format B—Institutions/MDAs).
(*Continued*)

Has a business continuity disaster recovery plan been completed?
- ○ **Yes**
- ○ **No**
- ○ **N/A**
- ○ **Don't Know**

Does your unit provide individuals equipped with University-owned desktop systems with the resources necessary to prevent or detect computer software viruses?
- ○ **Yes**
- ○ **No**
- ○ **N/A**
- ○ **Don't Know**

Are all drives and files on your system scanned for viruses?
- ○ **Yes**
- ○ **No**
- ○ **N/A**
- ○ **Don't Know**

Does your unit prohibit the use of personally owned software or University computer equipement?
- ○ **Yes**
- ○ **No**
- ○ **N/A**
- ○ **Don't Know**

Does your unit provide safeguards against fire, flood, theft, etc.?
- ○ **Yes**
- ○ **No**
- ○ **N/A**
- ○ **Don't Know**

Does your unit ensure that all software installed on University-owned computing systems are properly acquired and that all software license restrictions are followed?
- ○ **Yes**
- ○ **No**
- ○ **N/A**
- ○ **Don't Know**

Does your unit currently possess software licenses for all software resident on the computers/networks within your department?
- ○ **Yes**
- ○ **No**
- ○ **N/A**
- ○ **Don't Know**

Is there a portable device policy?
- ○ **Yes**
- ○ **No**
- ○ **N/A**
- ○ **Don't Know**

Figure 6.8 (Continued)   **Self-Audit Questionnaire (Format B—Institutions/MDAs).**
(Continued)

3. For each computing system, does your unit perform and verify the integrity of regular system backups?

○ Yes

○ No

If no, why not? _____

4. For each computing system, does your unit provide for off-site storage of system backup media?

○ Yes

○ No

If no, why not? _____

5. Does your unit utilize any computer applications developed within your unit?

○ Yes

○ No

If yes, please describe these applications: _____

10. Procurement Process
1. Are procurement cards used for the following transactions?:

Travel and entertainment expenses

○ Yes

○ No

Advertising and printing

○ Yes

○ No

Service payments (e.g., legal services, computer programming, or consultation services)

○ Yes

○ No

Individual or professional membership dues

○ Yes

○ No

Personal or other unauthorized charges per the APPM Section 2.7

○ Yes

○ No

2. Please answer the following:

Are procurement cards being issued to students, guests, individual contractors, or other nonemployees?

○ Yes

○ No

○ N/A

○ Don't Know

Figure 6.8 (Continued)   Self-Audit Questionnaire (Format B—Institutions/MDAs).
(*Continued*)

Have all procurement cardholders and Procurement Card coordinators (including noncardholders) attended the mandatory procurement card training?

- ○ **Yes**
- ○ **No**
- ○ **N/A**
- ○ **Don't Know**

Do cardholders share their cards with other empoyees?

- ○ **Yes**
- ○ **No**
- ○ **N/A**
- ○ **Don't Know**

Are you aware of the policies and procedures for procurement card use?

- ○ **Yes**
- ○ **No**
- ○ **N/A**
- ○ **Don't Know**

If you answered yes to the above question, is there a copy of the cardholder agreement on file for each cardholder?

- ○ **Yes**
- ○ **No**
- ○ **N/A**
- ○ **Don't Know**

Do cardholders split transactions (purchase one good or service, greater than $1000 and separate the payments into two or more transactions)?

- ○ **Yes**
- ○ **No**
- ○ **N/A**
- ○ **Don't Know**

Has anyone contacted the Purchasing Department to negotiate discounts when making repetitive purchases from the same vendor?

- ○ **Yes**
- ○ **No**
- ○ **N/A**
- ○ **Don't Know**

Are cardholders aware that University purchases are exempt from sales tax?

- ○ **Yes**
- ○ **No**
- ○ **N/A**
- ○ **Don't Know**

Are there copies of detailed receipts on file for each procurement card transaction? Receipts should note the quantity, description, and unit price for all items purchased (packing slips do not meet this requirement.)

- ○ **Yes**
- ○ **No**
- ○ **N/A**
- ○ **Don't Know**

Figure 6.8 (Continued)   Self-Audit Questionnaire (Format B—Institutions/MDAs).
(*Continued*)

Does the procurement cardholder provide a signed copy of cardholder statement and all applicable receipts to the procurement card coordinator?

- ○ **Yes**
- ○ **No**
- ○ **N/A**
- ○ **Don't Know**

Are monthly reviews of the cardholder statement being performed by the procurement card coordinator?

- ○ **Yes**
- ○ **No**
- ○ **N/A**
- ○ **Don't Know**

Does the procurement card coordinator sign each cardholder statement?

- ○ **Yes**
- ○ **No**
- ○ **N/A**
- ○ **Don't Know**

Do the procurement card coordinator(s) submit the Monthly Billing Cycle Report (MBCR) to the Procurement Card Office by the 10th of each month?

- ○ **Yes**
- ○ **No**
- ○ **N/A**
- ○ **Don't Know**

Are copies of each cardholder's monthly statement (with MBCR) provided to the unit
Business Officer/Business Manager/Administrator for his/her monthly review?

- ○ **Yes**
- ○ **No**
- ○ **N/A**
- ○ **Don't Know**

Do MBCR's document all violations, misrepresentation, and/or omissions for all cardholders for which the procurement card coordinator is responsible?
In cases of missing receipts, has the cardholder or the procurement card coordinator made every reasonable effort to obtain documentation for missing receipts?

- ○ **Yes**
- ○ **No**
- ○ **N/A**
- ○ **Don't Know**

If you answered yes to the above question, are notes documenting their effort retained in place of the missing receipt?

- ○ **Yes**
- ○ **No**
- ○ **N/A**
- ○ **Don't Know**

Figure 6.8 (Continued)   Self-Audit Questionnaire (Format B—Institutions/MDAs).
(*Continued*)

If you answered no, has there been any action taken to suspend or revoke the cardholder's procurement card privileges?

- ○ **Yes**
- ○ **No**
- ○ **N/A**
- ○ **Don't Know**

Do the cardholder and/or the department coordinator review the procurement card transactions every month before the 4th working day of the subsequent month, to ensure that the transactions are being charged to the appropriate FOAPAL (Fund Organization Account Program Activity Location)?

- ○ **Yes**
- ○ **No**
- ○ **N/A**
- ○ **Don't Know**

In the event that there is a discrepancy on the cardholder's monthly statement, is a Charge Dispute Form completed and forwarded to the procurement card office?

- ○ **Yes**
- ○ **No**
- ○ **N/A**
- ○ **Don't Know**

Does your department/unit have a Procurement Card Transaction Log?

- ○ **Yes**
- ○ **No**
- ○ **N/A**
- ○ **Don't Know**

Are copies of monthly cardholder statements being kept by the cardholder for at least one year?

- ○ **Yes**
- ○ **No**
- ○ **N/A**
- ○ **Don't Know**

Are copies of receipts for each procurement card purchase being retained by the department for seven years?

- ○ **Yes**
- ○ **No**
- ○ **N/A**
- ○ **Don't Know**

3. Was there a departmental or transactional audit conducted of your department's Procurement Card process?

- ○ **Yes**
- ○ **No**

4. If you answered yes to the above question, which one?

- ○ **Departmental**
- ○ **Transactional**

5. When? _____

Figure 6.8 (Continued)   Self-Audit Questionnaire (Format B—Institutions/MDAs).
(*Continued*)

6. Was the Audit Document Request sent to the Procurement Card Manager by the stated deadline?

    ○ Yes

    ○ No

7. Have any requests for cancellation of procurement cards been sent to the Procurement Card Manager after the cardholder is terminated or transferred from employment?

    ○ Yes

    ○ No

8. Is there an employee to act on the Procurement Card/Form on coordinator's behalf during their absence?

    ○ Yes

    ○ No

11. Governance

1. Does management meet with senior management to discuss the financial condition and review the goals and objectives of the dept./unit?

    ○ Yes

    ○ No

If so, how often? _____

2. Are reports provided to senior management?

    ○ Yes

    ○ No

If so, what types of reports and how often? _____
_____

3. Does the Dean or management receive financial reports from the Business Manager to be aware of the financial condition of the dept./unit?

    ○ Yes

    ○ No

If so, what types of reports? _____

4. Does management monitor progress towards established goals and objectives?

    ○ Yes

    ○ No

5. Does management ensure that goals and objectives are aligned with University goals and objectives?

    ○ Yes

    ○ No

6. Does the school/college have a separate governing board (i.e., board of visitors)?

    ○ Yes

    ○ No

Figure 6.8 (Continued) Self-Audit Questionnaire (Format B—Institutions/MDAs).
(Continued)

If so, what is their goal and mission, how often do you meet with them, and what types of reports are provided to them? _____

_____

7. Has management identified and analyzed risks that could prevent goals and objectives from being achieved?

      ○ Yes

      ○ No

8. Have controls been established to mitigate the above risks?

      ○ Yes

      ○ No

12. Fraud Risk and Awareness

1. Does management have knowledge of any fraud or suspected fraud affecting your school/college/division?

      ○ Yes

      ○ No

2. If the answer to question #1 is yes, has it been reported to anyone?

      ○ Yes

      ○ No

If yes, whom? _____

3. Have adequate controls been established to deter, prevent, or mitigate specific fraud risks? Examples include:

a. Segregation of duties
b. Management reviews
c. Authorization
d. Reconciliation
e. Safeguarding of assets
f. Periodic rotation of jobs

      ○ Yes

      ○ No

4. How does management monitor the above controls? _____

_____

_____

5. Please provide any additional information regarding your unit that you feel was not touched on through this questionnaire:

_____

_____

_____

_____

Figure 6.8 (Continued) Self-Audit Questionnaire (Format B—Institutions/MDAs). (Adapted from Wayne State University. Self-Audit Questionnaire, http://internal audit.wayne.edu/pdf/self_audit_questionnaire.pdf.)

PATRICKONSULT LTD
Office of Internal Audit
(Area audited)
(Audit period)

(Audit Project Title and No.)

Internal Control Questionnaire Form

Prepared by: _____

Date: _____

Reviewed by: ____

Date: _____

Department:	Auditable Function:
Discussed with:	Date:

Question	Yes	No	N/A	Comments

107-ICQ.doc

Figure 6.9 Internal Control Questionnaire Form. (Adapted from AuditNet. Copyright 2014 AuditNet LLC, by AuditNet.)

PATRICKONSULT LTD
Office of Internal Audit
(Area audited)
(Audit period)

INTERNAL CONTROL REVIEW CHECKLIST

Initials_____ Date_____

Reviewer_____ Date_____

| **Audit Procedures** | **Auditor/Date** |

1. Based on the nature of risks associated with activities being audited, determine what controls should be in place and what weaknesses may exist. Develop interview notes or Internal Control Questionnaires (ICQ) to use as a tool in conducting control interviews.

2. Obtain an understanding of tasks, work flow, procedures, and control techniques by conducting interviews with individuals responsible for activities being audited. If policy and procedure manuals or similar documentation exists, these can be used to supplement the control review.

3. Document your understanding of each activity using narratives, flowcharts, or other methods that reflect the process being audited and the strengths and weaknesses in the process.

4. Obtain copies of all significant auditee standard forms, reports, logs, etc., which are referenced within flowcharts, data flow diagrams, or narratives.

5. Verify the accuracy of the flowcharts, data flow diagrams, or narratives through examination of documentation, observation, or inquiry. Document the results of verification.

6. Identify and analyze control strengths. Determine if the controls identified in step #1 exist, how they work, and whether they are likely to achieve their intended purpose. Identify which controls will be tested and reference to applicable audit program step(s).

7. Identify and explain control weaknesses. Weaknesses may be inefficient or unnecessary steps as well as poor/missing fiscal controls. Indicate whether compensating controls exist or evaluate cause and significance of each weakness. Indicate if testing is needed to determine impact of a weakness. Prepare Point Sheets for significant weaknesses.

8. Based on the review of internal controls, conclude on the adequacy of the system of internal controls (i.e., the system, as designed, provides reasonable assurance that the activities being audited are functioning as intended.

Approval of Adequate Completion of Review of Internal Controls:

Name Date_____

Figure 6.10 Internal Control Review Checklist.

PATRICKONSULT LTD
Office of Internal Audit
(Area audited)
(Audit period)

RISK EVALUATION FORM

Date: _____

Division: _____

Department: _____

Business Function:

_____

DEFINITION OF SCOPE OF THE BUSINESS FUNCTION UNDER EVALUATION

Provide a definition of the scope of the risk evaluation.

_____
_____
_____
_____

_____

BUSINESS FUNCTION / BUSINESS REASON

Provide a high level overview of the area, function, or application being evaluated.

_____
_____
_____
_____
_____
_____

Figure 6.11 Risk Evaluation Form. *(Continued)*

ACCESS RISK	Probability	Exposure
Access risk refers to the impact of unauthorized access to any company assets, such as customer information, passwords, computer hardware and software, confidential financial information, legal information, cash, checks, and other physical assets. When evaluating access risk the nature and relative value of the company's assets need to be considered.	☐ High ☐ Medium ☐ Low ☐ N/A	☐ High ☐ Medium ☐ Low ☐ N/A

Rationale_____

_____

_____

BUSINESS DISRUPTION RISK	Probability	Exposure
Business disruption risk considers the impact if the function or activity was rendered inoperative due to a system failure, or a disaster situation. Consideration is given to the impact on Company customers as well as other Company operations.	☐ High ☐ Medium ☐ Low ☐ N/A	☐ High ☐ Medium ☐ Low ☐ N/A

Rationale_____

_____

_____

_____

Figure 6.11 (Continued)   Risk Evaluation Form.   *(Continued)*

CREDIT RISK	Probability	Exposure
Credit risk considers the potential that extensions of credit to customers may not be repaid. There is an element of credit risk in each extension of credit. When setting lending policies and procedures, the company must consider what level of credit risk is acceptable. Extension of credit includes the use of debit cards and credit cards by customers to make EFT purchases.	□ High □ Medium □ Low □ N/A	□ High □ Medium □ Low □ N/A

Rationale_____

_____

_____

_____

_____

_____

CUSTOMER SERVICE RISK	Probability	Exposure
Customer service risk considers the likely impact on customers if a control should fail. A customer may be external or internal to the company. For example, the line units are customers of the support units. When the customer is internal, assessment of customer service risk should also consider how problems with internal services will likely impact the level of service offered to the outside customer.	□ High □ Medium □ Low □ N/A	□ High □ Medium □ Low □ N/A

Rationale_____

_____

_____

_____

_____

Figure 6.11 (Continued)   Risk Evaluation Form.   (*Continued*)

DATA INTEGRITY RISK	Probability	Exposure
Data integrity risk addresses the impact if inaccurate data are used to make inappropriate business or management decisions. This risk also address the impact if customer information such as account balances or transaction histories were incorrect, or if inaccurate data are used in payment to/from external entities. The release of inaccurate data outside the Company to customers, regulators, shareholders, the public, etc. could lead to a loss of business, possible legal action or public embarrassment.	☐ High ☐ Medium ☐ Low ☐ N/A	☐ High ☐ Medium ☐ Low ☐ N/A

Rationale_____
_____
_____
_____

FINANCIAL/EXTERNAL REPORT MISSTATEMENT RISK	Probability	Exposure
Financial/external report misstatement risk is similar to data integrity risk. However, this risk focuses specifically on the company's general ledger and the various external financial reports which are created from the G/L. Consideration of Generally Accepted Accounting Principles and regulatory accounting principles is an important factor in evaluating financial report misstatement. This risk includes the potential impact of negative comments on the external auditor's Notes to Financial Statements or Management Letter.	☐ High ☐ Medium ☐ Low ☐ N/A	☐ High ☐ Medium ☐ Low ☐ N/A

Rationale_____
_____
_____
_____
_____

Figure 6.11 (Continued) Risk Evaluation Form.   (*Continued*)

FLOAT RISK	**Probability**	**Exposure**
Float risk considers the opportunity cost (lost revenues) if funds are not processed or invested in a timely manner. This risk also addresses the cost (additional expenses) if obligations are not met on a timely basis. Receivables, payables, and suspense accounts are subject to float risk.	☐ High ☐ Medium ☐ Low ☐ N/A	☐ High ☐ Medium ☐ Low ☐ N/A

Rationale_____

FRAUD RISK	**Probability**	**Exposure**
Both internal and external fraud risks need to be considered. Internally, employees may misappropriate company assets, or manipulate or destroy company records. Externally, customers and noncustomers may perpetrate a fraud by tapping into communication lines, obtaining confidential company information misdirecting inventories or assets, etc.	☐ High ☐ Medium ☐ Low ☐ N/A	☐ High ☐ Medium ☐ Low ☐ N/A

Rationale_____

Figure 6.11 (Continued) Risk Evaluation Form.   (*Continued*)

LEGAL AND REGULATORY RISK	Probability	Exposure
In evaluating legal and regulatory risk, consider whether the product, service, or function is subject to legal and regulatory requirements. Regulatory requirements may be federal, state, or local. The relative risk level of an objective may be high if the related law/regulation is currently on the most dangerous violation list. Legal risk also considers the likelihood of the company being sued under a civil action for breach of contract, negligence, misrepresentation, product liability, unsafe premises, etc.	□ High □ Medium □ Low □ N/A	□ High □ Medium □ Low □ N/A

Rationale_____

_____
_____
_____

PHYSICAL HARM RISK	Probability	Exposure
Physical harm risk considers the risk of harm to both employees and customers while in the Company premises or while performing company business. This risk also applies to company assets such as computers or other equipment that may be damaged due to misuse or improper setup and storage, or negotiable instruments and other documents that may be damaged or destroyed.	□ High □ Medium □ Low □ N/A	□ High □ Medium □ Low □ N/A

Rationale_____

_____
_____
_____

Figure 6.11 (Continued)   Risk Evaluation Form.   *(Continued)*

OTHER CONSIDERATIONS	Probability	Exposure
Consider the impact of all other relevant factors on risk. Consider, for instance, the transaction volumes (items and dollars), and financial impact on the balance sheet and income statement.	☐ High	☐ High
	☐ Medium	☐ Medium
	☐ Low	☐ Low
	☐ N/A	☐ N/A

Rationale_____
_____
_____
_____
___

OVERALL RATING	Probability	Exposure	Overall Risk
Based on the evaluation of: What can go wrong ? (probability), and what is the cost if what can go wrong, does go wrong? (the exposure), evaluate the overall magnitude of the risk in the area/function. Evaluate the Probability and Exposure, then combine the two for an estimate of Overall Risk of business mission failure.	☐ High	☐ High	☐ High
	☐ Medium	☐ Medium	☐ Medium
	☐ Low	☐ Low	☐ Low

Rationale_____
_____
_____

AUDIT APPROVALS

Prepared by: _____ Date: _____

Approved by: _____ Date: _____

CLIENT APPROVAL

Approved by: _____ Date: _____

Figure 6.11 (Continued)   Risk Evaluation Form. (Adapted from AuditNet. Copyright 2014 AuditNet LLC, by Jim Miller.)

Table 6.8   Planning Paperwork Index Template W/P Reference

PATRICKONSULT LTD **Office of Internal Audit** **(Area audited)** **(Audit period)** **PLANNING PAPERWORK INDEX TEMPLATE** **PROJECT TITLE** **WORK PAPER INDEX**
1. Audit Program _____
2. Survey Planning Memo _____
3. Program Descriptions and Funding _____
4. Organization and Resources _____
5. Budget Analysis _____
6. Financial Analysis _____
7. Governing Board Actions, Issues, Interests _____
8. Applicable Laws and Regulations _____
9. Significant Policies and Procedures _____
10. Professional and Performance Standards _____
11. Other Audits and Studies _____
12. Professional Audit Resource Materials _____
13. Entrance Conference _____
14. Audit Notification Memo _____
15. Strategy Meetings _____
16. Audit Assignment Form _____

Source: Adapted from AuditNet. Copyright 2014 AuditNet LLC, by AuditNet .plnindex.wpd.

PATRICKONSULT LTD
Office of Internal Audit
(Area audited)
(Audit period)

(Audit Project Title and No.)

AUDITOR ASSIGNMENT AND INDEPENDENCE STATEMENT

Government Auditing Standard 3.02 states:

"In all matters relating to the audit work, the audit organization and the individual auditor, whether government or public, must be free from personal, external, and organizational impairments to independence, and must avoid the appearance of such impairments of independence."

International Standards for the Professional Practice of Internal Auditing Standard 1120 Individual Objectivity states:

Internal auditors must have an impartial, unbiased attitude and avoid any conflict of interest.

By my signature below, I acknowledge my assignment to the above project and profess I know of nothing that might impair my independence and impartiality on the project

In-Charge Auditor:	_____	**Date:** _____
Staff Auditor:	_____	**Date:** _____
Supervisor:	_____	**Date:** _____

Assignment Source:

Audit Type:

Audit Objectives:

Audit Scope:

Special Instructions:

Start Date:

Estimated Audit Completion Date:

Audit Director's Verification of Auditor's Assignment and Independence:

I have assigned the above staff and have determined they are adequately skilled to work on the stated project. I am not aware of anything that might impair their independence and impartiality on the project.

Audit Director Signature _____ **Date:** _____

Figure 6.12 Auditor Assignment and Independence Statement Form. (Adapted from AuditNet. Copyright 2014 AuditNet LLC, by AuditNet.)

Table 6.9   Quality Control Checklist—Survey Phase

PATRICKONSULT LTD
Office of Internal Audit
(Area audited)
(Audit period)
(Audit Project Title and No.)

Prepared by: _____
Date: _____
Reviewed by: _____
Date: _____

SURVEY AND RESEARCH PHASE

The purpose of the survey and research process is to gain a working knowledge of the entity or function under review, identify problem areas warranting detailed analysis, and gain sufficient information to define audit objectives, scope, and methodology. In addition, the survey should consider management controls and legal and regulatory requirements that are relevant to the audit. Auditors should be alert to situations or transactions that could be indicative of illegal acts or abuse.

The survey Phase should be documented in its own set of work papers before proceeding to the fieldwork. To facilitate reviewing work for the survey phase, the following checklist is provided. Yes answers are acceptable work, and No answers require some response or action on the part of the auditor in charge.

Item	Yes	No	Review Comments
1. Are the work papers in good order? If the answer to any of the following questions is no, then stop the review and return them to the auditor in charge to be corrected: • Are the work papers logically organized, legible, and neatly bound? • Is there a completed Survey Section Index? • Are the work papers cross-indexed to the Standard Audit Program for the Survey Phase?			
2. Are/do work papers • Indexed in lower right corner? • Initialed and dated by preparer? • Include a descriptive title? • Include an appropriate heading?			
3. Prior to starting the audit, did the audit team meet with the director to agree on the preliminary audit scope, objectives, methodology, and special instructions?			

(*Continued*)

Table 6.9 (Continued)   Quality Control Checklist—Survey Phase

Item	Yes	No	Review Comments
4 If this was an unplanned assignment from one of our customers, did the director or the audit team meet with that customer to clarify audit type, scope, objectives, and any special instructions?			
5. Was a notification memo prepared and provided to the customer along with the brochure The Audit Process?			
6. Was an entrance conference conducted with the auditee? Was it documented?			
7. Was an Auditor Assignment and Independence Statement form completed?			
8. Was the Risk Assessment/Internal Control Evaluation completed and approved by the audit supervisor?			
9. Has an audit program been prepared for the fieldwork, which lists the objectives identified from the Risk Assessment/Internal Control Evaluation? Was the audit program reviewed and approved by the audit supervisor?			
10. Have all work papers been reviewed and approved?			
11. Have finding development sheets been drafted to identify areas holding the greatest risk or potential for material findings?			
12. Was the work performed within the agreed upon time budget?			
13. Has the Introduction, Purpose and Scope, and Methodology been drafted for inclusion in the discussion draft report?			

_____   _____
Auditor-in-Charge   Date

Source: Adapted from AuditNet. Copyright 2014 AuditNet LLC, by AuditNet.

Note: All quality control review points have been cleared.

6.3.6 *Internal Audit Fieldwork and Templates (Appendix B)*

Fieldwork involves the process of implementing the audit program. And it includes all efforts to collect or accumulate, analyze, classify, appraise, interpret, and document information so that we can express an opinion and provide recommendations for improvement.

Fieldwork implies measurement and evaluation of the existence or development of standards. Fieldwork can be performed through survey or detailed tests. The techniques used will depend on the particular situation but may include observing, questioning, analyzing, comparing, investigating, and evaluating.

The internal audit fieldwork concentrates on transaction testing and informal communications. It is during this phase that the auditor determines whether the controls identified during the preliminary review are operating properly and in the manner described by the client. The fieldwork stage concludes with a list of significant findings from which the auditor will prepare a draft of the audit report (AuditNet, LLC, 2014, p. 2).

As pointed out in Chapter 5, after the preliminary review is completed, the auditor performs the procedures adopted in the audit program. These procedures usually test the major internal controls and the accuracy and propriety of the transactions. Various techniques including sampling are used during this phase of the audit.

Testing techniques are ways in which auditors gather evidence to support testing objectives. There is no restriction to such testing as long as it makes sense and leads to desired results; examples of some of the techniques include but are not limited to

   i. **Observation** (see Table 6.11)

     This is when an audit uses the senses to assess certain activities, for example, observing inventory stock-taking to assess whether employees are doing the right thing.

  ii. **Confirmation**

     This involves receipt of a written or oral response from an independent third party, for example, confirmations of bank balances.

 iii. **Inquiries**

     Inquiries of client/auditee could be written based on oral information from the client/auditee; Examples of this technique include internal control questionnaires or asking employees if certain procedures are being followed.

 iv. **Re-performance**

     Re-performance or mechanical accuracy involves rechecking computations for arithmetic accuracy or re-performing accounting routines.

  v. **Vouching**

     Vouching involves agreeing amounts of two or more different documents, for example, agreeing amounts on purchase orders to supplier invoices and receiving reports.

vi. **Physical examination**

This is an inspection or counting by the auditor of tangible assets, e.g., cash, inventory, etc.

vii. **Scrutiny or scanning**

Scrutiny is a searching review of data in order to locate significant items that require further investigation, e.g., scrutiny of the general ledger for unusual or unexpectedly high or low values, etc.

viii. **Inspection**

Inspection is the examination of documents other than source documents for a transaction, e.g., inspection of lease agreements, or legal advisor's letter reporting on a land purchase.

Testing broadly involves determining standards and defining population.

The various forms or templates used in this phase includes but not limited to the following.

6.3.6.1 Compliance Issues (Figure 6.13)

6.3.6.2 Internal Control Questionnaire (Deposit Accounts) (Table 6.10)

6.3.6.3 Interview Summary Form (Figure 6.14)

6.3.6.4 Project Observation Form (Table 6.11)

6.3.6.5 Internal Audit Finding Record

6.3.6.5.1 Internal Audit Finding Report (Format A) (Table 6.12)

6.3.6.5.2 Internal Audit Finding Report (Format B) (Figure 6.15)

6.3.6.5.3 Developing a Finding (Format C) (Figure 6.16)

6.3.6.6 Internal Audit Review Point Sheet (Table 6.13)

6.3.6.7 Quality Control Checklist—Fieldwork Phase (Table 6.14)

We should review fieldwork work papers to be sure that work was performed in a professional and thorough manner and that work and work papers adequately support the findings and recommendations.

To facilitate reviewing work for the fieldwork phase, a checklist is provided in Table 6.14. *Yes* answers are acceptable work and *no* answers require some response or action on the part of the auditor in charge.

PATRICKONSULT LTD
Office of Internal Audit
(Area audited)
(Audit period)

(Audit Project Title and No.) e.g.:

Compliance Issue No. CI-01-007

\<Insert Date\>
\<Insert Position\>
\<Insert Dept.\>
\<Insert Street Address\>
\<Insert City, State, Zip\>
Date:

Auditor:	
Issue:	
Condition:	
Criteria:	
Effect:	

Noncompliance with (tick as appropriate)**:**
Laws/Regulations: ☐
   Contract/Agreement: ☐
   Policies/Procedures: ☐
   Accounting/Reporting Standards: ☐

Cause:	
Recommendation:	
Method of Identification:	

Management's Response (tick as appropriate) **:**   ☐ Agree ☐ Disagree
Dept. Personnel:
Date:
Summary of Management's Response:

Comments:

Disposition (Tick as appropriate)**:**   ☐ Memorandum   ☐ Oral Comment

Follow-up (Tick as appropriate)**:** ☐ Yes   ☐ N/A
Comments:
Date:

Figure 6.13   Compliance Test Form (Format A). (Adapted from Compliance and Internal Audit Division. Highlands County, FL.)

Table 6.10   Internal Control Questionnaire (Deposit Accounts)

	PATRICKONSULT LTD Office of Internal Audit (Area audited) (Audit period) (Audit Project Title and No.) Tick as Appropriate				
S/N	*Description*	*Yes*	*No*	*N/A*	*Remarks*
1	Are demand deposit personnel prohibited from acting as relief tellers?				
2	Are deposit tickets and cancelled checks filed in locking cabinets or vaults not accessible to tellers?				
3	Is a daily listing of closed accounts prepared and submitted to bank management?				
4	Are listings mentioned in no. 3 above checked for zero balances by someone other than tellers or deposit services personnel?				
5	Are statements of closed accounts mailed to depositors immediately following the account closing by someone other than a teller or deposit services employee?				
6	Are statements mailed or delivered to depositors monthly, with the exception of depositors who have requested that their statements be received over the counter?				
7	Are over-the-counter statements delivered to someone other than a deposit services employee or teller for control and handling?				
8	Is written authorization on file from customers who want their statements held for pickup at the bank?				

(Continued)

Table 6.10 (Continued)   Internal Control Questionnaire (Deposit Accounts)

S/N	Description	Yes	No	N/A	Remarks
9	Are customers required to sign for statements when picking them up?				
10	Are all over-the-counter statements that are not picked up mailed at least once each quarter?				
11	Are employee deposit accounts properly identified and reviewed periodically by an officer for unusual activity?				
12	Are inactive accounts properly identified?				
13	Are checking accounts reviewed regularly for the purpose of transferring accounts that have become inactive?				
14	Are new accounts opened by employees who are not tellers or deposit services personnel?				
15	Is a daily list of new accounts produced and signature cards reviewed and approved in writing by an officer?				
16	Are there proper procedures in effect for stop-payment orders received?				
17	Is a daily overdraft report generated?				
18	Are checks and return items promptly charged to the respective accounts?				
19	Is there a system in place for follow-up on unpaid overdrafts?				
20	Are deposit system records being reconciled to the ledger control accounts on a daily or monthly basis?				
21	Is the reserve supply or inventory of blank passbooks kept under dual control?				

(Continued)

Table 6.10 (Continued)   Internal Control Questionnaire (Deposit Accounts)

S/N	Description	Yes	No	N/A	Remarks
22	Is there a numbering scheme utilized by all branches for new deposits of all types?				
23	Are interest computations frequently tested for accuracy?				
24	Are IS department personnel prohibited from initiating transactions?				
25	Are trial balances reconciled to the general ledger periodically?				
26	Are account numbers of closed accounts cancelled and prohibited from being used again?				
27	Are signature cards stamped CLOSED at the time the account is closed?				
28	Are all deposits and withdrawals identified by teller's initials, teller stamp, or other means?				
29	Are signatures on inactive and dormant deposit account withdrawal tickets rechecked by someone other than the teller processing the transaction?				
30	Are all deposit account withdrawal tickets cancelled at the end of the day?				
31	Is there a large withdrawal procedure or policy that requires the approval of an officer?				
32	Are signatures on large withdrawals verified by an officer?				
33	Are disks and tapes containing daily processing kept locked in a fireproof cabinet or vault?				

Deposit services/deposit accounts ICQ (rev. 3/16)

Compiled by: _____ Date:_____

Employee interviewed: _____ Date:_____

Source: Adapted from Compliance and Internal Audit Division. Highlands County, Florida.

PATRICKONSULT LTD
Office of Internal Audit
(Area audited)
(Audit period)

(Audit Project Title and No.)
INTERVIEW SUMMARY

Prepared by: -------

Date: -----------------

Reviewed by: -------

Date: -----------------

Individual Interviewed:
Title:
Agency/Division:
Time/Date of Interview:
Auditor:
Others Present at Interview:
Name:
Title:
Name:
Title:
Summary of Discussion:

Figure 6.14   Interview Summary Form.

Table 6.11 Project Observation Form

PATRICKONSULT LTD Office of Internal Audit (Area audited) (Audit period) (Audit Project Title and No.) **PROJECT OBSERVABLE CONDITIONS** Prepared by: _____ Date: _____		
Purpose: Document an observation made during the course of the audit		
Procedure: Complete the following for each observable condition		
Observed Condition		*W/P Ref.*
When was the observation made?		
Where was the observation made?		
What was observed?		
What is the implication of this observation?		
What is done?		
Who does it?		
Why is it done?		
How is it done?		
Where is it done?		
When is it done?		
How is it monitored?		
How much does it cost?		

Source: Adapted from Fairfax County Public Schools, as cited in AuditNet Working Papers Templates, Project Observable Conditions. Observations, AuditNet, Audit Library: The Internal Audit Process from A to Z How It Works: Audit Working Paper.

Table 6.12   Internal Audit Finding Report (Format A)

<table>
<tr>
<td colspan="6">

PATRICKONSULT LTD
Office of Internal Audit
(Area audited)
(Audit period)
(Audit Project Title and No.)
PROJECT OBSERVABLE CONDITIONS

Finding No.
</td>
</tr>
<tr>
<td>*S/N*</td>
<td colspan="5">*Items*</td>
</tr>
<tr>
<td>1</td>
<td colspan="5">Date:</td>
</tr>
<tr>
<td>2</td>
<td colspan="5">Audit title:</td>
</tr>
<tr>
<td>3</td>
<td colspan="5">Auditor(s):</td>
</tr>
<tr>
<td>4</td>
<td colspan="5">Finding:</td>
</tr>
<tr>
<td>5</td>
<td colspan="5">Condition:</td>
</tr>
<tr>
<td>6</td>
<td colspan="5">Criteria:</td>
</tr>
<tr>
<td>7</td>
<td colspan="5">Effect:</td>
</tr>
<tr>
<td>8</td>
<td colspan="5">Cause:</td>
</tr>
<tr>
<td>9</td>
<td colspan="5">Recommendation:</td>
</tr>
<tr>
<td>10</td>
<td colspan="5">Work paper reference or method of identification of finding:</td>
</tr>
<tr>
<td>12</td>
<td colspan="5">Responsible department:</td>
</tr>
<tr>
<td>13</td>
<td>Management's response:</td>
<td>☐ Agree</td>
<td>☐ Disagree</td>
<td>Dept. personnel:</td>
<td>Date:</td>
</tr>
<tr>
<td>14</td>
<td colspan="5">Comments:</td>
</tr>
<tr>
<td>15</td>
<td>Disposition:</td>
<td>☐ Audit report</td>
<td>☐ Oral comment</td>
<td colspan="2">☐ Deleted from consideration</td>
</tr>
</table>

Source: Adapted from Compliance and Internal Audit Division, Highlands County, Florida.

PATRICKONSULT LTD **Office of Internal Audit** **(Area audited)** **(Audit period)** **(Audit Project Title and No.)** **INTERNAL AUDIT FINDING REPORT**		
Audited Entity:_____Audit No_____Date_____AFR No_____		
Procedure_____ Procedure No_____ ISO 9001 Clause No_____		
	Observation	Non-Conformance
Finding and Cause: Auditor_____Date_____Auditee_____Date_____		
Recommendation (optional); Auditor_____Date_____		
Immediate Actions to Correct the Finding _____		Date Due_____
Corrective and Preventive Actions _____		Date Due_____
Audit Leader: _____Date_____ Auditee Manager:_____Date:_____		
Actions Closed: Audit Leader:_____Date:_____		

Figure 6.15 Internal Audit Finding Report (Format B). (Adapted from ESCC 11100: Internal Audit Procedure for the ESCC System, February 2005.)

PATRICKONSULT LTD	

PATRICKONSULT LTD
Office of Internal Audit
(Area audited)
(Audit period)

(Audit Project Title and No.)
DEVELOPING A FINDING

Prepared by:_____

Date:_____

This worksheet is designed to assist the Auditor in writing findings and recommendations for the report.

Same finding disclosed in the last audit? Yes   No

The Recommendation solves/matches the Condition and the Cause.

CONDITION

EFFECT

CAUSE

CRITERIA

RECOMMENDATION 1— Solves the Condition

RECOMMENDATION 2— Solves the Cause

Figure 6.16   Developing a Finding (Format C).

Table 6.13 Internal Audit Review Point Sheet

PATRICKONSULT LTD **Office of Internal Audit** **(Area audited)** **(Audit period)** **(Audit Project Title and No.)** Auditor: _____ Reviewer: _____ Date: _____		Page _____ of _____
Point # and Page #	*Reviewer Points*	*Resolution*

Source: Adapted from AuditNet. Copyright 2014 AuditNet LLC, by AuditNet.

Table 6.14   Quality Control Checklist (Fieldwork Phase)

PATRICKONSULT LTD Office of Internal Audit (Area audited) (Audit period) (Audit Project Title and No.) Prepared by: _____ Date: _____			Reviewed by: _____ Date: _____
Item	*Yes*	*No*	*Review Comments*
1. Has an audit program been prepared and used which lists audit procedures to be performed, objectives of those procedures, estimated time to perform, and initial, date, and with workpaper reference when completed?			
2. Have all facts, findings, and recommendations contained in the draft report been cross referenced to supporting workpapers?			

3. Are workpapers
  a. Neat and uniform?
  b. Indexed lower right corner?
  c. Initialed and dated by preparer?			

4. Do workpapers
  a. Include a descriptive title?
  b. Include an appropriate heading?
  c. Include section objectives?
  d. Reflect the source of information?
  e. Include a summary of work preformed with cross-references?
  f. Include a conclusion?			

5. Are workpapers neatly bound with a cover sheet and a table of contents?			
6. Is there adequate support for findings and recommendations?			

(Continued)

Table 6.14 (Continued)   Quality Control Checklist (Fieldwork Phase)

Item	Yes	No	Review Comments
7. Were all findings and recommendations discussed with agency management and their feedback obtained throughout the course of the audit?			
8. Do all workpapers clearly indicate audit procedures performed?			
9. Have all workpapers been reviewed and approved?			
10. Was the work performed within the allotted time budget? If not, why not?			
NB: All quality control review points have been cleared			

_____	_____
Auditor-In-Charge	Date

Source: Adapted from AuditNet. Copyright 2014 AuditNet®, LLC by AuditNet.

6.4 Communicating Internal Audit Results

After the Exit Conference, the audit leader prepares a formal draft report taking into account the agreements reached at the exit conference. When the changes have been reviewed by audit, management, and the client/auditee, the final report is prepared and issued.

The Communicating Results Procedures summarize the report process of internal audit assignment as shown in Figure 6.17.

6.4.1 Communicating Results Procedures (Figure 6.17)

CONTINENTAL SHIPYARD LTD
OFFICE OF INTERNAL AUDIT
(Area audited)
(Audit period)
COMMUNICATING RESULTS PROCEDURES

Initials: _____ Date: _____
Reviewer: _____ Date: _____

Audit Procedures   **W/P Ref.**   **Auditor/Date**

1. If necessary, issue interim report to provide information about unexpected delays in completing the project or to notify them of critical control weaknesses.
2. Discuss progress and results throughout the project. Possible control weaknesses and exceptions should be discussed before Point Sheets are written to give management an opportunity to provide information that may clear potential findings or to begin corrective action. Document results of discussion in supporting work papers.
3. Prepare Point Sheets for all findings or explain why a point sheet was not necessary.
4. Hold an exit conference to discuss findings and recommendations.
5. Provide management with copies of Point Sheets in advance of the meeting.
6. Document results of exit conference using the Exit Conference Form and individual point sheets. Show whether auditee agreed with finding and any significant discussion about findings and recommendations.
7. Prepare draft report; report should follow standard format and should be referenced to supporting work papers. Issue report (stamped "DRAFT") to management for review.
8. If necessary, contact auditee to arrange a meeting to discuss report and process of responding. Once report wording has been agreed on, ask management for written responses (give specific due date for responses).
9. Obtain and evaluate auditee responses. Determine whether responses address the issues described in the findings, promise action that will correct the weakness reported, and Include reasonable completion date.
10. If auditee disagrees with findings or provides an inadequate response, take action to resolve such as
(a) Discussing issues with auditee
(b) Trying to resolve conflict with next level(s) of management
(c) Including auditee's views in report (give auditee opportunity to review revisions before issuing report)
(d) Documenting that senior management has been informed of the risk of not taking necessary corrective action and has accepted that risk
11. Incorporate auditee's responses in report and forward to next level of University/Corporate management for review.
12. Prepare corrective action forms and cover memorandum to be sent to department head. Set tickler date for each comment based on date management has indicated corrective action will be complete; tracking number should match finding number for follow-up database.
13. File final report in project binders and cross-referenced to supporting working papers; provide explanations for comments deleted or changed significantly since original draft.
14. Obtain signatures on final report and distribute copies to appropriate recipients. Include corrective action forms with copy sent to department head.

Approval of Adequate Completion of Communicating Results Procedures:

Name Date _____

Figure 6.17   Communicating results procedures.

Below are the forms and format used to communicate internal audit results for each audit assignment as captioned in Appendix C.

6.4.2 Exit Conference Document (Figure 6.18 [Format A] and Table 6.15 [Format B])

Purpose: The purpose of an exit meeting with the auditee is to develop a mutual understanding of the content of the draft report and of any other audit concerns that are not set out in the report. It is intended to avoid any misunderstandings or

---

Continental Shipyard LTD
Office of Internal Audit
(Area audited)
(Audit period)

(Audit Project Title and No.)

EXIT CONFERENCE DOCUMENT

Prepared by: _____
Date: _____

Reviewed by: _____
Date: _____

Purpose:	To document the exit conference.
Source:	Exit Conference meeting.
Date/Time:	
Auditors Present:	
Auditees Present: *(Include titles)*	

Meeting Discussion

Explained audit resolution and follow-up policy?   Yes ☐   No ☐

Concerns or Comments discussed at the Exit Conference:

Auditee(s)' Response to Potential Audit Comments:

Report Item	Auditee Response

Figure 6.18 Exit Conference Document (Format A). (Adapted from Fairfax County Public Schools Internal Audit.)

Table 6.15 Exit Conference Memorandum (Format B)

<table>
<tr><td colspan="2">

Continental Shipyard LTD
Office of Internal Audit
(Area audited)
(Audit period)
(Audit Project Title and No.)

Purpose: To document the exit conference.
Source: Exit Conference (exitconf.rpt)
</td></tr>
<tr><td>Audit Title</td><td></td></tr>
<tr><td>Internal audit</td><td></td></tr>
<tr><td>Staff present</td><td></td></tr>
<tr><td>Auditees present (include titles)</td><td></td></tr>
<tr><td>Overall opinion on audit discussed?</td><td>YES____ NO ____</td></tr>
<tr><td>Explained audit resolution and follow-up policy?</td><td>YES____ NO ____</td></tr>
<tr><td>Other concerns or comments discussed at the exit conference:</td><td></td></tr>
<tr><td colspan="2">Auditee Response to Potential Audit Comments</td></tr>
<tr><td>PAC #</td><td>Auditee Response</td></tr>
<tr><td></td><td></td></tr>
<tr><td></td><td></td></tr>
<tr><td></td><td></td></tr>
<tr><td></td><td></td></tr>
</table>

Source: Adapted from FairFax County Public Schools, as shown in the table, Exit Conference Memorandum, Exit Conference Template, AuditNet.

misinterpretations of fact by providing the opportunity for the auditee to clarify specific items and to express views on the significant audit concerns, recommendations, and other information presented in the draft report.

This meeting should also ensure that the formal response from the auditee does not contain any surprises for the auditor. Additionally, the exit meeting should serve as an opportunity to develop a feeling that the report is offered in a spirit of working together to improve the way things are being done.

Timing: The chief internal auditor should contact management to determine a suitable time and location for the exit meeting.

Attendees: Attendees should include anyone who may be able to object to the validity of the report's contents and anyone having responsibility for the area or the situation needing corrective action—whether or not they personally would take the action or would be affected by the action.

Discussion: The exit meeting can be either a difficult confrontation or an open and courteous discussion. The discussion topics at each exit meeting will vary depending on the specific audit concerns identified and who is attending the meeting. At a minimum, the auditor should:

- Summarize the audit including what was done (objectives, scope, procedures)
- Give justification for the approach used when ascertaining findings, conclusions, and recommendations from the audit
- Outline the risks identified
- Outline the significant audit concerns and the recommendations for dealing with the associated risk
- Indicate the significant audit concerns that have already been corrected
- Refer to any less significant concerns identified in the audit

The auditor should be willing and able to discuss all matters in whatever detail is necessary. It is also important to make it clear that all significant audit concerns have been discussed with management and that the report contains no surprises. You may also want to thank them for the cooperation obtained during the audit—if that is appropriate.

Avoiding confrontation: The auditor should be prepared for the possibility of conflict when presenting the concerns in the audit report and should be able to retrieve information, support facts, and amplify findings without difficulty or delay. To encourage the avoidance of confrontation during the exit meeting, the auditor should

- Be polite throughout the meeting.
- Avoid the use of nonpersonal phrases (e.g., try not to start a sentence with *you* when disagreeing).
- Make efforts to get on common ground.
- Avoid boxing the auditee into a corner.
- Distinguish the expression of different postures from disagreements.

6.4.3 Internal Audit Report (Appendix C)

The IIA Performance Standard 2400 requires internal auditors to communicate the results of their audit findings, taking into account issues of quality, accuracy, clarity, objectivity, conciseness, constructiveness, completeness, and timeliness of such communications.

Reports are the internal auditor's opportunity to get management's complete attention, and a perfect occasion to show management how internal auditors can be of help.

6.4.3.1 Definition of Internal Audit Report

According to IIA Standard 2410 (Criteria for Communicating), an internal audit report is a formal communication of engagement results. This communication includes the engagement's objectives and scope, as well as applicable conclusions, recommendations, and action plans.

6.4.3.2 Objective and Function of the Internal Audit Report

Internal audit reports serve three main objectives: to *cause* management to *act* and support such *action*. However, management will not act until internal auditors have recorded the audit findings, and informed and convinced the management on the findings. The principal objectives of audit reports are (Figure 6.19)

- To communicate the problems identified and the causes of those problems
- To assure management that risks are well controlled
- To inform them of the areas where this is not the case and where there are defined risk exposures
- To advise (and convince) them on steps to improve risk management strategies
- To explain the effects and repercussions of those problems and quantify them where necessary
- To measure performance—by providing analyses and appraisals—and to highlight areas in which greater efficiency and effectiveness may be achieved, and waste eliminated

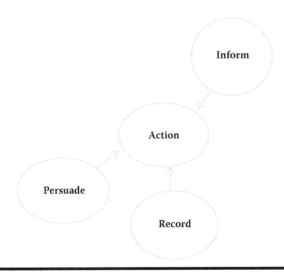

Figure 6.19 Objectives of internal audit reports. (From Lyer, AVANT Garde Academy, as cited in Blume, 2014.)

- To convince management of the need for change
- To suggest practical and cost-effective solutions
- To provide a basis for follow-up to ensure that appropriate action has been taken

There are three main functions of an audit report, namely

1. **It is an action document:** Unless the report achieves action, it would have been a waste of time for everyone involved in the audit. To achieve action, the report should provide the client with a brief objective assessment of control in the area under review and highlight any significant weaknesses identified. It should also bring out the impact of those weaknesses on the level of control and demonstrate to management that they need to do something about it
   - By explaining the risks involved
   - By quantifying, where possible, those risks and any potential benefits
2. **It acts as a formal, permanent record:** The audit work undertaken and the conclusions drawn from it, and the level of control that exists in a particular area at a specific point in time, must all feature as a permanent record in the audit report.
3. **Objectivity, independence, and competence:** A good report communicates professionalism and competence, which demonstrates the internal auditor's objectivity and independence in carrying out the assignment, and shows that auditors can help improve efficiency and effectiveness in the organization.

6.4.3.3 Types of Audit Procedure Reports (Table 6.16)

The following reports as shown in Table 6.16 are required by audit procedure.

Table 6.16 Types of Audit Procedure Reports

Report	From	To	Periodicity
Audit report	Lead auditor	Head of audit unit, audit point of contact	At each audit
Audit program status report	Head of audit unit	Board of directors or audit committee	At each board meeting

Note: Reports as required by internal audit procedure.

6.4.3.4 Report Writing Planning Worksheet

The process of writing an audit report begins when the audit is initiated rather than at the end of the fieldwork. To have an idea of where you are going, you need to have a plan for how to get there. This worksheet is meant to start you thinking and planning for some of the basics that will be incorporated into the report. The following questions should come to mind:

What is the topic or subject of the audit?
What is the main idea (message, conclusion, theme or point of view)?
What are the supporting points?
What are the audit objectives?
What corrective action do you want the reader to take as a result of your report?
What impression do you want to make on the reader, or what tone do you want to convey?

Audit reports should provide an assurance on the system under review, and form the basis of the overall assurance on the internal control system, risk management, and governance process to be provided in reports to the head of the organization.

It is vital to remember that the audit report is the only tangible product of an audit and, as such, is the internal audit's *shop window*. It is the culmination of the planning, time, and effort that goes into an audit, and reflects the quality and thoroughness of the audit. The quality of the report will have an important influence on the view of internal audit held by senior management of the organization.

An inadequate audit report may negate the best audit work and finest conclusions. It may also damage the reputation and status of the internal auditor.

6.4.3.5 Types of Internal Audit Reports

Internal audit reports can be categorized into three major types:

i. **Engagement reports**
   – Reports on results of individual assurance audit assignments.
ii. **Periodic reports**
   – Quarterly audit reports summarizing the audit and nonaudit activities performed by the internal audit unit over a quarter period. That is, it is a summary of the individual engagement reports and other nonaudit activities that were undertaken during the quarter.
   – Annual reports summarize the audit activities or services that were undertaken by the internal audit unit during the year. They are prepared based on quarterly reports.

iii. **Special audit reports**
   - Report on special audit arrangements by management and other special investigations. However, they need to be tailored to suit the specific terms of reference that gave rise to such special assignments, for example, fraud investigation.

6.4.3.6 Elements of an Effective Engagement Report

Lessans and Roslewics (undated, as cited in Blume, 2014) recognized, on a Quality Action Team on Reports that audit findings are most effectively communicated in reports if the following five key elements are included:

i. **Solid substance**

   Here auditors should ask themselves if the report has all the five attributes of a finding. Also, when drafting the report, auditors should make sure that each audit objective is addressed by an audit report whose attributes can be readily identified in a five-attribute format.

   Table 6.17 gives an example of how to structure an audit finding into a five-attribute format.

ii. **Logically sound**

   Does the report make sense, and is it easily readable?

   The best way to make sound logic is to write in a *deductive manner*; that is, to state conclusions first, and then support them with facts. Such report highlights the points/concerns first, which captures a busy reader's attention, and then presents the most important details that support it.

iii. **Balanced tone**

   Does the report present a tone that is respectful of the auditee?

   Since the audit reports usually convey critical information to senior official(s) who are in a position to take decisions, it is important that the auditor's report accords the auditee due respect as the contrary may present the auditor in the light of overzealousness or unnecessarily put the auditee on the spotlight, particularly where such official may be reluctant to accept criticism or negative message.

   The best approach is to commend and convey the positive information (e.g., good or noteworthy job) that is done by the auditee along with negative audit findings.

   For example, use the background section to *give the auditee credit where it is due*; this will help soften the mood before going into detailed negative findings.

Table 6.17   Example of How to Write an Audit Finding in a Five-Attribute Format

Attribute	Description
Condition	Statement of the issue: What is the key point you want to communicate to your readers? **Example:** Capital expenditure of USD 110 million for power equipment upgrade project was not monitored, and time and budget overruns were not approved.
Criteria	Description of *what should be*: What is the policy, standard, principle, or business practice in the project evaluation? **Example:** Finance policy requires continuous monitoring by the project manager and CEO/minister and approval of capital expenditure over USD 20 million.
Effect/risk/ consequence	Explanation of the *significance* or *impact*: What is the impact or materiality? What has gone or could go wrong as a result of the condition? **Example:** The equipment upgrade project was overbudgeted by 30% and the contractors paid no penalties.
Cause	Explanation of *what allowed the condition to occur*: What is the root cause of the problem? Why was the condition not detected or corrected? **Example:** A project manager had not been appointed to manage the power equipment upgrade project.
Corrective action (recommendations)	Description of action necessary to correct the condition **Example:** The finance manager will require the CEO/minister's written approval of all capital expenditure project plans in excess of USD 20 million, including monthly reports and cost overruns. Also, the CEO/minister should appoint a project manager for each capital expenditure project.

Source: Adapted from Blume, A. (2014). *Risk Management: Participants' Handbook* (April, 2014). Support to Local Governance Processes (SULGO) in Tanzania. Project: Strengthening internal controls at sub-national level.

iv. **Printed visual clarity**

Does the report's appearance guide the busy reader through the logic of the material? This aims at providing *instant visual understanding*.

Example:

– Use of tables of contents and an executive summary
– Separating the report sections with descriptive subcaptions
– Listing information using bullets, numbers, letters, or dashes
– Using italics or underlining, bold, and capitalization for key words and phrases
– Incorporating visual aids (e.g., charts, tables, graphs, and photographs) to illustrate key points
– Reserving *white space* on each page to make the text more appealing to read

v. **Good mechanics**

Do the report's words and sentences clearly and effectively communicate the message?

This requires the audit team to pay attention to the words in the verbal weaknesses of the report. This is achieved by avoiding the *overuse* of certain types of words, including jargons, acronyms, legalese, prepositions, and weak nouns, and by checking grammar.

6.4.3.7 Nature of the Internal Audit Report

The internal audit report can be of the nature of a *standard report* or an *audit memoranda*.

1. The *standard report* is the type most commonly used. It comprises three main sections—the executive summary, the detailed report, and the action plan.

   Standard audit reports typically should contain
   – Report cover
   – Contents page
   – Executive summary
   – Detailed report
   – Action plan
   – Appendices/annexes
2. *Audit memoranda* are normally shorter than standard reports and are used
   – For quick and special reviews carried out at the request of management to report the results of follow-up audits
   – Where only relatively minor points arise from the audit
   – As an interim report on longer audits

Audit memoranda will comprise

- An introduction
- A conclusion
- A series of separate paragraphs, with appropriate headings for the detailed findings and recommendations

6.4.3.8 Know Your Reader (Figure 6.20)

1.	**Define who the reader(s) of your report is (Position, Title).**
	_____
2.	**How familiar is the reader with the subject?**
3.	**What amount of explanation or background does the reader need?**
	☐ Detailed procedures or history
	☐ Definition of terms
	☐ Overview of the subject
4.	**What is your purpose in addressing this reader?**
	☐ Inform or provide requested information
	☐ Get action
	☐ Summarize results
	☐ Present detailed results
5.	**How will the reader use this information?**
	☐ Gain an understanding
	☐ Make a decision
	☐ Implement a procedure
6.	**What is the reader's likely reaction?**
	☐ Accepting
	☐ Resistant
	☐ Skeptical
	☐ Sensitive or defensive
7.	**What opposition does the reader have to your ideas?**
8.	**On what basis is the reader likely to react positively?**
9.	**What is the reader's communication style?**

Figure 6.20 Know your reader.

6.4.3.9 Internal Audit Standard Report Content

The audit report shall use the document style defined by the head of the audit unit and have the following structure:

Report Cover

This should set out the report title, date of issue, and report number. Some audit units adopt logos that are printed on the cover. It may also be worth considering the use of different color covers for different types of audit reviews (financial, operational, compliance, systems, vale for money, etc.).

Contents Page

This should include the report title, details of each of the main sections of the report, and a list of all appendices.

Executive Summary

The executive summary should stand alone and convey the main points to the reader without the need to refer to the detailed report. It should enable senior management to establish quickly and easily

- The scope and main objectives of the audit
- Why it was done
- The nature and scale of the system or activity reviewed
- The main conclusions of the audit
- The principal recommendations

This is the most important part of the report, as it is the main opportunity to encourage the reader to look at the detailed report, and either take action or ensure that appropriate action is taken. It should not be too lengthy; a maximum of three typed pages is recommended depending on the scope of the audit and should include the following sections.

Introduction and background: Covering

- General information of the revised area, including indications of the importance of the topic/system and why it is audited
- The scope and principal objectives of the audit
- Any important areas excluded from the review, and why
- When and why it has been audited

Main conclusions: This should paraphrase the most important conclusions reached in the detailed report. These are often set out on a section-by-section basis, but sometimes it can be more effective to identify any common *themes* that run through the report. Any overall opinion must reflect accurately the findings and comments in the detailed report. Keep to the major issues arising and try to avoid raising any minor conclusions in this section.

Principal recommendations: This should list only the key (high-priority) recommendations that feature in the action plan, and each of them should relate to one or more of the main conclusions.

The key thing to remember when drafting the executive summary is that it should stimulate interest that will lead to action.

Detailed Report

Format: The main body of the report should be divided into suitable sections, each clearly headed. The order of the sections will be determined during the report planning process. It may reflect the relative significance of the audit findings, a chronological sequence, or simply follow the order in which events occur in the system.

Content: Each section should contain details of the relevant findings. It is important to highlight the underlying causes of weaknesses and their impact on performance or the level of control. Failure to do so is one of the biggest single weaknesses of audit reports. Auditors should bear the following questions in mind:

- Why is this happening or not happening?
- What is the effect on performance, control, efficiency etc.?
- Why does management need to know this?

Descriptive material should be restricted to what is needed to establish the nature and extent of any weaknesses identified. It is not necessary to provide full and detailed descriptions of every part of the system under review.

It is often helpful to include graphs, tables, and charts to quantify and illustrate facts and data; however, this should not be overused as it can obscure the message and sometimes irritate the reader.

The report must be factual and objective. Subjective comments are not acceptable. Where it is necessary to make value judgments or assumptions, their basis should be clearly stated. Avoid the use of long paragraphs wherever possible.

Do not be afraid to commend something being done well, or to refer to good points you came across, but do not overdo it.

Recommendation: Usually, recommendations should be placed at the end of each section. However, where a section is particularly long, or deals with a variety of issues, recommendations can be inserted at appropriate points in the section. Recommendations should be placed in a separate paragraph(s) preceded by the subheading **Recommendations** in bold type.

In developing your recommendations, there are some simple things that should come to your mind, including that they should

- Be based on reliable information
- Deal with the underlying cause of the problem, and not just the symptoms
- Describe precisely what needs to be done
- Suggest who should be responsible for taking action
- Be clear, concise, and simple
- Be unambiguous
- Be achievable
- Refer to a discrete action point, that is, each recommendation deals with a single point

Note that where an auditee has already taken action, or agreed to do so, this should be stated in the report.

Paragraph Numbering—Some Simple Rules

Reports should adopt a simple one-part numbering system (1, 2, 3, etc.) beginning with the executive summary and continuing to the end of the report.

Recommendations should be numbered (R1, R2, R3, etc.) so that they can be readily identified.

Headings and subheadings should not be numbered.

Finalizing the Report

Before finalizing the audit report, there are a number of key checks that need to be made. The following questions are necessary as a checklist:

1. Executive Summary
   a. Does it motivate the reader to want to read the detailed report?
   b. Do the main conclusions reflect accurately the major issues and conclusions contained in the detailed report?
   c. Does each key recommendation relate to one or more of the main conclusions?
2. Detailed Report
   a. Are the conclusions appropriate and meaningful?
   b. Are weaknesses and benefits quantified where appropriate?
   c. Is the need for corrective action sold? Have we explained the effects of the issues we have identified? Use the "so what?" test.
   d. Do our recommendations deal effectively with the underlying causes of the problem?
3. General
   a. Is the tone of the report appropriate?
   b. Where appropriate and possible, have we tried to be positive?

    c. Is the report easy to read and understand?

    d. Have we deleted all unnecessary words and phrases?

6.4.3.10 Summary of Audit Results and Potential Recommendations (Table 6.18)

Table 6.18 contains summary of the audit result together with potential recommendations.

Notes:

- A summary of audit results and potential recommendations should be included in the audit tests binder.
- The *Developing a Finding* worksheet should be used to develop each audit result/potential recommendation that is going to be in the report.

Table 6.18   Summary of Audit Results and Potential Recommendations

Continental Shipyard LTD **Office of Internal Audit** **(Area audited)** **(Audit period)** **(Audit Project Title and No.)**		
Date: **Reviewed by:** **Date:** **General Questions**		
W/P Reference	*Audit Results/Potential Recommendation*	*Resolution (to Report or Reason for Not Taking to Report)*

6.4.3.11 *Specimen Internal Audit Report* Covering Letter

Audit report cover letter
<On the letterhead of the certified internal auditor or chartered accountant or audit unit's memo>

February 14, 201X
Report No. <Number>

CEO,
<Company Name> Limited
<Address>

Attention: Mr.<CEO>

Dear Sir/Madam

The audit team has concluded an operational review of the internal control structure and the recently implemented financial system IFRS. The objective of our review was to evaluate controls in the financial system, compliance with policy and regulations, and the effectiveness and efficiency of the current organization authority structure.

The review covered operations of the period <date> to <date>. Please find enclosed two copies of the Audit Report of <Company Name> Limited completed on February XX, 201X. I am pleased to inform you that the review found that the financial department is well managed with generally good controls. However, controls need to be strengthened in a few areas and documentation policies need to be more strictly enforced for travel expenses. A summary of the most significant audit findings is provided in Part II of the report.

The company must respond in writing to each audit finding. The proposed Corrective Action Plan should detail both short-term corrective action to correct the specific deficiencies cited and, where applicable, long-term corrective action. Long-term corrective action should focus on modifying the system to prevent recurrence of similar deficiencies in the future.

We wish to express our appreciation for the cooperation extended to the audit team by you and your staff during the audit.

Yours truly,

<Name>
<Designation>
Membership No.<number>

6.4.3.12 Specimen Internal Audit Report

AUDIT NAME
AUDIT REPORT
TABLE OF CONTENTS

AUDIT NAME
DATE
INTRODUCTION
Background
Audit Perspective
    Present audit status—
    Recent past audits—
    External audit coverage—

Scope and Objectives
Scope of the (audit or review):
The scope statement should be brief and should include the timing, type and purpose of the work, and the standards used when conducting the audit. The types of audits or reviews are financial, operational, compliance, and EDP (electronic data processing).

For example, the scope of the audit was financial and operational in nature. This routine audit was conducted on Tasty Foods Limited during the period of (month) (year). The audit covered the period from dd-mm-yyyy to dd-mm-yyyy. The audit was performed to ensure that financial data were properly recorded and adequate operational procedures exist in all the operational areas. The audit was conducted in accordance with the applicable accounting and auditing standards. It included reviews in the following areas:

a. Royalty payments
b. Rent received from subtenants

    c. Compliance with food safety and hygiene regulations
    d. Cash receipts
    e. Invoice receivables

The last day of fieldwork was _____.
The objectives of the audit were as follows:

- Determine that cash receipts were recorded correctly as to account, amount, and period, and are deposited promptly (recording, safeguarding)
- Verify that invoice receivables were correctly accounted, recorded, and payments received from the debtors
- Determine whether food safety inspections have been regularly carried out at various locations and appropriate hygiene levels are maintained
- Review inspection reports—internal and external—and steps taken to correct shortcomings, if any.
- Review whether royalty has been calculated correctly and has been paid to the brand owners timely
- Review whether contract has been drawn up with subtenants, and floor space, rent, and facilities have been agreed upon

Note: Audit is used in the report when actual tests are performed to corroborate the opinion. Review is used in the report when no tests are performed to corroborate the opinion. Comment should speak directly as to what was done. That is, if a test was performed, the word *test* should be used. If a review was performed, the word *review* should be used.

Company—General

Tasty Foods Limited
Provide information on the background of the company and its operations. Provide details of functions and personnel in departments. Mention any major change in the organization since the last audit. (For example, the company has opened new food centers at 12 more locations. The staff strength has risen to 15,000. The company is now undertaking a massive exercise to centralize its processing and accounting at the main office.)

Audit Synopsis

Mr. R. Xyz, senior partner of XYZ associates, was in charge of the audit. The audit was conducted in accordance with auditing standards and the policy and procedures detailed in Tasty Food Limited's manual. These techniques included interviews with key personnel, review of approved documents, sampling of relevant files, and random inspections throughout Tasty Food Limited's system.

The audit entry meeting was held in Tasty Food Limited's main office on <date>. During this meeting, the audit manager briefed the operator's management on the audit process and the team's audit plans. The officials of the company were regularly updated on the audit progress and of all audit findings submitted. The audit was completed and the exit meeting was held in Tasty Food Limited's main office on <date> with the senior officials namely <name>.

Corrective Action Plan

The audit findings identify a situation where a company policy, procedure, or activity does not conform to policies and procedures specified in the company's internal audit manual or to the applicable regulatory standard. The company must respond in writing to each audit finding, detailing short-term corrective action to correct the specific examples listed, and long-term systemic corrective action to prevent recurrence of similar situations.

XYZ Associates will monitor implementation of Tasty Food Limited's Corrective Action Plan through the audit follow-up process.

EXECUTIVE SUMMARY

Purpose and Limitations

The executive summary is intended to provide an overview of the audit process, and summarize the significant findings (discussed in the detailed audit report) and the conclusions reached. The reader should not frame an opinion solely on the basis of this summary. The detailed report should be read to obtain the complete understanding of the background, ramifications, and recommendations.

General

The audit examined Tasty Foods Limited's operations and finance divisions using applicable checklists referenced from the internal audit manual. A total of xx operations and xy finance audit findings are reported. These findings identified examples of nonconformance to the standards, regulations, and Tasty Foods Limited's policies and procedures. A number of the findings were administrative in nature and can be easily corrected, whereas others were systemic and will require particular attention to ensure that corrective actions are effected in addressing the identified system faults.

Audit Opinion

As discussed more fully in our opinion on page _____ of this report,

Relevant Findings

List a summary of each finding (without ramification/implication statement). Cross reference to detail section of report.

AUDIT NAME
INTERNAL AUDIT OPINION
In our opinion, we found the _____ to be adequate, or inadequate (detail of inadequacies to follow the word inadequate).

We have identified opportunities to improve the controls of the (offices/areas/departments) involved in the ... as discussed in this report.

_____   _____

AUDITOR-IN-CHARGE   DATE

(**Example:** In our opinion, we found that the financial transactions were properly recorded and the operational procedures adequate for the period under audit. However, there is still some scope for improving the operating efficiency and effectiveness, which are discussed in this audit report.

In our opinion, we found the financial transactions to be properly recorded, but the operational procedures inadequate for the period under audit. We have made some recommendations on improving efficiency and effectiveness of certain operating procedures as discussed in this audit report.

The areas requiring immediate attention are <area>, which currently lacks some essential elements; <area>, which requires a detailed system to ensure that all requirements have been met; and procedures to monitor and report on <area> activities.

The above deficiencies notwithstanding, the review revealed that Tasty Foods Limited is maintaining strict quality control standards and that a knowledgeable, competent management team has been assembled to oversee its staff and employees that have the ability and desire to operate within the regulatory framework. The company's response upon learning of any deficiency was immediate and indicative of their focus on quality control.)

AUDIT NAME
DETAILED REPORT
Overview
Pages X through XX outline the *specific findings* resulting from our substantive audit testing. These issues are discussed in detail in our report and are categorized first on the basis of departments. Within each division, the major primary findings (significant internal control deficiencies and items potentially having a significant or adverse effect on the unit's operations) are mentioned first, and then other matters (items of a lesser nature requiring attention, but not likely to have a significant or adverse effect on the unit's operations).

Primary Findings

I. COMMENT
   Insert summary of the finding included in the Executive Summary
   Finding
   Ramifications/Implications
   Recommendation(s)
   Auditee's Response
   Other Matters
II. COMMENT
   Insert summary of the finding included in the Executive Summary
   Finding
   Ramifications/Implications
   Recommendation(s)
   Auditee's Response

6.4.3.13 Quality Control Checklist for Audit Reports (Table 6.19)

Table 6.19 contains the quality control checklist for internal audit report.

Table 6.19 Quality Control Checklist for Audit Reports

Continental Shipyard LTD Office of Internal Audit (Area audited) (Audit period) (Audit Project Title and No.)		
Prepared by: **Date:** **Reviewed by:** **Date:** **General Questions**		

Description	Yes	No
Are the appropriate sections included?		
Is there an executive summary?		
Does the outline of the report give the reader a quick overview?		
Are enough headings used to guide the reader?		
Are titles written in a consistent style?		
Is the formatting inviting?		
Are the most important comments presented first?		
Does the report balance positive and negative?		
Are related comments combined?		
Is repetition avoided?		
Is detail presented in appendices?		

Report Content

S/N	Description	Draft Report	Final Report	N/A
1.	The audit report includes: – Transmittal letter – Title page – Table of contents			
2.	The audit report contains an executive summary (two to three pages maximum)			

(Continued)

Table 6.19 (Continued)   Quality Control Checklist for Audit Reports

S/N	Description	Draft Report	Final Report	N/A
3.	The detailed report includes – The purpose of the audit, including the reason (whether planned with the annual plan or was exceptional) – The scope of the audit, time period covered, functions or processes reviewed, and audit techniques used – Background information describing – The system, process, or the activity – The audit finding – The audit conclusion – The audit recommendations – The action plan – All the correct appendices			
4.	A draft report is clearly labeled draft			

Report Quality, Tone, and Appearance

S/N	Description	Draft Report	Final Report	N/A
1.	The report is clear and concise, free of unnecessary detail.			
2.	The conclusions expressed in the executive summary and the body of the report are consistent.			
3.	The report is divided into sections, and each section is clearly labeled.			
4.	Descriptions of operating procedures, if required, are kept short and concise.			
5.	The structure of the report is logical and easy to follow.			
6.	Jargon, technical language, clichés, and colloquialisms are avoided.			
7.	Acronyms and abbreviations are defined before being used.			
8.	The active voice predominates.			

(Continued)

Table 6.19 (Continued)   Quality Control Checklist for Audit Reports

S/N	Description	Draft Report	Final Report	N/A
9.	The report is direct and to the point.			
10.	The headings are informative and descriptive.			
11.	The opening sentences are strong and attention getting.			
12.	The main points are presented first.			
13.	The report has a balanced tone.			
14.	The findings are worded constructively.			
15.	The recommendations are directed toward achieving desired results without prescribing step-by-step actions.			
16.	The report has a professional appearance.			
17.	The spelling, grammar, and punctuation are correct.			

6.4.3.14 Action Plans

Action plans are very important for recording and monitoring the action taken by management on the internal audit's recommendations. They make follow-up audits easier and more effective. An action plan should be prepared for every standard audit report. It details what management has agreed to.

It lists every recommendation contained in the audit report and shows for each of them

- The comments of management
- Who is responsible for the action
- The date by which action will be taken

Table 6.20 shows a template for an action plan.

Recommendation number (rec. no.)—This is the number given to each recommendation in the detailed report (R1, R2, etc.). The action plan should include every recommendation made in the audit report, and the recommendations should be listed in the order in which they appear in the detailed report.

Recommendation—Each recommendation is included here, worded exactly as it appears in the detailed report.

Table 6.20 Action Plan Template

					Audit Report No._____
1	*2*	*3*	*4*	*5*	*6*
Rec. No.	Recommendation	Priority	Action Agreed Y/N	Person Responsible	Implementation Date
R1					
R2					
R3					
R4					
R5					
R6					
R7					
R8					
R9					
R10					
R11					
R12					
...					
Prepared by:_____			Approved by:_____		

Priority—This indicates the level of importance of the recommendation: high/medium/low.

Action agreed—It should be pointed, concerted activity.

Person responsible—This should record the name and title of the person who is to take responsibility for implementing the recommendation. Depending on the nature of the recommendation, this could be either the person who will actually be making the changes, or the manager who is responsible for the unit, department, or sector to which the recommendation relates.

Implementation date—The date by which management intend to make the recommended changes.

Note: The lead internal auditor is to submit the action plan template of the previous audit report to the head(s) of the audited unit(s) with a completed column 2 (Recommendation). The head(s) of the audited units, in return, shall within 2 weeks or 10 days of receipt provide the same response as contained in the audit report, and sign an action plan to implement the recommendations with timeline and the person(s) responsible.

The action plan should be sent out with the draft audit report, and the chief internal auditor should ensure that it is completed and returned—together with any other management comments within 10 working days. The completed action plan should be reviewed to ensure that

- Recommendations have been accepted.
- Any alternative proposals by management are acceptable.
- An appropriate person has been made responsible for implementing each recommendation.
- Suitable dates for implementation are proposed.

The completed action plan should be inserted as Appendix 1 in the final report and a copy of it placed on the permanent audit file. On the basis of the action plan, the chief internal auditor should schedule a follow-up audit, if necessary before the next planned audit.

6.5 Internal Audit Resolution and Follow-Up

6.5.1 Introduction

Internal audit follow-up of its recommendations is one of the most important stages of any audit that should not be neglected or incorrectly implemented. If the internal audit fails to make sure that its recommendations are implemented, then all of the investment in doing the audit may be wasted.

The timing of the follow-up should be determined in relation to the significance and impact of the recommendations and the criticality of the system that has been audited. It should also take account of the implementation timeline given in the action plan. It is important that time for follow-up audits is provided in the short-term (annual) plan and that any specific follow-up audits are scheduled upon completion of each audit.

There are three main ways of following-up an audit, namely,

1. **By letter asking the auditee to confirm action has been taken**
   In many cases, and certainly for those audits containing minor audit findings, this will be the most appropriate approach. Checks should then be made at the next scheduled audit to ensure that appropriate action had actually been taken and that the controls had been implemented properly.

2. **Scheduling a specific follow-up audit**

 This may involve either

 – An interim review of the systems and controls that have been introduced, discussions with management to determine how they are operating, and a limited program of testing to ensure they are working as intended, or

 – A full system audit to establish that the correct action has been taken and controls are working effectively or, where no action has been taken by management, to determine the impact of the lack of control

 In deciding whether to do an interim review or a full systems audit, some things to consider are

 – The risk, importance, and materiality of the system

 – Known changes in organizational objectives or priorities since the audit was done

 – The stability of the system (systems that are subject to frequent change are less likely to be suitable for interim reviews)

 – The extent of the changes recommended in the audit report

 – Any indication that significant changes or new systems developments may have taken place

3. **Follow-up as part of the next audit**

 It should be standard practice on any scheduled audit to carry out a follow-up to establish the extent of implementation of the recommendations made at the last audit. This should be done at the start of the audit so that audit testing can be adjusted appropriately. The audit report should highlight clearly any further action that needs to be taken in relation to the last audit.

6.5.2 Audit Resolution and Follow-Up Templates (Appendix D)

6.5.2.1 Sample: Internal Audit Follow-Up Status Report

OFFICE OF THE CITY AUDITOR
Audit Report
October 12, 2007
Stockton City Council
AUDIT FINDINGS FOLLOW-UP: STATUS OF MANAGEMENT ACTION PLANS—2007

In accordance with our 2006–2007 audit plan, we have completed the annual follow-up of management action plans to improve conditions reported in audits.

The objective of our audit was to determine whether management's plans for corrective action had been implemented, and whether audit finding conditions were corrected. We verified management's corrective actions through interview, observation, and testing.

Included in this year's audit findings follow-up were 17 management action plans with implementation dates of June 30, 2007, or earlier.

We have verified management's correction of seven of the audit finding conditions reviewed.

Management's corrective actions have resulted in

- Revision of various city administrative directives
- Strengthened practices and controls over employee salary adjustments
- Improved risk management of insurance provisions
- Implementation of written procedures on performing golf inventory counts
- Improved practices and controls of golf course videotapes from surveillance cameras
- Implementation of written procedures for transactions at the golf pro shops
- Documenting asset accountability of noncapital assets of the organization

The remaining 10 findings to be resolved relate to

- Strengthening internal controls over golf course passes and gift certificates
- Revision of various administrative directives
- Use of temporary workers to staff essential positions
- Developing procedures for effective construction contract management and monitoring
- Retention of records in accordance with the city's records retention schedule
- Implementation of an electronic document management system
- Strengthening internal controls over inventory of fixed assets
- Developing and documenting procedures for payroll processing and time sheet submittal

The responsible department managers for human resources, parks and recreation, administrative services, and the city manager are to be commended for their efforts to improve the city's systems of internal control by resolving audit findings in a timely manner.

Additional information about our audit can be found in the attached audit report.

F. MICHAEL TAYLOR, CIA   NANCY XIONG
CITY AUDITOR   DEPUTY CITY AUDITOR I

emc: J. Gordon Palmer, Jr., City Manager
Ren Nosky, City Attorney
Katherine Gong Meissner, City Clerk
All Department Heads
Connie Cochran, Public Information Officer
Macias, Gini, O'Connell LLP
The Record

TABLE OF CONTENTS
Audit Findings Follow-Up: Status of Management Action Plans—2007

In accordance with the city auditor's 2006–2007 audit plan, we have completed the annual follow-up of management's action plans to improve conditions reported in audit reports.

BACKGROUND

As each audit assignment is completed, the auditor categorizes the conditions found as either audit findings, suggestions for improvement, or other comments. How a condition is categorized depends on its significance and relationship to the audit objectives.

Audit findings are presented to responsible city management in writing. Management responds to the audit findings with action plans and target dates to make needed improvements. We incorporate management's action plans into the final audit report.

We provide our audit reports to the city council and city management. Additionally, we discuss any significant findings identified in our audit reports with the audit committee.

After report issuance, we track audit findings, including the related management action plans and target dates, in a database application. On a quarterly basis, we provide a listing of all open findings to the city manager's office to assist in monitoring progress toward corrective action. On an annual basis, we conduct a follow-up review of open audit findings to assess the status of all management's action plans and to verify the implementation of management's corrective action.

Suggestions for improvement are those conditions deemed by the auditor to be of less significance than audit findings. Generally, these are areas where procedures could be more efficient, or where opportunities exist to make minor internal control improvements. These items are reported in a separate memorandum to management, and no follow-up work is performed.

Other comments may appear in the body of our audit reports. These comments may be included to highlight issues that apply to related areas in addition to the specific audit assignment, or to call attention to actions or events that may be of significant interest to the city council.

OBJECTIVES AND SCOPE

Much of the benefit from audit work is not in the findings reported or the recommendations made, but in the effective resolution of control weaknesses.

Management is responsible for resolving audit findings, and the office of the city auditor performs follow-up procedures to determine whether prompt and appropriate corrective action has been taken on reported findings. We conducted our audit follow-up on management's action plans with target implementation dates of June 30, 2007, or earlier.

METHODOLOGY

On an annual basis, the city auditor sends a written inquiry to management requesting the status of planned actions that have passed their target implementation date. For planned actions that have not been implemented, management is asked to provide revised plans and target dates. Auditing verifies through interview, observation, and testing those actions represented by management as implemented.

Our audit was conducted in accordance with GAGAS.

RESULTS

During the 2006–2007 fiscal year, there were 17 reportable audit findings with management action plans due to be implemented by June 30, 2007, or earlier. The reportable audit findings and their status are summarized in Tables 6.21 and 6.22.

Table 6.21 List of Seven Resolved Audit Findings

Department	Audit Title	Finding Number	Status	Original Target Date	Revised Target Date
City Manager	IFG Facilities Management Agreement	160-03	Closed	05/17/2007	
City Manager	Fixed Assets	310-02	Closed	11/01/2006	
City Manager	Payroll	321A-05	Closed	06/30/2006	
Human Resources	Administrative Directives	460-10	Closed	12/01/2002	
Parks & Recreation	Golf Pro Shop Inventory	129-02	Closed	10/15/2004	
Parks & Recreation	Golf Course Receipts	187-07	Closed	06/30/2004	
Parks & Recreation	Golf Course Receipts	187-10	Closed	06/30/2004	

Source: Adapted from Office of the City Auditor. Copyright 2007 by the City of Stockton, USA.

Table 6.22 List of Remaining 10 Open Audit Findings

Department	Audit Title	Finding Number	Status	Original Target Date	Revised Target Date
City Manager	Internal Control Evaluation: Events Center	159-02	Open	06/30/2007	01/31/2008
City Manager	City Clerk	306-03	Open	12/31/2006	12/31/2010
City Manager	City Clerk	306-03	Open	12/31/2005	01/31/2008
City Manager	Fixed Assets	310-01	Open	06/30/2007	12/31/2007
City Manager	Payroll	321A-01	Open	06/30/2007	12/31/2007
City Manager	Payroll	321A-04	Open	11/30/2007	11/31/2007
City Manager	Administrative Directives	460-03	Open	12/31/2002	06/30/2008
Human Resources	Management Information Services	182-09	Open	09/30/2001	06/30/2008
Parks & Recreation	Golf Course Receipts	187-02	Partially	05/19/2004	12/31/2007
Parks & Recreation	Golf Course Receipts	187-03	Partially	09/30/2004	12/31/2007

Source: Adapted from Office of the City Auditor. Copyright 2007 by the City of Stockton, USA.

Management's corrective actions during the year have resolved seven of the audit finding conditions.

In resolving the above audit findings, management's corrective actions have resulted in the following improvements:

- Revision of various city administrative directives
- Strengthened practices and controls over the adjustment of employee salaries due to changes in classification

- Improved risk management by meeting all insurance provisions of the IFG and professional sport teams' contracts, risk management, and insurance reporting requirements will be included into the city's contract compliance program
- Implementation of written procedures on performing golf inventory count
- Improved control on the handling, storage, and access of golf course videotapes from surveillance cameras
- Implementation of written procedures for cash handling and deposits for the golf pro shops
- Strengthening of the city departments' responsibility to control all noncapital assets of the organization

Table 6.22 is a list of the remaining 10 open audit findings. For each open audit finding, we have attached copies of the most recent follow-up reports, which detail the condition, management's action plan, and current status.

It should be standard practice on any scheduled audit to carry out a follow-up to establish the extent of implementation of the recommendations made at the last audit. This should be done at the start of the audit so that audit testing can be adjusted appropriately. The audit report should highlight clearly any further action that needs to be taken in relation to the last audit.

We would like to express our appreciation to the staff of all departments for their assistance during this audit.

REPORT OF OPEN AUDIT FINDINGS

The following are the finding numbers with their audit name (auditee) and departments, respectively: 159-02, Internal Control Evaluation—Events Center; 306-03, City Clerk; 306-05, City Clerk; 310-01, Fixed Assets; 321A-01, Payroll; 321A-04, Payroll; 460-03, Administrative Directives (Department: City Manager); 182-09, Management Information Services (Department: Human Resources); 187-02, Golf Course Receipts; 187-03, Golf Course Receipts (Department: Parks & Recreation).

Audit Name: Internal Control Evaluation—Events Center	**Finding Number:** 159-02
Department: City Manager	**Implemented:** No
Division:	
Original Target Date: 06/30/2007	**Current Target Date:** 01/31/2008

Condition

During our audit, we noted several internal control weaknesses related to the management of citywide construction projects.

1. The city's contract with Treadwell & Rollo did not contain standard contract clauses. The contract lacked specific terms describing what was to be provided, the basis for making payments, and how progress would be measured and monitored.

2. The city contracted for specific services to assist in contract management but did not ensure these services were rendered.
   a. Based on the architects' observations on site, they were required to review and comment on Swinerton's percentage of completion and quality of work in accordance with the construction documents. As evidence of their review, they were to execute the "Architect's Certification of Application for Payment." We noted both architects did not review and certify all of Swinerton's applications for payment. HKS Architects Inc. (HKS), the architect for the ballpark, certified only 2 of 19 payment applications. For payment application numbers 14 to 19, HKS notified the city that they would not perform the work until the city resolved the payment issues with their invoices. Accordingly, the city reduced the final settlement amount with HKS to adjust for the work that was not performed. 360 Architecture (ThreeSixty), the architect for the arena, stated that the initial payment applications provided to them for review were payment application numbers 7, 9, and 10. ThreeSixty did review and certify the remaining payment applications related to the arena as required.
   b. The city's contract with Regent Event Center LLC (Regent) was in place to address project controls, schedule, and budget issues. According to the contract, Regent was to provide monthly budget reports to the city. Regent was unable to prepare the reports as the city did not provide them with access to financial data for the project.
3. The total project costs for the Events Center were difficult to determine as not all costs were recorded under assigned project numbers. Costs for the Events Center were recorded under two project numbers as well as allocated to various departments, thus making it difficult to determine the total cost of the project. The project also experienced turnover of key staff responsible for tracking project costs. Each individual used a different methodology to track project costs. Costs charged outside the assigned project numbers were overlooked unless the individual tracking the costs knew the specific accounts in which costs were originally recorded.
4. Citywide procedures addressing supporting documentation to be submitted to accounts payable with requests for payment are lacking. Payments to Regent, F&H Construction, HKS, and ThreeSixty were processed without adequate supporting documentation submitted to accounts payable. The amount of supporting documentation provided to accounts payable varied depending on the individual submitting the invoice for payment. It was unclear whether the detail in support of the invoices was maintained by individuals submitting the invoices. Accounts payable is often viewed as a control point as all documentation submitted in support of payments is eventually scanned and maintained electronically by check number. Supporting documentation for Events Center invoices was voluminous in some instances and may explain why it was not submitted to accounts payable.

Management's Action Plan

Management agrees with the need for effective construction contract management and orderly organization of supporting documentation. As pointed out in this finding, management's current administrative directive regarding contracts expresses the importance of contract monitoring for progress, performance, and payment.

Management will ensure that all construction contracts include provisions for deliverables, milestones, and payment terms in order that contract performance can be monitored and payment processing expectations are clear.

All contract managers will be expected to monitor the performance of the contracts under the terms of the construction contracts.

Project numbers will be assigned to all projects for which establishing such numbers is Date Printed: 07/10/2007 necessary to facilitate accurate financial reporting.

Supporting documentation will be maintained by project managers who will note where supporting documentation can be found on all invoices submitted for payment to accounts payable that do not have the complete documentation attached.

Management Follow-Up Comments

Status at June 30, 2007, follow-up: Staff is currently reviewing standard processes used by project managers for construction contract management. The next step is to develop a plan for communicating to all city project managers the standards for construction contract management, including contract terms, supporting documentation, contract monitoring, payment processing, and the use of project numbers.

Audit Name: City Clerk **Finding Number:** 306-03
Department: City Manager **Implemented:** No
Division:
Original Target Date: 12/31/2006 **Current Target Date:** 12/31/2010

Condition

The city council has recently adopted a record retention and management policy citywide. While there are numerous manual records that are kept by the city, electronic records make up a significant portion of the city records. In the development of a record retention plan, there needs to be an emphasis on policies, procedures, and practices relating to how computer records are managed and retained, as well as manual records.

Citywide controls and accountability over computer records is necessary because creators of records, users of records, city departments, city attorney, and administrative services–information technology all have a degree of control and influence over vital records. Each of the above has significant control over how records are managed and placed on the record retention schedule, and which records are retained after the required retention period has passed.

There are significant issues in which coordination of effort between groups is needed, such as

- Computer records often have a paper copy kept. It is uncertain whether the record retention schedule for the same document in both paper and computer form is adhered to simultaneously.
- The city's record retention in many cases is longer than two years and varies in accordance with each department's record retention needs. GroupWise may not be capable of handling the diverse record retention schedules needed by the city.
- Other technologies storing public records, GroupWise, or other computer technology that can handle different record retention schedules need to be explored. There are issues involving responsibilities over records and what procedures should be used to monitor the process of electronic record management. Issues that need to be resolved include access rights to records, periodic review of records for determination of record retention, record security, hardware and software used to store records, and naming conventions of records so they can be located more easily.
- Software and other computer systems may store information for long periods of time. If a computer software system becomes obsolete, the transfer of data from one medium to another is necessary to preserve key records. Public records are at risk if technology cannot successfully transfer records to other technology.
- Departments testing disaster recovery systems periodically to determine electronic records can be recovered in an efficient and effective manner.

Management's Action Plan

On December 14, 2004, City Council Resolution 04-0803 was adopted authorizing the city to enter into a contract with THIRDWAVE CORPORATION to provide enterprise document management consulting services in the amount of $95,165 to evaluate its stand-alone document and records management systems and to make recommendations for an electronic document management system. The consulting services will include recommendations regarding the city's current electronic document management system, the management of electronic records to include an imaging solution and suggestions of policies and procedures for the city to adopt. It will take some time for the study to be done, recommendations to be drafted, and decisions to be made regarding policies and procedures to be implemented.

Management Follow-Up Comments

Status at June 30, 2007, follow-up: A consulting firm has been hired to assess internal readiness, help with vendor selection, perform cost–benefit analysis, and to assist with vendor contract negotiations (should the first two items show environmental readiness/fitness). The target date for starting implementation is January 2008, with completion estimated within 36 months.

Status at June 30, 2006, follow-up: An electronic document management system has been approved in the 2006–2007 budgets. City staff is coordinating implementation efforts.

Audit Name: City Clerk	**Finding Number:** 306-05
Department: City Manager	**Implemented:** No
Division:	
Original Target Date: 12/31/2005	**Current Target Date:** 01/31/2008

Condition

In our observation and review of record storage, we noted contents that were several years old and possibly kept in excess of the established retention periods. We also reviewed and observed records outside our sample at various storage sites. In some cases, we observed records in excess of 70–80 years old. Many records appear to have exceeded their useful life, and the cost–benefit to the city in retaining the above records needs to be assessed.

Management's Action Plan

The city manager's office will draft a memo to all city departments who may have old and outdated records at various sites that may no longer serve any legal, operational, or enduring purpose. The memorandum will mandate that records be inventoried and retained in accordance with the city's records retention schedule. Because the above records involve more analysis in order to determine records status, it may take a period of time to properly evaluate each record's status in accordance with the records retention schedule and handle records appropriately.

Management Follow-Up Comments

Status at June 30, 2007, follow-up: All files were removed from the old Fire Company No. 1 location. Additional file cleanup is still needed in the City Hall attic. It is anticipated that this next phase will be completed by January 31, 2008.

Status at June 30, 2006, follow-up: A memo was drafted to all city departments. Individual departments are in the process of reviewing files stored at various sites.

Audit Name: Fixed Assets	**Finding Number:** 310-01
Department: City Manager	**Implemented:** No
Division:	
Original Target Date: 06/30/2007	**Current Target Date:** 12/31/2007

Condition

The city's annual physical inventory of fixed asset equipment is performed by the same staff that has custody or access to the assets, with no independent verification. On an annual basis, resource managers send equipment listings to departments identifying equipment for which the department is accountable. Departments are to compare the lists to equipment on hand, noting any discrepancies, and return them to the resource managers. There is no independent verification to provide assurance that counts performed by the departments are complete and accurate.

Management's Action Plan

The proposed Administrative Directive FIN-003, Asset Accountability, requires departments to develop appropriate criteria for tracking assets assigned to their department. The directive includes considerations that should be taken into account by departments when developing their criteria. Resource managers will apply sampling techniques during their normal work processes to verify the accuracy of inventories for which they are responsible, on a sample basis.

Management Follow-Up Comments

Status at June 30, 2007, follow-up: Administrative Directive FIN-003, Asset Accountability, was presented to the executive committee and received final approval effective June 25, 2007. The revised directive incorporates the changes recommended by the audit. Resource managers will perform periodic sampling techniques to verify the accuracy of inventories for which they are responsible. Accounting will work with the resource managers to obtain documentation of these sampling procedures.

Audit Name: Payroll   **Finding Number:** 321A-01
Department: City Manager   **Implemented:** No
Division:
Original Target Date: 06/30/2007   **Current Target Date:** 12/31/2007

Condition

Though there are payroll-related administrative directives, the city does not maintain comprehensive, written, citywide policies and procedures related to payroll processing. The responsibility for complete and accurate payroll extends to every city employee, in every department. In the absence of citywide guidance, the city is missing an opportunity to promote uniformity in processing, and to emphasize critical roles and activities of the internal control structure. In addition, policies and procedures could formalize segregation of duties by describing the responsibilities of each participant in the payroll process, while listing incompatible activities for each.

To be effective, employees in critical positions should receive training to ensure they understand the policies and procedures, written guidance should be made readily available, and each department's operational processes should be surveyed and monitored to ensure correct implementation.

Management's Action Plan

The Human Resources Department and the Administrative Services Department—Payroll Unit will collaboratively review the segregation of duties between the departments to ensure that proper internal controls are in place to properly safeguard the assets of the City of Stockton. Written policies and procedures will be developed that clearly define the division of responsibilities. The Human Resources Department and the Administrative Services Department—Payroll Unit will develop a meeting schedule to develop these documents.

In addition, both departments will review the payroll processes in each department and develop consistent procedures for the user departments. To develop uniformity, training will be conducted for the payroll users in each department. A first training on the proper use of the payroll system will be conducted by HTE in July 2006.

Management Follow-Up Comments

Status at June 30, 2007, follow-up: The Human Resources Department and the Administrative Services Department have been meeting consistently to address this finding. The segregation of duties between departments has been reviewed, and it has been determined that proper internal controls are in place to safeguard city assets. The payroll processing responsibilities of the Human Resources Department are documented and procedures have been developed. The Administrative Services Department is continuing to document citywide policies and procedures related to payroll processing, including the responsibilities of the user departments. The Finance Division has assigned an internal auditor to work with payroll staff to assist with the development of the documentation. Training will be provided to the payroll users in each department.

Audit Name: Payroll	**Finding Number:** 321A-04
Department: City Manager	**Implemented:** No
Division:	
Original Target Date: 01/31/2007	**Current Target Date:** 11/30/2007

Condition

Though time sheets are identified as the official source document and audit trail, in practice other records are required to fully document payroll. Time sheets are often not signed by employees, or are signed with known inaccuracies under the assumption that corrections will be made in future pay periods. For the Police Department, overtime hours are not documented on the time sheets submitted to payroll.

Management's Action Plan

Automated time entry is the desired method of tracking and archival of payroll attendance and will continue to be explored as part of the citywide electronic document management system project. In the short term, FIN-004 will be reviewed and revised as needed. In addition, the necessity for accurate, timely filing of an employee's time sheet will be reaffirmed and communicated by the city manager to all departments. Departments will be required to submit to payroll documents and procedures that are a variation to the current official record for acceptance and filing.

Management Follow-Up Comments

Status at June 30, 2007, follow-up: The Human Resources Department and the Administrative Services Department have worked together to update FIN-004 to address the necessity for the accurate and timely filing of employee time sheets. The revised draft has been finalized and submitted to the executive committee for adoption.

Audit Name: Administrative Directives **Finding Number:** 460-03
Department: City Manager **Implemented:** No
Division:
Original Target Date: 12/31/2002 **Current Target Date:** 6/30/2008

Condition

Administrative directives are not being reviewed annually for current accuracy and relevancy. As part of our audit, we sent letters to the departments requesting that they review the directives and determine if they are current and relevant. If they were not current or relevant, we requested the department to provide a target date for the revision or deletion. On the basis of our review of the department's response, we have determined that the directives listed in the attachment are not current and relevant and have not been revised (Table 6.23).

Table 6.23 List of Directives Not Current and Relevant and Have Not Been Revised

Audit Name:	Administrative Directives	Finding Number:	460-03			
Department:	City Manager					
Directive	*Title*	*Effective Date*	*Current Target Date*	*Exhibit Appendix Updated*	*Status*	*Date Verified*
MAN-13[a]	City Manager's Agenda Report to the City Council	4/1/1998	6/30/2008	No	Open	
MAN-13E	Resolution Memo Sample		6/30/2008	No	Open	
MAN-13F	Committee Meeting Sample		6/30/2008	No	Open	
MAN-13G	Staff Report Sample		6/30/2008	No	Open	
MAN-13H	Legislation Adoption Sample		6/30/2008	No	Open	
MAN-13M	Multiple Committee Meeting Sample		6/30/2008	No	Open	
MAN-13T	Transmittal of Material for City Council Agenda		6/30/2008	No	Open	
MAN-15[a]	Emergency Plans	9/15/1982	6/30/2008	No	Open	
MAN-17	Health Insurance Advisory Committee	11/15/1989	6/30/2008		Open	
MAN-19	Economic Review Committee (ERC)	6/1/1994	6/30/2008		Open	
MAN-03[a]	Budget Transfer Administrative Policy	9/2/1997	9/30/2003	Yes	Closed	12/19/2003

(Continued)

Table 6.23 (Continued) List of Directives Not Current and Relevant and Have Not Been Revised

Directive	Title	Effective Date	Current Target Date	Exhibit Appendix Updated	Status	Date Verified
MAN-04	Departmental Orientations	5/8/1995	9/30/2003		Closed	6/24/2004
MAN-04A	Departmental Orientation Form		9/30/2003		Closed	6/24/2004
MAN-04B	Departmental Orientation Critique Sheet		9/30/2003		Closed	6/24/2004
MAN-07[a]	City Council Injuries/Complaints	3/15/1979	9/30/2003	No	Closed	6/24/2004
MAN-08	Correspondence: External	1/1/1997	9/30/2003		Closed	12/13/2004
MAN-08S	Sample Simplied Letter		9/30/2003		Closed	12/13/2004
MAN-09	Correspondence: Internal (Memorandum)	1/1/1997	9/30/2003		Closed	12/13/2004
MAN-09S	Sample Memorandum		9/30/2003		Closed	12/13/2004
MAN-11	Administrative Procedure Directive Changes	3/15/1979	9/30/2003		Closed	6/24/2004
MAN-12[a]	Grants—Application Procedure	12/2/1992			Closed	12/17/2002
MAN-18	Affirmative Action Guidelines for Federal Funded Pro	10/8/1997	9/30/2003		Closed	10/5/2004

(Continued)

Table 6.23 (Continued) List of Directives Not Current and Relevant and Have Not Been Revised

Directive	Title	Effective Date	Current Target Date	Exhibit Appendix Updated	Status	Date Verified
MAN-20[a]	Electronic Monitoring System (CityLink)	2/1/1991	9/30/2003	No	Closed	5/24/2004
MAN-22	Employee Suggestion Program	9/1/1996	7/31/2005		Closed	3/19/2005
MAN-23[a]	Communication Policy	10/20/1999	9/30/2003	Yes	Closed	10/5/2004
MAN-24	Cable T.V. Channel 42—Government Channel Prog.	3/15/1994	9/30/2003		Closed	10/5/2004
MAN-25	Contracts, Management of	8/2/2000	9/30/2003		Closed	10/5/2004
MAN-26	Staff Committee Structure	6/3/1996			Closed	3/27/2003
MAN-26A	Committee Formation Form				Closed	3/27/2003
P&R-02	Civic Memorial Auditorium	3/15/1979	9/30/2003		Closed	10/2/2004

Source: Retrieved from Office of the City Auditor, City of Stockton, California. Copyright 2007 by Stockton City Council. Reprinted with permission.

Note: [a], Directive references that an appendix or exhibit is attached but is not available in GroupWise.

Management's Action Plan
The city manager's department proposes a target date of December 31, 2002, for each of the directives listed. Staff will manage a tickler system to ensure compliance.

Management Follow-Up Comments
Status at June 30, 2007, follow-up: The city manager's staff dedicates time regularly to organize administrative directives, set timelines, coordinate departmental action according to schedule, and coordinate the revision approval process to ensure compliance. Updates require approval of proposed changes by the city manager and secondly require placement on agenda for approval action at a weekly executive team meeting.

Status at June 30, 2006, follow-up: Administrative Directive MAN-13 is awaiting implementation of the city's document management system.

Status at June 30, 2005, follow-up: Directives are in the process of being revised.

Status at June 30, 2004, follow-up: This high-priority project (the organization and update of administrative directives) has been delegated to a staff member. She has dedicated time to organize the directives, set a timeline and coordinate departmental action according to schedule, and coordinate revision approval process to ensure compliance. Updates require approval of proposed changes by the city manager and secondly require placement on agenda for approval action at a weekly department head meeting. The revised target date for review of the administrative directives project is December 31, 2004.

Audit Name: Management Information Services	**Finding Number:** 182-09
Department: Human Resources **Division:**	**Implemented:** Partially
Original Target Date: 09/30/2001	**Current Target Date:** 06/30/2008

Condition
MIS temporary workers are being used on a long-term basis and are being used to staff essential positions within the city, therefore subjecting the city's computer and network system to security risk. The city's MIS Help Desk for PC and network support is critical to the city's daily operations. City employees rely on the help desk to correct computer and network problems promptly. On February 6, 2001, temporary help desk workers appeared to conduct what The Record characterized as a *sick-out* in an attempt to resolve a contract rate dispute. The city's reliance on the temporary workers may have forced the city to resolve the contract dispute rather than dismissing the temporary workers. In addition, temporary workers may accept full-time positions with other companies at any time, thus leaving the city understaffed in essential positions.

Management's Action Plan

The director of personnel services has scheduled time to perform a complete review of the staffing and organization of the MIS Division. [The administrative services officer] will be working with him to implement portions of the review as soon as possible before his scheduled completion date of September 2001.

Management Follow-Up Comments

Status at June 30, 2007, follow-up: A long-term solution (multiyear) was proposed but was not adopted in the 2006–2007 or 2007–2008 fiscal year budget. Critical (vulnerable) positions were identified for conversion for fiscal year 2007–2008 in particular; five temporary agency positions will be eliminated. The Human Resources Department is awaiting council approval. Once an IT director is hired, an in-depth strategic review will be performed and a plan developed.

Status at June 30, 2006, follow-up: The director of Human Resources and the director of Administrative Services will continue to address the staffing of the IT Division with temporary agency employees.

Status at June 30, 2005, follow-up: Review of the staffing and organization of the IT Division has been completed. The director of Human Resources and the director of Administrative Services will continue to address the staffing of the IT Division with temporary workers.

Status at June 30, 2004, follow-up: Review of the staffing and organization of the IT Division has been completed. The director of Human Resources and the director of Administrative Services will continue to address the staffing of the IT Division with temporary workers.

Status at June 30, 2003, follow-up: At the request of the city manager, beginning in September 2001 and concluding in February 2002, Cooperative Personnel Services (CPS) conducted a review of the IT Division's organization, structure, classification, staffing, and position requirements to promote growth and increase the department's effectiveness.

CPS concluded that the city should consider replacing the large number of temporary staff with full-time employees for operational efficiency and reliability. It was noted that although the use of temporary staff may have the appearance of short-term cost savings, it was determined that this process is costing the city more resources in its long-term operation in the following quality and quantity measures: productive time, level of deliverables and service products, continuity of services, quality control, reliability of operation, skill set and knowledge consistency, training and learning curve, work assignment and scheduling flexibility, and accountability of service qualities.

Specifically, their recommendation was to allocate temporary staff to full-time positions of administrative assistants and micro-computer specialists. This recommendation has not been implemented by the city manager because of the excessive costs associated with the allocation of eight additional positions.

The City Information Technology Committee is also reviewing the IT organization structure and staffing. This committee is tasked with making recommendations to the city manager that will increase overall IT effectiveness in meeting the city's current and future needs.

Status at June 30, 2002, follow-up: A management study recommended converting temporary positions at the Help Desk and Administrative personnel into regular positions. A City IT Committee formed after being recommended in the audit report is currently exploring alternatives to the recommendation identified in the management study. Such alternatives may be to contract out with an agency to provide technical support (Help Desk). The IT Committee is meeting monthly to discuss this issue. However, this is not the only alternative. As previously stated, alternatives are still being considered. Also, the ability of converting temporary staff to permanent status requires council action along with the budgetary process.

Audit Name: Golf Course Receipts
Department: Parks & Recreation
Division: Golf
Original Target Date: 05/19/2004

Finding Number: 187-02
Implemented: Partially

Current Target Date: 12/31/2007

Condition

Early in our work, we communicated to management that gift certificates were not monitored or properly controlled by the Parks & Recreation Department. The weak controls were serious enough that the risk of financial loss appeared to be high. Certificates were not prenumbered, and there was no tracking of sales or redemptions.

In response, the Parks & Recreation Department began using prenumbered two-part forms for gift certificates. This design change provided an opportunity to improve controls over gift certificates, but control weaknesses remain.

Outstanding gift certificates represent a liability to the city, yet the city has no way of determining the number or value of outstanding certificates. As certificates are sold, the certificate number and amount are not recorded. In addition, the city's copy of the issued certificate is not always retained; many are immediately placed in the trash. We observed this practice during one of our on-site interviews.

As gift certificates are redeemed, the city does not retain any documentation to support the actual use of the gift certificate. It is possible to enter a transaction, accept payment by cash, check, or credit card, but record the tender type as a gift certificate. We have documented instances of this occurring at Swenson Park Golf Course when a credit card was used to make a purchase but the transaction was recorded as paid by gift certificate. This allowed cash to be removed from the cash register.

Management's Action Plan

Effective immediately, copies of all gift certificates sold will be retained and logged. As customers use gift certificates, the certificate number and remaining balance will also be logged.

We will change the form of gift certificates to handle them under the same procedures as golf passes, as referenced in our response to our management action plan for golf passes. The gift certificates will be designed to have prenumbered magnetic strip cards similar to a credit card.

Staff will have the ability to include the amount of the certificate on the magnetic strip. Once the new gift cards are in place, we will recall outstanding gift certificates and issue gift cards for the remaining balances.

Management Follow-Up Comments

Status at June 30, 2007, follow-up: We anticipate the installation of a golf-specific point of sale (POS) system in August or September of 2007. This program will interface with the CLASS operating system that is used for our recreation program registrations. All gift certificates and golf passes will be purchased and managed through this system. Two-part paper certificates and logbooks will no longer be used. The system tracks sales, tee times, inventory, and scheduling through one point. Because the POS will be networked to our main CLASS server, patrons will have the flexibility to use certificates and passes at either of our courses. All aspects of our golf operation will be streamlined and more secure by implementing this system.

Status at June 30, 2006, follow-up: A procedure on handling gift certificates was developed and implemented in April 2006. This procedure has been added to the *Golf Operations Manual*. The department is looking at the possibility of limiting the use of the gift certificates to the golf course where the gift certificates were issued due to the issues identified with maintaining and reconciling separate logs at both golf courses. Adding magnetic strips or converting the gift certificates to magnetic cards will be postponed due to cost considerations.

Status at June 30, 2005, follow-up: The Parks & Recreation Department is currently recruiting a new golf manager and needs to give the person hired for the position time to establish procedures.

Status at June 30, 2004, follow-up: Effective May 19, 2004, all golf course staff were required to log all gift certificates sold with the amount of that certificate. Parks & Recreation is also working with the Purchasing Division of Administrative Services to select a vendor for magnetic card gift certificates. We anticipate having the magnetic strip gift cards by October 1, 2004.

Audit Name: Golf Course Receipts
Department: Parks & Recreation
Division: Golf
Original Target Date: 09/30/2004

Finding Number: 187-03
Implemented: Partially

Current Target Date: 12/31/2007

Condition

The Parks & Recreation Department sells golf passes. Our review of the golf pass system of sales, distribution, and monitoring indicated the following internal control weaknesses.

The physical stock of golf passes is not adequately controlled. We noted that the monthly logs maintained to track the sale of passes were missing. The most recent instance involved missing logs for Swenson from October 2001 through February 2002. Missing logs on sales of monthly passes make monitoring difficult.

We observed that golfers who hold golf passes do not always present their pass to the cashier when checking in. They may simply call out their pass number to the cashier. Because the system does not flag an attempted use of an expired pass, it is possible for play to occur on expired passes. Additionally, when this occurs, the golfer is not given a receipt to demonstrate that he or she has checked-in, as required.

In addition, we noted that cashiers did not always enter the use of a golf pass in the cash register at the time of play. One cashier entered all pass play into the cash register at the end of their shift, making the information less useful for monitoring activity or management decision making.

Management's Action Plan

The Parks & Recreation Department is developing a magnetic card program for golf passes similar to a credit card. Golf course staff will have the ability to include the number of golf games on the magnetic strip and the number of games played can be deducted. Because the City of Stockton is considering changing banking institutions, this program will not be implemented until the city determines what bank it will be utilizing for their banking needs. This will allow us to use the same credit card processing services.

Management Follow-Up Comments

Status at June 30, 2007, follow-up: We anticipate the installation of a golf-specific POS system in August or September of 2007. This program will interface with the CLASS operating system that is used for our recreation program registrations. All gift certificates and golf passes will be purchased and managed through this system. Two-part paper certificates and logbooks will no longer be used. The system tracks sales, tee times, inventory, and scheduling through one point. Because the POS will be networked to our main CLASS server, patrons will have the flexibility to use certificates and passes at either of our courses. All aspects of our golf operation will be streamlined and more secure by implementing this system.

Status at June 30, 2006, follow-up: A procedure on proper handling of passes has been developed and implemented to strictly monitor and control the use of the golf passes. The procedure will be incorporated in the *Golf Operations Manual*. Conversion of passes to magnetic cards is postponed due to cost considerations. The department is looking at the possibility of limiting the use of the passes to the golf course where the pass was issued. The department will make this determination by December 31, 2006.

Status at June 30, 2005, follow-up: The Parks & Recreation Department is currently recruiting a new golf manager and needs to give the person hired for the position time to establish procedures.

Status at June 30, 2004, follow-up: The Parks & Recreation Department is working with the Purchasing Division of Administrative Services to select a vendor for providing a magnetic card program that can be used for golf passes as well as gift certificates. We anticipate having the magnetic strip cards by October 1, 2004 (Stockton City Council, 2007, pp. 1–19).

Prepared by: _____
Date: _____
Reviewed by: _____
Date: _____

6.5.2.2 Audit Resolution and Follow-Up Quality Control Checklist

The purpose of audit resolution and follow-up procedures is to ensure that management implements audit recommendations or corrective action aimed at the audit finding.

The follow-up phase should be documented in its own set of work papers. To facilitate reviewing work for the audit resolution and follow-up phase, the checklist in Table 6.24 is provided. *Yes* answers mean acceptable work and *no* answers require some response or action on the part of the auditor in charge.

Table 6.24 Audit Resolution and Follow-Up Quality Control Checklist

Item	Yes	No	Review Comments

1. Are work papers
  a. Neat and uniform?
  b. Indexed in lower right corner?
  c. Initialed and dated by preparer?			

2. Do work papers
  a. Include a descriptive title?
  b. Include an appropriate heading?
  c. Reflect the source of information?
  d. Include a work paper cover, index, and follow-up summary?
  e. Include a department updated action plan?
  f. Include a copy of the original IAO report?			

3. Was a memo prepared and provided to the department head to communicate the results of the follow-up along with an updated Status of Major Audit Recommendations?			
4. Was a Status of Major Audit Recommendations prepared and updated to reflect the results of follow-up procedures?			
5. Have all work papers been reviewed and approved?			
6. Was the work preformed within the agreed upon time budget? If not, why?			
All quality control review points have been cleared			

_____   _____

Auditor-in-Charge   Date

References

Adukia, R. S. (n.d.). *Manual on Internal Audit.*

AICPA. (2006). AU Section 339. Audit Documentation. Retrieved July 8, 2016, from: https://www.aicpa.org/Research/Standards/AuditAttest/DownloadableDocuments/AU-00339.pdf.

AuditNet LLC. (2014). The-internal-audit-process-from-a-to-z-how-it-works. Retrieved July 1, 2014, from: http://www.auditnet.org/audit-library/the-internal-audit-process-from-a-to-z-how-it-works, http://www.auditnet.org/audit-library/the-internal-audit-process-from-a-to-z-how-it-works/audit-working-papers.

AuditNet LLC. (2014). The-internal-audit-process-from-a-to-z-how-it-works. *Audit Working Papers (Engagement Letter).* Retrieved July 1, 2014, from: http://www.auditnet.org/system/resources/BAhbBlsHOgZmSSI~MjAxMy8wMy8wNC8xMy8yMy8wNy84NzIvQXVkaXROZXRfMjAyX0VuZ2FnZW1lbnRfTGV0dGVyLmRvYwY6BkVU/AuditNet 202-Engagement Letter.doc.

AuditNet LLC. (2014). The-internal-audit-process-from-a-to-z-how-it-works. *Audit Working Papers (Self-Assessment Questionnaire).* Retrieved July 1, 2014, from: http://internalaudit.wayne.edu/pdf/self_audit_questionnaire.pdf.

AuditNet LLC. (2014). The-internal-audit-process-from-a-to-z-how-it-works. *Audit Working Papers (Internal Control Template Questionnaire).* Retrieved July 1, 2014, from: http://www.auditnet.org/system/resources/BAhbBlsHOgZmSSIwMjAxMy8wMy8wNC8xMy8yMy8wOC80MS9BdWRpdE5ldF8yMDZfSUNRLmRvYwY6BkVU/AuditNet 206-ICQ.doc.

AuditNet LLC. (2014). The-internal-audit-process-from-a-to-z-how-it-works. *Audit Working Papers (Planning Workpaper Index).* Retrieved July 1, 2014, from: http://www.auditnet.org/system/resources/BAhbBlsHOgZmSSJCMjAxMy8wMy8wNC8xMy80MC80Ny85ODEvUGxhbm5pbmdfV29ya3BhcGVyX0luZGV4X1RlbXBsYXRlLmRvYwY6BkVU/Planning Workpaper Index Template.doc.

AuditNet LLC. (2014). The-internal-audit-process-from-a-to-z-how-it-works. Audit Working Papers (Quality Control Checklist—Survey Phase). Retrieved July 1, 2014, from: http://www.auditnet.org/system/resources/BAhbBlsHOgZmSSJBMjAxMy8wMy8wNC8xMy8yMy8wNi8xNTYvQXVkaXROZXRfMTA3X1FDX0NoZWNrbGlzdF9TdXJ2ZXkuZG9jBjoGRVQ/AuditNet 107-QC Checklist-Survey.doc.

Balovich, D. (2007). Sarbanes-Oxley document retention and best practices. Creditworthy News. Copyrighted 3JM Company Inc., Dallas. Retrieved July 7, 2016, from: http://www.creditworthy.com/3jm/articles/cw90507.html.

Blume, A. (2014). *Risk Management: Participants' Handbook.* Support to Local Governance Processes (SULGO) in Tanzania. Project: Strengthening internal controls at sub-national level. Deutsche Gesellschaftfür, Internationale Zusammenarbeit (GIZ) GmbH.

City of Stockton, California. (2007). *List of Remaining Ten Open Audit Findings, 2006–2007 Fiscal Year [Table].* Office of the City Auditor, Stockton, CA.

ESCC 11100. (2005). Internal Audit Procedure for the ESCC, Issue 1, p. 11. European Space Agency (https://escies.org).

Government of the Virgin Islands. (2005). Archives and Records Management: Specific Schedules. Retrieved July 9, 2016, from: http://www.nationalarchives.gov.vg/inc/forms/C-Specific%20Schedule%20C.pdf.

HM Treasury. (2011). Internal Audit Records Management. The National Archives, Kew, London. Copyright 2011 Crown. Retrieved July 8, 2016, from: https://www.gov.uk /government/uploads/system/uploads/attachment_data/file/207215/Internal_Audit _Records_Management.pdf.

Miller, J. (1991). (MillerJim@amstr.com)—Risk Evaluation Form.

Miller, J. (n.d.). *Risk Evaluation Form*. Retrieved from: http://www.auditnet.org/system /resources/BAhbBlsHOgZmSSIzMjAxMy8wMy8wNC8xMy80MC81MS8y OTQvUmlza0V2YWx1YXRpb25Gb3JtLmRvYy6BkVU/RiskEvaluationForm.doc.

Public Sector Internal Audit Standards. (PSIAS, 2012). Applying the IIA International Standards to the UK Public Sector. ISBN 978 1 84508 356 4. Retrieved July 8, 2016, from: https://www.gov.uk/government/uploads/system/uploads/attachment_data/file /207064/public_sector_internal_audit_standards_december2012.pdf.

Chapter 7

Internal Audit
Peer Review

7.1 Overview

A one-time Nigerian president, Gen. Olusegun Obasanjo (Rtd), apparently not comfortable with the state of the economy, wrote a book, *My Watch*. On the other hand, a human rights activist, Yinka Odumakin, not impressed with the character and the publication of former president Olusegun Obasanjo, published what appears a counter book, *Watch The Watcher*. This scenario describes the subject *peer review*.

A peer review, also known as a quality assurance review (or QAR), is the evaluation of an internal audit department by independent professionals in the same field as required by the Institute of Internal Auditors (IIA).

A peer review examines the internal audit department's compliance with professional standards and suggests improvements in order to align the department with best practices recognized in the profession.

Generally, internal audit departments can decide for themselves whom to select as audit partners.

The peer review usually goes through the normal audit project phases, that is, planning, preparation, execution, reporting, and follow-up (Boecker et al., 2007, p. 537).

In recent years, recognition and public scrutiny of auditors has increased, thereby enhancing the importance of independent peer reviews. As a result of this, the American Institute of Certified Public Accountants (AICPA) revised its Practice-Monitoring Program and issued new standards with effect from January 1, 2005.

In the same manner, internal audit institutes have enhanced their peer review programs. For example, IIA Standard 1312 (External Assessments) advises that a peer review should be conducted by an independent body, once every five years.

Furthermore, since this standard came into effect on January 1, 2002, every internal audit department seeking accreditation for its activities according to the International Standard for the Professional Practice of Internal Auditing must conduct a peer review by December 31, 2006.

In this practice manual, we shall be using samples provided by North Carolina Office of State Budget and Management (NCOSBM), Office of Internal Audit (OIA), as developed in its Peer Review Program, to help state agencies and universities comply with the IIA Standards for the Professional Practice of Internal Auditing (Standards) and the Internal Auditing Act (G.S. 143-745) (NCOSBM, 2013).

In this chapter, we shall look at the objectives of peer review/external quality assessment (EQA); how it is developed; procedures for selecting them as enunciated by NCOSBM; main focus areas of EQA; and how audit evidences are collected, and how conclusions are reached and report generated. In doing this, we shall make extensive use of NCOSBM guidelines. We shall also describe the various phases in peer review program, which include Planning, Execution (questionnaire, gathering evidence through document reviews, physical observation, focus group discussion, interview, survey, etc.), Reporting, and Follow-up as given in the following diagram (Royal Audit Authority of Bhutan, n.d.) (Figure 7.1):

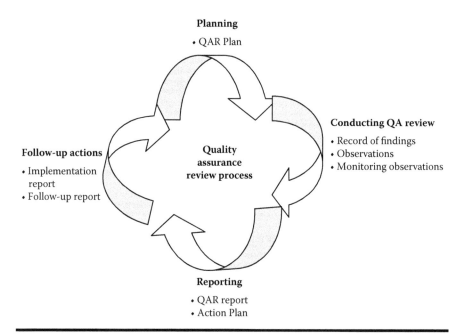

Figure 7.1 Quality assurance review process. (Adapted from Royal Audit Authority of Bhutan, (n.d.). Handbook on Quality Assurance Review Process.)

7.1.1 Planning

Planning is the first phase, where the review team will plan the review before it takes place. The inputs will include the terms of reference, budgets, and background information. The output of this phase will be a plan for conducting the review. This can be a long-term plan in case of an institutional level review and an annual plan in case of a financial/individual audit level review. As soon as the plan has been approved, it becomes a working tool of the second phase (Conducting QA Review).

7.1.2 Conducting QA Review

The second phase is Conducting Quality Assurance Review; the review team will conduct the review using the Quality Assurance work programs, which details the specific methods and checklists for getting evidence. The outputs of this phase are the findings and observations. This should be discussed with the senior management in the case of institutional level review and with the audit staff for individual level review to obtain feedback.

7.1.3 Reporting

Reporting is the third phase where the review team will use the outputs from the second phase (Conducting, i.e., findings and observations) as inputs to prepare a report.

7.1.4 Follow-Up Action

The final phase is the Follow-up, where the review team will use the action plan prepared by the line functions as inputs and assess the extent of implementation of the action plan agreed upon and reasons for non-implementation of any items in the action plan. It should be noted that appropriate follow-up actions are necessary to ensure that the agreed action plan is implemented or adequate steps are being taken to implement it.

7.2 Objectives

The main objective of a peer review is to improve the quality of audit as a whole by way of evaluating, documenting, and reporting on the effectiveness and quality of an internal audit department to internal (e.g., corporate management, board of directors, etc.) and external bodies (e.g., external auditors). It also serves as a means of providing valuable suggestions for improving internal audit practices.

In 2005, the IIA at SAP (Systems, Applications, and Products) implementation initiated a peer review process with the following objectives:

- To obtain objective confirmation from professional third parties that the audit procedures practiced by Group Internal Auditors (GIAS) conform to IIA Standards
- To gain a certified substantive basis for the development of an SAP software solution for audit management
- To enhance the profile and status of GIAS both within SAP and among third parties
- To gain credibility among contacts as well as internal and external customers by reversing the roles (auditing the auditors)
- To allow internal audit employees to gather valuable personal experience throughout the process
- To facilitate benchmarking against internal audit departments of other companies
- To motivate internal audit employees because the peer review should give them confidence that they are using an internationally recognized and effective audit model (Boecker et al., 2007, pp. 537–538)

7.3 Development of the Peer Review Concept

The development of the peer review concept involves preliminary considerations and general planning for conducting a peer review, which comprises the following (Boecker et al., 2007):

- Initial assessment of the project to obtain a clear understanding of the expected benefits
- Appointment of an internal project team
- Presentation of a first project plan to the entire department to establish its primary readiness to conduct a peer review
- Definition of the period covered by the review
- Testing of the internal quality assurance program, which is the basis for the processes to be subjected to peer review

7.4 Selection of Peer Review Partner

The professional standards of the IIA (Boecker et al., 2007) only require that an external QAR be conducted by qualified, independent auditors. To this effect, the internal audit department is at a liberty to decide for themselves whom to select for this assignment. However, in taking this decision, a peer review should be conducted according to IIA principles in terms of content and topic because they represent the current best practices in the profession.

Many consulting firms offer quality assessment reviews as one of their audit-related services. The professional internal audit institutes also offer peer review services, as well as government agencies established by Act for this purpose.

Participating in peer review teams provides training opportunities for internal auditors in both performing and receiving peer reviews. The process offers a chance to network with other professionals from state agencies, internal audit institutes, and consulting firms, and provides insights into best practices peer reviewers can take back to their own internal audit functions.

Team lead requirements:

1. Is a certified audit professional (CIA, CPA, CISA, etc.) with current in-depth knowledge of the Standards
2. Is well versed in the best practices of the profession
3. Has at least five years of recent experience in the practice of internal auditing or consulting at a management level
4. Has at least five years of recent experience in the practice of leading an audit engagement (State Agency Internal Audit Forum [SAIAF], 2013)

Team member requirements:

1. Is a certified audit professional (CIA, CPA, CISA, etc.) with current in-depth knowledge of the Standards
2. Has at least two years of recent experience in the practice of leading an audit engagement (SAIAF, 2013)

7.5 Main Focus Areas of the Peer Review

The peer review mostly focuses on assessing the following areas of audit assignment (Boecker et al., 2007):

■ Organizational positioning and structure of the internal audit: Here, the organizational fundamentals of the department are considered (e.g., the charter, mission, target agreements, and the audit handbook).
■ Definition and implementation of a risk-based audit approach: This involves reviewing the audit reports, working papers, and audit planning documents as part of the assessment of the audit approach and project management.

- Personnel management within internal audit (i.e., the qualification, training plan, and career development of its employees).
- Definition of and compliance with quality assurance programs as defined by the IIA Standards.
- Audit of IT-related issues.

7.6 Evidence

Evidence is obtained throughout the peer review process, which includes (SAIAF, 2013):

- The internal audit function's self-assessment (involves completion of the Master Peer Review Program, Working Paper Review Tool, reference file, and self-assessment report)
- The peer review team's evaluation of the self-assessment and related documents
- Additional working paper review
- Management surveys
- Interviews
- On-site reviews of additional information

Interviews are typically conducted with

- A sample of board members, usually including the chairman and a representative of the audit committee
- Representatives of auditee management, preferably individuals who have received audits during the time period being reviewed
- The chief audit executive/internal audit director
- Internal audit staff
- External auditors, if relevant and cost-effective

7.7 Conclusions and Reporting

Peer reviews are to be performed by experienced auditors who have been trained in the peer review process. The peer review team must use professional judgment based on evidence obtained during the peer review to reach a conclusion about the rating to give the internal audit function. Reasonable professionals may differ in the conclusions they draw based on the same set of facts. Therefore, it may be helpful to base the opinion on the impact of the risk created by instances of noncompliance: high risk pertains to actions or inactions that could have a material adverse impact on the organization, medium risks typically result in inefficiencies or uneconomical use of resources, and low risks typically do not have a significant impact on the organization (Boecker et al., 2007).

When performing peer reviews and issuing opinions, peer review teams should give consideration to the size of the internal audit activity being reviewed. This is important because small internal audit departments may operate somewhat differently from larger ones. For example, they may have less supervisory review or documentation of policies and procedures.

At the conclusion of the peer review, a report describing the result is written, which, if applicable, will confirm that internal audit complies with IIA Standards. In addition to confirming compliance to IIA Standards, the report should also suggest improvements by highlighting best practices. It is also important to inform those for internal audit in the company of the result of the peer review (e.g., CEO, board of directors, audit committee) (SAIAF, 2013).

7.8 Ratings for Reporting Results

The peer review team's opinion is expressed as one of the three following ratings: *generally complies/pass*, *partially complies/pass with deficiencies*, or *does not comply/fail* (SAIAF, 2013).

- *Generally complies/pass* means that the audit organization's system of quality control (relevant structures, policies, and procedures, as well as processes by which they are applied) has been suitably designed and complied with to provide the audit organization with reasonable assurance of performing and reporting in conformity with applicable professional standards or element of the *code of ethics* in all material respects.
- *Partially complies/pass with deficiencies* means that the audit organization's system of quality control has been suitably designed and complied with to provide the audit organization with reasonable assurance of performing and reporting in conformity with applicable professional standards and the *code of ethics* in all material respects with the exception of a certain deficiency or deficiencies that are described in the report.
- *Does not comply/fail* means that, based on the significant deficiencies that are described in the report, the audit organization's system of quality control is not suitably designed to provide the audit organization with reasonable assurance of performing and reporting in conformity with applicable professional standards or elements of the *code of ethics* in all material respects, or the audit organization has not complied with its system of quality control to provide the audit organization with reasonable assurance of performing and reporting in conformity with applicable professional standards or elements of the *code of ethics* in all material respects.

7.9 Internal Audit Response

The internal audit should have the confidence to communicate the peer review on their results within the company with a commendation. This is a strong point in achieving one of the major objectives of peer review, which is to strengthen internal audit standing in the company.

7.10 Implementation of Recommendations and Follow-Up

The minimum objective of the peer review is to confirm that the internal audit department reviewed performs its activities in accordance with IIA Standards. If this objective is not met, the peer review partner should specify corrective actions and deadlines within which the actions are to be implemented. If the minimum objective has been met, the internal audit should continue aligning itself with recognized best practice. For this purpose, the peer review partner should point out potentials for improvement and, if possible, specific steps to best tap this potential.

These communications should then be implemented in a sustainable way as part of a structured followed-up process, that is, with firm responsibilities, deadlines, and escalation procedures if necessary.

7.11 Quality Assurance Review Forms

7.11.1 Planning Phase

The planning process involves preparation of an operational plan and selection of the type of review to be conducted according to the conditions present in the terms of reference and stipulated standards.

The quality assurance review forms as used in this section include the following.

7.11.1.1 A1: Peer Review Volunteer Application Form (Figure 7.2)

The purpose of this questionnaire is to obtain information from applicants to serve on peer review teams. The OIA will use the information to select qualified peer review team members.

Minimum Qualifications

Qualifications of an individual serving on peer review teams are dependent on their role as follows:

Team Leader Requirements

- Is a certified audit professional (CIA, CPA, CISA, etc.) with current in-depth knowledge of the Standards
- Is well versed in the best practices of the profession
- Has at least three years of recent experience in the practice of internal auditing or consulting at a management level
- Has at least three years of recent experience in the practice of leading an audit engagement

Team Member Requirements

- Is a certified audit professional (CIA, CPA, CISA, etc.) with current in-depth knowledge of the Standards
- Has at least two years of recent experience in the practice the of leading an audit engagement

Employment Information:

Name: ………………………………………………………………..

Job Title: ………………………………………………………………...

State Agency: ………………………………………………………..

Business Phone: ………………………………………………………..

E-mail Address: ………………………………………………………

Supervisor Name: ……………………………………………………

Supervisor Title: ……………………………………………………

Supervisor Phone: …………………………………………………

Certifications/Licenses:

CPA ☐ CIA ☐ CISA ☐ CMA ☐ Other: _____ (Please State)

Education:

Name of College or University: _____

Location: _____

Figure 7.2   A1: Peer review volunteer application form.   (*Continued*)

Degree: Bachelors   Major: _____

Experience:

Agency/Company. _____	From	To
Agency/Company: _____	From	To
Agency/Company: _____	From	To
Agency/Company: _____	From	To
Agency/Company: _____	From	To
Agency/Company: _____	From	To
Agency/Company: _____	From	To
Agency/Company: _____	From	To
Agency/Company: _____	From	To
Agency/Company: _____	From	To

Provide a brief description of current duties: _____

Audit Skills: Check the skills below you have acquired from audit experience.

☐ Prepare audit plan   ☐ Apply sampling techniques

☐ Perform audit survey   ☐ Prepare working papers

☐ Review internal controls   ☐ Review working papers

☐ Prepare audit programs   ☐ Write reports

☐ Comply with IIA standards   ☐ Edit reports

☐ Auditor in charge—number of years:

☐ Manage multiple audits—number of years:

Primary Audit Area: ☐ Internal Audit ☐ External Audit

Figure 7.2 (Continued)   A1: Peer review volunteer application form.   (*Continued*)

Comments: _____

Do you wish to be considered for a team leader position? Yes ☐　No ☐

Statement of Knowledge:

By checking the boxes below, I certify the following statements regarding my knowledge and abilities to participate in the OIA Peer Review Program:

☐ I have current knowledge of the IIA Standards.

☐ I am well versed with auditing best practices.

☐ I am a certified audit professional.

☐ I have at least two years of internal auditing experience.

☐ I have greater than three years of auditing experience.

☐ I confirm that my supervisor approves that I participate in the Peer Review Program on behalf of my Department.

☐ I agree to disclose, as required by Section 1312 of the IIA Standards, if I am placed on a Review Team in which I am aware of any possible impairments to my appearance, in fact or appearance, in conducting the review.

Signed:_____　Date:_____

Figure 7.2 (Continued)　A1: Peer review volunteer application form. (Adapted from State of North Carolina, Council of Internal Auditing, Office of Internal Audit, Peer Review Program, Peer Review Volunteer Application [Form A1].)

7.11.1.2 A2: Peer Review Request Form (Figure 7.3)

The purpose of this form is to request a peer review through the OIA Peer Review Program. Please respond to all questions. The information provided in this form assists the office in prioritizing, scheduling, and assigning peer review teams. This form should be completed by the agency's director of internal audit.

Contact Information

Please provide the following information about your Agency or University:

Department Name _____

Internal Audit Function Address _____

Name of the Director of Internal Audit _____

Director of Internal Auditing Phone Number _____

Director of Internal Auditing Email Address _____

Background Information

1. Please provide the following background information about your Internal Audit function:

   When was the Internal Audit function created? _____

   Current year budget for your Internal Audit function _____

   Number of auditors in your Internal Audit function _____

   Number of IT auditors/specialists _____

   Number of contracted auditors in your Internal Audit function _____

   Number of administrative support staff in your Internal Audit function _____

   Number of other staff in your Internal Audit function _____

   Average years of audit experience (not including support staff) _____

   Are work papers centrally located? _____

   Number of reports issued per year _____

2. Has your Internal Audit function ever had an external review? ☐ Yes ☐ No
   If yes, when: Month _____ Year _____
   Was the Council Peer Review program used? ☐ Yes ☐ No

Figure 7.3   A2: Peer review request form. *(Continued)*

☐ By checking this box, I confirm the following:

1. I have reviewed the Council Peer Review Guide in its entirety and I understand the requirements necessary for my agency to participate in the Council Peer Review Program.

2. My Internal Audit function has completed Tool 2 and can provide these documents to the review team once selected and are prepared to provide the necessary paperwork requested during the external review.

3. My agency management is aware of this request.

Signed:_____ Date:_____

_____
For the Peer Review Program, the Internal Audit Director refers to the audit professional who oversees the internal audit function in the agency/university.

Figure 7.3 (Continued) A2: Peer review request form. (Adapted from State of North Carolina, Council of Internal Auditing, Office of Internal Audit, Peer Review Program, Peer Review Request Form [Form A2].)

7.11.1.3 A3: Memorandum of Understanding Sample (Figure 7.4)

The purpose of Memorandum of Understanding (MOU) is to sign a mutual contract between the organization's internal audit and the QAR team. The MOU must state the purpose of the review and the scope to be covered by the review, which must be in accordance with Peer Review Program Guidelines and the Institute of Internal Auditors Quality Assessment Manual. The MOU must also state the terms and conditions of the agreement; the MOU must be signed by authorized and responsible members from both sides.

Purpose:

This Memorandum of Understanding is entered into this *date* day of *month*, 20*xx* between the peer review team (on behalf of the Council of Internal Auditing Peer Review Program) and the *Requesting Agency/University Name* for the purpose of providing/receiving an external review.

Scope:

The scope of the review is to conduct a *quality assessment* peer review in accordance with the *Peer Review Program Guidelines* and the *Institute of Internal Auditors Quality Assessment Manual*. The objectives are to review the internal audit function and operations for compliance with the *International Professional Practice Mandatory Requirements* (Standards). The scope will include *Requesting Agency/University Name* internal audit projects completed during the period from *Month, Day, Year* through *Month, Day, Year*.

The peer review team will provide a written report of the results of the external review, including

- A written opinion as to whether the internal audit function *generally complies, partially complies,* or *does not comply* with the Standards
- Recommendations for improvement
- Identification of leading practices and value-added services (Limited work performed if a self-assessment with independent validation is selected)

The team members are

- *Team Lead Name, title, and agency/university*
- *Team Member Name, title, and agency/university*

The peer review will begin in *Month, Year* with fieldwork scheduled for *Month, Year*. A draft report will be provided to the director of internal auditing for review by *Date*, with a final report to be released by *Date*. An exit conference will be held with the director of internal audit and executive management on or about *Date*.

Terms of agreement:

The undersigned agree to the following terms and conditions in order to accomplish the purpose of this agreement:

The (*Requesting Agency/University Name*) agree to

- Provide the internal audit director as the primary contact for the peer review team.
- Provide adequate working space, necessary office supplies and equipment (i.e., printer, copier, and facsimile machine), and access to phones and incidental office supplies to the review team.
- Provide complete and timely responses to team inquiries.
- Fully cooperate with the review team including providing all documents referenced in the *Peer Review Program Guidelines*.
- Reimburse all travel expenses incurred, including transportation, lodging, and per diem (in accordance with the policies/procedures of the requesting agency/university).
- Provide a timely, constructive response to the draft report (including a corrective action plan, if necessary).
- Provide the review team unrestricted access to all audit staff.
- Allow the peer review committee or council to resolve any disputes related to the outcome of the peer review and abide by the resolution of these groups.
- Hold the council of internal auditing, the office of internal audit, the peer review committee, the team leader, and the team members harmless for any damage or liability occurring by the performance or nonperformance of activities in association with this peer review.

Figure 7.4 A3: Memorandum of Understanding sample.   (*Continued*)

The Team Leader agrees to

- Certify that he or she is qualified to perform as a team leader.
- Perform the assigned external review in accordance with the *Peer Review Program Guidelines* and the *Institute of Internal Auditors Quality Assessment Manual*.
- **Any audit engagement outsourced to a contractor hired from the State Term Contract 961A Supplemental Staff Internal Audit MUST be included for review during this process.**
- Direct and supervise the work of the team member(s) assigned to the peer review.
- Ensure that all impairments or appearances of impairments are reported to the OIA prior to the commencement of audit work.
- Obtain assurance from his/her agency/university to allow the team leader to work on the peer review on a continuous basis until the assignment is complete and the final report is issued to *Requesting Agency/University Name*.
- Maintain confidentiality of information obtained during this process or conclusions draw from the review. This information will only be discussed when appropriate with the requesting agency, OIA, committee, or council.

The Team Member(s) agrees to

- Certify that he or she is qualified to perform as a team member.
- Perform the assigned external review in accordance with the *Peer Review Program Guidelines* and the *Institute of Internal Auditors Quality Assessment Manual* under the direction of the team leader.
- Complete the assigned activities and submit the work papers to the team leader for review in a timely manner.
- Ensure that all impairments or appearance of impairments are reported to the OIA prior to the commencement of audit work.
- Obtain assurance from his/her agency/university to allow the team member to work on the peer review on a continuous basis until the assignment is complete and the final report is issued to *Requesting Agency/University Name*.
- Maintain confidentiality of information obtained during this process or conclusions draw from the review. This information should only be discussed when appropriate with the requesting agency, peer review team, OIA, or council.

The OSBM OIA will

- Ensure that all impairments or appearances of impairments are reported prior to the commencement of audit work.
- Assist the peer review team and the *Requesting Agency/University Name* with any questions they have on the peer review program process in a timely manner.
- Provide technical assistance to the team when needed.
- Maintain the original work papers and a final copy of the peer review report.

The Peer Review Committee will

- Review the external review documentation and resolve discrepancies on an as-needed basis as requested by the Team Leader or the Director of Internal Auditing for *Requesting Agency/University Name*.
- Maintain confidentiality of information obtained during this process or conclusions draw from the review. This information will only be discussed when appropriate with the requesting agency, OIA, committee, or council.

The council of internal auditing will

- Review the external review documentation and resolve discrepancies on an as-needed basis as requested by the peer review committee and the office of internal audit.

Figure 7.4 (Continued)   A3: Memorandum of Understanding sample.   (*Continued*)

The peer review team will conduct the review with due regard for any applicable professional ethics, including the requirements of confidentiality, and no information will be divulged by quality assessment (QA) team members to anyone not associated with the peer review. The restrictions on the disclosure of information shall not apply to any information that is required to be disclosed by law. Questions regarding this agreement should be directed to the OIA.

Director of Internal Audit:

_____

Signature   Date

_____

Printed Name & Title

Team Leader:

_____

Signature   Date

_____

Printed Name & Title

Office of Internal Audit:

_____

Signature   Date

Barbara Baldwin, Internal Audit Director and Assistant State Budget Officers, OSBM
_____
Printed Name & Title

Team Member:

_____

Signature   Date

_____

Printed Name & Title

Figure 7.4 (Continued) **A3: Memorandum of Understanding sample. (From State of North Carolina, Council of Internal Auditing, Office of Internal Audit, Peer Review Program, Memorandum of Understanding Sample [Form A3].)**

7.11.1.4 A4: Statement of Independence—Reviewer (Figure 7.5)

This form is intended to document the independence and willingness to conduct the review in accordance with the IIA *Code of Ethics, Standards for the Professional Practice of Internal Auditing* (Standards), and the OIA *Peer Review Program Guidelines*. This statement should be completed by each member of the peer review team.

Peer Review Information

Internal Audit Function under Review   <u>Department of Revenue</u>

Peer Reviewer Name   _____

Peer Reviewer Title   _____

Peer Reviewer Agency   _____

Statement of Independence

☐ **By checking this box, I confirm the following:**

1. I am a qualified Peer Reviewer in accordance with the IIA Standards and the OIA Peer Review Program or have received training to perform peer reviews or have experience conducting peer reviews.

2. I have no personal impairments that might cause me to limit the extent of the inquiry, limit disclosure, or weaken or slant findings in any way.

3. As required by Section 1312 of IIA Standards, I am not aware of any possible impairment to my independence, in fact or appearance, in conducting the review.

4. As required by Section III-D of the Council's Peer Review Program Manual, I am not aware of any possible impairment to my independence, in fact or appearance, in conducting the review.

5. I agree to perform the review under the direction of the Office of Internal Audit and the Peer Review Committee in accordance with the Office of Internal Audit *Peer Review Program Guidelines.*

Signed:_____   Date:_____

Figure 7.5   A4: Statement of Independence—Reviewer. (Adapted from State of North Carolina, Council of Internal Auditing, Office of Internal Audit, Peer Review Program, Statement of Independence—Reviewer [Form A4].)

7.11.1.5 A5: Statement of Independence—Mediator (Figure 7.6)

This form is intended to document the independence and willingness to conduct dispute resolution services in accordance with the policies and procedures in the OIA *Peer Review Program Guidelines* Section IIB.

Mediator Information

Mediator Name   _____

Mediator Title   _____

Mediator's Agency   _____

Peer Review Team Information

Peer Review Lead Name   _____

Peer Reviewer Lead Title   _____

Peer Reviewer Lead's Agency   _____

Peer Review Member Name   _____

Peer Reviewer Member Title   _____

Peer Reviewer Member's Agency   _____

Internal Audit Function Under Review

Internal Audit Function under Review   _____

Internal Audit Director   _____

Statement of Independence

☐ **By checking this box, I confirm the following:**

1. I have read and understand the policy and procedures delineated in the OIA Peer Review Program Section II-B.
2. I am a qualified to mediate since I have received training to perform peer reviews or have experience conducting or receiving a peer reviews.
3. I have no personal or professional impairments that might cause me to limit the extent of the inquiry, limit disclosure, or weaken or slant my decision in any way.
4. As required by Section 1312 of IIA Standards, I am not aware of any possible impairment to my independence, in fact or appearance, in conducting the dispute resolution.
5. As required by Section III-D of the Council's Peer Review Program Manual, I am not aware of any possible impairment to my independence, in fact or appearance, in conducting the dispute resolution.
6. I agree to perform the dispute resolution in accordance with the Office of Internal Audit *Peer Review Program Guidelines.*

Signed:_____   Date:_____

Figure 7.6 A5: Statement of Independence—Mediator. (Adapted from State of North Carolina, Council of Internal Auditing, Office of Internal Audit, Peer Review Program, Statement of Independence—Mediator [Form A5].)

7.11.1.6 A6: Planning Questionnaire (Table 7.1)

The purpose of the planning questionnaire is to obtain general information about the internal audit to be reviewed. This can be likened to a self-assessment form for internal audit planning in Chapter 6. This questionnaire covers what would be a standard internal audit charter.

Table 7.1   A6: Planning Questionnaire

Background Information	*Governance*	*Staff*	*Management*	*Process*
1. Briefly describe the structure and major activities of your state agency (**Attachment 1**).				
2. Provide the following summary information about your state agency:				
Approximate number of employees in the state agency you audit				
Current year budget for the state agency you audit				
Internal Audit (IA) Function				
3. Give a brief history of the IA function, including when it was started, any change(s) of internal audit directors during the past 10 years, an indication of its growth in the past 10 years, and significant changes in its lines of reporting, authority, scope of work, and internal organization. Comment on how these changes have enhanced the IA function's effectiveness (**Attachment 2**).				
4. Name and title of the person to whom the internal audit director administratively reports (name and title):				
5. Name and title of the person to whom the internal audit director functionally reports (name and title):				
6. Name and address of the chair of the audit committee, or other board/commission member(s) with oversight of the IA function:				
7. Name of the state agency's external auditor:				
GOVERNANCE				
Internal Audit Practice Environment (Support, Authority, and Scope)				

(Continued)

Table 7.1 (Continued) A6: Planning Questionnaire

Background Information	Governance	Staff	Management	Process
8. Attach the state agency organization chart showing placement of the IA function. Comment as to whether or not this is the optimum placement of the department to ensure independence, access to appropriate executives, ease of communication, support, and resources. Comment on any proposed or potential enhancements in these areas (**Attachment 3**).	1110			
9. Attach a copy of the IA function's charter or a similar authority's document. Comment on how the IA function's charter fosters the independence, access, resources, etc., necessary to the effective functioning of the IA function. Mention any proposed or potential enhancements to the IA function's charter (**Attachment 4**).	1000			
10. Provide a copy of the IA function policy and procedures manual electronically. If you do not have it electronically, please provide the table of contents. Provide any explanatory comments or future plans (**Attachment 5**).			2040	

(*Continued*)

Table 7.1 (Continued) A6: Planning Questionnaire

Background Information	Governance	Staff	Management	Process
11. Does the IA function have full access to all areas of the state agency? If no, describe restrictions on the IA function regarding access to information considered necessary to conduct audits and consulting engagements or access to relevant managers and employees. Yes/No (**Attachment 6**).	1130			
12. Describe the procedures to ensure that the IA function's staff are objective (e.g., conflict of interest statements, auditor rotation, etc.); describe the procedure for reporting conflicts of interest or bias to the internal audit director and subsequently dealing with them (**Attachment 7**).		1100 1110 1120 1130		
13. Describe the philosophy of the IA function, its core values, and mission/ goals/objectives for serving its customers (**Attachment 8**).				
14. Describe the objectives against which the IA function's periodically measures its performance and describe how management evaluates the performance of the IA function (**Attachment 9**).		1300 1310 1311 1312		

(Continued)

Table 7.1 (Continued)   A6: Planning Questionnaire

Background Information	Governance	Staff	Management	Process
15. List the IA function's additional best practices and indicate how these practices enhance the IA function's effectiveness. Comment on any proposed or potential additional practices that would add further value or enhance effectiveness. If there are such practices that the IA function is not planning to implement (or if it is prevented from doing so), discuss the related reasons and the potential impact of the decisions not to implement them **(Attachment 10).**	1000 1300			
16. List other oversight/monitoring units outside the IA function; describe their authority, scope, and functions (e.g., safety, environment, evaluation, security, investigations, process improvement, and other compliance/consulting activities). Describe (a) how their separation from the IA function impacts their overall effectiveness; (b) how they relate to senior management, the board, and other governance responsibilities and accountabilities; (c) how the separation impacts risk management, management control, efficiency, or resource utilization; and (d) comment on the potential for combining (any of) these functions and whether or not this is planned in the near future **(Attachment 11).**			2110 2130	

(*Continued*)

Table 7.1 (Continued)   A6: Planning Questionnaire

Background Information	Governance	Staff	Management	Process
17. Briefly describe (and be prepared to furnish documentation and discuss further during the on-site visit) the IA function's quality improvement processes, including internal quality assessments, benchmarking, measurement criteria, empowerment policies, and accountability mechanisms **(Attachment 12).**	1311 1312 1320			
STAFF				
18. Provide a list of the IA function's staff, classified by staff level and type, along with an indication of time in the IA function and prior experience **(Attachment 13).** Have available for later review the IA function's organization chart, job descriptions, records showing skills requirements, staff qualifications, sources of staff, unfilled positions, use of outside services, recent turnover, and outplacement of staff.	1210			
19. Describe the IA function's staff development policies and programs, including use of the IA function as a part of management training in the state agency and other staff rotation programs **(Attachment 14).** Have available for later review information on internal and external staff training courses, staff performance appraisal and career planning, staff surveys, and related records.	1230			

(Continued)

Table 7.1 (Continued) A6: Planning Questionnaire

Background Information	Governance	Staff	Management	Process
20. Briefly describe (and have detailed information available for later review) the IA function's planning, administration, supervision, communicating results, and follow-up of remedial implementation for individual assurance and consulting engagements (**Attachment 15**).		1210		2410 2500
MANAGEMENT				
Risk Management, Governance, Accountability, and Oversight				
21. Describe the process to identify, measure, and manage enterprise risks in your state agency; list the most significant risks that have been identified (**Attachment 16**).			2120	
22. Describe the regulatory constraints that affect the IA function with emphasis on recently enacted legislations or regulations (**Attachment 17**).	1100 1120			
23. Describe how strategies are selected in your state agency; how objectives are established, measured, and reported; and indicate how managers are held accountable for achievement for their assigned objectives (**Attachment 18**).			2110	
24. Attach a copy of the policy for controlling your state agency (e.g., management control policies, delegations of authority, accountabilities, etc.). Comment on any planned or potential changes (**Attachment 19**).			2130	

(*Continued*)

Table 7.1 (Continued) A6: Planning Questionnaire

Background Information	Governance	Staff	Management	Process
25. Describe the extent to which the IA function's priorities, scope of work, and use of resources are aligned with your state agency's enterprise risk management framework; describe how the IA function contributes to achievement of the goals. Comment on potential or planned changes to the IA function's priorities, scope, or use of resources to enhance that alignment **(Attachment 20)**.			2000 2030	
26. Attach a copy of the audit committee's charter, or similar document relating to board oversight of the IA function and other monitoring functions in the state agency. Comment as to the extent to which this current audit committee charter gives the audit committee adequate authority, scope, resources, information, and access to management to discharge its responsibilities. Comment on any proposed or potential enhancements to the audit committee's current charter **(Attachment 21)**.			2060	
Relationship of the Internal Audit Office with Senior Management				
27. Describe interactions of the internal audit director and senior management: involvement in management meetings for strategic and technology planning, periodic management briefings, etc. **(Attachment 22)**.	1110		2060	

(Continued)

Table 7.1 (Continued)   A6: Planning Questionnaire

Background Information	Governance	Staff	Management	Process
28. Describe how senior management and the board (audit committee) are kept informed about the work of the IA function (**Attachment 23**). Include how often the internal audit director is scheduled to meet with them, who attends such meetings, what is typically discussed, how often senior management and the board receive status reports, etc. Comment on any additional formal or informal contacts.			2060	
Management of the Internal Audit Office				
29. Provide a brief description of risk assessment and engagement planning (**Attachment 24**). Discuss how the IA function's assurance/consulting universe is determined, and how the planning considers:			2010 2030	
a. Alignment of the IA function's risk assessment and engagement planning with the state agency's strategic plans, objectives, and enterprise risk framework.				
b. Technology plans, current systems, those under development, and technology management issues.				
c. The management control environment and accountability processes.				
d. Management input regarding their plans, concerns, priorities, etc.				
e. Potential partnering opportunities and other value-adding activities.				
f. Staffing numbers/skills needed, along with opportunities to leverage IA resources through empowerment, joint efforts with customers, selective outsourcing, fostering self-assessment, etc.				

(*Continued*)

Table 7.1 (Continued)   A6: Planning Questionnaire

Background Information	Governance	Staff	Management	Process
g. Long-range engagement planning to achieve appropriate coverage of the IA function's universe.				
30. Provide a copy of the following:				
a. The engagement plan versus actual for the current period, including engagements currently in progress and details of engagements completed and reports issued (**Attachment 25**).				
b. The engagement plan versus actual for the prior period, including details of engagements completed and reports issued (**Attachment 26**).				
c. The IA function's financial budget versus actual for the current period (**Attachment 27**).				
d. The IA function's financial budget versus actual for the prior period (**Attachment 28**).				
e. (*Note:* These reports should be available as part of the IA function's management information and its reports to senior management and the board. They should include information on the type of engagement, customer name, staff assigned, time budgets, starting, completion, and report issuance dates, etc. If this is not the case, the IA function should not prepare them especially for this assessment project, but should have the relevant information available in a form that can be reviewed readily on site by the external assessment team.)	2060			
31. Show the percentage of the IA function's staff time and contract (outsourced) services applied to each of the following types of assurance and consulting activities (*Note:* If the IA function's timekeeping system does not facilitate classifying time in this manner, provide a rough estimate and also show a separate breakdown based on the IA function's system. The IA function's timekeeping/time management system will be reviewed during the peer review team's on-site visit.):	2030			

(*Continued*)

Table 7.1 (Continued)   A6: Planning Questionnaire

Background Information	Governance	Staff	Management	Process
	Percentage			
Results of operations, programs, or projects, including accomplishment of objectives and effective use of resources:				
Reliability and integrity of financial and operating information:				
Compliance with policies, laws, regulations, and ethical standards:				
The means to safeguard assets, loss prevention, and fraud detection:				
Management of technology and information systems audits:				
Process improvement and related consulting activities:				
Other productive time (describe):				
Training, vacations, illness, general management, and other *unassigned*				
Total				
32. Describe the relationship between the IA function and the state agency's external auditors, covering coordination of audit work, reciprocal review of audit universe and annual plans, reliance placed on the work of the IA function, loaning or exchange of staff, joint training, joint engagements, compatibility of methodologies and tools, sharing of reports, and remedial implementation follow-up **(Attachment 29).**			2050	

Source: State of North Carolina, Council of Internal Auditing, Office of Internal Audit, Peer Review Program, Planning Questionnaire (Form A6).

7.11.1.7 A7: Peer Review Program Checklist (Table 7.2)

As in the case of Internal Audit, the QAR (Peer Review) Program Checklist of consists of a detailed schedule of plan of the work to be performed and includes the steps required to achieve review objectives. It consists of the Planning Phase, the Fieldwork (Conducting) Phase, and the Concluding (Report) Phase.

Table 7.2   A7: Peer Review Program Checklist

Work Program
Agency: _____
Review Period: _____
Review Planning Document The team lead is responsible for developing a review planning document (typically known as a work program). The purpose of this document is to outline each step that must be completed and the tentative time frame for completion. It is highly recommended that this document be used; however, it is optional, and the team lead can create a review planning document. The team lead should review this document and make appropriate modifications. The column labeled *Due Date* includes tentative time frames and should be modified to reflect the actual due date. The *Done* column denotes when a step is complete. This column may include a check mark for completion, the date completed, or the initials for the individual that completed the work. The *W/P Reference* column should clearly identify where this item can be found in the work papers. The team lead should determine the schematics for work paper numbering. If the step is not applicable, the W/P Reference should denote NA.
A. Planning Phase
This section of the work program serves as a guide to ensure that essential steps are completed before the team arrives at the offices of the internal audit organization (hereafter *the organization*). Throughout the preliminary phase, the team leader should emphasize to all team members that advance preparation facilitates the fieldwork portion of the review. This phase generally begins two to three months before the start of fieldwork. Obtain and review the most applicable version of the IIA *Quality Assurance Review Manual* and the OIA *Peer Review Manual.* Pay particular attention to policies and procedures and the documents to be used for review of all audits. At least two weeks prior to the on-site work, the peer review team lead finalizes the peer review plan. This includes identifying individuals for interviews, scheduling interviews, and selecting a sample of engagements for review. The peer review team coordinates on-site work with the internal audit director, including contacts with state agency management and board members. In addition, the team lead prepares and copies necessary paperwork for the site visit.

(Continued)

Table 7.2 (Continued)   A7: Peer Review Program Checklist

	Work Program Agency: _____ Review Period: _____			
1	Execute Memorandum of Understanding (A3). The internal audit director and team lead work out the logistic of the review.	Ten weeks prior on-site to visit		
2	Complete the Statement of Independence and submit to OIA (A4).	Ten weeks prior on-site to visit		
3	Review prior review QAR report and working papers. (NA if there are no prior peer reviews.)	Ten weeks prior on-site to visit		
4	Obtain and review the OIA *Peer Review Manual* and all forms and tools in a word document form from the OIA office.	Ten weeks prior on-site to visit		
5	Obtain and review the most recent IIA *Quality Assurance Review Manual* (optional but may be useful).	Ten weeks prior on-site to visit		
6	Review the Institute of Internal Auditors (IIA) *International Standards for the Professional Practice of Internal Auditing* (Standards) and *Code of Ethics*.	Ten weeks prior on-site to visit		
7	Contact the organization to obtain the Planning Questionnaire (A6).	Ten weeks prior on-site to visit		
	a. Review all information within the Planning Questionnaire. Ensure it contains all required elements.			
	b. Obtain (electronically, if possible) the organization's policies and procedures manual(s) (for use by team members; not for inclusion in the working papers).			

(*Continued*)

Table 7.2 (Continued)   A7: Peer Review Program Checklist

		Work Program Agency: _____ Review Period: _____			
8	Distribute the data obtained in step 7 to the team members once received from the internal audit director.	Ten weeks prior on-site to visit			
9	Assess the size, adequacy, and experience of the review team. Every effort should be made to ensure that the experience of the review team, as a whole, matches the types of engagements performed by the organization. Consult with OIA staff about any necessary additions, deletions, or substitutions.	Ten weeks prior on-site to visit			
10	Coordinate with the internal audit director a preliminary meeting, which may be via conference call or in person:	Eight weeks prior to on-site visit			
	a. Introduce the internal audit staff members and peer review team members.				
	b. Discuss the review process including sending out surveys.				
	c. Confirm the review period.				

	d. Request a list of names and contact information of:
	    i. State agency managers who have been involved in internal audits during the time period being reviewed from the internal audit director
	    ii. Internal audit staff names and contact information
	    iii. Individuals the internal audit director reports to functionally and administratively				

(Continued)

Table 7.2 (Continued)   A7: Peer Review Program Checklist

		Work Program Agency: _____ Review Period: _____		
	e. Request a list of all internal audits completed during the selected review period.			
	f. Discuss the process for selecting a representative sample of audit working papers to be reviewed.			
	g. Familiarize the team members with the policies and procedures of the internal audit function.			
	h. Select or confirm the date for on-site visit.			
	i. Discuss office space for the team members.			
	j. Discuss parking for the team members.			
	k. Discuss reporting requirements (Opinion Report, Letter of Comments, due date, number of copies, and distribution).			
	l. Discuss travel arrangements with the internal audit director and determine how internal audit director wants expenses submitted.			
11	Immediately following the preliminary meeting, obtain from the internal audit director the following:	Eight weeks prior to on-site visit		
	a. A list of names and contact information for all of the state agency managers who have been involved in internal audits during the time period being reviewed from the internal audit director			

(Continued)

Table 7.2 (Continued)   A7: Peer Review Program Checklist

		Work Program Agency: _____ Review Period: _____			
	b. A list of all internal audit staff names and contact information				
	c. A list of individuals the internal audit director reports to functionally and administratively				
	d. A list of all internal audits completed during the selected review period				
12	Request the internal audit director to send an e-mail notification to the individuals listed in 11.a, 11.b, and 11.c above, that a peer review is occurring and that they may be contacted to complete an electronic survey or for an interview.	Seven weeks prior to on-site visit			
13	a. Determine who will receive the surveys and notify the program development officer with the OIA to establish links for surveys using B1, B2b, and B3b.	Six weeks prior to on-site visit			
	b. At least six weeks prior to the on-site visits, send link for surveys to the internal audit director, internal audit staff, and clients via e-mail. Be sure to CC the OIA program development officer.				
14	Request survey responses received from the program development officer with the OIA.	Four weeks prior to on-site visit			
	a. Compile survey responses and analyze results. Summarize comments, as appropriate, editing them to maintain anonymity of staff (B4).				

(Continued)

Table 7.2 (Continued)   A7: Peer Review Program Checklist

		Work Program Agency: _____ Review Period: _____			
	b. Note, by standard, on the Observations and Issues Worksheet (E1), the potential weaknesses in the organization's quality control system or noncompliance with professional standards reported by staff.				
	c. Distribute the results of the survey analysis and any comments made on the Observations and Issues Worksheet to team members.				
15	Engagement selection and summary of audit coverage.	Three to five weeks prior to on-site visit			
	a. Utilizing the listing of engagements and based on risk and other relevant factors, select the engagements to be reviewed by the team. Identify which engagement(s) will be selected on-site, but do not identify them to the organization at this time. The review team will select an additional engagement after arriving on site as a check to see if working paper changes are made by the audit organization before the review is performed.				
	b. Document the engagements selected for testing (D7). Include the following: 1) name of engagement, 2) report date, 3) audit hours, and 4) audit hours covered as a percentage of total audit hours in the review period.				

(Continued)

Table 7.2 (Continued)   A7: Peer Review Program Checklist

		Work Program Agency: _____ Review Period: _____		
	c. Document team assignments for all engagements tested (D7).			
16	Notify internal audit director of engagements selected for review. Discuss and document conversations with organization personnel concerning the engagements selected to ensure that working papers will be on hand and audit personnel will be available to answer questions during the field review.	Two to three weeks prior to on-site visit		
17	Provide the following documents to team members at least one month in advance of the on-site review, and document that action in the working papers:	Four weeks prior to on-site visit		
	a. Organization's policies and procedure manual(s)			
	b. Completed Planning Questionnaire (A6)			
	c. Reports for engagements selected for review. (If the reports are not yet completed or if they are not available on-line, ask the organization to send the reports to the appropriate team member as soon as possible.)			
18	Finalize the peer review plan.	Two weeks prior to on-site visit		
	a. Distribute assignments to team members and all appropriate document related to these assignments.			

(Continued)

Table 7.2 (Continued) A7: Peer Review Program Checklist

		Work Program *Agency:* _____ *Review Period:* _____			
	b. Explain how you want team members to prepare questionnaires and working papers. Working papers should be indexed in accordance with the working paper references identified in this program.				
	c. Explain how you want team members to document 1) deficiencies or deviations identified during the review that could be significant with respect to the organization's quality control system, or 2) other matters for further consideration.				
19	Contact state agency individuals to schedule interviews. (The team lead or IA director can schedule the interviews.)	Two weeks prior to on-site visit			
B. Fieldwork Stage					
The on-site work is the most comprehensive part of the peer review. The work is usually conducted for a period of one week, depending on the scope of the work, and involves the review of the internal audit function including audits and consulting engagements; reports and supporting documentation; administrative and operating policies, procedures, and records; staffing knowledge and skills; evaluation of the capabilities and adequacy of the audit coverage in information technology areas; risk assessment; controls monitoring; interaction with governance participants; best practices; and other evidence of continuous improvement. All this work should be completed on-site. On-site visits are typically one week. For large entity with several engagements being reviewed, more time may be needed. The team lead should assign due dates for each step.					
1	Hold an entrance conference with the internal audit director to discuss the on-site process.				

(*Continued*)

Table 7.2 (Continued)   A7: Peer Review Program Checklist

	Work Program Agency: _____ Review Period: _____			
2	Evaluate whether or not the internal audit office reports to a level within the agency/university that allows the internal audit activity to accomplish its responsibilities, maintains effective audit committee relationships, and maintains a quality assurance and improvement program that covers all aspects of the internal audit activity and continuously monitors its effectiveness. Complete the Governance Program Section (D1). Findings and conclusions should be documented on the Observations and Issues Worksheet (E1).			
3	Evaluate whether the recruitment, development, and assignment of the right mix of staff skills achieves the internal audit activity's mission/goals. When evaluating competencies, the reviewer should refer to the applicable practice advisories published by the IIA. Complete the Staff Program Section (D2). Findings and conclusions should be documented on the Observations and Issues Worksheet (E1).			

(Continued)

Table 7.2 (Continued)   A7: Peer Review Program Checklist

	Work Program Agency: _____ Review Period: _____			
4	Evaluate activity reports and determine how the IA activity monitored program accomplishments and added value to the agency/university. Complete the Management Program Section (D3). Findings and conclusions should be documented on the Observations and Issues Worksheet (E1).			
5	Evaluate whether the internal audit activity's planning process considered the agency/university's enterprise risk framework, management control environment, and accountability processes, as well as the agency/university's strategic and technology plans and significant business activities to arrive at the annual and longer-term plan.			
	The risk assessment and planning process should involve four stages: risk assessment, audit plans, staff analysis, and budgeting. The following procedures and considerations will guide the team through the most important aspects of managing an IA activity. Complete the Process Program Section (D4). Findings and conclusions should be documented on the Observations and Issues Worksheet (E1).			

(Continued)

Table 7.2 (Continued)   A7: Peer Review Program Checklist

	Work Program Agency: _____ Review Period: _____			
6	Review and evaluate the IT audit processes/activities in the following key result areas: risk identification, audit coverage, staff expertise/training, prospective risk-based auditing focus, and use of CAATs (computer-assisted audit tools). Complete IT Procedures Program Section (D5). Findings and conclusions should be documented on the Observations and Issues Worksheet (E1).			
7	Develop interview questions and conduct interviews with the following:			
	a. Executive to whom the IA director reports (C2)			
	b. A sample of agency managers who received audits or consulting engagements during the time period begin reviewed (C3)			
	c. A sample of board members, preferably including the chair and an audit committee representative (C1)			
	d. Director of internal audit (C5)			
	e. Internal audit staff (C6).			
	f. External auditors, if relevant and cost-effective (C7).			

(Continued)

Table 7.2 (Continued)   A7: Peer Review Program Checklist

		Work Program Agency: _____ Review Period: _____			
8	Document the individual interview results. Summarize all of the interview results using the Summary Form for Interview Results (C8). Findings and conclusions should be documented on the Observations and Issues Worksheet (E1).				
9	Ensure that team members obtain and evaluate working papers and reports of audit engagements selected for review using the Work Paper Review (D6) for each engagement selected for review. Findings and conclusions should be documented on the Observations and Issues Worksheet (E1).				
10	Monitor the review process and document the following in the working papers, as appropriate:				
	a. Review the progress of team members on a continuing basis and provide necessary assistance. Review documents completed by team members.				
	b. Consider the need to modify the standard work program or the general approach to the review.				

(Continued)

Table 7.2 (Continued)   A7: Peer Review Program Checklist

		Work Program Agency: _____ Review Period: _____			
	c. Consult with the OIA director in any of the following situations:				
		1. A *does not conform* rating is being considered.			
		2. The review may be discontinued before completion.			
		3. Major difficulties are encountered or circumstances appear to indicate a significant departure from established guidelines.			
11	As team members complete the on-site work, any observations and issues realized through the peer review process are recorded on the Observations and Issues Worksheet. In the end, each member of the review team completes the Conformance with Standards—Master Framework (E2—Part IV) to help determine the overall level of compliance for the internal audit function being reviewed. The team lead should review all Conformance with Standards—Master Framework (E2—Part IV) completed by each team member and consolidate the evaluation to the Standards Conformance Evaluation Summary document (E2—Part III).				

(*Continued*)

Table 7.2 (Continued)   A7: Peer Review Program Checklist

<table>
<tr><td colspan="5">*Work Program*
Agency: _____
Review Period: _____</td></tr>
<tr><td>12</td><td>Gather team members to discuss overall results and issues and recommendations gathered during the on-site work.</td><td></td><td></td><td></td></tr>
<tr><td></td><td>a. Summarize the issues and recommendations for the closing conference.</td><td></td><td></td><td></td></tr>
<tr><td></td><td>b. Evaluate results of review and determine final overall ratings based on the peer review the work conducted.</td><td></td><td></td><td></td></tr>
<tr><td>13</td><td>Conduct closing conference. The purpose of the closing conference is to share the findings/recommendations, Conformance Evaluation Summary document (E2—Part III) and obtain any responses to the recommendations.</td><td></td><td></td><td></td></tr>
</table>

C. Conclusion Phase

The conclusion phase is completed at the review team's office and comprises the final steps to close the review. The team lead ensures that all steps have been completed adequately, the report has been drafted, and the internal audit director's response has been included in the final report. The review team and internal audit director will respond to survey that will aid in the improvement of the peer review program.

	Procedures	Due Date	Done	W/P Reference
1	Following completion of the on-site work and closing conference, draft the final report. Provide the draft report to the internal audit director for response. The internal audit director has two weeks to respond.	Two weeks after on-site visit		

(Continued)

Table 7.2 (Continued)   A7: Peer Review Program Checklist

	Work Program *Agency: _____* *Review Period: _____*			
2	Provide the working papers to the OIA Director for a quality review.	One week after draft report completed		
3	Once written comments are received back from the internal audit director, incorporate the comments into the report, obtain signatures of the Team members, and issue the final report.	One day after responses received		
4	Submit final report and original work papers to OIA office.	One week after final report issued		
5	To close out the peer review process, complete the *Peer Review Survey.* All team members and the internal audit staff participating in the peer review process should complete the QAR Process Survey (E5) and submit it to the OIA Office. The internal audit director receiving the peer review should complete the Client Satisfaction Survey (E6) and submit it to the OIA Office.	One week after work paper submitted		

Source: State of North Carolina, Council of Internal Auditing, Office of Internal Audit, Peer Review Program, Peer Review Program Checklist (Form A7).

7.11.1.8 A8: Self-Assessment Checklist (Table 7.3)

The purpose of quality assurance reviews (internal and external) is to understand how an internal audit function is conforming, or not conforming, to the IIA Standards. This document contains a sample checklist of questions to consider when conducting an *internal self-assessment.* This is *not* a requirement of the peer review program, but is to aid internal audit directors with positioning their function for a peer review.

Table 7.3   A8: Self-Assessment Checklist

Standard	*Questions to Consider*
1000	• Does the internal audit charter document the expectation that auditors will conform to the IIA code of ethics? • Does your internal audit policy and procedure document specify that all internal audit personnel must abide by the code of ethics? • Is the nature of assurance services defined in the audit charter? • If assurances are provided to parties outside the organization, is the nature of these assurances also defined in the charter? • Is the nature of consulting services defined in the audit charter? • Are the purpose, authority, and responsibility of the internal audit activity formally defined in a charter consistent with the Standards, and approved by the board or appropriate agency authority?
1100	• Does the auditor overseeing audit activities report to a level within the state agency that allows the internal audit function to fulfill its responsibilities? • Is the internal audit activity free from interference in determining the scope of internal auditing, performing work, and communicating results?
1120	• Do the internal auditors have an impartial, unbiased attitude and avoid conflicts of interest?
1130	• If independence or objectivity is impaired in fact or appearance, are the details of the impairment disclosed to appropriate parties? (The nature of the disclosure will depend on the impairment.) • Do the internal auditors refrain from assessing specific operations for which they were previously responsible within the previous year? • Does a party outside the internal audit function oversee assurance services over functions for which the internal audit director has been responsible? • If internal auditors provide consulting services relating to operations for which they had previous responsibilities, are potential impairments to independence or objectivity disclosed to the client prior to performing consulting services?

(Continued)

Table 7.3 (Continued)   A8: Self-Assessment Checklist

Standard	Questions to Consider
1210	• Do internal auditors possess the knowledge, skills, and other competencies needed to perform their individual responsibilities? • Does the internal audit function collectively possess or obtain the knowledge, skills, and other competencies needed to perform its responsibilities? • Does the internal audit director obtain competent advice and assistance if the internal audit staff lack the knowledge, skills, or other competencies needed to perform all or part of the engagement? • Do the internal auditors have sufficient knowledge to identify the indicators of fraud? (*Note:* Internal auditors are not expected to have the expertise of a person whose primary responsibility is detecting and investigating fraud.) • Do the internal auditors have knowledge of key information technology risks and controls and available technology-based audit techniques to perform their assigned work? (*Note:* Not all internal auditors are expected to have the expertise of an internal auditor whose primary responsibility is information technology auditing.) • Does the internal audit director decline the consulting engagement or obtain competent advice and assistance if the internal audit staff lack the knowledge, skills, or other competencies needed to perform all or part of the engagement?

1220	• Do the internal auditors apply the care and skill expected of a reasonably prudent and competent internal auditor? (*Note:* Due professional care does not imply infallibility.)
	• Do the internal auditors exercise due professional care by considering the
	  • Extent of work needed to achieve the engagement's objectives
	  • Relative complexity, materiality, or significance of matters to which assurance procedures are applied
	  • Adequacy and effectiveness of risk management, control, and governance processes
	  • Probability of significant errors, irregularities, or noncompliance
	  • Cost of assurance in relation to potential benefits
	• In exercising due professional care, does the internal auditor consider the use of computer-assisted audit tools and other data analysis techniques?

(*Continued*)

Table 7.3 (Continued)   A8: Self-Assessment Checklist

Standard	Questions to Consider

	• Are the internal auditors alert to the significant risks that might affect objectives, operations, or resources? (*Note*: Assurance procedures alone, even when performed with due professional care, do not guarantee that all significant risks will be identified.)
	 • Do the internal auditors exercise due professional care during a consulting engagement by considering the
	   • Needs and expectations of clients, including the nature, timing, and communication of engagement results?
	   • Relative complexity and extent of work needed to achieve the engagement's objectives?
	   • Cost of the consulting engagement in relation to potential benefits?

1230	• Do the internal auditors enhance their knowledge, skills, and other competencies through continuing professional development?
1310	• Does the internal audit function have a process to monitor and assess the overall effectiveness of the quality program, and does it include both internal and external assessments?

1311	• Do internal assessments include
	   • Ongoing reviews of the performance of the internal audit activity?
	   • Periodic reviews performed through self-assessment or by other persons within the state agency that have knowledge of internal audit practices and the standards?

1312	• Are external assessments, such as quality assurance reviews, conducted at least once every five years by a qualified, independent reviewer or review team from outside the state agency?
1320	• Does the internal audit director communicate the results of external assessments to the board?
1330	• Use of *Conducted in Accordance with the Standards*—Do the internal auditors report that their activities are "conducted in accordance with the *International Standards for the Professional Practice of Internal Auditing*" only if assessments of the quality improvement program demonstrate that the internal audit function is in compliance with the standards?

(*Continued*)

Table 7.3 (Continued) A8: Self-Assessment Checklist

Standard	Questions to Consider
1340	• Although the internal audit function should achieve full compliance with the standards, and internal auditors should fully comply with the code of ethics, when instances in which full compliance is not achieved impact the overall scope or operation of the internal audit function, is disclosure made to senior management and the board?
2010	• Has the internal audit director established risk-based plans to determine the priorities of the internal audit function, consistent with the state agency's goals? • Is the internal audit function's plan of engagements based on a risk assessment, undertaken at least annually, and is the input of senior management and the board considered in this process? • Does the internal audit director consider accepting proposed consulting engagements based on the engagement's potential to improve management of risks, add value, and improve the agency/university's operations? • Are engagements that have been accepted included in the plan?
2020	• Does the internal audit director communicate the internal audit activity's plans and resource requirements, including significant interim changes, to senior management and to the board for review and approval? • Has the internal audit director also communicated the impact of resource limitations?
2030	• Does the internal audit director ensure that internal audit resources are appropriate, sufficient, and effectively deployed to achieve the approved plan?
2040	• Has the internal audit director established policies and procedures to guide the internal audit activity?
2050	• Does the internal audit director share information and coordinate activities with other internal and external providers of relevant assurance and consulting services to ensure proper coverage and minimize duplication of efforts?
2060	• Does the internal audit director report periodically to the board and senior management on the internal audit function's purpose, authority, responsibility, and performance relative to its plan? • Does the reporting include significant risk exposures and control issues, corporate governance issues, and other matters needed or requested by the board and senior management?

(Continued)

Table 7.3 (Continued)   A8: Self-Assessment Checklist

Standard	Questions to Consider

2110	• Does the internal audit activity assist the state agency by identifying and evaluating significant exposures to risk and contributing to the improvement of risk management and control systems?
	• Does the internal audit function monitor and evaluate the effectiveness of the agency/university's risk management system?
	• Does the internal audit function evaluate risk exposures relating to the state agency's governance, operations, and information systems regarding the
	  • Reliability and integrity of financial and operational information
	  • Effectiveness and efficiency of operations
	  • Safeguarding of assets
	  • Compliance with laws, regulations, and contracts
	• During consulting engagements, do the internal auditors address risk consistent with the engagement's objectives, and are they alert to the existence of other significant risks?
	• Do the internal auditors incorporate their knowledge of risks gained from consulting engagements into the process of identifying and evaluating significant risk exposures of the state agency?

2120	• Does the internal audit function assist the state agency in maintaining effective controls by evaluating their effectiveness and efficiency and by promoting continuous improvement?
	• On the basis of the results of the risk assessment, does the internal audit activity evaluate the adequacy and effectiveness of controls encompassing the state agency's governance, operations, and information systems? Does this include evaluation of the
	  • Reliability and integrity of financial and operational information
	  • Effectiveness and efficiency of operations
	  • Safeguarding of assets
	  • Compliance with laws, regulations, and contracts
	• Do the internal auditors ascertain the extent to which operating and program goals and objectives have been established and conform to those of the state agency?
	• Do the internal auditors review operations and programs to ascertain the extent to which results are consistent with established goals and objectives in order to determine whether operations and programs are being implemented or performed as intended?

(Continued)

Table 7.3 (Continued)   A8: Self-Assessment Checklist

Standard	Questions to Consider
	• Do the internal auditors ascertain the extent to which management has established adequate criteria to determine whether objectives and goals have been accomplished? • If adequate, do internal auditors use such criteria in their evaluation? • If inadequate, do internal auditors work with management to develop appropriate evaluation criteria? • During consulting engagements, do internal auditors address controls consistent with the engagement's objectives, and are they alert to the existence of any significant control weaknesses? • Do the internal auditors incorporate knowledge of controls gained from consulting engagements into the process of identifying and evaluating significant risk exposures of the state agency?

2130	• Does the internal audit function assess and make appropriate recommendations for improving the governance process in its accomplishment of the following objectives:
	  • Promoting appropriate ethics and values within the state agency
	  • Ensuring effective organizational performance management and accountability
	  • Effectively communicating risk and control information to appropriate areas of the state agency
	  • Effectively coordinating the activities of and communicating information among the board, external and internal auditors, and management
	• Does the internal audit function evaluate the design, implementation, and effectiveness of the state agency's ethics-related objectives, programs, and activities?
	• Are consulting engagement objectives consistent with the overall values and goals of the state agency?

2200	• Do the internal auditors develop and record a plan for each engagement, including the scope, objectives, timing, and resource allocations?
2300	• Do the internal auditors identify, analyze, evaluate, and record sufficient information to achieve the engagement's objectives?
2400	• Do the internal auditors properly communicate the engagement results?

(Continued)

Table 7.3 (Continued)   A8: Self-Assessment Checklist

Standard	Questions to Consider
2500	• Has the internal audit director established a follow-up process to monitor and ensure that management actions have been effectively implemented or that senior management has accepted the risk of not taking action? • Does the internal audit function monitor the disposition of results of consulting engagements to the extent agreed upon with the client?
2600	• When the internal audit director believes that senior management has accepted a level of residual risk that may be unacceptable to the state agency, does the internal audit director discuss the matter with senior management? If the decision regarding residual risk is not resolved, do the internal audit director and senior management report the matter to the board for resolution?
Standard	Supporting Documentation
1000	• Internal audit (IA) charter
1100	• Organization chart • Board meeting agendas or minutes • Independence (conflict of interest) policy or statements
1200	• Job descriptions • Staff resumes (include certifications) • Staff training records • Use of outside service providers
1300	• Working paper review checklist • Performance evaluation form, example, and dates • IA goals and performance measures • IA customer feedback • Implementation status of last peer review results
2000	• Risk assessment • Annual audit plan • Department operating budget • Annual internal audit report • IA department policies and procedures • Activity reports (from staff, to board or management) • Project timekeeping system and reports • Other performance monitoring tools (budget to actual hours, project milestones) • Coordination with other audit and consulting activities

(Continued)

Table 7.3 (Continued) A8: Self-Assessment Checklist

Standard	Supporting Documentation
2100	• Agency strategic plan excerpts • Analysis of IA scope of work (strategic plan; risk, control, and governance processes) • Other audit planning documents
2200	• Engagement planning procedures (refer to section V) • Examples of audit engagement planning documentation (e.g., entrance conference notes, planning memo, plan/program) • Example of consulting engagement planning documentation
2300	• Performing the audit procedures (refer to section V) • Working paper review comments
2400	• Examples of audit engagement reporting • Examples of consulting engagement reporting • Report distribution list
2500	• Issue/recommendation follow-up tracking system • Follow-up work (refer to section V)
2600	• Memo to board

Source: State of North Carolina, Council of Internal Auditing, Office of Internal Audit, Peer Review Program, Self-Assessment Checklist (Form A8).

7.11.2 Conducting the QAR Phase

As stated earlier, this is the second phase in QAR and involves the review team conducting the review using the Quality Assurance work programs, which details the specific methods and checklists for getting evidence. The primary objective here is to find evidence to support conformance or nonconformance.

Note that according to RAA, Bhutan (n.d.), a sound system of monitoring and supervision is essential for high-quality QARs. Supervision involves directing the QA team and monitoring their work to ensure that the QA objectives are met. Supervision involves assigning responsibilities and providing sufficient guidance to team members. It also involves staying informed about significant problems encountered, reviewing the work performed, overseeing individual development, coaching, and providing periodic feedback and effective on-the-job training.

Note also that all works are reviewed by the team leader before the QA reports are finalized. This is to bring more than one level of experience and judgment in the review process and to ensure that evaluations and conclusions are based on sound work and are supported by sufficient, relevant, and reliable evidence as a foundation for the final opinion or report.

For the purpose of simplicity, we shall delineate the process into three: Survey phase, Interview phase, and Program phase.

7.11.2.1 Survey Phase

Survey is the detailed study of a market or geographical area or entity to gather data on attitudes, impressions, opinions, satisfaction level, etc. Survey phase in Peer Review involves a detailed study of the internal audit unit to extract relevant information as review evidence by the use of special forms designed for each category of the internal audit unit. Below are the various forms and categories of internal audit unit.

7.11.2.1.1 B1: Sample Survey—Internal Audit Director (Figure 7.7)

This is a survey questionnaire used to extract relevant information from the internal audit director bothering on his functions, relationship with the board and management, the IA charter, the IA management function, and other relevant activities.

Please respond in brief narrative form and with relevant attachments to the questions deemed applicable to your state agency and internal audit function.

General Information

Internal Audit Office:

Internal Audit Director:

Due Date:

Peer Review Team Lead:

A. Board and Management Oversight
1. Does the board (audit committee) get involved in the annual planning/budgeting for the internal audit (IA) activity? If so, do you consider their input adequate?
2. Are you satisfied with the method and frequency of reporting to, and meeting with, the board?
3. Is your position in the organization demonstrated through participation in strategic planning meetings, other executive gatherings, and receipt of timely communications?
4. Are you content with executive management's expectations, support, and satisfaction?

B. Charter and Audit Practice Environment
1. Does the IA charter set the tone for the mission of the IA activity and your interaction with the board (audit committee) and senior management? Do you have their formal approval?
2. Is the charter current and relevant in view of any significant changes in the organization and in the IIA's *International Standards for the Professional Practice of Internal Auditing* (Standards)?
3. Does the charter establish an adequate role, authority, and scope of work of the IA activity, and provide unrestricted access to records, information, locations, and employees?
4. Do the environment, culture, and empowerment within the IA activity promote a customer orientation by providing appropriate frequent contact, quality work, and partnering relationships?
5. Does the IA activity foster an identifiable culture of professionalism and continuous improvement?
6. Does staff exhibit an awareness and understanding of enterprise risk, corporate governance, business goals, and objectives, as well as of opportunities for service beyond traditional audit activities?
7. Does the charter define consulting activity provided by the IA activity or comment on the provision of consulting? If not, why not?

Figure 7.7   B1: Sample survey—internal audit director.   *(Continued)*

C. Planning
1. Were the organization's risk framework, strategic business plan, and technology plan all used in the planning process?
2. Was sufficient attention given to the IA activity's approach to auditing information technology?
3. Was the need for extensive and productive use of technology by the IA activity taken into account?
4. Are funding, staff mix and skills, technology, and other resources sufficient to fulfill the plan?
5. Do planned engagements include appropriate statements of risks; control objectives; compliance with policies, plans, laws, and regulations; reliability/integrity of information; safeguarding of assets; effective use of resources; and accomplishment of objectives/goals for operations/programs?

D. Organizing
1. Does your organization structure promote achievement of the IA activity's mission/goals?
2. Do your policies, procedures, and practices contribute to achieving the mission/goals?
3. Are the competency models (position descriptions), performance standards, or other means used to enunciate the expectations and accountabilities of the staff?

E. Staffing
1. Are you satisfied with the staff's understanding of your vision, goals, and objectives?
2. Do the IA activity's recruiting and development policies and practices provide the necessary numbers and skills mix, giving particular attention to information technology skills?
3. Are staff views sought and considered for management and audit policy/planning deliberations?
4. Do supervisory practices support staff members in improving their empowerment and accountability in areas such as the scope of audit coverage during the audit, rather than relying on a post-audit review?
5. Is the IA activity involved in an executive development, rotation, or similar program using IA as a management resource for the organization? If so, please explain.
6. Do your auditors comply with the IIA's Standards and code of ethics?

F. Directing and Coordinating
1. Are audit planning procedures and control assessments used to understand the organization's risks and control processes to ensure significant coverage/focus on the important business processes?
2. Does the scope of work in the individual audits satisfy the broader objectives set out in the annual planning process?
3. Are the audits of business processes designed and conducted to assess all the significant risks and controls for a value-added result for management?
4. Are issues disclosed in audit and consulting engagements reported in a timely manner?
5. Do your reports consider management's comments, and are the issues presented in a manner to best serve management, with the focus on managing risk and improving business processes?
6. Are you satisfied with the extent to which the external auditors rely on your work?

Figure 7.7 (Continued)   B1: Sample survey—internal audit director.   (*Continued*)

G. Quality/Process Improvement
1. What are the significant quality/process improvement actions currently under way or planned for the near term in the following areas:
   • Customer relations (e.g., partnering, self-assessment, and consulting on management processes)
   • Reducing audit cycle time (e.g., early and frequent customer involvement in audit planning and audit results, reduction of reporting and follow-up intervals, and streamlining audit procedures)
   • Empowerment of staff and customers (e.g., self-review and accountability, organizational flattening and reduction of supervisory time, and team auditing)
   • New technology and other enhancements to audit techniques
   • Other areas—describe other quality processes and *successful practices*
2. Describe the IA activity's internal review and quality assessment program. Has it had an external assessment? If so, how recently?

H. Other
1. Describe the types of benchmarking data from industry groups, associations, or networking groups (local, national, or global) used to measure your annual internal audit efforts.
2. Can you describe any additional successful practices currently in place within the IA activity not noted in the Successful Practices section of Tool 2?

Figure 7.7 (Continued) B1: Sample survey—internal audit director. (From State of North Carolina, Council of Internal Auditing, Office of Internal Audit, Peer Review Program, Sample Survey—Internal Audit Director [Form B1].)

7.11.2.1.2 B2a: E-Mail with Client Survey (Figure 7.8)

This is an electronic mail to the internal audit clients by QAR team leader intimating them of the proposed review and request for their full cooperation. This email also provides them a link to the survey questionnaire to answer and submit.

TO: Client
FROM: Peer Review Team Lead Name
SUBJECT: Internal Audit Survey Request

The internal audit function is undergoing a quality assessment review through the peer review program (website). The purpose of peer reviews is to assess the efficiency and effectiveness of the activity, identify opportunities and offer ideas for improving the performance of the internal audit activity, and provide an opinion as to whether the activity confirms with the *Internal Standards for the Professional Practice of Internal Auditing* (Standards). Your candid response to the survey will assist the peer review team in assessing strengths and identifying areas for improvements. Click on the link below to respond to the survey.

The internal audit director will be provided with a summary of the results, not the detailed results or the source of the comments. Feel free to contact me if you have questions or need more information.

Thank you in advance for participating in the survey,

Name of Team Leader

Figure 7.8 B2a: E-mail with client survey. (State of North Carolina, Council of Internal Auditing, Office of Internal Audit, Peer Review Program, E-mail with client survey [Form B2a].)

7.11.2.1.3 B2b: Client Survey (Table 7.4)

The overall objective of this form (B2b Client Survey) is to assess the functions of internal audit and its compliance or otherwise to standards stated in the *Internal Standards for the Professional Practice of Internal Auditing* (Standards).

Table 7.4   B2b: Client Survey

The purpose of this form is to assess the internal audit function's performance and compliance with the *Internal Standards for the Professional Practice of Internal Auditing* (Standards). Your candidness on the survey will assist the peer review team in assessing strengths and identifying areas for improvements. Thank you in advance for your help!					
Relationships with Management					
	Excellent	*Good*	*Fair*	*Poor*	*N/A*
1. Internal audit as a valued member of the management team.	○	○	○	○	○
2. Organizational placement of the internal audit activity to ensure its independence and ability to fulfill its responsibilities.	○	○	○	○	○
3. Auditors have free and unrestricted access to records, information, locations, and employees during the performance of their engagements.	○	○	○	○	○
4. The internal audit activity promotes customer orientation by providing quality work.	○	○	○	○	○
Audit Staff					
5. Objectivity of the internal auditors.	○	○	○	○	○
6. Professionalism of the internal auditors.	○	○	○	○	○
7. Technical proficiency of the internal auditors.	○	○	○	○	○
8. Knowledge of your industry/ organization/processes/success factors.	○	○	○	○	○

(Continued)

Table 7.4 (Continued)   B2b Client Survey

	Excellent	Good	Fair	Poor	N/A
9. Communication skills of the internal auditors.	○	○	○	○	○
Scope of Audit Work					
10. Selection of important areas or topics for audit.	○	○	○	○	○
11. Pre-audit notification to you of audit purpose and scope.	○	○	○	○	○
12. Inclusion of your suggestions for areas or topics to audit.	○	○	○	○	○
Audit Process and Report					
13. Feedback to you on emerging issues during audits.	○	○	○	○	○
14. Duration of the audit.	○	○	○	○	○
15. Timeliness of the audit report.	○	○	○	○	○
16. Accuracy of the audit findings.	○	○	○	○	○
17. Clarity of the audit report.	○	○	○	○	○
18. Usefulness of the audit in improving business process and controls.	○	○	○	○	○
19. Internal audit follow-up on corrective action.	○	○	○	○	○
20. Communication of results.	○	○	○	○	○
Management of the Internal Audit Activity					
21. Your understanding of the internal audit activity's purpose.	○	○	○	○	○
22. Effectiveness of internal audit management.	○	○	○	○	○
23. Quality of staff development for subsequent transfer to/from other departments.	○	○	○	○	○

Source: Adapted from State of North Carolina, Council of Internal Auditing, Office of Internal Audit, Peer Review Program, Client Survey (Form B2b).

7.11.2.1.4 B3a: E-Mail with Internal Audit Staff Survey (Figure 7.9)

This is an electronic mail to the staff of the internal audit client by the QAR team leader intimating them of the proposed review, the purpose of the review, and request for their full cooperation. This email also provides them a link to the survey questionnaire to answer and submit.

TO: Internal Audit Office Staff
FROM: Peer Review Team Lead Name
SUBJECT: Internal Audit Survey Request

As you may know, your internal audit function is undergoing a quality assessment review through the OIA peer review program. The purposes of peer reviews are to assess efficiency and effectiveness of the activity, identify opportunities and offer ideas for improving the performance of the internal audit activity, and provide an opinion as to whether the activity confirms with the *Internal Standards for the Professional Practice of Internal Auditing* (Standards).

Please find below a link for the Internal Audit Staff Survey. While we plan to conduct some individual and group interviews, we want to receive feedback from all staff. Your candid response to the survey will assist the review team in assessing strengths and identifying areas for improvement. Please submit your responses by <date>. You may choose to put your name on your response as you see fit. Without identifying specific respondents, a summary of the responses will be shared with the internal audit director.

Thank you in advance for participating in the survey,

Name of Team Leader

Figure 7.9 B3a: E-mail with internal audit staff survey. (From State of North Carolina, Council of Internal Auditing, Office of Internal Audit, Peer Review Program, E-mail with Internal Audit Staff Survey [Form B3a].)

7.11.2.1.5 B3b: Internal Audit Staff Survey (Table 7.5)

The purpose of this form is to rate the internal audit function's activity in terms of knowledge, skills, understanding, training, and experience, among others.

Table 7.5   B3b: Internal Audit Staff Survey

The purpose of this form is to rate the internal audit function's activity. Your candidness on the survey will assist the peer review team with the peer review process. Thank you in advance for your help!					
How do you rate your knowledge, skills, or understanding of the following:					
	Excellent	*Good*	*Fair*	*Poor*	*N/A*
1. Audit committee expectations	○	○	○	○	○
2. Management expectations	○	○	○	○	○
3. Understanding of corporate governance and mission	○	○	○	○	○
4. Understanding of the IA function, mission, and goals	○	○	○	○	○
5. IA function policies and procedures	○	○	○	○	○
6. Relationships with auditing customers	○	○	○	○	○
7. Internal auditing standards	○	○	○	○	○
8. Knowledge of the agency/ university operations and processes	○	○	○	○	○
9. Documentation and review of systems or processes	○	○	○	○	○
10. Evaluation of internal control	○	○	○	○	○
11. Audit risk	○	○	○	○	○
12. General auditing tools/techniques	○	○	○	○	○
13. Current technology, equipment, and software	○	○	○	○	○
14. Information technology auditing tools/techniques	○	○	○	○	○

(Continued)

Table 7.5 (Continued)   B3b: Internal Audit Staff Survey

	Excellent	Good	Fair	Poor	N/A
15. Interviewing skills	○	○	○	○	○
16. Performance audit concepts	○	○	○	○	○
17. Report writing	○	○	○	○	○
18. Communication and interpersonal skills	○	○	○	○	○
Rate whether the internal audit function has provided you with appropriate opportunities in training/experience.					
19. In-house training seminars: specific subjects	○	○	○	○	○
20. In-house training seminars: broad topics	○	○	○	○	○
21. Outside seminars: audit topics	○	○	○	○	○
22. Outside seminars: other	○	○	○	○	○

Source: Adapted from State of North Carolina, Council of Internal Auditing, Office of Internal Audit, Peer Review Program, Internal Audit Staff Survey (Form B3b).

7.11.2.1.6 B4: Survey Response Summary (Table 7.6)

The purpose of this form is to rate the internal audit function's activity in terms of knowledge, skills, understanding, training, experience, and consulting services, among others. This summary form goes to the internal audit director.

Table 7.6   B4: Survey Response Summary

How do you rate your knowledge, skills, or understanding of the following:					
Time Submitted *February 16, 2014, 9:43 PM*	Excellent	Good	Fair	Poor	N/A
1. Audit committee expectations	○	○	○	○	○
2. Management expectations	○	○	○	○	○
3. Understanding of corporate governance and mission	○	○	○	○	○

(Continued)

Table 7.6 (Continued) B4: Survey Response Summary

Time Submitted *February 16, 2014, 9:43 PM*	Excellent	Good	Fair	Poor	N/A
4. Understanding of the IA function, mission, and goals	○	○	○	○	○
5. IA function policies and procedures	○	○	○	○	○
6. Relationships with auditing customers	○	○	○	○	○
7. Internal auditing standards	○	○	○	○	○
8. Knowledge of the agency/ university operations and processes	○	○	○	○	○
9. Documentation and review of systems or processes	○	○	○	○	○
10. Evaluation of internal control	○	○	○	○	○
11. Objectivity and independence of internal auditors	○	○	○	○	○
12. Audit risk	○	○	○	○	○
13. General auditing tools/ techniques	○	○	○	○	○
14. Current technology, equipment, and software	○	○	○	○	○
15. Information technology auditing tools/techniques	○	○	○	○	○
16. Interviewing skills	○	○	○	○	○
17. Performance audit concepts	○	○	○	○	○
18. Report writing	○	○	○	○	○
19. Communication and interpersonal skills	○	○	○	○	○

(Continued)

Table 7.6 (Continued)   B4: Survey Response Summary

Time Submitted *February 16, 2014, 9:43 PM*	*Excellent*	*Good*	*Fair*	*Poor*	*N/A*
Rate whether the internal audit function has provided you with appropriate opportunities in training/experience:					
20. In-house training seminars: specific subjects	○	○	○	○	○
21. In-house training seminars: broad topics	○	○	○	○	○
22. Outside seminars: audit topics	○	○	○	○	○
23. Outside seminars: other	○	○	○	○	○
24. Receiving specific training for auditing assignments	○	○	○	○	○
25. On-the-job training	○	○	○	○	○
26. Rotation between auditing and operating departments	○	○	○	○	○
27. Membership/participation in professional organizations	○	○	○	○	○
Rate whether the IA function has provided you with appropriate opportunities to apply these practices:					
28. Ability to be objective/activity independence	○	○	○	○	○
29. Understanding/application of function's core values	○	○	○	○	○
30. Empowerment and self-accountability	○	○	○	○	○
31. Staff involvement in audit planning	○	○	○	○	○
32. Input into individual audit scope	○	○	○	○	○
33. Staff allowed to change audit objectives and procedures	○	○	○	○	○

(Continued)

Table 7.6 (Continued)   B4: Survey Response Summary

Time Submitted February 16, 2014, 9:43 PM	Excellent	Good	Fair	Poor	N/A
How would you rank the following:					
34. Consulting and partnering with management	○	○	○	○	○
35. Helpfulness of supervision to strengthen auditing work	○	○	○	○	○
36. Satisfaction with performance review process	○	○	○	○	○
37. Career satisfaction	○	○	○	○	○
1. Add any comments you may have on any of the above items.					
2. List three of the items you like most about your job.					
3. What are the three things (e.g., policies, practices, culture, resources, etc.) you would change to improve the IA activity?					
4. Additional comments:					
I request an opportunity to discuss these matters further with the review team.					

Source: Adapted from State of North Carolina, Council of Internal Auditing, Office of Internal Audit, Peer Review Program, Survey Response Summary (Form B4).

7.11.2.2 Interview Phase

The On-Site Work commences with the interview phase. This is another important phase in conducting the QAR or Peer Review process; similar to the survey phase, a questionnaire is used to extract relevant information from the respondents. However, unlike the survey phase, the answers are extracted face to face from the selected respondents.

According to NCOSBM (2014), the on-site work is the most comprehensive part of the peer review. The work is usually conducted for a period of one week, depending on the scope of the work, and involves the review of the internal audit function including

1. Audits and consulting engagements
2. Reports and supporting documentation
3. Administrative and operating policies, procedures, and records
4. Staffing knowledge and skills
5. Risk assessment
6. Controls monitoring
7. Interaction with governance participants
8. Best practices
9. Other evidence of continuous improvement

During the on-site work, the internal audit director is expected to assist the Peer Review Team throughout the process in performing the following actions such as rescheduling of interviews; providing the team with requested work papers; providing the team with requested documents; and scheduling entrance (the preliminary meeting may replace the entrance conference if agreed upon by the Peer Review Team and internal audit director) and exit conferences. This assistance is necessary to enable the Peer Review Team complete its assignment in a timely manner.

The Peer Review Team keeps to its time schedule in the performance of the On-Site-Work in addition to Lead maintaining open communication with the internal audit director during the peer review regarding project status and results.

During the on-site work, the following process is undertaken by all members involved in the review:

1. Hold an entrance conference with the internal audit director, internal audit staff, if the internal audit director deems necessary, and Peer Review Team Members to discuss the on-site process.
2. The Review Team conducts interviews using the under listed Forms, which shall be modified according to need.
3. They should document the individual interview results then summarize all of the interview results using the Summary Form for Interview Results (C8, Figure 7.17).

7.11.2.2.1 C1: Sample Interview Questionnaire— Board/Committee Member (Figure 7.10)

Prior to the interview, the interviewer should familiarize himself/herself on the background of the interviewee. Explain briefly to the interviewee the purposes of the peer review and how this interview is important to those purposes.

Person Interviewed: _____ Date: _____

MANAGEMENT
IIA Code of Ethics
1. Do the Internal Auditors demonstrate and promote ethical behavior?

1000 Purpose, Authority, and Responsibility
2. Do you think the Internal Audit charter that was approved by the Commission/Board provides Internal Audit with sufficient authority to fulfill its responsibilities?
3. The Charter specifies the scope of internal audit activities to be performed. Do you think the charter provides sufficient guidance on what you expect from Internal Audit, or do you have to provide the auditors with additional guidance regarding what you expect from them? If additional guidance is necessary, how is it provided?

1100 Independence and Objectivity
4. The Director of Internal Audit currently reports operationally to the *Board/Commission*, and administratively to the *Agency Head.* Do you think this reporting relationship is effective, and why?
5. Does Internal Audit appear to be independent and objective?
6. Are you and/or the other Board/Commission members involved in the appointment or removal of the Director of Internal Audit? If so, is this responsibility documented?

1300 Quality Assurance and Improvement Program
7. Are the results of external quality assurance reviews (peer reviews) communicated to you and the rest of the Board/Commission?

STAFF
1200 Proficiency and Due Professional Care
8. What is your opinion of the Internal Audit Director and Internal Audit staff:
   - Ability?
   - Professionalism?
   - Communication Skills?

MANAGEMENT
2000 Managing the Internal Audit Activity
1. Internal Audit develops a risk-based Annual Audit Plan to determine its priorities. Do you provide input to the risk assessment? Does the Board/Commission approve the Annual Audit Plan?
2. Do you think Internal Audit's priorities align with the agency/university's goals? Please explain.

Figure 7.10   C1: Sample interview questionnaire—board/committee member.
(Continued)

3. Does Internal Audit add value to the agency/university? If so, in what ways?
4. Does the Director of Internal Audit periodically report to the board its performance relative to its Annual Audit Plan, including any significant interim changes? If so, how is this information reported?

2100 Nature of Work
5. Does Internal Audit help identify significant risks and improve the agency/university's control systems? Please explain.

2600 Management's Acceptance of Risks
6. If management accepts a level of risk that Internal Audit considers inappropriate, how would the Director of Internal Audit report it to you and the rest of the Board/Commission?

PROCESS
2400 Communicating Results
7. Do you receive copies of the audit reports? If so, approximately how many do you receive per year?
8. Are the reports clear, concise, and accurate?
9. Do the reports provide practical and cost-effective recommendations for correcting problems?

2500 Monitoring Progress
10. Does Internal Audit monitor whether the issues and recommendations identified in audit reports are resolved?

GENERAL QUESTIONS
1. If you were to give Internal Audit a letter grade of A through F, what grade would you give it, and why?
2. What changes would you make to Internal Audit, if any?

Figure 7.10 (Continued)   C1: Sample interview questionnaire—board/committee member. (Adapted from State of North Carolina, Council of Internal Auditing, Office of Internal Audit, Peer Review Program, Sample Interview Questionnaire—Board/Committe Member [Form C1].)

7.11.2.2.2 C2: Sample Interview Questionnaire— Executive Management (Figure 7.11)

Prior to the interview, the interviewer should familiarize himself/herself on the background of the interviewee. Explain briefly to the interviewee the purposes of the peer review and how this interview is important to those purposes. The sample survey questions in this document should be used for whom the internal audit director reports.

Person Interviewed: _____ Date: _____

GOVERNANCE
IIA Code of Ethics
1. Do the Internal Auditors demonstrate and promote ethical behavior?

1000 Purpose, Authority, and Responsibility
2. What do you consider the purpose of an internal audit?
3. Do you think Internal Audit has the appropriate authority to carry out its purpose?
4. Does Internal Audit perform consulting engagements as well as audits? If so, what do you consider the most significant differences between an audit and a consulting engagement?

1100 Independence and Objectivity
5. Do you think the reporting relationship for Internal Audit is appropriate?
6. Does Internal Audit appear to be independent?
7. Do you consider Internal Audit objective?
8. Is Internal Audit free from the management decision-making and operating responsibilities?

1300 Quality Assurance and Improvement Program
9. Does Internal Audit obtain management's feedback about its effectiveness? If so, how is this done?

STAFF
1200 Proficiency and Due Professional Care
10. Do you think the internal auditors have the knowledge and skills to perform their responsibilities?
11. How would you rate their professionalism?
12. Do the internal auditors enhance their knowledge and skills through continuing professional development?

MANAGEMENT
2000 Managing the Internal Audit Activity
13. Do you provide input to the risk assessment and planning process? If so, please describe how your input is obtained and used?
14. Are Internal Audit's priorities aligned with the agency/university's goals?
15. Does Internal Audit add value to the agency/university?
16. Does Internal Audit have any resource limitations that you are aware of?
17. Are there any areas that you think Internal Audit should cover that are not currently covered?
18. Are there any areas that are audited that you think should not be? If so, why?
19. Do you think the Internal Audit Director manages the internal audit function effectively?

Figure 7.11 C2: Sample interview questionnaire—executive management.
(*Continued*)

2100 Nature of Work
20. Do you think the internal audit coverage, including information technology audit, is adequate?
21. Does Internal Audit help identify significant risks to the agency/university, including fraud risks?
22. Does it help improve the agency/university's risk management and control systems?

2600 Management's Acceptance of Risks
23. Does Internal Audit discuss with you the implications of accepting risks?

PROCESS
2200 Engagement Planning
24. Has audit work been adequately planned?

2400 Communicating Results
25. Are the results of audits and consulting projects communicated promptly?
26. Are the reports clear, accurate, and concise?
27. Do the reports acknowledge satisfactory performance when appropriate?
28. Do the reports provide practical and cost-effective recommendations for correcting problems?

2500 Monitoring Progress
29. Does Internal Audit monitor whether the issues identified in reports are resolved? If so, how is this done?

GENERAL QUESTIONS

30. Have you had any problems or disagreements with Internal Audit? If so, were they resolved and how?
31. If you were to give Internal Audit a letter grade of A through F, what grade would you give it?
32. What changes would you make to Internal Audit, if any?

Figure 7.11 (Continued)   C2: Sample interview questionnaire—executive management. (Adapted from State of North Carolina, Council of Internal Auditing, Office of Internal Audit, Peer Review Program, Sample Interview Questionnaire— Executive Management [Form C2].)

7.11.2.2.3 C3: Sample Interview Questionnaire— Management (Figure 7.12)

Prior to the interview, the interviewer should familiarize himself/herself with the background of the interviewee. Explain briefly to the interviewee the purposes of the peer review and how this interview is important to those purposes.

Person Interviewed: _____ Date: _____

GOVERNANCE
IIA Code of Ethics
1. Do the Internal Auditors demonstrate and promote ethical behavior?

1000 Purpose, Authority, and Responsibility
2. What do you consider the purpose of an internal audit?
3. Do you think Internal Audit has the appropriate authority to carry out its purpose?
4. Does Internal Audit perform consulting engagements as well as audits? If so, what do you consider the most significant differences between an audit and a consulting engagement?

1100 Independence and Objectivity
5. Who does Internal Audit report to? Do you think the reporting relationship is appropriate?
6. Does Internal Audit appear to be independent?
7. Do you consider Internal Audit objective?
8. Is Internal Audit free from the management decision-making function and operating responsibilities?

1300 Quality Assurance and Improvement Program
9. Does Internal Audit obtain management's feedback about its effectiveness? If so, how is this done?

STAFF
1200 Proficiency and Due Professional Care
10. Do you think the internal auditors have the knowledge and skills to perform their responsibilities?
11. How would you rate their professionalism?
12. Do the internal auditors enhance their knowledge and skills through continuing professional development?

MANAGEMENT
2000 Managing the Internal Audit Activity
13. Do you provide input to the risk assessment and planning process? If so, please describe the type of input and how it is used.
14. Are Internal Audit's priorities aligned with the agency/university's goals?
15. Does Internal Audit add value to the agency/university?
16. Does Internal Audit have any resource limitations that you are aware of?
17. Are there any areas that you think Internal Audit should cover that are not currently covered?
18. Are there any areas that are audited that you think should not be? If so, why?
19. Do you think the Internal Audit Director manages the internal audit function effectively?

Figure 7.12 C3: Sample interview questionnaire—management. (*Continued*)

2100 Nature of Work
20. Do you think the internal audit coverage, including information technology audit, is adequate?
21. Does Internal Audit help identify significant risks to the agency/university, including fraud risks?
22. Does it help improve the agency/university's risk management and control systems?

2600 Management's Acceptance of Risks
23. Does Internal Audit discuss with you the implications of accepting risks?

PROCESS
2200 Engagement Planning
24. For audits of your area, has the work that was performed been adequately planned?
25. Were you informed of the audit scope and objectives in a timely manner?

2400 Communicating Results
26. Are the results of audits and consulting projects communicated promptly?
27. Are the reports clear, accurate, and concise?
28. Do the reports acknowledge satisfactory performance when appropriate?
29. Do the reports provide practical and cost-effective recommendations for correcting problems?

2500 Monitoring Progress
Does Internal Audit monitor whether the issues identified in reports are resolved? If so, how is this done?

General Questions
30. Have you had any problems or disagreements with Internal Audit? If so, were they resolved and how?
31. If you were to give Internal Audit a letter grade of A through F, what grade would you give it?
32. What changes would you make to Internal Audit, if any?

Figure 7.12 (Continued) C3: Sample interview questionnaire—management. (Adapted from State of North Carolina, Council of Internal Auditing, Office of Internal Audit, Peer Review Program, Sample Interview Questionnaire—Management [Form C3].)

7.11.2.2.4 C4: Sample Interview Questionnaire—CIO (Figure 7.13)

Prior to the interview, the interviewer should familiarize himself/herself on the background of the interviewee. Explain briefly to the interviewee the purposes of the Peer Review and how this interview is important to those purposes. The sample survey questions in this document should be used for the Chief Information Officer (CIO).

Person Interviewed: _____ Date: _____

INFORMATION SYSTEMS ENVIRONMENT

1. **Describe the inherent risk present in your IT environment (hardware, operation systems, databases, and desktop) because of its diversity, nature, etc. What are the implications for IA (i.e., critical skills needed to audit)?** (Note to interviewer: It is not necessary to get exact detailed information. You should already have obtained these details from Tool 2 and the IT audit department manager, if the organization has one. Use this question to fill in gaps, verify any areas of concern, or as a more general warm-up to get a feel for the complexity and diversity of the IT environment from the chief information officer's (CIO's) perspective to better understand IT risks that affect the IT audit program and the diversity of audit skills required by the internal audit staff).

IT RISK MANAGEMENT, CONTROL, AND ACCOUNTABILITY

2. **How effective is IT governance in your organization? (From Tool 2, IT governance, question, and confirm information about governance.) Are the existing processes adequate and functioning?**

    2.1 **What is the role the IA activity is/should be playing in governance?**

    2.2 **Comment on the IT control environment and management processes.** Is a framework such as Control Objectives for Information and related Technology Systems (COBIT), ISO framework, or Information Technology Infrastructure Library (ITIL) being used?

3. **What are the mission critical (most important five to seven) applications in the organization from your perspective? Is the IA activity involved at an appropriate level?** Does the IA activity audit those applications regularly/periodically? Does it perform consulting engagements? Is the IA activity involved when important systems are under development or being implemented? What does it contribute?

4. **What IT processes are at highest risk in your organization? Are they audited by the IA activity? IT processes include such things as network security, system development life cycle, computer operations, IT governance, communications, etc. (refer to Tool 15 for a list of IT processes). What are the most important risks and opportunities in your area of responsibility? How do you decide to accept, mitigate, share, transfer, etc., these risks? How are these risks communicated to the audit committee and senior management? How is risk management in your area aligned/integrated with that for the organization as a whole?**

5. **Give additional comments on the IT organization's overall control environment and management processes.** Provide any other comments on IT governance, communication of information, management structure, delegation of authority, or oversight/evaluation functions and processes. Is management information timely, reliable, and at the right level of detail for your area of responsibility?

Figure 7.13 C4: Sample interview questionnaire—CIO.   (*Continued*)

THE INTERNAL AUDIT ACTIVITY AND OTHER MONITORING/ OVERSIGHT FUNCTIONS

6. **Comment generally on the independence, structure, and scope of work of the IA activity. Is the IA activity free to audit all aspects of IT? Is the IA activity auditing the critical IT areas? What areas should it audit that it has not? Why do you think that is the case? Is the IA activity IT structure aligned with your structure?**

7. **Are there groups in IT that perform control and risk mitigation functions?** If so, what areas are covered? If so, is this coordinated with the IA activity? Describe the information security function in IT. How do these groups work with the IA activity?

8. **Describe IT governance practices.** Does a member of the IA activity attend the strategy committee meetings? Do internal auditors? Are governance issues audited? How is the IA activity kept informed about IT changes, strategy, new projects, etc. What could be done to improve information flow?

9. **Comment on the credibility and effectiveness of the IA activity.** Is the CAE considered a key member of management? Do you think the IA activity is performing a critical function — or is it only useful to have, but not critical?

10. **Based on your experience and observations, comment on the IT capabilities and professionalism of the IA activity's staff.** Are staff members objective/professional? What IT skills does the IA activity need or need more of? Does the IA activity demonstrate a sufficient understanding of the technologies in use at your organization? Does the IA activity IT audit manager demonstrate an appropriate level of understanding of the technologies and governance of IT in your organization? Do you consider the IA activity a staffing resource for your area? Would you consider sending high-potential staff for a rotational assignment in the IA activity? Would you support a formal rotation program for staff between IT and the IA activity? Do you hold any joint training?

11. **Does the IA activity help management identify significant risks and improve the organization's control and governance systems? Does it involve you in annual audit planning?** Do you have adequate input into the IA activity's risk assessment and planning of services to your area? How? And how frequently is that input obtained? How are disagreements resolved? Is there sufficient emphasis on IT issues? How have the IA activity's audits/consulting engagements assisted in dealing with your risks and other concerns?

Figure 7.13 (Continued)   C4: Sample interview questionnaire—CIO.   (*Continued*)

12. **Do you receive internal audit reports or summaries**? How many reports do you receive annually? Are reports reasonably balanced, and do they properly reflect the existing conditions? Are they too technical or not technical enough from an IT perspective? Are reports and feedback during audits given on a timely basis? Is your input or the input of your senior management team solicited in the opening and closing meetings?

13. **Express your opinion of the quality/value added of the IA activity's services in your area of responsibility.** Do recommendations relate to important issues and have you found them to be valuable and able to be implemented reasonably? Is there adequate and timely implementation follow-up by the IA activity? On a scale of 1 to 10, how would you currently rate internal auditing overall?

14. **Give your views on ways to improve the effectiveness/value and technical competence of the IA activity.** What could be done to improve the audit process as it relates to your area of responsibility?

15. **Does the IA activity perform consulting engagements as well as assurance audits?** Do you request the IA activity's advisory assistance beyond scheduled audits? Does it have the ability to respond in a timely manner? Do internal audit staff members participate in system development and/or implementation projects as controls/consultants? Do they review security policies?

16. **Express additional observations/conclusions about the IA activity or other matters discussed during the interview or ways that the IA activity could help IT.**

Figure 7.13 (Continued)   C4: Sample interview questionnaire—CIO. (Adapted from State of North Carolina, Council of Internal Auditing, Office of Internal Audit, Peer Review Program, Sample Interview Questionnaire—CIO [Form C4].)

7.11.2.2.5 C5: Sample Interview Questionnaire— Internal Audit Director (Figure 7.14)

Prior to the interview, the interviewer should familiarize himself/herself on the background of the interviewee. Explain briefly to the interviewee the purposes of the Peer Review and how this interview is important to those purposes. The sample interview questions in this document should be used for the internal audit director.

<u>General Information</u>

Internal Audit Office: _____

Internal Audit Director: _____

Due Date: _____

Peer Review Team Lead: _____

ENTERPRISE RISK MANAGEMENT, CONTROL, AND ACCOUNTABILITY
1. **Comment on the agency/university's overall control environment, governance, and management processes.**
   A. Which policies (e.g., ethics/conflict of interest policy, department/corporate reporting, etc.) are in place to ensure appropriate management control processes? (If a control policy has been already provided by the IA activity, ask the interviewee to comment on the completeness of the policy.)
   B. Do you consider the policy(ies) adequate (e.g., covering enterprise risk, authorities and responsibilities, management controls, and accountabilities)?

2. **Describe how risks are identified, measured, and managed in the agency/university.**
   A. What are the most important risks and opportunities?
   B. How is risk management *rolled up* so that the CEO can evaluate and oversee the *big picture*?
   C. How does the IA activity assist management in the identification and management of significant risks?

3. **Indicate how objectives and expected results are established in the agency/university. Comment on measurement and reporting of results.**
   A. How well are objectives and accountabilities aligned with risk management processes?
   B. Describe the nature and frequency of evaluation of operating results and management performance.
   C. Do management information systems and reports provide adequate decision support information and documentation of the organization's results and accountability processes?

4. **Give additional comments on the agency/university's overall control environment, governance, and management processes.**
   A. Any other comments on management structure, delegation of authority, or oversight/evaluation functions and processes?
   B. Is management information timely, reliable, and at the right level of detail for your area of responsibility?

Figure 7.14 C5: Sample interview questionnaire—internal audit director. *(Continued)*

**THE INTERNAL AUDIT (IA) ACTIVITY AND OTHER MONITORING/
OVERSIGHT FUNCTIONS**

5. **Comment on the charter and audit practice environment.**
    A. Does the CAE meet privately with the audit committee? If so, how often?
    B. Has the charter been kept current and relevant? Did the board approve it?
    C. Does the charter establish adequate role, authority, and scope of work of the IA activity? If not, please define what areas the IA activity is not allowed to review.
    D. Is the charter easily accessible (web, manual) to management and staff in the agency/university?
    E. Do the work environment, culture, and empowerment within the IA activity promote a customer orientation by providing frequent contact, quality work, and partnering relationship?
    F. Is the IA activity free from management decision-making functions and operational responsibilities?

6. **Comment on the independence, structure, and scope of work of the IA activity.**
    A. Does the nature/level of the IA activity's reporting lines to senior management and the board ensure its independence?
    B. How is the board involved in the appointment, replacement, dismissal, and compensation of the Internal Audit Director?
    C. Does the organization structure of the IA activity promote achievement of its mission/goals?
    D. Do you have adequate budgetary resources to enable you (as the Internal Audit Director) to provide adequate audit coverage of the risk and exposure of the activities and special projects as outlined in the annual audit plan?
    E. Are you aware of any impediment to independence?

7. **Describe the board/audit committee's oversight of the IA activity.**
    A. Are you satisfied with the support (availability of committee members, resources, follow-up) that you receive from the board?
    B. Is the board's input sought during the annual planning and risk assessment of the IA activity?
    C. Does the board approve the annual audit plan?
    D. Describe the method and frequency of your meetings with and reporting to the board?
    E. Do you meet privately with the board or the chair of the audit committee?

8. **Describe the frequency and nature of your interactions with the senior executive to whom you report.**

    A. Who do you report to administratively?
    B. How often do you meet with the senior executive?
    C. Describe the methods of your meetings with and reporting to the senior executive.
    D. Do you seek the senior executive's input during the IA activity's annual risk assessment and planning?
    E. Is the annual audit plan discussed with the senior executive before the board approves the plan?
    F. Do you attend strategic planning meetings or other senior management meetings? Do you receive a copy of the minutes from those meetings?

Figure 7.14 (Continued)   C5: Sample interview questionnaire—internal audit director. *(Continued)*

9. **Comment on other oversight or monitoring functions (such as evaluation, process improvement, control self-assessment, or special investigations) and on the independent audit firm in relation to the IA activity.**
    A. Indicate the roles of other *monitoring functions* in the agency/university.
    B. How do you ensure adequate coordination with the monitoring functions and prevent overlapping work while providing sufficient coverage?
    C. Does the IA activity follow up or assist in implementation of the recommendations of the other monitoring functions?
    D. Is there an adequate coordination of review work between the IA activity and the external auditor (and regulators) to minimize duplication or redundancy?
    E. How often do you meet with the external auditor?
    F. Are you satisfied with the extent to which the external auditor relies on your work?

10. **Comment on the credibility and effectiveness of the IA activity.**
    A. Are you considered a key member of the management team?
    B. How do you ensure that internal auditors have the knowledge and skills to perform their responsibilities?
    C. How do you obtain management and the board's feedback about the effectiveness of the IA activity?
    D. Does the IA activity add value to the agency/university? If so, how does IA add value?

11. **Comment on the capabilities/professionalism of the IA activity's staff.**
    A. Does the IA activity foster an identifiable culture of professionalism and continuous improvement?
    B. Are you satisfied with the staff's understanding of the IA activity's core values, mission, and goals/objectives?
    C. Does the IA staff have a reasonable understanding of enterprise risk, corporate governance, and opportunities for service beyond traditional audit activities?
    D. Does staff have the right skills to audit operational, financial, performance, and information technology areas of the agency/university?
    E. Are the staff's views sought and considered for management and audit policy/planning deliberations?
    F. Are the competency models (position descriptions), performance standards, or other means used to define the expectations and accountabilities of the staff?
    G. Do the auditors comply with the IIA's Standards and Code of Ethics?

12. **Comment on the IA activity risk assessment and audit planning.**
    A. Is there an audit universe of enterprise risks, management controls, and accountabilities that is systematically assessed to arrive at the annual and longer-term IA activity plan?
    B. Were the agency/university's risk framework, strategic business plan, and technology plan all used in the planning process?
    C. Was input sought from key stakeholders (board, senior management, and external auditor) during the IA activity's annual risk assessment and planning?

Figure 7.14 (Continued)   C5: Sample interview questionnaire—internal audit director.   **(*Continued*)**

D. Was sufficient attention given to the IA activity's approach to auditing information technology?

E. Are funding, staff mix and skills, technology, and other resources sufficient to fulfill the plan?

13. How satisfied are you with the IA activity's processes for overseeing the planning and performing of consulting engagements?

A. Is there an up-to-date procedure that sets forth the guidelines for audit consultants?

B. Are consulting engagements performed in accordance with established methodologies and working practices?

C. Are the audit consultant's work papers made available to the IA activity?

D. Are appropriate audit plans established for each engagement that includes scope, objectives, timing, and resource allocations?

E. How are the consulting engagements supervised and do you think the level of supervision is adequate?

F. Do you review the consulting reports before they are released to management?

14. Comment on the IA's Quality Assurance and Improvement Program, including ongoing monitoring mechanisms (engagement supervision, benchmarking, measurement criteria) and internal and external quality assessments.

A. What are the significant quality/process improvement actions currently under way or planned for the near term in the following areas:

    i. Customer relations (e.g., partnering, self-assessment, and consulting on management processes)

    ii. Reducing audit cycle time (e.g., early and frequent involvement in audit planning and audit result, reduction of reporting and follow-up intervals, and streamlining audit procedures)

    iii. Empowerment of staff and customers (e.g., self-review and accountability, team auditing)

    iv. Benchmarking

    v. Other areas (adoption of leading practices)

B. How do you monitor effectiveness of the Quality Assurance and Improvement Program?

15. Any additional observations/comments about the IA activity or other matters discussed in the interview.

Figure 7.14 (Continued) C5: Sample interview questionnaire—internal audit director. (Adapted from State of North Carolina, Council of Internal Auditing, Office of Internal Audit, Peer Review Program, Sample Interview Questionnaire— Internal Audit Director [Form C5].)

7.11.2.2.6 C6: Sample Interview Questionnaire— Internal Audit Staff (Figure 7.15)

Prior to the interview, the interviewer should familiarize himself/herself on the background of the interviewee. Explain briefly to the interviewee the purposes of the Peer Review and how this interview is important to those purposes. The sample interview questions in this document should be used for the Internal Audit Staff.

Person Interviewed: _____ Date: _____

GOVERNANCE:
IIA Code of Ethics
1. In what ways does Internal Audit demonstrate and promote ethical behavior?

1000 Purpose, Authority, and Responsibility
2. What do you consider the mission of an internal audit?
3. Do you think Internal Audit has the appropriate authority to carry out its mission?
4. Do you think the internal audit coverage, including information technology audit, is adequate?
5. Does Internal Audit perform consulting engagements as well as audits? If so, what do you consider the most significant differences between an audit and a consulting engagement?

1100 Independence and Objectivity
6. Who does Internal Audit report to, and do you think the reporting relationship is appropriate?
7. Is Internal Audit free from the management decision-making function and operating responsibilities?
8. What actions are taken to ensure Internal Audit is independent and objective?
9. How are impairments to independence or objectivity addressed?

1300 Quality Assurance and Improvement Program
10. Does Internal Audit obtain management's feedback about its effectiveness? If so, how is this done?
11. How is your work supervised, and do you think the supervision is adequate?
12. What is the performance evaluation process used for internal auditors? (e.g., annual evaluations, project evaluations, etc.)

Management's Acceptance of Risks
13. Does the Internal Audit Director inform the board if Internal Audit believes that senior management has accepted a level of residual risk that is unacceptable to the agency/university?

STAFF:
1200 Proficiency and Due Professional Care
14. Do you think the internal auditors have the knowledge and skills to perform their responsibilities?
15. Do internal auditors have opportunities to enhance their knowledge and skills through continuing professional development?
16. Do internal auditors have access to specialized training when needed?

MANAGEMENT:
2000 Managing the Internal Audit Activity
17. Does Internal Audit develop a risk-based plan at least annually to determine its priorities? If you are involved in the process, please describe it.

Figure 7.15   C6: Sample interview questionnaire—internal audit staff. (*Continued*)

18. Who provides input to the risk assessment and planning process, and how is the input used?
19. Does Internal Audit have any resource limitations? If any, how are they addressed?

2100 Nature of Work
20. What kinds of audits does Internal Audit perform?
21. In what ways does Internal Audit contribute to the improvement of risk management, control, and governance systems of the agency/university?

PROCESS:
2200 Engagement Planning
22. How is audit planning performed, who is involved, and what approvals are required?
23. How are the scope and objectives of audits determined, and who approves them?
24. How and when are auditees informed of the audit objectives and scope?

2300 Performing the Engagement
25. What is the process for ensuring the conclusions internal audit reports are based on sufficient factual evidence?

2400 Communicating Results
26. How is the reporting process performed, who is involved, and what approvals are required?
27. Are the results of audits and consulting projects communicated promptly?
28. Are the reports constructive, and do they acknowledge satisfactory performance when appropriate?
29. Do the reports provide recommendations for correcting problems that are practical and cost-effective?
30. Do you think internal audit reports are disseminated to the appropriate individuals?

2500 Monitoring Progress
31. How does internal audit monitor whether the issues identified in reports are resolved?

MANAGEMENT:
2000 Managing the Internal Audit Activity
32. Does Internal Audit develop a risk-based plan at least annually to determine its priorities? If you are involved in the process, please describe it.
33. Who provides input to the risk assessment and planning process, and how is the input used?
34. Does Internal Audit have any resource limitations? If any, how are they addressed?

2100 Nature of Work
35. What kinds of audits does Internal Audit perform?
36. In what ways does Internal Audit contribute to the improvement of risk management, control, and governance systems of the agency/university?

Figure 7.15 (Continued)   C6: Sample interview questionnaire—internal audit staff. *(Continued)*

PROCESS:
2200 Engagement Planning
37. How is audit planning performed, who is involved, and what approvals are required?
38. How are the scope and objectives of audits determined, and who approves them?
39. How and when are auditees informed of the audit objectives and scope?

2300 Performing the Engagement
40. What is the process for ensuring that the conclusions internal audit reports are based on sufficient factual evidence?

2400 Communicating Results
41. How is the reporting process performed, who is involved, and what approvals are required?
42. Are the results of audits and consulting projects communicated promptly?
43. Are the reports constructive, and do they acknowledge satisfactory performance when appropriate?
44. Do the reports provide recommendations for correcting problems that are practical and cost-effective?
45. Do you think internal audit reports are disseminated to the appropriate individuals?

2500 Monitoring Progress
46. How does internal audit monitor whether the issues identified in reports are resolved?

General Questions
47. If you were to give Internal Audit a letter grade of A through F, what grade would you give it?
48. What changes would you make to Internal Audit, if any?

Figure 7.15 (Continued) C6: Sample interview questionnaire—internal audit staff. (Adapted from State of North Carolina, Council of Internal Auditing, Office of Internal Audit, Peer Review Program, Sample Interview Questionnaire—Internal Audit Staff [Form C6].)

7.11.2.2.7 C7: Sample Interview Questionnaire— External Auditor (Figure 7.16)

Prior to the interview, the interviewer should familiarize himself/herself with the background of the interviewee. Explain briefly to the interviewee the purposes of the Peer Review and how this interview is important to those purposes.

Person Interviewed: _____   Date: _____

GOVERNANCE:
1100 Independence and Objectivity
1. In your opinion, does the Internal Audit Director report to a level in the agency/university that is adequate to ensure independence?
2. Are you aware of any restrictions or limitations that prevent the internal audit activity from determining the scope of internal auditing, performing its work, or communicating its results?
3. Do the internal auditors appear to have impartial, unbiased attitudes and to avoid conflicts of interest?

STAFF:
1200 Proficiency and Due Professional Care
4. Based on your observations, do the internal auditors have the knowledge and skills to perform their responsibilities, including identifying indicators of fraud?
5. Do the staff members receive adequate training to carry out their audit responsibilities?
6. Do you think the internal auditors receive adequate supervision?
7. To what extent do you rely on or use the work of the internal auditors?

MANAGEMENT:
2000 Managing the Internal Audit Activity
8. Does the Internal Audit Director establish risk-based plans to determine the priorities for the internal audit function?
9. Are the audit plans consistent with the agency/university's goals?
10. Does the Internal Audit Director share information and coordinate activities with you to ensure proper coverage and minimize duplication of efforts?

GENERAL QUESTIONS:
11. Have you had any problems or disagreements with Internal Audit? If so, were they resolved and how?
12. If you were to give Internal Audit a letter grade of A through F, what grade would you give it?
13. What changes would you make to Internal Audit, if any?

Figure 7.16 C7: Sample interview questionnaire—external auditor. (Adapted from State of North Carolina, Council of Internal Auditing, Office of Internal Audit, Peer Review Program, Sample Interview Questionnaire—External Auditor [Form C7].)

7.11.2.2.8 C8: Interview Results Summary Form (Figure 7.17)

This form is used to summarize individual interview results.

Based on the interviews conducted, does it appear that the internal audit function adheres to the following:
GOVERNANCE: IIA Code of Ethics **1000 Purpose, Authority, and Responsibility** **1100 Independence and Objectivity** **1300 Quality Assurance and Improvement Program**
STAFF: **1200 Proficiency and Due Professional Care**
MANAGEMENT: **2000 Managing the Internal Audit Activity** **2100 Nature of Work** **2600 Management's Acceptance of Risks**
PROCESS: **2200 Engagement Planning** **2300 Performing the Engagement** **2400 Communicating Results** **2500 Monitoring Progress**
GENERAL QUESTIONS:

Figure 7.17   C8: Interview results summary form. (Adapted from State of North Carolina, Council of Internal Auditing, Office of Internal Audit, Peer Review Program, Interview Results Summary Form [Form C8].)

7.11.2.3 Program Phase

This is the phase of evaluating the internal audit function; accordingly, the Peer Review Team will evaluate the internal audit function based on the survey and interview results using the forms shown below (see D1–D4). As team members complete the on-site work, any observations and issues realized through the peer review process are recorded in each individual program spreadsheet (Form). If additional documentation is necessary, the Observations and Issues Worksheet—E1 is an optional tool.

7.11.2.3.1 D1: Governance (See Table 7.7, pp. 391–398)

This form is used to evaluate the Governance process and cover issues such as Internal Audit Charter, Independence and Objectivity, Functional Reporting, Administrative Reporting, Quality Assurance and Improvement Program, Monitoring Quality Programs, Assessing Quality Programs, Continuous Improvement, Communicating Results, Conformance with Standards, and Disclosure of Nonconformance.

7.11.2.3.2 D2: Staff (See Table 7.8, pp. 399–404)

This form evaluates IA Staff Matters including Continuing Professional Development and Performance Appraisals.

7.11.2.3.3 D3: Management (See Table 7.9, pp. 405–415)

This form is used to evaluate the quality of IA assurances to management and will cover such areas as Enterprise Risk Management (ERM), Coordination, Resolution of Management's Acceptance of Risk, Planning—Policies and Procedures, Planning—Audit Universe, Risk Assessment Process, Audit Plans, Completion of Audit Plans, Reporting to Senior Management, and the Board and Resource Allocation.

7.11.2.3.4 D4: Process (See Table 7.10, pp. 416–433)

This form is used to evaluate the quality of IA Process and includes such areas as engagement planning, planning considerations, key conformance criteria, engagement objectives, engagement scope, engagement resource allocation, engagement work program, performing the engagement, identifying information, analysis and evaluation, documenting information, engagement supervision, communicating results, criteria for communicating results, quality of communications, errors and omissions, disseminating results, engagement disclosure of nonconformance, monitoring progress, adequacy of IA follow-up procedures, etc.

7.11.2.3.5 D5: Information Technology (See Table 7.11, pp. 434–441)

With form D5, the Peer Review Team evaluates the quality and adequacy of the organization's information technology and its relationship with the internal audit

Table 7.7 D1: Governance

Area of Review	Governance	Staff	Management	Process	Exception Noted	Initial/Date
Governance						
Internal Audit Activity Charter						
Ensure the charter, role, and activities of the internal audit function are clearly understood and responsive to the needs of the audit committee and board.	1000					
A. Is the charter consistent with the IIA model and the *International Standards for the Professional Practice of Internal Auditing* (Standards) in defining the purpose, authority, and responsibility of the IA activity?	1010					
B. Has the charter been approved by the board?	1000					
C. Is the charter periodically reviewed and updated as necessary?	1000					

(Continued)

Table 7.7 (Continued)   D1: Governance

Area of Review	Governance	Staff	Management	Process	Exception Noted	Initial/Date
D. Does the charter note conformance with the Standards? The IA activity's reports should use this clause, "conducted in accordance with the Standards," if current with their external review.	1321					
Independence and Objectivity						
Regardless of which reporting relationship the state agency chooses, several key actions can help assure that the reporting lines support and enable the effectiveness and independence of the internal auditing activity	1100					
Functional Reporting						
A. Is the functional reporting line directly to the audit committee chair or its equivalent to ensure the appropriate level of independence and effective communication?	1110 / 1111					
B. Does the internal audit director meet privately with the audit committee or its equivalent? Do discussions include if materials and information being furnished to the committee are meeting their needs?	1110		2060			

(Continued)

Table 7.7 (Continued)   D1: Governance

Area of Review	Governance	Staff	Management	Process	Exception Noted	Initial/Date
C. Does the audit committee have final authority to review and approve the annual risk assessment and audit plan and all major changes to the plan?	1110		2020 / 2060			
D. Does the internal audit director, at all times, have open and direct access to the chair of the audit committee and its members, or the chair of the board or full board, if appropriate?	1110					
E. Determine that at least once a year, the audit committee reviews the performance of the internal audit director and approves the annual compensation and salary adjustment.	1110					
F. Assess whether the audit committee determines whether there are scope or budgetary limitations that impede the ability of the IA activity to execute its responsibilities.	1110		2020			

(Continued)

Table 7.7 (Continued)   D1: Governance

Area of Review	Governance	Staff	Management	Process	Exception Noted	Initial/Date
Administrative Reporting						
G. Does the internal audit director report to the CEO or another executive with sufficient authority to provide appropriate support for the IA activity?	1110					
H. Does the positioning of the function and the internal audit director in the organization's structure support the independence and effective operations of the IA activity?	1110					
I. Are there indications that the administrative reporting line exercises undue influence over the scope and reporting of results of the IA activity?	1110					
J. Does the administrative reporting line facilitate open and direct communications with executive and line management? The internal audit director should be able to communicate directly with any level of management, including the CEO.	1110					

(Continued)

Table 7.7 (Continued)   D1: Governance

Area of Review	Governance	Staff	Management	Process	Exception Noted	Initial/Date
K. Does the administrative reporting line enable adequate communications and information flow such that the IA activity have adequate information concerning the activities, plans, and business initiatives of the organization?	1110					
L. Determine that the internal audit director considers the impact of performing consulting engagements and that appropriate actions have been taken to ensure independence and objectivity.	1110 / 1120					
Quality Assurance and Improvement Program						
Determine whether the internal audit director has implemented processes that are designed to provide reasonable assurance to the various stakeholders that the IA activity:	1300					
A. Conducts activities in accordance with its charter.	1300					

(Continued)

Table 7.7 (Continued)   D1: Governance

Area of Review	Governance	Staff	Management	Process	Exception Noted	Initial/Date
B. Operates in an effective and efficient manner (see also Tool 16).	1300					
C. These processes should include appropriate supervision, periodic internal assessment, and ongoing monitoring of quality assurance, and periodic external assessments.	1310 / 1311 / 1312					
Monitoring Quality Programs—Determine whether monitoring includes ongoing measurements and analyses of performance metrics, e.g., cycle time and recommendations accepted.	1311					
Assessing Quality Programs—Determine whether assessments evaluate and conclude on the quality of the internal audit activity and lead to recommendations for appropriate improvements. Assessments of quality programs should include evaluations of	1320					
A. Adequacy of the internal audit activity's charter, goals, objectives, policies, and procedures.			2040			

(Continued)

Table 7.7 (Continued) D1: Governance

Area of Review	Governance	Staff	Management	Process	Exception Noted	Initial/Date
B. Contribution to the agency/university's risk management, governance, and control processes.			2100			
C. Compliance with applicable laws, regulations, and government or industry standards. The *Internal Audit Act* compliance should be included here.	1311					
D. Effectiveness of continuous improvement activities and adoption of best practices.	1300					
E. Whether the IA activity adds value and improves the agency/university's operations.	1300		2000			
Continuous Improvement—Determine whether all quality improvement efforts include a communication process designed to facilitate appropriate modification of resources, technology, processes, and procedures as indicated by monitoring and assessment activities.	1320		2030			

(Continued)

Table 7.7 (Continued)   D1: Governance

Area of Review	Governance	Staff	Management	Process	Exception Noted	Initial/Date
Communicating Results—Determine whether the internal audit director shared the results of external and, as appropriate, internal quality program assessments with the various stakeholders of the IA activity, such as senior management, the board, and external auditors.	1310 1320					
Conformance with the Standards—IA activity's reports should use this clause, "conducted in accordance with the Standards," if current with their external review.	1321					
Disclosure of Nonconformance—Throughout the quality assessment, note any violations of the IIA's code of ethics. Were any such violations identified by the IA activity reported to senior management and the board? Be alert during interviews and work paper review for any potential code violations.	1322					

Source: Retrieved from State of North Carolina, Council of Internal Auditing, Office of Internal Audit, Peer Review Program, Program Phase—Governance (Form D1).

Table 7.8   D2: Staff

Area of Review	Governance	Staff	Management	Process	Exception Noted	Initial/ Date
Staff						
A. Review the education and background of the IA activity's staff. Internal auditors should possess the knowledge, skills, and other competencies needed to perform their individual responsibilities. The internal audit activity collectively should possess or obtain the knowledge, skills, and other competencies needed to perform its responsibilities.		1210				
B. Review staff and management job descriptions.		1210				
Determine whether job descriptions identify career paths for staff.						
Determine whether job descriptions provide suitable criteria of education and experience for filling IA positions.						
Determine whether current auditors meet the specified criteria of education and experience.						
C. Obtain and review information pertaining to specialized skills required by the IA activity.		1210				

(Continued)

Table 7.8 (Continued) D2: Staff

Area of Review	Governance	Staff	Management	Process	Exception Noted	Initial/ Date
Determine whether the current IA activity staff possess adequate IT audit skills.		1210. A3				
Determine whether any other specialized skills or expertise (i.e., fraud detection skills, consulting skills, etc.) are required to effectively meet unique needs of the agency/university.		1210. A2				
If specialized skills are needed, determine whether the current staff possess these skills.		1210				
Evaluate whether the qualifications of any consultants used during the review period, and the type of assistance provided, were appropriate.		1210. A1				
Conclude as to whether the IA activity possesses or obtains the necessary knowledge, skills, and disciplines needed to carry out its audit responsibilities.						

(Continued)

Table 7.8 (Continued)   D2: Staff

Area of Review	Governance	Staff	Management	Process	Exception Noted	Initial/ Date
D. Staffing analysis						
Review the current organization chart of the audit activity. Consider the number and levels of the staff (both approved and filled).			2030			
Determine whether a staffing analysis was prepared by the audit activity as part of the planning process.						
Determine whether the number and levels of existing staff are in accordance with the staffing analysis prepared by the audit activity.			2020			
If the size of the audit staff does not permit complete coverage based on the risk assessment, determine that the process used to defer or reschedule audits is reasonable and that the board of directors or responsible management officials have been made aware of the effects of the reduced audit coverage of high-risk areas.						
Conclude as to the adequacy of the number and levels of the internal auditing staff.			2020			

(Continued)

Table 7.8 (Continued)   D2: Staff

Area of Review	Governance	Staff	Management	Process	Exception Noted	Initial/ Date
Continuing Professional Development: Using the criteria from the *Staffing Proficiency* section above, consider the development program as the means to increase the knowledge, understanding, and skills of the staff.		1230				
A. Obtain and review information regarding continuing education.		1230				
Determine whether there is a written IA activity policy regarding continuing education.						
Evaluate IA activity policy as to the required number of hours per year of continuing professional education for each auditor and its adequacy.						

(Continued)

Table 7.8 (Continued)   D2: Staff

Area of Review	Governance	Staff	Management	Process	Exception Noted	Initial/ Date
B. Obtain training records and review courses taken by internal auditors during the past 12 months.		1230				
Assess the training received and determine whether it represented the necessary courses to maintain proficiency, especially with regard to specialized skills.						
Determine whether supervisors have received training in management skills.						
C. Assess policy for emphasizing professional certifications (i.e., CIA, CPA, CISA, CMA, CISSP, CBA, etc.), including review courses and examinations. Review reward practices and continuing education for those who receive certification.		1230				
D. Review the policy and practice for encouraging staff to attend and participate in professional associations, such as IIA.		1230				
E. Conclude as to the adequacy of the IA activity's continuing education.		1230				

(Continued)

Table 7.8 (Continued) D2: Staff

Area of Review	Governance	Staff	Management	Process	Exception Noted	Initial/ Date
Performance Appraisals						
A. Review documented performance standards used for evaluations and whether they are consistent with the needs of the IA activity.			2030			
B. Review policy for at least annual performance appraisals and whether evaluations are made of internal auditors after each audit. Assess how the appraisals are used for measuring and improving performance, career counseling, and development of staff.			2030			
C. Assess the potential for, and implementation of, empowerment principles including changes in supervision practices, accountability, self-directed teams, and moving the decision-making and customer relations processes downward in the IA activity.			2030			
D. Conclude as to the adequacy of the personnel performance appraisal process.			2030			

Source: Retrieved from State of North Carolina, Council of Internal Auditing, Office of Internal Audit, Peer Review Program, Program Phase—Staff (Form D2).

Table 7.9   D3: Management

Area of Review	Governance	Staff	Management	Process	Exception Noted	Initial/ Date
Management						
Enterprise Risk Management (ERM)—IA activity's core role with regard to ERM is to provide objective assurance to the board on the effectiveness of an agency/university's ERM activities to help ensure key business risks are being managed appropriately and that the system of internal control is operating effectively. Is the IA activity's role in ERM reasonable?			2120			
The IA activity should assess and make appropriate recommendations for improving the governance process in its accomplishment of the following objectives:			2110			
A. Promoting appropriate ethics and values within the agency/university.			2110			
B. Ensuring effective organizational performance management and accountability.			2110			
C. Effectively communicating risk control information to appropriate areas of the agency/university.			2110			

(Continued)

Table 7.9 (Continued) D3: Management

Area of Review	Governance	Staff	Management	Process	Exception Noted	Initial/Date
D. Effectively coordinating the activities of and communicating information among the board, external and internal auditors, and management.			2110			
E. Determining the IA activity's role in governance within the agency/university.			2110			
Coordination—Determine whether the CAE shares information and coordinates activities with other internal and external providers of relevant assurance and consulting services to ensure proper coverage and minimize duplication of efforts.			2050			
Resolution of Management's Acceptance of Risks— Determine if the internal audit activity has developed a process to discuss and document management's acceptance of risk, including possible escalation of these risks to the audit committee or board.			2600			

(Continued)

Table 7.9 (Continued)   D3: Management

Area of Review	Governance	Staff	Management	Process	Exception Noted	Initial/ Date
Planning—Policies and Procedures						
A. Obtain and review the IA activity's policies and procedures for the annual planning and risk assessment processes.			2000			
B. Determine the level of compliance with the IA activity's policies and procedures in conjunction with completion of the next steps of this tool.						
C. Conclude as to the compliance with IA activity's policies and procedures.						
Planning—Audit Universe						
A. Determine the completeness of the audit universe. Assess the approach taken to develop the audit universe. When doing this, you may find some of the following elements helpful:			2010			
Senior management's responses to inquiries regarding major risk areas of the agency/university						

Table 7.9 (Continued)   D3: Management

Area of Review	Governance	Staff	Management	Process	Exception Noted	Initial/ Date
Entity organization charts and other applicable agency/university documentation (such as annual report, listing of legal entities, strategic planning documents, budget documents, etc.)						
Lists of major information technology systems or applications						
Business products, services, and organizational products						
Charts of accounts						
B. Evaluate how executive management was involved and how the agency/university's strategic and technology plans were used from the standpoints of both controls and business strategy/operating effectiveness			2010			
Organizational budget documents						
New and emerging risks (mergers and acquisitions, new systems, etc.)						
C. Determine if information technology systems/ applications were appropriately included within or as audit entities.			2010			

(Continued)

Table 7.9 (Continued)   D3: Management

Area of Review	Governance	Staff	Management	Process	Exception Noted	Initial/ Date
D. Determine the appropriateness of size and number of audit entities (e.g., too detailed or general, too many or too few, inconsistencies between different areas in the agency/university, logical division of systems or areas).			2010.A1			
E. Conclude as to appropriateness of approach taken to identify the entities in the audit universe.			2010.A1			
Risk Assessment Process			2010			
A. Determine whether the audit activity conducted a formal risk analysis of auditable entities at least annually. The following are aspects that they might have considered:			2010.A1			
The date and results of the last audit			2010.C1			
Financial exposure						
Potential loss and risk						
Requests by management						
Major changes in operations, programs, systems, and controls						

(Continued)

Table 7.9 (Continued)   D3: Management

Area of Review	Governance	Staff	Management	Process	Exception Noted	Initial/Date
Stability or continuity of management						
Significant business or volume changes						
Changes in governance structure						
B. Is the risk assessment updated annually (e.g., based on subsequent audit results, changes in audit entities)?						
C. Conclude on the appropriateness of the risk assessment approach used by the IA activity.						
Audit Plans			2000			
A. Assess how the results of the risk assessment were used to develop audit plans. Consider the following:			2010			

(Continued)

Table 7.9 (Continued) D3: Management

Area of Review	Governance	Staff	Management	Process	Exception Noted	Initial/ Date
Is the IA activity following its approved audit frequency guidelines?			2010.A1			
How was audit time budgeted for each auditable entity?						
If applicable, determine if the audit activity adequately coordinated with other audit groups (e.g., the external auditor, Tool 11).						
Has client management been consulted regarding concerns or issues that might impact the audit plan?						
Does the audit plan include time for follow-up on reported audit comments and recommendations to ensure that effective and timely corrective action has been accomplished, as appropriate?						
B. Assess how the internal audit director and his/her team participate in the planning process to arrive at the final plan.						
C. Determine if plans were approved by the audit committee or responsible management officials and included matters needed or requested by the board and senior management.						

(Continued)

Table 7.9 (Continued)   D3: Management

Area of Review	Governance	Staff	Management	Process	Exception Noted	Initial/ Date
D. Assess whether/how streamlining the audit process/practices, staff empowerment, use of technology, self-assessments, team audits, and other opportunities to reduce audit cycle time and improve cost.						
E. Assess whether/how an *added value* discipline was applied to the planning process.						
Completion of Audit Plans			2030			
A. Review the audit plans for current and prior years.						
B. Review the listing of audits currently in process.						
C. Obtain information on the current status of audits in process including actual or expected completion dates.						
D. For audit plan projects included in the prior year's plan that were not executed, determine whether they are scheduled to roll forward or be canceled.						

(Continued)

Table 7.9 (Continued)   D3: Management

Area of Review	Governance	Staff	Management	Process	Exception Noted	Initial/ Date
E. For nonplan projects completed, determine the adequacy of consideration/approval to add them to the plan.						
F. Evaluate the internal audit director's methods to track engagement in-process, completed, management requests, and other priorities not foreseen during risk assessment/planning.						
G. Determine direct time percentage: take IA activity's total available time and subtract administrative categories, then divide remainder by total available time.						
Determine whether hours utilized for administrative work adversely affected coverage of audit plans.						
Conclude as to appropriateness of the percentage of hours charged as direct time and administration.						

(*Continued*)

Table 7.9 (Continued)   D3: Management

Area of Review	Governance	Staff	Management	Process	Exception Noted	Initial/ Date
Reporting to Senior Management and the Board			2060			
A. Review the periodic reports sent to the board and senior management on the IA activity's purpose, authority, responsibility, and performance relative to its plans.						
How does the internal audit director inform the board (audit committee) and his/her superior on factors affecting plan accomplishment?						
What value-added factors (i.e., cost savings) are communicated?						
Does the internal audit director report on results of consulting engagements or other activity without a formal reporting mechanism?						
B. Determine if these reports include significant risk exposures and control issues, corporate governance issues, and other matters needed or requested by the board and senior management.						

(Continued)

Table 7.9 (Continued) D3: Management

Area of Review	Governance	Staff	Management	Process	Exception Noted	Initial/ Date
Resource Allocation						
A. Determine whether the resource allocation process reflects the risk and planning process.			2030			
B. Apart from the audit plan, were the following activities built into the resource allocation?						
Special requests						
Consulting engagements						
Administrative categories, such as training						
C. If the size of the staff does not permit complete coverage based on the risk assessment, determine that the process to defer or reschedule audits is reasonable and the board of directors or responsible management officials have been made aware of and approved the reduced coverage of high-risk areas. Was the use of external resources considered?						
D. Conclude as to the adequacy of the resource allocation process to allow the IA activity achieve the approved plan.						

Source: Retrieved from State of North Carolina, Council of Internal Auditing, Office of Internal Audit, Peer Review Program, Program Phase—Management (Form D3).

Table 7.10 D4: Process

Area of Review	Governance	Staff	Management	Process	Exception Noted*	Initial/Date
Process						
A. Engagement Planning				2200		
Internal auditors must develop and document a plan for each engagement, including the engagement's objectives, scope, timing, and resource allocations.						
Planning Considerations				2201		
In planning the engagement, internal auditors must consider:						
• The objectives of the activity being reviewed and the means by which the activity controls its performance						
• The significant risks to the activity, its objectives, resources, and operations, and the means by which the potential impact of risk is kept to an acceptable level						
• The adequacy and effectiveness of the activity's risk management and control processes compared to a relevant control framework or model						

(Continued)

Table 7.10 (Continued)   D4: Process

Area of Review	Governance	Staff	Management	Process	Exception Noted	Initial/ Date
• The opportunities for making significant improvements to the activity's risk management and control processes						
Key Conformance Criteria—Tool 19						
Internal auditors systematically conduct a preliminary risk assessment of the organization's audit universe in order to determine the engagement objectives.						
Internal auditors develop and record a program for each engagement.						
In the case of outside engagements, the internal auditors establish a written understanding about the objectives, scope, and respective responsibilities of each party.						

(Continued)

Table 7.10 (Continued)   D4: Process

Area of Review	Governance	Staff	Management	Process	Exception Noted	Initial/ Date
• When planning an engagement for parties outside the organization, internal auditors must establish a written understanding with them about objectives, scope, respective responsibilities, and other expectations, including restrictions on distribution of the results of the engagement and access to engagement records.				2201.A1		
• Internal auditors must establish an understanding with consulting engagement clients about objectives, scope, respective responsibilities, and other client expectations. For significant engagements, this understanding must be documented.				2201.C1		
B. Engagement Objectives						
Objectives must be established for each engagement.				2210		
• Internal auditors must conduct a preliminary assessment of the risks relevant to the activity under review. Engagement objectives must reflect the results of this assessment.				2210.A1		

(Continued)

Table 7.10 (Continued) D4: Process

Area of Review	Governance	Staff	Management	Process	Exception Noted	Initial/ Date
• Internal auditors must consider the probability of significant errors, fraud, noncompliance, and other exposures when developing the engagement objectives.				2210.A2		
• Adequate criteria are needed to evaluate controls. Internal auditors must ascertain the extent to which management has established adequate criteria to determine whether objectives and goals have been accomplished. If adequate, internal auditors must use such criteria in their evaluation. If inadequate, internal auditors must work with management to develop appropriate evaluation criteria.				2210.A3		
• Consulting engagement objectives must address governance, risk management, and control processes to the extent agreed upon with the client.				2210.C1		
Conclude as to adequacy of the IA activity's audit objectives.						
C. Engagement Scope				2220		
The established scope must be sufficient to satisfy the objectives of the engagement.						

(Continued)

Table 7.10 (Continued)   D4: Process

Area of Review	Governance	Staff	Management	Process	Exception Noted*	Initial/ Date
Engagement scope is consistent with the audit objectives. If relevant, there is a written understanding and communication of consulting objectives, scope, and responsibilities and results subsequently communicated in accordance with consulting standards.						
• The scope of the engagement must include consideration of relevant systems, records, personnel, and physical properties, including those under the control of third parties.				2220.A1		
• If significant consulting opportunities arise during an assurance engagement, a specific written understanding as to the objectives, scope, respective responsibilities, and other expectations should be reached and the results of the consulting engagement communicated in accordance with consulting standards.				2220.A2		

(Continued)

Table 7.10 (Continued)   D4: Process

Area of Review	Governance	Staff	Management	Process	Exception Noted	Initial/ Date
• In performing consulting engagements, internal auditors must ensure that the scope of the engagement is sufficient to address the agreed-upon objectives. If internal auditors develop reservations about the scope during the engagement, these reservations must be discussed with the client to determine whether to continue with the engagement.				2220.C1		
D. Engagement Resource Allocation				2230		
Internal auditors must determine appropriate and sufficient resources to achieve engagement objectives based on an evaluation of the nature and complexity of each engagement, time constraints, and available resources.						
Key Conformance Criteria—Tool 19						
There is evidence of appropriate evaluation of staffing after scoping that is based on the nature and complexity of the engagement, time constraints, and available resources.						

(Continued)

Table 7.10 (Continued)   D4: Process

Area of Review	Governance	Staff	Management	Process	Exception Noted	Initial/ Date
Conclude as to the adequacy of the IA activity's resources allocated to the engagement.						
E. Engagement Work Program				2240		
Internal auditors must develop and document work programs that achieve the engagement objectives.						
The internal auditor has developed a formal engagement work program outlining the resources and procedures needed to achieve the audit objectives. Fraud was considered in the program.						
The engagement work program and subsequent program adjustments are approved in writing by the chief audit executive or designee before the engagement is commenced.						
• Work programs must include the procedures for identifying, analyzing, evaluating, and documenting information during the engagement. The work program must be approved prior to its implementation, and any adjustments must be approved promptly.				2240.A1		

(Continued)

Table 7.10 (Continued) D4: Process

Area of Review	Governance	Staff	Management	Process	Exception Noted	Initial/ Date
• Work programs for consulting engagements may vary in form and content depending upon the nature of the engagement.				2240.C1		
Conclude as to the adequacy of the IA activity's work program.						
F. Performing the Engagement				2300		
Internal auditors must identify, analyze, evaluate, and document sufficient information to achieve the engagement's objectives.						
Working papers include all the relevant information to achieve the objectives.						
Audit conclusions and engagement results are based on appropriate analyses and evaluations that identify the root cause(s) of irregularities.						
Analysis and evaluation:						
• Sufficient information was recorded to support the conclusions and audit results.						

(Continued)

Table 7.10 (Continued)   D4: Process

Area of Review	Governance	Staff	Management	Process	Exception Noted	Initial/ Date
• Work papers have controlled access according to the policy of the organization.						
• There is evidence that the chief audit executive obtains appropriate approvals prior to releasing records.						
• There is evidence of policy on retention requirements.						
• There is evidence engagements are properly supervised and the work reviewed on a timely basis.						
• **Identifying Information**				2310		
Internal auditors must identify sufficient, reliable, relevant, and useful information to achieve the engagement's objectives.						
• **Analysis and Evaluation**				2320		
Internal auditors must base conclusions and engagement results on appropriate analyses and evaluations.						

(Continued)

Table 7.10 (Continued)   D4: Process

Area of Review	Governance	Staff	Management	Process	Exception Noted	Initial/ Date
• **Documenting Information**				2330		
Internal auditors must document relevant information to support the conclusions and engagement results.						
• The chief audit executive must control access to engagement records. The chief audit executive must obtain the approval of senior management or legal counsel prior to releasing such records to external parties, as appropriate.				2330.A1		
• The chief audit executive must develop retention requirements for engagement records, regardless of the medium in which each record is stored. These retention requirements must be consistent with the organization's guidelines and any pertinent regulatory or other requirements.				2330.A2		

(Continued)

Table 7.10 (Continued)   D4: Process

Area of Review	Governance	Staff	Management	Process	Exception Noted	Initial/ Date
• The chief audit executive must develop policies governing the custody and retention of consulting engagement records, as well as their release to internal and external parties. These policies must be consistent with the organization's guidelines and any pertinent regulatory or other requirements.				2330.C1		
• **Engagement Supervision**				2340		
Engagement must be properly supervised to ensure objectives are achieved, quality is assured, and staff is developed.						
Conclude as to the adequacy of the IA activity's engagement performance.						
G. Communicating Results				2400		
Internal auditors must communicate the engagement results.						
There is evidence of appropriate, timely communication with management.						

(Continued)

Table 7.10 (Continued) D4: Process

Area of Review	Governance	Staff	Management	Process	Exception Noted	Initial/ Date
An overall opinion or conclusion is included in the audit report.						
Satisfactory performance is acknowledged in engagement communications.						
Communications outside the organization are limited in distribution and use of results.						
There is evidence of progress and results on consulting engagements that is reasonable to the engagement.						
Communications are appropriate as described in *quality of communications.*						
Audit reports are timely.						
Where appropriate, there is communication of corrected information to all parties concerned.						
Audit reports are distributed to an appropriate level of senior management.						
Consulting engagement reports are distributed appropriately.						

(Continued)

Table 7.10 (Continued)   D4: Process

Area of Review	Governance	Staff	Management	Process	Exception Noted*	Initial/ Date
• **Criteria for Communicating**				2410		
Communications must include the engagement's objectives and scope as well as applicable conclusions, recommendations, and action plans.						
• Final communication of engagement results must, where appropriate, contain internal auditors' overall opinion or conclusions.				2410.A1		
• Internal auditors are encouraged to acknowledge satisfactory performance in engagement communications.				2410.A2		
• When releasing engagement results to parties outside the organization, the communication must include limitations on distribution and use of the results.				2410.A3		
• Communication of the progress and results of consulting engagements will vary in form and content depending upon the nature of the engagement and the needs of the client.				2410.C1		

(Continued)

Table 7.10 (Continued)   D4: Process

Area of Review	Governance	Staff	Management	Process	Exception Noted	Initial/ Date
• **Quality of Communications**						
Communications must be accurate, objective, clear, concise, constructive, complete, and timely.				2420		
• **Errors and Omissions**						
If a final communication contains a significant error or omission, the chief audit executive must communicate corrected information to all parties who received the original communication.				2421		
• **Use of "Conducted in Conformance with the International Standards for the Professional Practice of Internal Auditing"**				2430		
Internal auditors may report that their engagements are "conducted in conformance with the International Standards for the Professional Practice of Internal Auditing," only if the results of the quality assurance and improvement program support the statement.						

(Continued)

Table 7.10 (Continued)   D4: Process

Area of Review	Governance	Staff	Management	Process	Exception Noted	Initial/ Date
• **Disseminating Results**				2440		
The chief audit executive must disseminate results to the appropriate parties.						
• The chief audit executive is responsible for communicating the final results to parties who can ensure that the results are given due consideration.				2440.A1		
• If not otherwise mandated by legal, statutory, or regulatory requirements, prior to releasing results to parties outside the organization the chief audit executive must				2440.A2		
Assess the potential risk to the organization.						
Consult with senior management or legal counsel, as appropriate.						
Control dissemination by restricting the use of the results.						
• The chief audit executive is responsible for communicating the final results of consulting engagements to clients.						

(Continued)

Table 7.10 (Continued)   D4: Process

Area of Review	Governance	Staff	Management	Process	Exception Noted	Initial/ Date
• During consulting engagements, governance, risk management, and control issues may be identified. Whenever these issues are significant to the organization, they must be communicated to senior management and the board.						
Conclude as to the overall adequacy of the IA activity's reporting process and resulting reports.						
H. Engagement Disclosure of Nonconformance				2431		
When nonconformance with the code of ethics or the Standards impacts a specific engagement, communication of the engagement results should disclose the						
• Principle or rule of conduct of the code of ethics or standard(s) with which full conformance was not achieved						
• Reason(s) for nonconformance						
• Impact of nonconformance on the engagement and the communicated engagement results						

(Continued)

Table 7.10 (Continued)   D4: Process

Area of Review	Governance	Staff	Management	Process	Exception Noted	Initial/Date
When there is noncompliance, and the standards are applicable and significant in the circumstances, communication of results must disclose this.						
If there was noncompliance with the Standards, conclude as to the adequacy of the IA activity's disclosure of it.						
I. Monitoring Progress				2500		
The chief audit executive must establish and maintain a system to monitor the disposition of results communicated to management.						
Key conformance criteria—Tool 19						
The chief audit executive has established a formal, documented follow-up process to monitor and ensure that management actions have been implemented effectively or risk accepted. (If there is evidence of residual risk that the chief audit executive considers unacceptable to the organization and these issues have not been resolved satisfactorily, see Tool 19, Standard 2600, key conformance criteria.)						

(Continued)

Table 7.10 (Continued)   D4: Process

Area of Review	Governance	Staff	Management	Process	Exception Noted	Initial/ Date
• The chief audit executive must establish a follow-up process to monitor and ensure that management actions have been effectively implemented or that senior management has accepted the risk of not taking action.				2500.A1		
• The internal audit activity must monitor the disposition of results of consulting engagements to the extent agreed upon with the client.				2500.C1		
Conclude as to the adequacy of the IA activity's follow-up process.						

Source: Adapted from State of North Carolina, Council of Internal Auditing, Office of Internal Audit, Peer Review Program, Program Phase—Process (Form D4).

Table 7.11 D5: Information Technology

Area of Review	Governance	Staff	Management	Process	Exception Noted	Initial/ Date
Information Technology						
Scope and Governance						
A. Determine the type and extent of IT activities in the agency/university. Are IT activities (data centers, system development and support, networks) in-house, outsourced, or a combination? If a combination, determine the extent of each.			2010 2030			
B. Inquire whether or not the agency/university has an IT strategy committee. Is IA a member of or invited to the committee or its equivalent management group? Does it have a committee that performs an IT strategy function?			2110.A2			
C. Determine if an information security function exists in the agency/university, the scope of its responsibilities, and how it interfaces with the IA activity.			2120.A1			
D. Determine if an enterprise policy on data ownership exists and its characteristics.			2130.A1			

(Continued)

Table 7.11 (Continued)   D5: Information Technology

Area of Review	Governance	Staff	Management	Process	Exception Noted	Initial/ Date
E. Determine whether the IT organization or the IA activity uses an IT control framework (e.g., COBIT, ISO 17799, and ITIL).				2201.A1		
F. Note any conclusions from the background (e.g., use of COBIT, ISO 17799, ITIL, and IT strategy committee).						
Organization and Staffing						
A. Determine how the IA activity is organized and staffed to address IT risk and control issues. Inquire if dedicated IT staff, integrated staff, outsourced resources, or some combination is used.		1210				
B. Determine the types of IT audit services provided, i.e., assurance, consulting, involvement in system development, or computer-assisted audit tools (CAATs) support.		1230				

(Continued)

Table 7.11 (Continued)   D5: Information Technology

Area of Review	Governance	Staff	Management	Process	Exception Noted	Initial/ Date
C. Using data collected in Tool 14 and from the results of the interviews with the IT staff, assess the qualifications, position descriptions, and ongoing training of the staff performing IT audits. Are there auditors with CISA certification on staff?			2030			
D. Evaluate IT staff ongoing education and training for both formal CPE coursework and informal participation in professional industry organizations, trade shows, and self-taught training (e.g., local college extension courses, online educational materials, etc.). Compare training and staff size to available benchmarks.						
E. Determine whether the entire audit staff is generally knowledgeable of key information technology process, controls, and risks (Standard 1210.A3).						
F. Using data on organization risk from the risk rating in Tool 13, statistics, and an analysis of the IT auditable units, determine the sufficiency of resources devoted to IT audits.						

(Continued)

Table 7.11 (Continued)   D5: Information Technology

Area of Review	Governance	Staff	Management	Process	Exception Noted	Initial/ Date
G. Conclude as to the appropriateness and adequacy of the IA activity and, in particular, the IT audit staff, to provide effective IT audit coverage and services (Staffing).						
Planning and Risk						
A. Review IT audit planning, polices, and procedures with the IT audit manager or the internal audit director.			2010			
B. Determine whether a risk assessment, which specifically includes IT topics in the list of auditable units, is performed at least annually. Refer to Tool 13 (Standard 2010.A1). Are IT risk and control topics given appropriate consideration (weighting) in the planning process?						
C. Is there a process of monitoring over time for the discovery/introduction of new risks to existing technology (e.g., subscription to security newsgroups, vendor notification mailing lists, etc.)?						

(Continued)

Table 7.11 (Continued)   D5: Information Technology

Area of Review	Governance	Staff	Management	Process	Exception Notea	Initial/ Date
D. Does IA specifically consider fraud as a risk factor in the assessment of IT (e.g., vendor selection/ purchasing, financial statements, etc.)?						
E. Review the IA activity's involvement in and awareness of						
Strategic/tactical plans for installing new IT within the agency/university						
Technologies being implemented, e.g., e-commerce, intranet, client/server, wireless technology, and networking.						
Long-range IT planning and systems development.						
F. Conclude as to the process of including IT auditable units in the annual audit planning process (Risk Rating IT).						

(Continued)

Table 7.11 (Continued)   D5: Information Technology

Area of Review	Governance	Staff	Management	Process	Exception Noted	Initial/Date
Audit Coverage						
A. To assess the adequacy of IT processes, the internal audit creates a table using the data collected in Tool 13, the planning process covered under C, and the IT framework (e.g., COBIT, ISO 17799, and ITIL). This table is for reference only and does not need to be completed in its entirety. The reviewer needs only indicate those areas determined to be inadequately covered.			2110.A2			
B. Audit coverage should also include periodic review of high-risk applications as well as new projects under development. List any appropriate projects here and determine coverage.			2120.A1			
Determine whether IT audit has a process to identify all high-risk IT applications.				2201.A1		
Determine whether IT audit has a plan to review outsourced/vendor-operated systems.						
Determine if auditors have identified computerized applications that process data and generate reports upon which management relies.						

(Continued)

Table 7.11 (Continued)   D5: Information Technology

Area of Review	Governance	Staff	Management	Process	Exception Noted	Initial/ Date
C. Development Projects						
What is the process by which IT audit is made aware of system development projects?						
Determine the nature of IT audit involvement in the system development process (Assurance and Consulting).						
D. Conclude as to the adequate identification and audit coverage of IT risk in the agency/university (Universe).						
Annual Audit Plan						
A. Compare the list of completed audits from Tool 2 to the list of high-risk systems, including major financial and human resources applications.			2120.A1			
Does the annual audit plan include IT consulting projects?						
Does the annual plan include the use of an IT framework and audit plans from sources such as COBIT, ISO 17799, or ITIL?						
Does the annual plan address the high-risk areas?						

(Continued)

Table 7.11 (Continued)   D5: Information Technology

Area of Review	Governance	Staff	Management	Process	Exception Noted	Initial/Date
B. Determine whether fraud is considered in implementation audits, consulting, and process audits.						
C. Conclude as to the adequate coverage of IT risk and control topics in the annual plan.						
Leveraging the power of IT with computer-assisted audit tools						
A. Determine whether audit tools are developed for auditors to extract and analyze data, identify areas of risk, and perform real-time/online testing?						
B. Determine whether auditors are educated and encouraged in the use of these tools.						
C. Inquire if support in using these tools is provided to auditors, either from within or outside the agency/university.						
D. Conclude as to the adequacy of audit tools and other technology for the IA activity.						

Source: Adapted from State of North Carolina, Council of Internal Auditing, Office of Internal Audit, Peer Review Program, Program Phase—Information Technology (Form D5).

function. This evaluation covers, scope and governance, organization and staffing, planning and risks, audit coverage, and annual audit plan.

7.11.2.3.6 D6: Testing Tool—Work Paper Review Assignment (Table 7.12)

The purpose of this tool is to assign engagements to each member for review.

Table 7.12   D6: Testing Tool—Work Paper Review Assignment

1. Name of audit/consulting engagement:	Audit Report Date:
	Audit Hours
	Audit hours as a percentage of all hours
Peer Review Team Member:	QA Review Completed Date:
2. Name of audit/consulting engagement:	Audit Dates Performed
	Audit Report Date:
Peer Review Team Member:	QA Review Completed Date:
3. Name of audit/consulting engagement:	Audit Dates Performed
	Audit Report Date:
Peer Review Team Member:	QA Review Completed Date:
4. Name of audit/consulting engagement:	Audit Dates Performed
	Audit Report Date:
Peer Review Team Member:	QA Review Completed Date:

Source: Adapted from State of North Carolina, Council of Internal Auditing, Office of Internal Audit, Peer Review Program, Program Phase—Testing Tool—Work Paper Review Assignment (Form D6).

7.11.2.3.7 D7: Testing Tool—Work Paper Review Summary (Figure 7.18)

Where there is more than one issue noted in the work paper assessment, this summary form is used to document major observations from the program—Process (D4).

If there is more than one issue noted in the work paper assessment, use this summary to document major observations from the program (D4). Major observations are usually those that are either of significant individual items or repeated patterns that support a potential recommendation (E1) or a potential Standards conformance issue (E2).

Summary Comments
(Potential reportable items, opportunities for improvement, and potential Standards compliance issues)

A. Planning—2200
B. Objectives—2210
C. Scope—2220
D. Resource Allocation—2230
E. Work Program—2240
F. Performing the Engagement—2300
G. Communicating Results—2400
H. Disclosure of Nonconformance—2431
I. Monitoring Progress—2500

Figure 7.18   D7: Testing tool—work paper review summary. (Retrieved from State of North Carolina, Council of Internal Auditing, Office of Internal Audit, Peer Review Program, Program Phase—Testing Tool—Work Paper Review Summary [Form D7].)

7.11.3 Evaluation Summary and Report Phase

As in the case of internal audit work, all QA findings and observations must be supported by sufficient, relevant, and reliable audit evidence. Working papers of the QAR team should be documented methodically to enable easy referencing. The draft findings and recommendations should be discussed with senior management before including them in the final report. Also, the report should include a summary of observations and recommendations.

7.11.3.1 E1: Evaluation Tool—Observations and Issues Worksheet (Figure 7.19)

Record any observations and issues realized through the peer review process. Provide a summary and hold a closing conference with the internal audit director. If necessary, more than one E1 can be used.

W/P Reference of issue(s) if identify:

Area/Topic/Issue:

Criteria/Other Documentation: Standard No._____ Practice Advisory No._____ Policies/Procedures No._____ Benchmark/Industry Standard_____

QA Team Member's Observations/Comments:

Recommendation(s):

Briefly comment on your validation of the observation with the internal audit activity's management, including the individuals with whom it was discussed:

Figure 7.19   E1: Evaluation tool—observations and issues worksheet.   (*Continued*)

Included in report? □ Yes □ No □ Verbally Only
If yes, report reference:
If no, briefly explain:

Reviewer's Name: _____ Date: _____

Team Leader: _____ Date: _____

Figure 7.19 (Continued) E1: Evaluation tool—observations and issues worksheet. (Retrieved from State of North Carolina, Council of Internal Auditing, Office of Internal Audit, Peer Review Program; Evaluation Summary and Report Phase— Evaluation Tool—Evaluation and Issues Worksheet [Form E1].)

7.11.3.2 E2: Standard Conformance Evaluation (Tables 7.13 and 7.14)

Part I: General Instructions/Definitions

Together with completion of all of the applicable tools in the *Peer Review Manual*, E2 should be used to provide an overall assessment of the organization's conformance with the IIA Standards.

When evaluating conformance, carefully read the Standards and relevant interpretations included and consider only the IIA Standards and corresponding interpretations, not the ideal situations, *successful practice*, etc. Please note that only the requirements included in the IIA Standards and interpretations are mandatory.

Pages E2-6 through E2-34 provide a master framework to aid in the overall assessment of conformance with the IIA Standards.

Each member of the peer review team must complete the master framework section (Part IV of this document). Consider each individual standard, including the relevant implementation standards, and conclude as to the degree of conformance by the activity to each individual standard using the key conformance criteria and examples of evidence for guidance.

Any of the key conformance criteria not achieved would strongly suggest a rating of *does not conform* or *partially conforms* for that individual standard.

Pages E2-3 through E2-5 provide the overall evaluation.

The team lead is responsible for completing this section (Part III of this document). Consider each section of the Standards with numbers ending in "00" (e.g., Standard 1200: Proficiency and Due Professional Care, Standard 2300: Performing the Engagement, etc.), and conclude as to the degree of conformance by the activity to each section taken as a whole, based on conclusions reached for the related individual Standards in the section and on other relevant observations made during

Table 7.13 Consolidated Conformance Evaluation Form

Team Lead Consolidates All Part IV Evaluations		GC	PC	DNC
Part III: Overall Evaluation				
GOVERNANCE				
IIA Code of Ethics				
Definition of Internal Auditing				
1000	**Purpose, Authority, and Responsibility**			
1010	Recognition of the Definition of Internal Auditing			
1100	**Independence and Objectivity**			
1110	Organizational Independence			
1111	Direct Interaction with the Board			
1120	Individual Objectivity			
1130	Impairments to Independence or Objectivity			
1300	**Quality Assurance and Improvement Program**			
1310	Requirements of the Quality Assurance and Improvement Program			
1311	Internal Assessments			
1312	External Assessments			
1320	Reporting on the Quality Assurance and Improvement Program			
1321	Use of "Conforms with the *International Standards for the Professional Practice of Internal Auditing*"			
1322	Disclosure of Nonconformance			

(Continued)

Table 7.13 (Continued)   Consolidated Conformance Evaluation Form

Team Lead Consolidates All Part IV Evaluations		GC	PC	DNC
STAFF				
1200	**Proficiency and Due Professional Care**			
1210	Proficiency			
1220	Due Professional Care			
1230	Continuing Professional Development			
MANAGEMENT				
2000	**Managing the Internal Audit Activity**			
2010	Planning			
2020	Communication and Approval			
2030	Resource Management			
2040	Policies and Procedures			
2050	Coordination			
2060	Reporting to Senior Management and the Board			
2100	**Nature of Work**			
2110	Governance			
2120	Risk Management			
2130	Control			
2600	**Communicating the Acceptance of Risks**			

(Continued)

Table 7.13 (Continued)   Consolidated Conformance Evaluation Form

Team Lead Consolidates All Part IV Evaluations		GC	PC	DNC
PROCESS				
2200	**Engagement Planning**			
2201	Planning Considerations			
2210	Engagement Objectives			
2220	Engagement Scope			
2230	Engagement Resource Allocation			
2240	Engagement Work Program			
2300	**Performing the Engagement**			
2310	Identifying Information			
2320	Analysis and Evaluation			
2330	Documenting Information			
2340	Engagement Supervision			
2400	**Communicating Results**			
2410	Criteria for Communicating			
2420	Quality of Communications			
2421	Errors and Omissions			
2430	Use of "Conducted in conformance with the *International Standards for the Professional Practice of Internal Auditing*"			
2431	Engagement Disclosure of Nonconformance			
2440	Disseminating Results			
2500	**Monitoring Progress**			

Table 7.14   Part IV: Standards Conformance Evaluation—Master Framework

Each peer review team member should complete this form separately.

1. Attribute Standards

Standard	Key Conformance Criteria	Examples of Evidence, Sound Practices, and Other Considerations
GOVERNANCE		
1000—Purpose, Authority, and Responsibility: The purpose, authority, and responsibility of the internal audit activity must be formally defined in an internal audit charter, consistent with the definition of internal auditing, the code of ethics, and the Standards. The chief audit executive must periodically review the internal audit charter and present it to senior management and the board for approval. **1000.A1**—The nature of assurance services provided to the organization must be defined in the internal audit charter. If assurances are to be provided to parties outside the organization, the nature of these assurances must also be defined in the internal audit charter. **1000.C1**—The nature of the consulting must be defined in the internal audit charter.	There is a charter containing the purpose, authority, and responsibility of the internal audit activity. The charter has been reviewed periodically and approved by the board. The charter defines the nature of assurance and consulting services.	Internal audit activity charter: The charter is approved by senior management. The purpose, authority, and responsibilities of the internal audit activity are defined in the charter. The charter establishes the position of the internal audit department within the organization. The charter provides unrestricted access to records, personnel, and physical properties relevant to the performance of engagements. The charter sets the tone for the internal audit activity's interaction with the board. The charter defines the nature of activities to be performed. Minutes of board meetings. Interviews of the CAE, senior management, etc. The code of conduct is referenced.

(Continued)

Table 7.14 (Continued)   Part IV: Standards Conformance Evaluation—Master Framework

Standard	Key Conformance Criteria	Examples of Evidence, Sound Practices, and Other Considerations
1000—Purpose, Authority and Responsibility		≤GC ≤PC ≤DNC
1010—Recognition of the Definition of Internal Auditing, the Code of Ethics, and the Standards in the Internal Audit Charter: The mandatory nature of the definition of internal auditing, the code of ethics, and the Standards must be recognized in the internal audit charter. The chief audit executive should discuss the definition of internal auditing, the code of ethics, and the Standards with senior management and the board.	The charter includes references to the definition of internal auditing and the code of ethics consistent with the Standards.	Audit committee minutes verify that discussion of the definition of internal auditing, code of ethics, and Standards periodically took place.
1010—Recognition of Definition of Internal Auditing		≤GC ≤PC ≤DNC
1000—Purpose, Authority and Responsibility	Sum of Standards 1000–1010	≤GC ≤PC ≤DNC

(Continued)

Table 7.14 (Continued) Part IV: Standards Conformance Evaluation—Master Framework

Standard	Key Conformance Criteria	Examples of Evidence, Sound Practices, and Other Considerations
1110—Organizational Independence: The chief audit executive must report to a level within the organization that allows the internal audit activity to fulfill its responsibilities. The chief audit executive must confirm to the board, at least annually, the organizational independence of the internal audit activity. **1110.A1**—The internal audit activity must be free from interference in determining the scope of internal auditing, performing work, and communicating results.	The CAE reports to a level in the organization that is adequate to discharge his or her responsibilities. Any reporting relationship (administrative or total) to management does not interfere with the CAE's responsibility to the board. There are no restrictions to the scope, resources, and access of internal audit activity.	Organizational charts. Annual audit plan. Engagement work programs. Interviews of the CAE, senior management, etc. The internal audit activity reports directly to the highest executive levels of the organization (e.g., senior management, the board). Audit committee charter includes: Appointment and removal of CAE; Salary of CAE; CAE performance appraisal; Annual planning of audit engagements; Resource allocations; Coverage of engagement objectives; Implementation of audit procedures; Communication of results; and Budget and staffing. Major restrictions on the scope of internal audit activities are systematically reported to board.
1110—Organizational Independence		≤GC ≤PC ≤DNC

(Continued)

Table 7.14 (Continued) Part IV: Standards Conformance Evaluation—Master Framework

Standard	Key Conformance Criteria	Examples of Evidence, Sound Practices, and Other Considerations
1111—Direct Interaction with the Board: The chief audit executive must communicate and interact directly with the board.		Evidenced through interviews and board minutes.
1111—Direct Interaction with the Board		≤GC ≤PC ≤DNC
1120—Individual Objectivity: Internal auditors must have an impartial, unbiased attitude and avoid any conflict of interest.	Auditors do not have assignments in conflict. Audit staff has background and experience that does not conflict with audit assignment. Results and conclusions of engagements are based on factual evidence and observation.	Interviews with audit staff. Interviews with senior management. Examination of auditor assignments—e.g., must not audit a function for which they were responsible. Evaluation of auditor background. Evidence of supervision. There is linkage between the audit objectives, factual evidence, and conclusions.

(Continued)

Table 7.14 (Continued)   Part IV: Standards Conformance Evaluation—Master Framework

Standard	Key Conformance Criteria	Examples of Evidence, Sound Practices, and Other Considerations
		≤GC ≤PC ≤DNC
1120—Individual Objectivity		
1130—Impairment to Independence or Objectivity: If independence or objectivity is impaired in fact or appearance, the details of the impairment must be disclosed to appropriate parties. The nature of the disclosure will be dependent on the impairment.	Auditors are aware they must report any real or perceived conflict of interest as soon as such conflict arises.	List of auditors including their date of appointment and responsibilities held prior to appointment. Engagement records. Internal auditors' assignments for previous three years.
1130.A1—Internal auditors must refrain from assessing specific operations for which they were previously responsible. Objectivity is presumed to be impaired if an internal auditor provides assurance services for an activity for which the internal auditor had responsibility within the previous year.	Assignment of internal audit personnel takes into account previous responsibilities. A policy exists to ensure that assurance engagements of areas that are under the control or direct influence of the CAE are overseen by a party external to the CAE.	Policies and procedures of the internal audit department. Disclosures on independence have been made to board per minutes of the board meetings. Formal commitment to code of ethics. An outside party oversees assurance services over functions for which the CAE has been responsible. Objectivity may be impaired if assigned to operations for which they were previously responsible within the previous year and relationships with the audited activities potential conflicts of interest.
1130.A2—Assurance engagements for functions over which the chief audit executive has responsibility must be overseen by a party outside the internal audit activity.		Areas of responsibility are rotated on a regular basis, thus ensuring that the same processes, activities, and entities are not audited by the same auditors.
1130.C1—Internal auditors may provide consulting services relating to operations for which they had previous responsibilities.		

(Continued)

Table 7.14 (Continued)   Part IV: Standards Conformance Evaluation—Master Framework

Standard	Key Conformance Criteria	Examples of Evidence, Sound Practices, and Other Considerations
1130.C2—If internal auditors have potential impairments to independence or objectivity relating to proposed consulting services, disclosure must be made to the engagement client prior to accepting the engagement.		
1130—Impairment to Independence or Objectivity		≤GC ≤PC ≤DNC
1300—Quality Assurance and Improvement Program: The chief audit executive must develop and maintain a quality assurance and improvement program that covers all aspects of the internal audit activity.	The internal audit activity has a process to monitor and assess the overall effectiveness of the quality program.	Documented quality assurance and improvement program. Quality program procedures. Performance indicators for the internal audit activity. Formal results of assessments performed. Responses given to assessment recommendations. Activity reports. Measurement of value added such as surveys. Assessments include the following aspects: Adherence to the Standards and code of ethics; Adequacy of the internal audit charter, objectives, policies, and procedures; Contribution to risk management, control, and governance processes; and

(Continued)

Table 7.14 (Continued)   Part IV: Standards Conformance Evaluation—Master Framework

Standard	Key Conformance Criteria	Examples of Evidence, Sound Practices, and Other Considerations
		Value added according to key stakeholders. Assessments include ongoing reviews of the performance of the internal audit activity and periodic reviews performed through self-assessment or by other persons within the organization who have knowledge of internal audit practices and the Standards.
1300—QAIP	≤GC ≤PC ≤DNC	
1310—Requirements of the Quality Assurance and Improvement Program: The quality assurance and improvement program must include both internal and external assessments.		
1310—Requirements of the QAIP	≤GC ≤PC ≤DNC	

(Continued)

Table 7.14 (Continued)   Part IV: Standards Conformance Evaluation—Master Framework

Standard	Key Conformance Criteria	Examples of Evidence, Sound Practices, and Other Considerations
1311—Internal Assessments: Internal assessments must include: Ongoing monitoring of the performance of the internal audit activity; and Periodic reviews performed through self-assessment or by other persons within the organization with sufficient knowledge of internal audit practices.	There is evidence of ongoing reviews of the performance of the internal audit activity. Periodic reviews were performed through self-assessment or by other persons within the organization, with knowledge of internal audit practices and the Standards.	Reports and documentation of internal reviews, including action plan. Periodic assessment of internal audit staff. Client surveys. Work paper reviews. Board minutes. Performance indicators.
1311—Internal Assessments		≤GC ≤PC ≤DNC
1312—External Assessments: External assessments must be conducted at least once every five years by a qualified, independent reviewer or review team from outside the organization. The chief audit executive must discuss with the board: The need for more frequent external assessments; and	There is evidence of comprehensive external reviews by qualified, independent reviewers.	Committee/board minutes. Report of external reviewer. List of competencies for the team leader and team.

(Continued)

Table 7.14 (Continued) Part IV: Standards Conformance Evaluation—Master Framework

Standard	Key Conformance Criteria	Examples of Evidence, Sound Practices, and Other Considerations
The qualifications and independence of the external reviewer or review team, including any potential conflict of interest		
1312—External Assessment	≤GC ≤PC ≤DNC	
1320—Reporting on the Quality Assurance and Improvement Program: The chief audit executive must communicate the results of the quality assurance and improvement program to senior management and the board.		Reports of the results of external assessments are submitted to the board.
1320—Reporting on the QAIP	≤GC ≤PC ≤DNC	Training and continuous development policy for internal audit function.
		List of CIA auditors or of auditors having obtained similar professional certifications.
		Training program fulfilling criteria for maintaining certification.
		Auditors participate in the activities of professional bodies.
		Auditors participate in conferences, seminars, and working groups.
		Auditors take part in internal and external training.
		The internal audit activity encourages internal auditors to obtain relevant professional certifications such as the CIA.

(Continued)

Table 7.14 (Continued)   Part IV: Standards Conformance Evaluation—Master Framework

Standard	Key Conformance Criteria	Examples of Evidence, Sound Practices, and Other Considerations
1321—Use of "Conforms with the *International Standards for the Professional Practice of Internal Auditing*": The chief audit executive may state that the internal audit activity conforms with the *International Standards for the Professional Practice of Internal Auditing* only if the results of the quality assurance and improvement program support this statement.		There is appropriate wording in audit reports.
1321—Use of "Conforms with the *International Standards for the Professional Practice of Internal Auditing"*	There is appropriate wording in report to the board.	≤GC ≤PC ≤DNC
1322—Disclosure of Nonconformance: When nonconformance with the definition of internal auditing, the code of ethics, or the *Standards* impacts the overall scope or operation of the internal audit activity, the chief audit executive must disclose the nonconformance and the impact to senior management and the board.		Interview with board or senior management as to whether the situation has occurred and has been reported. Board minutes. External assessment report.
1322—Disclosure of Nonconformance		≤GC ≤PC ≤DNC
1300—Quality Assurance and Improvement Program	Sum of Standards 1300–1322	≤GC ≤PC ≤DNC

(Continued)

Table 7.14 (Continued)   Part IV: Standards Conformance Evaluation—Master Framework

Standard	Key Conformance Criteria	Examples of Evidence, Sound Practices, and Other Considerations
1310—Requirements of the QAIP		≤GC ≤PC ≤DNC
1311—Internal Assessments: Internal assessments must include: Ongoing monitoring of the performance of the internal audit activity; and Periodic reviews performed through self-assessment or by other persons within the organization with sufficient knowledge of internal audit practices.	There is evidence of ongoing reviews of the performance of the internal audit activity. Periodic reviews were performed through self-assessment or by other persons within the organization, with knowledge of internal audit practices and the Standards.	Reports and documentation of internal reviews, including action plan. Periodic assessment of internal audit staff. Client surveys. Work paper reviews. Board minutes. Performance indicators.
1311—Internal Assessments		≤GC ≤PC ≤DNC

(Continued)

Table 7.14 (Continued)   Part IV: Standards Conformance Evaluation—Master Framework

Standard	Key Conformance Criteria	Examples of Evidence, Sound Practices, and Other Considerations
1312—External Assessments: External assessments must be conducted at least once every five years by a qualified, independent reviewer or review team from outside the organization. The chief audit executive must discuss with the board: The need for more frequent external assessments; and The qualifications and independence of the external reviewer or review team, including any potential conflict of interest.	There is evidence of comprehensive external reviews by qualified, independent reviewers.	Committee/board minutes. Report of external reviewer. List of competencies for the team leader and team.
1312—External Assessment		≤GC ≤PC ≤DNC
1320—Reporting on the Quality Assurance and Improvement Program: The chief audit executive must communicate the results of the quality assurance and improvement program to senior management and the board.	Reports of the results of external assessments are submitted to the board.	Board minutes. Action plan. External assessment report.
1320—Reporting on the QAIP		≤GC ≤PC ≤DNC

(Continued)

Table 7.14 (Continued)   Part IV: Standards Conformance Evaluation—Master Framework

Standard	Key Conformance Criteria	Examples of Evidence, Sound Practices, and Other Considerations
1321—Use of "Conforms with the *International Standards for the Professional Practice of Internal Auditing"*: The chief audit executive may state that the internal audit activity conforms with the *International Standards for the Professional Practice of Internal Auditing* only if the results of the quality assurance and improvement program support this statement.	There is appropriate wording in audit reports.	Audit reports. Audit procedures manual. IA activity charter. External assessment report with a general conform opinion.
1321—Use of "Conforms with the *International Standards for the Professional Practice of Internal Auditing"*		≤GC ≤PC ≤DNC
1322—Disclosure of Nonconformance: When nonconformance with the definition of internal auditing, the code of ethics, or the *Standards* impacts the overall scope or operation of the internal audit activity, the chief audit executive must disclose the nonconformance and the impact to senior management and the board.	There is appropriate wording in report to the board.	Interview with board or senior management as to whether the situation has occurred and has been reported. Board minutes. External assessment report.
1322—Disclosure of Nonconformance		≤GC ≤PC ≤DNC

(Continued)

Table 7.14 (Continued)   Part IV: Standards Conformance Evaluation—Master Framework

Standard	Key Conformance Criteria	Examples of Evidence, Sound Practices, and Other Considerations
1300—Quality Assurance and Improvement Program	Sum of Standards 1300–1322	≤GC ≤PC ≤DNC
Code of Ethics—The auditors adhere to the IIA code of ethics (Code).	Department policy establishes the expectation that audit staff will conform to the code of ethics requirements. There is evidence that the policy is communicated to and understood by the internal audit activity staff.	Audit policies and procedures. Interviews of selected auditors. Interviews of selected clients. Annual evaluation. The code of ethics is included in department policies and procedures. On the basis of surveys of a cross-section of auditors and clients, determine if internal auditors are familiar with and adhere to the code of ethics. Instances of nonconformance have been adequately addressed.
Code of Ethics		≤GC ≤PC ≤DNC
Definition of Internal Auditing		≤GC ≤PC ≤DNC
Governance—Overall		≤GC ≤PC ≤DNC

(Continued)

Table 7.14 (Continued)   Part IV: Standards Conformance Evaluation—Master Framework

Standard	Key Conformance Criteria	Examples of Evidence, Sound Practices, and Other Considerations
STAFF		
1200—Proficiency and Due Professional Care: Engagements must be performed with proficiency and due professional care.		
1210—Proficiency: Internal auditors must possess the knowledge, skills, and other competencies needed to perform their individual responsibilities. The internal audit activity collectively must possess or obtain the knowledge, skills, and other competencies needed to perform its responsibilities. **1210.A1**—The chief audit executive must obtain competent advice and assistance if the internal auditors lack the knowledge, skills, or other competencies needed to perform all or part of the engagement. **1210.A2**—Internal auditors must have sufficient knowledge to evaluate the risk of fraud and the manner in which it is managed by the organization, but are not expected to have the expertise of a person whose primary responsibility is detecting and investigating fraud.	Auditors undergo specific training based on collective staff training needs analysis. Staff performance is reviewed on a regular basis and the criterion used is adequate and appropriate for the needs of the activity. Where skills are lacking, CAE has engaged capable assistance. Auditors have fraud training or proficiency in identification of fraud indicators.	Job descriptions and competency requirements (especially information systems and fraud). Staff date of appointment, prior responsibilities and qualifications. Hiring plans and selection procedures. Training plans. Annual and engagement performance evaluations. Interviews of clients. Contracts for supplemental resources or outsourcing. Review of third-party reports. Reports and work papers of third party. Performance and knowledge requirements are clearly documented in the contract. Professional certifications. Resumes of staff. There is evidence that IT tools are used when appropriate in audit plans.

(Continued)

Table 7.14 (Continued) Part IV: Standards Conformance Evaluation—Master Framework

Standard	Key Conformance Criteria	Examples of Evidence, Sound Practices, and Other Considerations
1210.A3—Internal auditors must have sufficient knowledge of key information technology risks and controls and available technology-based audit techniques to perform their assigned work. However, not all internal auditors are expected to have the expertise of an internal auditor whose primary responsibility is information technology auditing. **1210.C1**—The chief audit executive must decline the consulting engagement or obtain competent advice and assistance if the internal auditors lack the knowledge, skills, or other competencies needed to perform all or part of the engagement.	Auditors have training or proficiency in IT concepts and computer aided audit tools. Where skills are lacking, the CAE has engaged capable assistance or has declined the engagement.	Performance and knowledge requirements are clearly documented in the contract. Autonomous data extraction. Evidence in work papers that fraud has been considered.
1210—Proficiency		≤GC ≤PC ≤DNC

(Continued)

Table 7.14 (Continued)   Part IV: Standards Conformance Evaluation—Master Framework

Standard	Key Conformance Criteria	Examples of Evidence, Sound Practices, and Other Considerations
1220—Due Professional Care: Internal auditors must apply the care and skill expected of a reasonably prudent and competent internal auditor. Due professional care does not imply infallibility.	Audit work papers provide evidence of due professional care in the conduct of the work performed.	Audit work papers. Reports. Tools used by internal auditors.
1220.A1—Internal auditors must exercise due professional care by considering the: Extent of work needed to achieve the engagement's objectives; Relative complexity, materiality, or significance of matters to which assurance procedures are applied; Adequacy and effectiveness of governance, risk management, and control processes; Probability of significant errors, fraud, or nonconformance; and Cost of assurance in relation to potential benefits.	Audit engagements are supported by appropriate tools, including information systems and used in an appropriate manner. There is evidence of a risk assessment of the audit engagement. Consulting engagement documentation provides evidence of due professional care in the conduct of the work performed.	Conclusions based on appropriate tests, analyses and supporting documentation, indexed and classified work papers, effective coverage of engagement work program objectives, etc. When making recommendations, the internal auditors consider the cost of implementing controls in relation to potential benefits. Data extraction and analysis techniques, risk assessment tools, tools for engagement planning and performance, communication, etc. Audit engagement risk assessment. Conclusions based on appropriate tests, analyses and supporting documentation, indexed and classified work papers, effective coverage of engagement work program objectives, etc. When making recommendations, the internal auditors consider the cost of implementing controls in relation to potential benefits.
1220.A2—In exercising due professional care the internal auditor must consider the use of technology-based audit and other data analysis techniques.		

(Continued)

Table 7.14 (Continued) Part IV: Standards Conformance Evaluation—Master Framework

Standard	Key Conformance Criteria	Examples of Evidence, Sound Practices, and Other Considerations
1220.A3—Internal auditors must be alert to the significant risks that might affect objectives, operations, or resources. However, assurance procedures alone, even when performed with due professional care, do not guarantee that all significant risks will be identified. **1220.C1**—Internal auditors must exercise due professional care during a consulting engagement by considering the: Needs and expectations of clients, including the nature, timing, and communication of engagement results; Relative complexity and extent of work needed to achieve the engagement's objectives; and Cost of the consulting engagement in relation to potential benefits.		Work papers should have evidence of use of technology-based tools. Staff interviews should reveal that auditors are familiar with advanced data analysis techniques.
1220—Due Professional Care		≤GC ≤PC ≤DNC

(Continued)

Table 7.14 (Continued) Part IV: Standards Conformance Evaluation—Master Framework

Standard	Key Conformance Criteria	Examples of Evidence, Sound Practices, and Other Considerations
1230—Continuing Professional Development: Internal auditors must enhance their knowledge, skills, and other competencies through continuing professional development.	There is continuing professional development to enhance the knowledge and competencies of internal auditors.	Training and continuous development policy for internal audit function. List of CIA auditors or of auditors having obtained similar professional certifications. Training program fulfilling criteria for maintaining certification. Auditors participate in the activities of professional bodies. Auditors participate in conferences, seminars, and working groups. Auditors take part in internal and external training. The internal audit activity encourages internal auditors to obtain relevant professional certifications such as the CIA.
1230—Continuing Professional Development		≤GC ≤PC ≤DNC
1200—Proficiency	Sum of Standards 1210–1230	≤GC ≤PC ≤DNC
Staff—Overall		≤GC ≤PC ≤DNC

(Continued)

Table 7.14 (Continued)   Part IV: Standards Conformance Evaluation—Master Framework

Standard	Key Conformance Criteria	Examples of Evidence, Sound Practices, and Other Considerations
2. Performance Standards		
MANAGEMENT		
2000—Managing the Internal Audit Activity: The chief audit executive must effectively manage the internal audit activity to ensure it adds value to the organization.		
2010—Planning: The chief audit executive must establish risk-based plans to determine the priorities of the internal audit activity, consistent with the organization's goals. **2010.A1**—The internal audit activity's plan of engagements must be based on a documented risk assessment, undertaken at least annually. The input of senior management and the board must be considered in this process. **2010.C1**—The chief audit executive should consider accepting proposed consulting engagements based on the engagement's potential to improve management of risks, add value, and improve the organization's operations. Accepted engagements must be included in the plan.	The CAE has established risk-based plans in consultation with the board and senior management. Where appropriate, consulting engagements are in the annual audit plan.	Annual audit plan: The audit plan risk assessment establishes a link between the proposed audit topics and the operational and strategic risks of the organization. The audit plan risk assessment takes account of feedback received from operational managers. Formal opinions of senior management and of the board, e.g., final approval of annual audit plan. Formal risk assessment. Strategic plan of organization. Annual audit plan. The engagement work program is based on a periodic, at least annual, comprehensive risk assessment.

(Continued)

Table 7.14 (Continued) Part IV: Standards Conformance Evaluation—Master Framework

Standard	Key Conformance Criteria	Examples of Evidence, Sound Practices, and Other Considerations
2010—Planning		≤GC ≤PC ≤DNC
2020—Communication and Approval: The chief audit executive must communicate the internal audit activity's plans and resource requirements, including significant interim changes, to senior management and the board for review and approval. The chief audit executive must also communicate the impact of resource limitations.	The CAE has communicated the internal audit activity's annual plans, including significant interim changes, to senior management and the board. The CAE also has communicated to senior management and the board the impact of resource limitations.	Annual audit plan. Final approval of annual audit plan. Evidence of action taken by CAE in the event of resource limitations. Formal assessment of needs prepared by CAE. The CAE informs senior management and the board of any audit engagements that have been rescheduled as well as the reasons for rescheduling and the degree of risk associated with the rescheduled engagements.
2020—Communication and Approval		≤GC ≤PC ≤DNC

(Continued)

Table 7.14 (Continued) Part IV: Standards Conformance Evaluation—Master Framework

Standard	Key Conformance Criteria	Examples of Evidence, Sound Practices, and Other Considerations
2030—Resource Management: The chief audit executive must ensure that internal audit resources are appropriate, sufficient, and effectively deployed to achieve the approved plan.	Staffing plans and financial budgets are determined from annual audit plans and activities of the internal audit department. The internal audit activity is organized to ensure proper coverage of the organization's audit universe.	Staffing analysis and annual operating plans. Annual audit plan. Program for selecting and developing human resources. Interviews of senior management. Interviews of the CAE. Procedures to notify CAE or any internal audit manager of any problems that arise during the audit. Evidence that the internal audit activity is organized to reflect the activities of the organization and to encourage interaction between internal auditors and their audit clients (e.g., internal audit is organized similar to audited organization). Administrative activities, training requirements, etc.

(Continued)

Table 7.14 (Continued) Part IV: Standards Conformance Evaluation—Master Framework

Standard	Key Conformance Criteria	Examples of Evidence, Sound Practices, and Other Considerations
		Staffing plans make provisions for the knowledge, skills, and other competencies required to perform the internal audit responsibilities.
		Utilization of staff.
		Budget to actual time.
		The CAE established a program for selecting and developing the human resources of the internal audit department.
		On-time performance of audit engagements monitored:
		If yes, budget to actual time comparisons are performed.
		If no, comparisons are analyzed.
2030—Resource Management		≤GC ≤PC ≤DNC
2040—Policies and Procedures: The chief audit executive must establish policies and procedures to guide the internal audit activity.	There are appropriate policies and procedures and they are communicated to and understood by the staff of the internal audit activity.	Policies and procedures.
		Audit manual.
		Interviews with staff.
		There is evidence that policies and procedures are followed.
		Policies and procedures are well documented.

(Continued)

Table 7.14 (Continued)   Part IV: Standards Conformance Evaluation—Master Framework

Standard	Key Conformance Criteria	Examples of Evidence, Sound Practices, and Other Considerations
2040—Policies and Procedures		≤GC ≤PC ≤DNC
2050—Coordination: The chief audit executive should share information and coordinate activities with other internal and external providers of assurance and consulting services to ensure proper coverage and minimize duplication of efforts.	Internal audit work is coordinated with that of the external auditors and with internal providers of assurance and consulting services.	Annual audit plans of internal and external auditors. Reports on meetings. Delegation of personnel or resource sharing. Common training courses. Compatible methods and tools. Follow-up by internal audit of the external auditors' recommendations. Comprehensiveness of their respective plans, proper coverage of the organization's audit universe, etc. Internal and external auditors share information about the results of their work (reciprocal exchanges of activity reports, etc.). Internal auditors meet regularly with the external auditors to discuss matters of mutual interest or concern.
2050—Coordination		≤GC ≤PC ≤DNC

(Continued)

Table 7.14 (Continued) Part IV: Standards Conformance Evaluation—Master Framework

Standard	Key Conformance Criteria	Examples of Evidence, Sound Practices, and Other Considerations
2060—Reporting to Senior Management and the Board: The chief audit executive must report periodically to senior management and the board on the internal audit activity's purpose, authority, responsibility, and performance relative to its plan. Reporting must also include significant risk exposures and control issues, including fraud risks, governance issues, and other matters needed or requested by senior management and the board.	There is evidence that the CAE reports appropriately to the board and senior management on the internal audit activity purpose, authority, responsibility, and performance as well as significant fraud and other risks.	Board minutes. CAE presentation to board. Activity reports. Interviews, management reports, reports on meetings. Senior management's responses to internal audit reports. Any tangible evidence (e-mail records, internal memos, reports on meetings, etc.) demonstrating that the board had been informed. Status of action plans from audit findings. Interview, where necessary, of a member of the board. CAE report includes: Performance measures; Risk exposures; Control issues; and Governance issues.
2060—Reporting to Senior Management and the Board		≤GC ≤PC ≤DNC

(Continued)

Table 7.14 (Continued)   Part IV: Standards Conformance Evaluation—Master Framework

Standard	Key Conformance Criteria	Examples of Evidence, Sound Practices, and Other Considerations
2000—Managing the Internal Audit Activity	Sum of Standards 2010–2060	≤GC ≤PC ≤DNC
2100—Nature of Work: The internal audit activity must evaluate and contribute to the improvement of governance, risk management, and control processes using a systematic and disciplined approach.	Sum of Standards 2110–2130	
2110—Governance: The internal audit activity must assess and make appropriate recommendations for improving the governance process in its accomplishment of the following objectives: Promoting appropriate ethics and values within the organization; Ensuring effective organizational performance management and accountability; Communicating risk and control information to appropriate areas of the organization; and Coordinating the activities of and communicating information among the board, external and internal auditors, and management.	Internal audit activity assesses and makes appropriate recommendations for improving the governance process in its accomplishment of the objectives specified in the Standards.	Code of ethics. Activity reports. Engagement records. Minutes of board meetings. Memoranda resulting from meetings with senior management. Job description for CAE. Work paper review. Annual audit plan. Promoting appropriate ethics and values within the organization. Establishing objectives, monitoring their accomplishment, and ensuring their accountability.

(Continued)

Table 7.14 (Continued)   Part IV: Standards Conformance Evaluation—Master Framework

Standard	Key Conformance Criteria	Examples of Evidence, Sound Practices, and Other Considerations
2110.A1—The internal audit activity must evaluate the design, implementation, and effectiveness of the organization's ethics-related objectives, programs, and activities. **2110.A2**—The internal audit activity must assess whether the information technology governance of the organization sustains and supports the organization's strategies and objectives. **2110.C1**—Consulting engagement objectives must be consistent with the overall values and goals of the organization.		Effectively communicating risk and control information to appropriate areas of the organization. Effectively coordinating the activities of and communicating information among the board, external and internal auditors, and management. The internal audit activity evaluates the design, implementation, and effectiveness of the organization's ethics-related objectives, programs, and activities. The internal audit activity actively contributes to improving the ethical culture within the organization. The internal audit activity ensures that the operations and projects are consistent with the overall values and goals of the organization. The internal audit activity has close relations with senior management. The internal audit activity has periodic relations with the board, e.g., participation by the CAE in board meetings, opportunities for the CAE to meet privately with the board chair, reporting to the board, relevancy of topics raised, etc.

(Continued)

Table 7.14 (Continued)   Part IV: Standards Conformance Evaluation—Master Framework

Standard	Key Conformance Criteria	Examples of Evidence, Sound Practices, and Other Considerations
		The internal audit activity has assessed whether the information technology governance of the organization sustains and supports the organization's strategies and objectives.
2110—Governance		≤GC ≤PC ≤DNC
2120—Risk Management: The internal audit activity must evaluate the effectiveness and contribute to the improvement of the risk management processes. **2120.A1**—The internal audit activity must evaluate risk exposures relating to the organization's governance, operations, and information systems regarding the: Reliability and integrity of financial and operational information; Effectiveness and efficiency of operations; Safeguarding of assets; and Conformance with laws, regulations, and contracts.	The scope of the internal audit includes appropriate evaluation of risk management and control systems. Consulting projects cover all significant risk activities within the scope. The potential for fraud and the organization's fraud risk has been addressed.	Risk mapping. Internal audit activity report. Annual audit plan. Charter. Engagement records. Audit report. Memoranda resulting from meetings or discussions with the risk department. Results of risk and controls self-assessments. Preliminary risk assessment report performed prior to commencement of the audit assignment. The audit engagement verifies the existence of a risk management program. If there is a risk management program, the program is evaluated.

(Continued)

Table 7.14 (Continued)   Part IV: Standards Conformance Evaluation—Master Framework

Standard	Key Conformance Criteria	Examples of Evidence, Sound Practices, and Other Considerations
2120.A2—The internal audit activity must evaluate the potential for the occurrence of fraud and how the organization manages fraud risk. **2120.C1**—During consulting engagements, internal auditors must address risk consistent with the engagement's objectives and be alert to the existence of other significant risks. **2120.C2**—Internal auditors must incorporate knowledge of risks gained from consulting engagements into their evaluation of the organization's risk management processes. **2120.C3**—When assisting management in establishing or improving risk management processes, internal auditors must refrain from assuming any management responsibility by actually managing risks.		If there is no risk management program, the internal auditors notify senior management. Assurance engagements periodically evaluate the risk exposure of the organization in respect of the: Reliability and integrity of financial information and operational management reporting. Effectiveness and efficiency of operations. Safeguarding of assets. Conformance with laws, regulations, and contracts. Are auditors permitted and encouraged to identify risks not identified in the original plan. There is a mechanism for auditors to take input from engagements into the risk evaluation process.
2120—Risk Management		≤GC ≤PC ≤DNC

(Continued)

Table 7.14 (Continued) Part IV: Standards Conformance Evaluation—Master Framework

Standard	Key Conformance Criteria	Examples of Evidence, Sound Practices, and Other Considerations
2130—Control: The internal audit activity must assist the organization in maintaining effective controls by evaluating their effectiveness and efficiency and by promoting continuous improvement.	Where appropriate, audit work papers reflect the elements specified in the implementation standards.	Audit work papers. Interview with auditors. Interview with clients.
2130.A1—The internal audit activity must evaluate the adequacy and effectiveness of controls in responding to risks within the organization's governance, operations, and information systems regarding the: Reliability and integrity of financial and operational information; Effectiveness and efficiency of operations; Safeguarding of assets; and Compliance with laws, regulations, and contracts.	Where appropriate, audit work papers reflect the elements specified in the implementation standards for consulting.	Audit work papers and reports reflect: Reliability and integrity of financial and operational information; Effectiveness and efficiency of operations; Safeguarding of assets; and Conformance with laws, regulations, and contracts. Audits address effectiveness of controls encompassing governance, operations, and information systems.
2130.A2—Internal auditors should ascertain the extent to which operating and program goals and objectives have been established and conform to those of the organization.		Work papers adequately reflect an identification and evaluation of the operating and program goals and objectives of the area audited. Work papers adequately reflect identification of the goals and objectives of the area audited. Evaluation (testing) must determine if results of the operation achieved the objectives.

(Continued)

Table 7.14 (Continued)   Part IV: Standards Conformance Evaluation—Master Framework

Standard	Key Conformance Criteria	Examples of Evidence, Sound Practices, and Other Considerations
2130.A3—Internal auditors should review operations and programs to ascertain the extent to which results are consistent with established goals and objectives to determine whether operations and programs are being implemented or performed as intended. **2130.C1**—During consulting engagements, internal auditors must address controls consistent with the engagement's objectives and be alert to significant control issues. **2130.C2**—Internal auditors must incorporate knowledge of controls gained from consulting engagements into the evaluation of the organization's control processes.		Work papers reflect auditor has analyzed extent to which management has established adequate criteria to determine whether objectives and goals have been accomplished. The audit program reflects that the auditor use criteria in their evaluation if criteria existed. If inadequate, the auditors work with management to develop appropriate evaluation criteria according to the work papers. Work papers adequately reflect an evaluation of the operating and program goals and objectives of the area audited to determine whether operations and programs are implemented or performed as intended. There is a mechanism by which knowledge of controls from consulting engagements is an input to risk assessment.
2130—Control	Sum of Standards 2110–2130	≤GC ≤PC ≤DNC
2100—Nature of Work		≤GC ≤PC ≤DNC

(Continued)

Table 7.14 (Continued)   Part IV: Standards Conformance Evaluation—Master Framework

Standard	Key Conformance Criteria	Examples of Evidence, Sound Practices, and Other Considerations
2600—Resolution of Management's Acceptance of Risks		≤GC ≤PC ≤DNC
Management—Overall		≤GC ≤PC ≤DNC
PROCESS		
2200—Engagement Planning: Internal auditors must develop and document a plan for each engagement, including the engagement's objectives, scope, timing, and resource allocations.	Sum of Standards 2201–2240	
2201—Planning Considerations: In planning the engagement, internal auditors must consider: The objectives of the activity being reviewed and the means by which the activity controls its performance; The significant risks to the activity, its objectives, resources, and operations and the means by which the potential impact of risk is kept to an acceptable level;	Internal auditors systematically conduct a preliminary risk assessment of the organization's audit universe in order to determine the engagement objectives.	Audit procedure. Audit engagement letter. Engagement work program. Engagement records. Agreement between the consulting engagement client and the internal auditor. Evidence that fraud is considered in each audit engagement plan. IT risks and controls are considered when appropriate in the audit plans.

(Continued)

Table 7.14 (Continued)   Part IV: Standards Conformance Evaluation—Master Framework

Standard	Key Conformance Criteria	Examples of Evidence, Sound Practices, and Other Considerations
The adequacy and effectiveness of the activity's risk management and control processes compared to a relevant control framework or model; and	Internal auditors develop and record a program for each engagement.	This plan specifies the following:
The opportunities for making significant improvements to the activity's risk management and control processes.	In the case of outside engagements, the internal auditors establish a written understanding about the objectives, scope, and respective responsibilities of each party.	Scope of work;
2201.A1—When planning an engagement for parties outside the organization, internal auditors must establish a written understanding with them about objectives, scope, respective responsibilities, and other expectations, including restrictions on distribution of the results of the engagement and access to engagement records.		Audit objectives;
		Engagement dates;
		Timing; and
		Resources allocated.
		The engagement plan reflects the expectations of senior management.
		The engagement plan is based on a preliminary survey of the activity to be audited.
		The preliminary survey takes into account:
		The objectives of the activity being reviewed;
		The significant risks to the activity;
		The means by which the activity controls its performance; and
2201.C1—Internal auditors must establish an understanding with consulting engagement clients about objectives, scope, respective responsibilities, and other client expectations.		The adequacy and effectiveness of the activity's risk management and control systems.
For significant engagements, this understanding must be documented.		Outside engagement documentation or contracts.
		Interviews with audit management.
		Consulting engagement documentation.
		Interviews with audit management.
		Interviews with consulting clients.

(Continued)

Table 7.14 (Continued) Part IV: Standards Conformance Evaluation—Master Framework

Standard	Key Conformance Criteria	Examples of Evidence, Sound Practices, and Other Considerations
		≤GC ≤PC ≤DNC
2201—Planning Considerations		
2210—Engagement Objectives: Objectives must be established for each engagement. **2210.A1**—Internal auditors must conduct a preliminary assessment of the risks relevant to the activity under review. Engagement objectives must reflect the results of this assessment. **2210.A2**—Internal auditors must consider the probability of significant errors, fraud, noncompliance, and other exposures when developing the engagement objectives. **2210.A3**—Adequate criteria are needed to evaluate controls. Internal auditors must ascertain the extent to which management has established adequate criteria to determine whether objectives and goals have been accomplished. If adequate, internal auditors must use such criteria in their evaluation. If inadequate, internal auditors must work with management to develop appropriate evaluation criteria.	Internal auditors refer back to the preliminary risk assessment (Standard 2201) of the organization's audit universe in order to determine the engagement objectives.	Audit procedure. Audit engagement letter. Engagement work program. Engagement records. Agreement between the consulting engagement client and the internal auditor. Internal auditors develop and record a program for each engagement, which Specifies the scope of work, audit objectives, engagement dates, timing, and resources allocated; Reflects the expectations of senior management; and Is based on a preliminary survey of the activity to be audited. The preliminary survey (mentioned above) takes into account: The objectives of the activity being reviewed; The significant risks to the activity; The means by which the activity controls its performance; and The adequacy and effectiveness of the activity's risk management and control systems.

(Continued)

Table 7.14 (Continued)   Part IV: Standards Conformance Evaluation—Master Framework

Standard	Key Conformance Criteria	Examples of Evidence, Sound Practices, and Other Considerations
2210.C1—Consulting engagement objectives must address governance, risk management, and control processes to the extent agreed upon with the client.		In the case of consulting engagements, the internal auditors establish a written understanding with consulting engagement clients about the objectives, scope, and respective responsibilities of each party.
2210—Engagement Objectives		≤GC ≤PC ≤DNC
2220—Engagement Scope: The established scope must be sufficient to satisfy the objectives of the engagement. **2220.A1**—The scope of the engagement must include consideration of relevant systems, records, personnel, and physical properties, including those under the control of third parties.	The engagement scope is consistent with the audit objectives. If relevant, a written understanding and communication of consulting objectives, scope, and responsibilities. There is evidence that results are communicated in accordance with consulting standards.	Engagement work program. Client interviews. Consulting documentation, including formal agreement and other correspondence. Consulting standards and practices. Interview with staff.

(Continued)

Table 7.14 (Continued) Part IV: Standards Conformance Evaluation—Master Framework

Standard	Key Conformance Criteria	Examples of Evidence, Sound Practices, and Other Considerations
2220.A2—If significant consulting opportunities arise during an assurance engagement, a specific written understanding as to the objectives, scope, respective responsibilities, and other expectations should be reached and the results of the consulting engagement communicated in accordance with consulting standards. **2220.C1**—In performing consulting engagements, internal auditors must ensure that the scope of the engagement is sufficient to address the agreed-upon objectives. If internal auditors develop reservations about the scope during the engagement, these reservations must be discussed with the client to determine whether to continue with the engagement.		
2220—Engagement Scope		≤GC ≤PC ≤DNC

(Continued)

Table 7.14 (Continued)   Part IV: Standards Conformance Evaluation—Master Framework

Standard	Key Conformance Criteria	Examples of Evidence, Sound Practices, and Other Considerations
2230—Engagement Resource Allocation: Internal auditors must determine appropriate and sufficient resources to achieve engagement objectives based on an evaluation of the nature and complexity of each engagement, time constraints, and available resources.	There is evidence of appropriate evaluation of staffing after scoping that is based on nature and complexity of engagement, time constraints, and available resources.	Staffing analysis. Interviews of audit management and staff. Staffing allocation makes provision for the knowledge, skills, and other competencies required to perform the internal audit. On-time performance of audit engagements is monitored: If yes, budget to actual time comparisons are performed. If yes, comparisons are analyzed.
2230—Engagement Resource Allocation		≤GC ≤PC ≤DNC
2240—Engagement Work Program: Internal auditors must develop and document work programs that achieve the engagement objectives. **2240.A1**—Work programs must include the procedures for identifying, analyzing, evaluating, and documenting information during the engagement. The work program must be approved prior to its implementation, and any adjustments approved promptly.	The internal auditor has developed a formal engagement work program outlining the resources and procedures needed to achieve the audit objectives.	Engagement work programs.

(Continued)

Table 7.14 (Continued)   Part IV: Standards Conformance Evaluation—Master Framework

Standard	Key Conformance Criteria	Examples of Evidence, Sound Practices, and Other Considerations		
2240.C1—Work programs for consulting engagements may vary in form and content depending upon the nature of the engagement.	Fraud was considered in the program. The engagement work program and subsequent program adjustments are approved in writing by the CAE or designee before the engagement is commenced.			
2240—Engagement Work Programs		≤GC	≤PC	≤DNC
2200—Engagement Planning	Sum of Standards 2201–2240	≤GC	≤PC	≤DNC
2300—Performing the Engagement: Internal auditors must identify, analyze, evaluate, and document sufficient information to achieve the engagement's objectives.	Sum of Standards 2310–2340			

(Continued)

Table 7.14 (Continued) Part IV: Standards Conformance Evaluation—Master Framework

Standard	Key Conformance Criteria	Examples of Evidence, Sound Practices, and Other Considerations
2310—Identifying Information: Internal auditors must identify sufficient, reliable, relevant, and useful information to achieve the engagement's objectives.	Work papers include all the relevant information to achieve the objectives.	Audit work papers. Interview with auditors. Interview with clients. Work papers are clear, properly indexed and classified, referenced to the engagement work program and the audit documentation, etc.
2310—Identifying Information		≤GC ≤PC ≤DNC
2320—Analysis and Evaluation: Internal auditors must base conclusions and engagement results on appropriate analyses and evaluations.	Audit conclusions and engagement results are based on appropriate analyses and evaluations that identify the root cause(s) of irregularities.	Audit work papers. Interview with auditors. Interview with clients. Work papers clearly show the results of tests and the conclusions and recommendations arising from such tests. Actual testing is conducted and sufficient to support the scope and objectives. Substantive testing is done where appropriate. Evidence by interview is also validated by secondary source. The elements of criteria, condition, cause, effect, and recommendation are considered.
2320—Analysis and Evaluation		≤GC ≤PC ≤DNC

(Continued)

Table 7.14 (Continued) Part IV: Standards Conformance Evaluation—Master Framework

Standard	Key Conformance Criteria	Examples of Evidence, Sound Practices, and Other Considerations
2330—Documenting Information: Internal auditors must document relevant information to support the conclusions and engagement results.	Sufficient information is documented to support the conclusions and audit results.	Audit work papers. Summary of findings. CAE interview. Approval documents. Audit policies. Organization and regulatory requirements. Requirements consistent with organization guidelines and other regulatory requirements. Findings and recommendations can easily be traced to supporting evidence. Adequate documentation per the IA activity's policy can be located.
2330.A1—The chief audit executive must control access to engagement records. The chief audit executive must obtain the approval of senior management and/or legal counsel prior to releasing such records to external parties, as appropriate.	Work papers have controlled access according to the policy of the organization.	
2330.A2—The chief audit executive must develop retention requirements for engagement records, regardless of the medium in which each record is stored. These retention requirements must be consistent with the organization's guidelines and any pertinent regulatory or other requirements.	There is evidence that CAE obtains appropriate approvals prior to releasing records.	

(Continued)

Table 7.14 (Continued) Part IV: Standards Conformance Evaluation—Master Framework

Standard	Key Conformance Criteria	Examples of Evidence, Sound Practices, and Other Considerations
2330.C1—The chief audit executive must develop policies governing the custody and retention of consulting engagement records, as well as their release to internal and external parties. These policies must be consistent with the organization's guidelines and any pertinent regulatory or other requirements.	There is evidence of policy on retention requirements for assurance and consulting engagements.	
2330—Documenting Information		≤GC ≤PC ≤DNC
2340—Engagement Supervision: Engagements must be properly supervised to ensure objectives are achieved, quality is assured, and staff is developed.	There is evidence engagements are properly supervised as specified in the Standards.	Internal policies and procedures for the internal audit activity. Approved engagement work program. Any written instructions issued by the supervisor. Signed work papers (or initialed and signed by the supervisor). Audit reports signed by the supervisor. Review reports with resolution of review comments. Annual training plans for auditors. Annual competency reviews for auditors and evaluations of training received. Audit plans and reports for decentralized audit departments.

(Continued)

Table 7.14 (Continued) Part IV: Standards Conformance Evaluation—Master Framework

Standard	Key Conformance Criteria	Examples of Evidence, Sound Practices, and Other Considerations
		Where a centralized internal audit department has a decentralized internal control structure: A common audit methodology has been adopted. The centralized internal audit department coordinates the audit plans, if applicable.
2340—Engagement Supervision		≤GC ≤PC ≤DNC
2300—Performing the Engagement	Sum of Standards 2310–2340	≤GC ≤PC ≤DNC
2400—Communicating Results: Internal auditors must communicate the engagement results.	Sum of Standards 2410–2440	
2410—Criteria for Communicating: Communications must include the engagement's objectives and scope as well as applicable conclusions, recommendations, and action plans. 2410.A1—Final communication of engagement results must, where appropriate, contain internal auditors' overall opinion or conclusions.	There is evidence of appropriate, timely communication with management. An overall opinion or conclusion is included in the audit report.	Records, internal memos, e-mail, etc. Report on opening kickoff meeting with audit client. Interviews of operational management of the audited organization. Work program, objectives, and scope of the engagement.

(Continued)

Table 7.14 (Continued)   Part IV: Standards Conformance Evaluation—Master Framework

Standard	Key Conformance Criteria	Examples of Evidence, Sound Practices, and Other Considerations
2410.A2—Internal auditors are encouraged to acknowledge satisfactory performance in engagement communications. **2410.A3**—When releasing engagement results to parties outside the organization, the communication must include limitations on distribution and use of the results. **2410.C1**—Communication of the progress and results of consulting engagements will vary in form and content depending on the nature of the engagement and the needs of the client.	Satisfactory performance is acknowledged in engagement communications. Communications outside the organization are limited in distribution and use of results. There is evidence of progress and results on consulting engagements that is reasonable to the engagement.	Engagement period covered and estimated completion dates. The procedures for validating and reporting audit results and following up to determine that corrective action is taken. The elements of criteria, condition, cause, effect, and recommendation are included. Audit report. Engagement communications. Outside communications. Consulting documentation.
2410—Criteria for Communicating		≤GC ≤PC ≤DNC

(Continued)

Table 7.14 (Continued)   Part IV: Standards Conformance Evaluation—Master Framework

Standard	Key Conformance Criteria	Examples of Evidence, Sound Practices, and Other Considerations
2420—Quality of Communications: Communications must be accurate, objective, clear, concise, constructive, complete, and timely.	Communications are appropriate as stated in the Standards. Audit reports are timely.	Audit records. Report on client debriefing meetings. Interviews of operational management of the audited organization. Audit reports must be understandable by anyone (not contain technical jargon). Audit reports must be concise in outlining what was tested, what was found, and its significance. Audit reports must clearly contain facts to support the conclusions. Determine that discussions, which help ensure that there have been no misunderstandings or misinterpretations of fact, have taken place during the audit engagement and during client debriefing meetings.
2420—Quality of Communications		≤GC ≤PC ≤DNC
2421—Errors and Omissions: If a final communication contains a significant error or omission, the chief audit executive must communicate corrected information to all parties who received the original communication.	Where appropriate, there is communication of corrected information to all parties.	Corrected correspondence.
2421—Errors and Omissions		≤GC ≤PC ≤DNC

(Continued)

Table 7.14 (Continued)   Part IV: Standards Conformance Evaluation—Master Framework

Standard	Key Conformance Criteria	Examples of Evidence, Sound Practices, and Other Considerations
2430—Use of "Conducted in conformance with the *International Standards for the Professional Practice of Internal Auditing*": Internal auditors may report that their engagements are "conducted in conformance with the *International Standards for the Professional Practice of Internal Auditing*," only if the results of the quality assurance and improvement program support the statement.	Use of "Conducted in conformance with the *International Standards for the Professional Practice of Internal Auditing*."	
2430—Use of "Conducted in conformance with the *International Standards for the Professional Practice of Internal Auditing*"	Where appropriate, communication of results discloses nonconformance.	≤GC ≤PC ≤DNC
2431—Engagement Disclosure of Nonconformance: When nonconformance with the definition of internal auditing, the code of ethics, or the Standards impacts a specific engagement, communication of the engagement results must disclose the: Principle or rule of conduct of the code of ethics or Standard(s) with which full conformance was not achieved; Reason(s) for nonconformance; and Impact of nonconformance on the engagement and the communicated engagement results.		Audit report or any other written summary of the results of the audit. There is a procedure to determine compliance with the Standards in audit engagements. Supervision policies. Communication of results discloses the: Standard(s) with which full compliance was not achieved; Reason(s) for noncompliance; and Impact of noncompliance on the engagement.

(Continued)

Table 7.14 (Continued) Part IV: Standards Conformance Evaluation—Master Framework

Standard	Key Conformance Criteria	Examples of Evidence, Sound Practices, and Other Considerations
2431—Engagement Disclosure of Nonconformance with the Standards		≤GC ≤PC ≤DNC
2440—Disseminating Results: The chief audit executive must communicate results to the appropriate parties. **2440.A1**—The chief audit executive is responsible for communicating the final results to parties who can ensure that the results are given due consideration. **2440.A2**—If not otherwise mandated by legal, statutory, or regulatory requirements, prior to releasing results to parties outside the organization, the chief audit executive must: Assess the potential risk to the organization; Consult with senior management or legal counsel as appropriate; and Control dissemination by restricting the use of the results.	Audit reports are distributed to an appropriate level of senior managers. If applicable, the CAE properly considered the elements of the standard prior to disclosure outside the organization. Consulting engagement reports are distributed appropriately.	Assessed the potential risk to the organization. Consulted with senior management or legal counsel as appropriate. Controlled dissemination by restricting the use of the results. Audit report distribution. Correspondence with senior management or legal. Interview with CAE. Consulting results communications. Board meeting minutes. Correspondence with senior management. CAE interview.

(Continued)

Table 7.14 (Continued)   Part IV: Standards Conformance Evaluation—Master Framework

Standard	Key Conformance Criteria	Examples of Evidence, Sound Practices, and Other Considerations
2440.C1—The chief audit executive is responsible for communicating the final results of consulting engagements to clients. **2440.C2**—During consulting engagements, governance, risk management, and control issues may be identified. Whenever these issues are significant to the organization, they must be communicated to senior management and the board.		
2440—Disseminating Results		≤GC ≤PC ≤DNC
2400—Communicating Results	Sum of Standards 2410–2440	≤GC ≤PC ≤DNC
2500—Monitoring Progress: The chief audit executive must establish and maintain a system to monitor the disposition of results communicated to management.	The CAE has established a follow-up process to monitor and ensure that management actions have been effectively implemented or risk accepted.	Records (e.g., follow-up report) or reports on meetings. The process includes a formal procedure for setting out reasons for not implementing follow-up action.

(Continued)

Table 7.14 (Continued)   Part IV: Standards Conformance Evaluation—Master Framework

Standard	Key Conformance Criteria	Examples of Evidence, Sound Practices, and Other Considerations
2500.A1—The chief audit executive must establish a follow-up process to monitor and ensure that management actions have been effectively implemented or that senior management has accepted the risk of not taking action.		If a management action has not been effectively implemented, the CAE has ensured that senior management has accepted the risk of not taking action and communicated this to relevant stakeholders.
2500.C1—The internal audit activity must monitor the disposition of results of consulting engagements to the extent agreed upon with the client.		
2500—Monitoring Progress		≤GC ≤PC ≤DNC

(Continued)

Table 7.14 (Continued)   Part IV: Standards Conformation Evaluation—Master Framework

Standard	Key Conformance Criteria	Examples of Evidence, Sound Practices, and Other Considerations
2600—Resolution of Senior Management's Acceptance of Risks: When the chief audit executive believes that senior management has accepted a level of residual risk that may be unacceptable to the organization, the chief audit executive must discuss the matter with senior management. If the decision regarding residual risk is not resolved, the chief audit executive must report the matter to the board for resolution.	Decisions regarding residual risk that are not resolved are reported by the CAE to the board for resolution. The subsequent resolution/disposition of such residual risk issues is appropriately documented.	Interview with CAE. Interview with board members. Board minutes.
Process—Overall		≤GC ≤PC ≤DNC

Source: Adapted from State of North Carolina, Council of Internal Auditing, Office of Internal Audit, Peer Review Program, Evaluation Summary and Report Phase—Standard Conformation Evaluation (Form E2).

the quality assessment. If all underlying Standards are rated *does not conform*, then the overall standard *does not conform*. Otherwise, the team must make a judgment based on the number of *does not conform* and the specific conditions present as to whether the overall rating is *does not conform* or *partially conforms*.

On the same basis as for sections of the Standards, conclude as to the degree of conformance by the activity to the major categories of the Standards (Attribute and Performance).

Consider the four principles and related rules of conduct in the code of ethics and conclude whether or not the activity's management and staff uphold each of the principles and apply the related rules of conduct.

Make an overall evaluation as to the activity's conformance with the Standards as a whole.

Part II: Definitions

GC—generally conforms means the evaluator has concluded that the relevant structures, policies, and procedures of the activity, as well as the processes by which they are applied, comply with the requirements of the **individual** Standard or element of the code of ethics in all material respects. For the **sections** and **major categories**, this means that there is general conformance to a majority of the individual Standards or elements of the code of ethics, and at least partial conformance to the others, within the section/category. There may be significant opportunities for improvement, but these must not represent situations where the activity has not implemented the Standards or the code of ethics, has not applied them effectively, or has not achieved their stated objectives. As indicated above, general conformance does not require complete/perfect conformance, the ideal situation, *successful practice*, etc.

PC—partially conforms means the evaluator has concluded that the activity is making good-faith efforts to comply with the requirements of the **individual** Standard or element of the code of ethics, **section**, or **major category**, but falls short of achieving some major objectives. These will usually represent significant opportunities for improvement in effectively applying the Standards or code of ethics, or achieving their objectives. Some deficiencies may be beyond the control of the activity and may result in recommendations to senior management or the board of the organization.

DNC—does not conform means the evaluator has concluded that the activity is not aware of, is not making good-faith efforts to comply with, or is failing to achieve many/all of the objectives of the **individual** Standard or element of the code of ethics, **section**, or **major category**. These deficiencies will usually have a significant negative impact on the activity's effectiveness and its potential to add value to the organization. These may also represent significant opportunities for improvement, including actions by senior management or the board.

Often, the most difficult evaluation is the distinction between *general* and *partial*. It is a judgment call keeping in mind the definition of *general conformance* above. Carefully read the Standard to determine if basic conformance exists. The existence of *opportunities for improvement*, better alternatives, or other successful practices do not reduce a *generally conforms* rating.

7.11.3.3 E3: Quality Assurance Review (Table 7.15)

The purpose of quality assurance review (QAR) for the peer review team is to properly review its work to ensure that work performed conforms and adequately supports the conclusions reached and the steps required for the assignment were adequately followed.

Table 7.15   E3: Quality Assurance Review

	Agency Reviewed: Lead Reviewer: Team Member:		Date: Reviewer:		
	The quality review must review all documents related to the QAR to ensure work perform supports the conclusions and the step required by the program were followed.				
	Included in Work Papers	*Yes*	*No*	*Comment*	
1.	Request for review (A2)				
2.	Independence statement (A4)				
3.	MOU (A3)				
4.	Planning tool (A6)				
5.	Preliminary meeting held				
6.	Travel arrangements discussed				
7.	Survey conducted of:				
7a.	Internal audit director (B1)				
7b.	Clients (B2b)				
7c.	Internal audit staff (B3b)				
8.	Review planned adequately				
8a.	Surveys results summarized (B4)				
8b.	Identified and set up interviews				
8c.	Selected engagements for review				
8d.	Finalized review program				
9.	On-site review				
9a.	Conducted entrance				
9b.	Conducted interviews and results (C1–C8)				

(*Continued*)

Table 7.15 (Continued)   E3: Quality Assurance Review

Agency Reviewed: Lead Reviewer: Team Member:		Date: Reviewer:		
The quality review must review all documents related to the QAR to ensure work perform supports the conclusions and the step required by the program were followed.				
	Included in Work Papers	*Yes*	*No*	*Comment*
9c.	Reviewed governance (D1)			
9d.	Reviewed staff (D2)			
9e.	Reviewed management (D3)			
9f.	Reviewed internal audit process (D4)			
9g.	Reviewed IT procedures (D5)			
10.	Documented observation and issues (E1)			
11.	Evaluated standards and compliance (E2)			
12.	Completed overall rating (E2)			
13.	Issues discussed with internal audit director			
14.	Report drafted (E4)			
15.	Satisfaction survey submitted to all appropriate individuals: • Internal audit director (E5 and E6) • Team lead (E5) • Team member (E5)			

Source: Retrieved from State of North Carolina, Council of Internal Auditing, Office of Internal Audit, Peer Review Program, Evaluation Summary and Report Phase—Quality Assurance Review (Form E3).

7.11.3.4 E4: Sample Draft Report (Figure 7.20 and Table 7.16)

Table 7.16 summarizes compliance (whether general compliance or partial compliance) or noncompliance to Standards, ethics and relevant legislatures. Figure 7.20 was intended to show readers how a standard peer review report looks like and comprises the purpose and objectives of the QAR, opinion of the peer review team as to conformance to Standards, Scope covered and Methodology adopted, Recommendations and Observations, and finally, Attachment A (Standards Conformance Evaluation Summary).

COUNCIL'S PEER REVIEW PROGRAM

EXTERNAL REVIEW

EXTERNAL QUALITY ASSESSMENT OF AGENCY/UNIVERSITY
INTERNAL AUDIT FUNCTION

MONTH 20XX

TABLE OF CONTENTS

PURPOSE AND OBJECTIVE

As requested by the internal audit director, we conducted a QA of the internal audit function at *agency/university*. The principal objectives of the QA were to assess internal audit function's conformity to the IIA's *International Standards for the Professional Practice of Internal Auditing* (Standards) as well as evaluate internal audit's effectiveness in carrying out its mission (as set forth in its charter and expressed in the expectations of the agency/university management), and identify opportunities to enhance its management and work processes, as well as its value to agency/university.

OPINION AS TO CONFORMANCE TO THE STANDARDS

It is our overall opinion that the IA activity [*insert outcome: generally, partially, or does not conform*] to the Standards and code of ethics. For a detailed list of conformance to individual Standards, please see Attachment A. The QA team identified opportunities for further improvement, details of which are provided in this report.

The IIA's *Quality Assessment Manual* suggests a scale of three ratings, *generally conforms*, *partially conforms*, and *does not conform*. *Generally conforms* is the top rating and means that an IA activity has a charter, policies, and processes that are judged to be in conformance with the Standards. *Partially conforms* means deficiencies in practice are noted that are judged to deviate from the Standards, but these deficiencies did not preclude the IA activity from performing its responsibilities in an acceptable manner. *Does not conform* means deficiencies in practice are judged to be so significant as to seriously impair or preclude the IA activity from performing adequately in all or in significant areas of its responsibilities.

Figure 7.20 E4: Sample draft report (complete dotted areas). *(Continued)*

SCOPE AND METHODOLOGY

As part of the preparation for the QA, the internal audit function prepared an advanced preparation document with detailed information and sent out surveys to its staff and a representative sample of agency/university managers. A summary of the survey results (without identifying the individual survey respondents) has been furnished to the internal audit function. Prior to commencement of the on-site work by the peer review team on Month XX, 20XX, the team lead worked with the internal audit director to gather additional background information, select executives for interviews during the on-site fieldwork, and finalize planning and administrative arrangements for the peer review. Extensive interviews with agency/university management and internal audit staff were conducted. We also reviewed the internal audit function's risk assessment and audit planning processes, audit tools and methodologies, engagement and staff management processes, and a representative sample of the internal audit function's working papers and reports.

RECOMMENDATIONS AND OBSERVATION

Recommendations and observations are divided into four groups:

- Recommendations that concern agency/management as a whole and suggest actions by senior management. Some of these are matters outside the scope of the peer review, as set out above, which came to our attention through the surveys and interviews. We include them because we believe they will be useful to agency/university management and because they impact the effectiveness of internal audit function and the value it can add.
- Recommendations that relate to internal audit function's structure, staffing, deployment of resources, and similar matters that should be implemented within the internal audit function, with support from senior management.
- Observations that recognize best practices employed by the internal audit activity leading to a level of performance beyond generally conforming to the mandatory guidance of the IIA.
- Observations of process improvement opportunities for the internal audit activity to consider in its continuous improvement efforts. These do not indicate a lack of conformance to mandatory IIA guidance. They are offered as suggestions for the continued growth of the internal audit activity's successful practice.

Highlights of the more significant recommendations are set forth below, with details in the main body of the report.

PART I—MATTERS FOR CONSIDERATION OF AGENCY/UNIVERSITY

1. Observation **EXAMPLE:** Enhance the audit committee charter by clarifying the responsibility to approve the annual audit plan and periodic review of the IA charter, staffing, and organizational structure (Standard 1110).

   Recommendation
   Senior Management Response

2. Observation (Standard xxxx)

   Recommendation
   Senior Management Response

Figure 7.20 (Continued)   E4: Sample draft report (complete dotted areas).
(Continued)

PART II—ISSUES SPECIFIC TO THE INTERNAL AUDIT ACTIVITY

1. Observation **EXAMPLE:** Improve the follow-up process by documenting and implementing a process that ensures all significant findings are addressed on a timely basis (Standard 2500).

   Recommendation
   Senior Management Response

2. Observation (Standard xxxx)

   Recommendation
   Senior Management Response

PART III—OBSERVATION OF BEST PRACTICES

1. Best practice **EXAMPLE:** Utilize online client satisfaction survey after every audit project to identify issues and improve the internal audit process, workplace ethics, or communications, etc.

2. Best practice

PART IV— OBSERVATION OF PROCESS IMPROVEMENT OPPORTUNITIES

1. Process improvement opportunity **EXAMPLE:** Implement use of CAATs for continuous monitoring.

   Recommendation
   Senior Management Response

2. Process improvement opportunity (Standard xxxx)

   Recommendation
   Senior Management Response

We appreciate this opportunity to be of service to agency/university. We will be pleased to respond to further questions concerning this report and to furnish any desired information.

Name, Credentials
Team Leader

Name, Credentials
Team Lead
Agency/University Internal Audit Function

Team Members:
Name, Credentials
Agency/University Internal Audit Function

Name, Credentials
Agency/University Internal Audit Function

Figure 7.20 (Continued) E4: Sample draft report (complete dotted areas). (Retrieved from State of North Carolina, Council of Internal Auditing, Office of Internal Audit, Peer Review Program [Form E4].)

Table 7.16 Attachment A: Standards Conformance Form—Overall Evaluation Summary

Standard	Generally Conforms	Partially Conforms	Does Not Conform
Attribute Standards			
1000—Purpose, Authority, and Responsibility	☐	☐	☐
1010—Recognition of the Definition of Internal Auditing, the Code of Ethics, and the Standards in the Internal Audit Charter	☐	☐	☐
1100—Independence and Objectivity	☐	☐	☐
1110—Organizational Independence	☐	☐	☐
1120—Individual Objectivity	☐	☐	☐
1130—Impairments to Independence or Objectivity	☐	☐	☐
1200—Proficiency and Due Professional Care	☐	☐	☐
1210—Proficiency	☐	☐	☐
1220—Due Professional Care	☐	☐	☐
1230—Continuing Professional Development	☐	☐	☐
1300—Quality Assurance and Improvement Program	☐	☐	☐
1310—Requirements the Quality Assurance and Improvement Program	☐	☐	☐
1311—Internal Assessments	☐	☐	☐
1312—External Assessments	☐	☐	☐
1320—Reporting on the Quality Program	☐	☐	☐

(Continued)

**Table 7.16 (Continued)   Attachment A: Standards Conformance Form—
Overall Evaluation Summary**

Standard	Generally Conforms	Partially Conforms	Does Not Conform
1321—Use of "Conforms with the *International Standards for the Professional Practice of Internal Auditing*"	☐	☐	☐
1322—Disclosure of Nonconformance	☐	☐	☐
Performance Standards			
2000—Managing the Internal Audit Activity	☐	☐	☐
2010—Planning	☐	☐	☐
2020—Communication and Approval	☐	☐	☐
2030—Resource Management	☐	☐	☐
2040—Policies and Procedures	☐	☐	☐
2050—Coordination	☐	☐	☐
2060—Reporting to the Board and Senior Management	☐	☐	☐
2100—Nature of Work	☐	☐	☐
2110—Governance	☐	☐	☐
2120—Risk Management	☐	☐	☐
2130—Control	☐	☐	☐
2200—Engagement Planning	☐	☐	☐
2201—Planning Considerations	☐	☐	☐
2210—Engagement Objectives	☐	☐	☐
2220—Engagement Scope	☐	☐	☐

(*Continued*)

Table 7.16 (Continued)   Attachment A: Standards Conformance Form—Overall Evaluation Summary

Standard	Generally Conforms	Partially Conforms	Does Not Conform
2230—Engagement Resource Allocation	☐	☐	☐
2240—Engagement Work Program	☐	☐	☐
2300—Performing the Engagement	☐	☐	☐
2310—Identifying Information	☐	☐	☐
2320—Analysis and Evaluation	☐	☐	☐
2330—Documenting Information	☐	☐	☐
2340—Engagement Supervision	☐	☐	☐
2400—Communicating Results	☐	☐	☐
2410—Criteria for Communicating	☐	☐	☐
2420—Quality of Communications	☐	☐	☐
2421—Errors and Omissions	☐	☐	☐
2430—Use of "Conducted in Conformance with the *International Standards for the Professional Practice of Internal Auditing*"	☐	☐	☐
2431—Engagement Disclosure of Nonconformance	☐	☐	☐
2440—Disseminating Results	☐	☐	☐
2500—Monitoring Progress	☐	☐	☐
2600—Resolution of Management's Acceptance of Risks	☐	☐	☐
IIA Code of Ethics	☐	☐	☐
IA Act	☐	☐	☐

(*Continued*)

Table 7.16 (Continued)   Attachment A: Standards Conformance Form—Overall Evaluation Summary

Source: Retrieved from State of North Carolina, Council of Internal Auditing, Office of Internal Audit, Peer Review Program, Evaluation Summary and Report Phase—Report Format (Form E4).

Note: **Definitions**

DNC—does not conform means the evaluator has concluded that the activity is not aware of, is not making good-faith efforts to comply with, or is failing to achieve many/all of the objectives of the individual Standard or element of the code of ethics, section, or major category. These deficiencies will usually have a significant negative impact on the activity's effectiveness and its potential to add value to the organization. These may also represent significant opportunities for improvement, including actions by senior management or the board.

GC—generally conforms means the assessor has concluded that the relevant structures, policies, and procedures of the activity, as well as the processes by which they are applied, comply with the requirements of the individual Standard or element of the code of ethics in all material respects. For the sections and major categories, this means that there is general conformity to a majority of the individual Standards or elements of the code of ethics, and at least partial conformity to the others, within the section/category. There may be significant opportunities for improvement, but these should not represent situations where the activity has not implemented the Standards or the code of ethics, has not applied them effectively, or has not achieved their stated objectives. As indicated above, general conformance does not require complete/perfect conformance, the ideal situation, *successful practice*, etc.

PC—partially conforms means the evaluator has concluded that the activity is making good-faith efforts to comply with the requirements of the individual Standard or element of the code of ethics, section, or major category, but falls short of achieving some major objectives. These will usually represent significant opportunities for improvement in effectively applying the Standards or code of ethics, or achieving their objectives. Some deficiencies may be beyond the control of the activity and may result in recommendations to senior management or the board of the organization.

7.11.3.5 E5: Specimen of Peer Review Results/ Reports (Figure 7.21)

This is an example result or report of the QAR and contains introduction indicating that the Review process has been concluded; indicates areas of weakness and strength; and expresses opinion on conformance or nonconformance and relevant recommendation.

The internal audit is expected to write in return to the peer review team acknowledging the report of the peer review team and showing appreciation, with a promise to implement their recommendation.

July 31, 2014

Association of Local Govt. Auditors
449 Hargett Circle
Suite 290, Lexington, KY 40503
www.governmentauditors.org

Director of Internal Audit
Yaba College of Technology
Yaba, Lagos
Nigeria

Dear P. O. Nzechukwu:

Re: External Quality Control Review: Yaba College of Technology (YCT), Office of Internal Audit

We have completed a peer review of Yaba College of Technology (YCT) Office of Internal Audit (IA) for the period January 1, 2009, through December 31, 2013. In conducting our review, we followed the standards and guidelines contained in the *Peer Review Guide* published by the Association of Local Government Auditors (ALGA, 2007).

We reviewed the internal quality control system of your audit organization and conducted tests in order to determine if your internal quality control system operated to provide reasonable assurance of compliance with the *Government Auditing Standards* issued by the Controller General of the United States. Due to variances in individual performance and judgment, compliance does not imply adherence to standards in every case, but does imply adherence in most situations.

Based on the results of our review, it is our opinion that Yaba College of Technology Office of Internal Audit internal quality control system was suitably designed and operating effectively to provide reasonable assurance of compliance with the *Government Auditing Standards* for audits and attestation engagements during the period of January 1, 2009, through December 31, 2013.

We have prepared a separate letter offering suggestions to further strengthen your internal quality control system.

Okeke J. Chijioke	**Garuba I. Gaya**	**Ogunnaike O. Durojaiye**
University of Nigeria	Federal Polytechnic	University of Lagos
Nsukka	Bauchi	Akoka

Figure 7.21   E5: Specimen of peer review results (reports).   *(Continued)*

July 31, 2014

Association of Local Govt. Auditors
449 Hargett Circle
Suite 290, Lexington, KY 40503
www.governmentauditors.org

Director of Internal Audit
Yaba College of Technology
Yaba, Lagos
Nigeria

Dear Mr. P. O. Nzechukwu:

Re: External Quality Control Review: Yaba College of Technology (YCT), Office of Internal Audit

We have completed a peer review of Yaba College of Technology Office of Internal Audit (YCT IA) for the period January 1, 2009, through December 31, 2013, and issued our report thereon dated July 31, 2014. We are issuing this companion letter to offer certain observations and suggestions stemming from our peer review.

We would like to mention some the areas that we believe your office excels:

- Each audit and/or project was consistently documented using a standard index and structure. Audit files were easy to review and were available in both hard copy and electronic format.

- Use of the Peer Review Guidance (Review of Audit/Engagement Documentation Checklists) in each audit and/or project file simplified the file review for the peer review team and also ensured staff compliance with all standards prior to completing the work papers.

We offer the following observations and suggestions to enhance your organization's demonstrated adherence to the *Government Auditing Standards:*

- Standard 1.33 states, "When performing nonaudit services for an entity for which audit organization performs a Generally Accepted Government Auditing Standards (GAGAS) audit or attestation engagement, the audit organization should communicate, as appropriate, with requestors and those charged with governance to clarify that the scope of work performed does not constitute an audit under GAGAS." In reviewing YCT IA's work papers, we did not note any documentation that management or those charged with governance were informed that the work did not constitute an audit under GAGAS. The director said that this information is discussed at each audit committee meeting.

We suggest that the discussion with management stating that any nonaudit services do not follow GAGAS be documented in the work papers.

- Standard 7.11d requires auditors to understand and assess risks and the potential for fraud and abuse. In reviewing the YCT IA work papers, we observed some documentation of a risk assessment. The director stated that some of the risks assessment is completed during a *brainstorming session* with staff that is not formally documented.

We suggest you capture the ideas discussed in the *brainstorming sessions* for the work papers. This documents how risks were identified and any reasons for elevating or dismissing the risks discussed.

- Standard 5.03 requires that American Institute of Certified Public Accountants (AICPA) standards be followed in the reporting process. The YCT IA's standard form GB-11 includes an acknowledgement of the AICPA fieldwork standards; it does not acknowledge the reporting standards of financial audits.

While all fieldwork and reporting standards were followed during the period reviewed, we suggest you consider adding the reporting standards to your standard form GB-11 to strengthen the acknowledgement of the required standards for financial audits.

We extend our thanks to you, your staff, and the other officials we met for the hospitality and cooperation extended to us during our review.

Sincerely,

Okeke J. Chijioke	**Garuba I. Gaya**	**Ogunnaike O. Durojaiye**
University of Nigeria	Federal Polytechnic	University of Lagos
Nsukka	Bauchi	Akoka

Figure 7.21 (Continued)   E5: Specimen of peer review results (reports). (*Continued*)

July 25, 2014

Director of Internal Audit
Yaba College of Technology
Yaba, Lagos
Nigeria

Okeke J. Chijioke
University of Nigeria
Nsukka, Enugu State

Garuba I. Gaya
Federal Polytechnic
Gwalameji, Bauchi

Ogunnaike O. Durojaiye
University of Lagos
Akoka, Lagos

Dear Peer Review Team:

Re: External Quality Control Review: Yaba College of Technology, Office of Internal Audit

On behalf of Yaba College of Technology, I would like to thank you, as well as the Association of Local Government Auditors (ALGA), for your time and effort in providing us with this valuable service. We appreciate the thorough and comprehensive peer review performed by your team. We are pleased that our office was found to be in full compliance in this peer review. We concur with the recommendations to strengthen our organization's adherence to the *Government Auditing Standards.* The following action plans will be implemented to address the observations and suggestions in the management letter dated March 29, 2012.

- We will add appropriate language in our nonaudit services certification to reflect communication with management and the audit committee. We will make this change immediately.

- We will include a summary of our *brainstorming sessions* in the audit work papers to formally document our discussions regarding the assessment of various risks. We will include this documentation in all future audit work papers.

- We will add appropriate language in our work papers that acknowledges that we are aware of the required AICPA reporting standards. We will make this change when we update our *Policies and Procedures Manual* and standardized work papers as a result of the recently revised *Government Auditing Standards.*

Yaba College of Technology appreciates your dedication to the profession. Please contact me if you have any further questions.

Sincerely,

Mr. P. O. Nzechukwu
Director of Internal Audit
Yaba College of Technology
Yaba, Lagos
Nigeria

Figure 7.21 (Continued)   E5: Specimen of peer review results (reports). (Adapted from Virginia Beach City Public Schools, Office of Internal Audit, March 29, 2012. Peer Review Report, www.vbschools.com.)

7.11.3.6 E6: Satisfaction Survey (See Table 7.17, pp. 512–514)

The purpose of this survey is to solicit the internal audit director's opinion concerning the quality of service provided during our QAR. Your input will help us gauge the effectiveness of the process and the quality of the review team.

7.11.3.7 E7: Peer Review Survey (See Table 7.18, pp. 515–518)

The primary objective of this survey is to rate the peer review processes, procedures, and manual by the entire internal audit team to ensure that the best quality program is deployed.

Table 7.17 E6: Satisfaction Survey

The primary objective of this survey is to seek the opinion of the Internal Audit Director or Chief Audit Executive or Head of Internal Audit as the case may be in relation to the quality of service provided by the Peer Review or Quality Assurance Review. Please feel free to expand on any areas that you wish to clarify in the comment area at the end. Your thoughts and input will help us continue to improve the value of our contributions. We sincerely appreciate your feedback.

Please indicate your level of satisfaction with the following statements:

	Strongly Agree	Somewhat Agree	Neither Agree nor Disagree	Somewhat Disagree	Strongly Disagree
The review team adequately explained the review process and scope before starting the review.	○	○	○	○	○
The review team adequately considered your suggestions and concerns during the review.	○	○	○	○	○
The review team maintained an adequate level of communication throughout the review.	○	○	○	○	○
The personal conduct of the review team was professional and courteous.	○	○	○	○	○
The review team displayed technical proficiency while conducting the review.	○	○	○	○	○
The review team demonstrated an understanding of the internal audit standards, the quality assurance review requirements, and your audit shop procedures.	○	○	○	○	○
The review team had good communication skills.	○	○	○	○	○

(Continued)

Table 7.17 (Continued)   E6: Satisfaction Survey

	Strongly Agree	Somewhat Agree	Neither Agree nor Disagree	Somewhat Disagree	Strongly Disagree
The quality assurance review report clearly represented the results of the review.	○	○	○	○	○
The recommendations in the report were reasonable, relevant, and actionable.	○	○	○	○	○
The draft report was adequately discussed and any problems resolved before the report was formally issued.	○	○	○	○	○
The review took a reasonable amount of time from start of review to issuance of final report.	○	○	○	○	○
The results of the review helped you achieve improved compliance with IIA internal audit standards.	○	○	○	○	○
The results of the review helped you achieve improved efficiency and effectiveness in operations.	○	○	○	○	○
Overall, you received benefits from this review that will assist you in the future.	○	○	○	○	○

(Continued)

Table 7.17 (Continued)   E6: Satisfaction Survey

	Outstanding	Very Good	Average	Needs Improvement	Poor	N/A
Team leader	○	○	○	○	○	○
Team member	○	○	○	○	○	○

Do you have any other comments, including how to improve this process?

Source: Adapted from State of North Carolina, Council of Internal Auditing, Office of Internal Audit, Peer Review Program, Evaluation Summary and Report Phase—Satisfaction Survey (Form E5).

Table 7.18 E7: Peer Review Survey

The purpose of this survey is to solicit your opinion concerning the peer review manual, processes, and procedures in place while receiving or conducting a QAR. The input of the internal audit director, team lead, and team members is needed to ensure the best-quality program. Please rate the peer review process and the *Peer Review Manual* on the following attributes:

General Attributes of the *Peer Review Manual*

	Outstanding	Very Good	Average	Needs Improvement	Poor	N/A
1. Accessibility	○	○	○	○	○	○
2. Usefulness	○	○	○	○	○	○
3. Content	○	○	○	○	○	○
4. Organization	○	○	○	○	○	○
Attributes of Specific Sections of the *Peer Review Manual*						
5. Sec. I Overview	○	○	○	○	○	○
6. Sec. II A Reciprocity Participation	○	○	○	○	○	○
7. Sec. II B Dispute Resolution	○	○	○	○	○	○
8. Sec. II C Confidentiality of Information	○	○	○	○	○	○
9. Sec. II D Records Retention	○	○	○	○	○	○
10. Sec. II E Conformance of Standards	○	○	○	○	○	○

(Continued)

Table 7.18 (Continued)   E7: Peer Review Survey

	Outstanding	Very Good	Average	Needs Improvement	Poor	N/A
11. Sec. II F Quality Assurance Review of Peer Review Program	○	○	○	○	○	○
12. Sec. III A Peer Review Preparation	○	○	○	○	○	○
13. Sec. III B Planning Tool Questionnaire	○	○	○	○	○	○
14. Sec. III C Requesting a Review	○	○	○	○	○	○
15. Sec. III D Independence Statement	○	○	○	○	○	○
16. Sec. III E Memorandum of Understanding	○	○	○	○	○	○
17. Sec. III F Preliminary Meeting	○	○	○	○	○	○
18. Sec. III G Travel Arrangements	○	○	○	○	○	○
19. Sec. III H Planning	○	○	○	○	○	○
20. Sec. III I Survey Questionnaires	○	○	○	○	○	○
21. Sec. III J On-Site Preparation	○	○	○	○	○	○
22. Sec. III K On-Site Work	○	○	○	○	○	○

(Continued)

Table 7.18 (Continued) E7: Peer Review Survey

	Outstanding	Very Good	Average	Needs Improvement	Poor	N/A
23. Sec. III L Evaluation and Closing Conference	○	○	○	○	○	○
24. Sec. III M Drafting the Report	○	○	○	○	○	○
25. Sec. III N Quality Assurance Review	○	○	○	○	○	○
26. Sec. III O Closing Items	○	○	○	○	○	○
27. Appendix A Steps, Time frame, and Responsibility	○	○	○	○	○	○
28. Appendix B Tools	○	○	○	○	○	○
General Attributes of the Peer Review Process						
29. Ease of obtaining a peer review	○	○	○	○	○	○
30. Time required to receive a peer review	○	○	○	○	○	○
31. Time required to perform a peer review	○	○	○	○	○	○

(Continued)

Table 7.18 (Continued)   E7: Peer Review Survey

	Outstanding	Very Good	Average	Needs Improvement	Poor	N/A
Overall Rating						
32. Overall rating for *Peer Review Manual* and process	○	○	○	○	○	○
33. Was there anything about the *Peer Review Manual* or process you especially liked?						
34. Was there anything about the *Peer Review Manual* or process you especially disliked?						
35. How can the peer review process be improved?						

Your Name (optional) ....

Your Agency ....

What role(s) did you perform in the peer review process? ....

Performed review ....

Received review ....

Prepared self-assessment ....

Source: Adapted from State of North Carolina, Council of Internal Auditing, Office of Internal Audit, Peer Review Program, Evaluation Summary and Report Phase—Peer Review Survey (Form E6).

References

ALGA (2007). *Peer Review Guide for Assessing Compliance with International Standards for the Professional Practice of Internal Auditing.* ALGA. Retrieved July 15, 2016, from: https://algaonline.org/DocumentCenter/View/201.

Boecker, C., Keil, Z., Kagermann, H., William, K., Busch, J., Karlheinz K., Bussiek, O., Claus-Peter, W., Christ, M. H., Eckes, P., Falk, M., Greenberg, P. S., Reichert, B., Wolf, M. (2007). *Internal Audit Handbook: Management with the SAP®—Audit Roadmap.* Springer Science & Business Media, Berlin.

North Carolina Office of State Budget and Management (NCOSBM) (2013). Council of Internal Auditing, NCOSBM. Retrieved from: http://www.osbm.state.nc.us/ncosbm/management/internal_audits.shtm.

North Carolina Office of State Budget and Management (NCOSBM) (2013). Council of Internal Auditing, Office of Internal Audit. Peer Review Program, Peer Review Volunteer Application (Form A1).

North Carolina Office of State Budget and Management (NCOSBM) (2013). Council of Internal Auditing, Office of Internal Audit, Peer Review Program, Peer Review Request Form (Form A2).

North Carolina Office of State Budget and Management (NCOSBM) (2013). Council of Internal Auditing, Office of Internal Audit, Peer Review Program, Memorandum of Understanding Sample (Form A3).

North Carolina Office of State Budget and Management (NCOSBM) (2013). Council of Internal Auditing, Office of Internal Audit, Peer Review Program, Statement of Independence- Reviewer (Form A4).

North Carolina Office of State Budget and Management (NCOSBM) (2013). Council of Internal Auditing, Office of Internal Audit, Peer Review Program, Statement of Independence—Mediator (Form A5).

North Carolina Office of State Budget and Management (NCOSBM) (2013). Council of Internal Auditing, Office of Internal Audit, Peer Review Program, Planning Questionnaire (Form A6).

North Carolina Office of State Budget and Management (NCOSBM) (2013). Council of Internal Auditing, Office of Internal Audit, Peer Review Program, Peer Review Program Checklist (Form A7).

North Carolina Office of State Budget and Management (NCOSBM) (2013). Council of Internal Auditing, Office of Internal Audit, Peer Review Program, Self-Assessment Checklist (Form A8).

North Carolina Office of State Budget and Management (NCOSBM) (2013). Council of Internal Auditing, Office of Internal Audit, Peer Review Program, Sample Survey— Internal Audit Director (Form B1).

North Carolina Office of State Budget and Management (NCOSBM) (2013). Council of Internal Auditing, Office of Internal Audit, Peer Review Program, E-mail with client survey (Form B2a).

North Carolina Office of State Budget and Management (NCOSBM) (2013). Council of Internal Auditing, Office of Internal Audit, Peer Review Program, Client Survey (Form B2b). Retrieved from: https://adobeformscentral.com/?f=vD-dproSFox*iwMQ*nGWSw&preview.

North Carolina Office of State Budget and Management (NCOSBM) (2013). Council of Internal Auditing, Office of Internal Audit, Peer Review Program, E-mail with Internal Audit Staff Survey (Form B3a).

North Carolina Office of State Budget and Management (NCOSBM) (2013). Council of Internal Auditing, Office of Internal Audit, Peer Review Program, Internal Audit Staff Survey (Form B3b). Retrieved from: https://adobeformscentral.com/?f=ARWIdk2Y6s McPimCtAzCoQ&preview.

North Carolina Office of State Budget and Management (NCOSBM) (2013). Council of Internal Auditing, Office of Internal Audit, Peer Review Program, Survey Response Summary (Form B4).

North Carolina Office of State Budget and Management (NCOSBM) (2013). Council of Internal Auditing, Office of Internal Audit, Peer Review Program, Sample Interview Questionnaire—Board/Committee Member (Form C1).

North Carolina Office of State Budget and Management (NCOSBM) (2013). Council of Internal Auditing, Office of Internal Audit, Peer Review Program, Sample Interview Questionnaire—Executive Management (Form C2).

North Carolina Office of State Budget and Management (NCOSBM) (2013). Council of Internal Auditing, Office of Internal Audit, Peer Review Program, Sample Interview Questionnaire—Management (Form C3).

North Carolina Office of State Budget and Management (NCOSBM) (2013). Council of Internal Auditing, Office of Internal Audit, Peer Review Program, Sample Interview Questionnaire—CIO (Form C4).

North Carolina Office of State Budget and Management (NCOSBM) (2013). Council of Internal Auditing, Office of Internal Audit, Peer Review Program, Sample Interview Questionnaire—Internal Audit Director (Form C5).

North Carolina Office of State Budget and Management (NCOSBM) (2013). Council of Internal Auditing, Office of Internal Audit, Peer Review Program, Sample Interview Questionnaire—Internal Audit Staff (Form C6).

North Carolina Office of State Budget and Management (NCOSBM) (2013). Council of Internal Auditing, Office of Internal Audit, Peer Review Program, Sample Interview Questionnaire—External Auditor (Form C7).

North Carolina Office of State Budget and Management (NCOSBM) (2013). Council of Internal Auditing, Office of Internal Audit, Peer Review Program, Evaluation Summary and Report Phase—Evaluation Tool—Evaluation and Issues Worksheet (Form E1).

North Carolina Office of State Budget and Management (NCOSBM) (2013). Council of Internal Auditing, Office of Internal Audit, Peer Review Program, Evaluation Summary and Report Phase—Standard Conformation Evaluation (Form E2).

North Carolina Office of State Budget and Management (NCOSBM) (2013). Council of Internal Auditing, Office of Internal Audit, Peer Review Program, Evaluation Summary and Report Phase—Quality Assurance Review (Form E3).

North Carolina Office of State Budget and Management (NCOSBM) (2013). Council of Internal Auditing, Office of Internal Audit, Peer Review Program, Evaluation Summary and Report Phase—Report Format (Form E4).

North Carolina Office of State Budget and Management (NCOSBM) (2013). Council of Internal Auditing, Office of Internal Audit, Peer Review Program, Evaluation Summary and Report Phase—Satisfaction Survey (Form E5).

North Carolina Office of State Budget and Management (NCOSBM) (2013). Council of Internal Auditing, Office of Internal Audit, Peer Review Program, Evaluation Summary and Report Phase—Peer Review Survey (Form E6). Retrieved February 16, 2014, from: https://adobeformscentral.com/?f=Tbwt*UoQyZYzTkVzP68QqA&preview.

North Carolina Office of State Budget and Management (NCOSBM) (2014). Council of Internal Auditing, Office of Internal Audit, Peer Review Program Manual. Retrieved July 14, 2016, from: http://ncosbm.s3.amazonaws.com/s3fs-public/QARmanual_20140914 .pdf.

Royal Audit Authority of Bhutan. (n.d.). Handbook on Quality Assurance Review Process (A Handbook). Retrieved July 12, 2016, from: http://www.bhutanaudit.gov.bt /publi%20cation/Handbook%20on%20Quality%20Assurance%20Review%20 Process.pdf.

State Agency Internal Audit Forum (SAIAF) (2013). *Peer Review Process Manual.* Texas Commission on Environmental Quality. Retrieved July 15, 2016, from: http://pub lishingext.dir.texas.gov/portal/internal/resources/DocumentLibrary/SACC-SAIAF %20Peer%20Review%20Manual%20-%20Feb%202013.doc.

Virginia Beach City Public Schools, Office of Internal Audit (2012). Peer Review Report. Virginia Beach City Public Schools. Retrieved from: www.vbschools.com.

Chapter 8

What the Standards Say

8.1 Introduction

Internal auditing is conducted in multilegal and multicultural environments of entities that vary in size, nature, purpose, complexity, and structure. While differences may affect the practice of internal auditing in each environment, conformance with the Institute of Internal Auditors (IIA) International Standards, commonly referred to as *Red Book*, for the Professional Practice of Internal Auditing (Standards) or Generally Accepted Auditing Practice (GAAP), is essential in meeting the responsibilities of internal auditors and the internal audit activity.

In this chapter, we shall consider the postulations of the IIA, International Organization for Standardization (ISO), International Organization of Supreme Audit Institutions (INTOSAI), Generally Accepted Government Auditing Standards (GAGAS), and International Standards on Auditing (ISA) in relation to internal auditing using the IIA's International Professional Practice Framework (IPPF) as a benchmark.

The primary objective of this is to help readers identify where they can source for information regarding generally accepted auditing standards (GAASs) for internal auditing as a whole; this chapter does not replace the sources of GAASs.

We have delineated the chapter into two broad perspectives:

- GAAS as it concerns government agencies and institutions
- GAAS or IPPF as it concerns every organization

Note: The IIA's IPPF is applicable to all sectors of the economy, whether government or nongovernment, profit or nonprofit organizations.

It is instructive to note that the IIA, in a survey research, has identified that some organizations are not standards compliant for some or all of the underlisted reasons:

- Not appropriate for small and medium enterprises (SME)
- Inadequate internal audit activity
- Too costly to comply
- Too time consuming
- Not perceived as adding value to the management/board
- Standards or practice advisory too complex
- Superseded by local laws
- Compliance not expected in a particular country
- Standards not adequate for a particular industry
- Standards not available in a particular language of choice

Any reason notwithstanding, for uniformity, best practices, and global acceptance, the internal audit activity must comply with GAAS or IPPF standards.

8.2 International Standards for the Professional Practice of Internal Auditing (Standards)

8.2.1 Purpose of the Standards

The purpose of the Standards (as provided in the IPPF-2011 updated 2012) is to

- i. Delineate basic principles that represent the practice of internal auditing
- ii. Provide a framework for performing and promoting a broad range of value-added internal auditing
- iii. Establish the basis for the evaluation of internal audit performance
- iv. Foster improved organizational processes and operations

The Standards employ terms that have been given specific meanings that are included in the Glossary. Specifically, the Standards use the word *must* to specify an unconditional requirement and the word *should* where conformance is expected, unless, when applying professional judgment, circumstances justify deviation.

It is necessary to consider the statements and their interpretations as well as the specific meaning from the Glossary to understand and apply the Standards correctly.

8.2.2 Types of the Standards

The structure of the Standards is divided between Attribute Standards, Performance Standards, and Implementation Standards.

i. **Attribute Standards (ASs)**

Attribute Standards address the attributes of organizations and individuals performing internal auditing. They are numbered in 1000 and cover Standards 1000 to 1322.

There are four Attribute Standards: Purpose, Authority, and Responsibility (1000); Independence and Objectivity (1100); Proficiency and Due Professional Care (1200); and Quality Assurance and Compliance (1300). This can be summarized as follows:

AS 1000: Purpose, Authority, and Responsibility

1010—Recognition of the Definition of Internal Auditing, the Code of Ethics, and the Standards in the Internal Audit Charter

AS 1100: Independence and Objectivity

1110—Organizational Independence

1111—Direct Interaction with the Board

1120—Individual Objectivity

1130—Impairment to Independence or Objectivity

1200—Proficiency and Due Professional Care

1210—Proficiency

1220—Due Professional Care

1230—Continuing Professional Development

AS 1300: Quality Assurance and Improvement Program

1310—Requirements of the Quality Assurance and Improvement Program

1311—Internal Assessments

1312—External Assessments

1320—Reporting on the Quality Assurance and Improvement Program

1321—Use of "Conforms with the International Standards for the Professional Practice of Internal Auditing"

1322—Disclosure of Nonconformance

ii. **Performance Standards (PSs)**

The Performance Standards describe the nature of internal auditing and provide quality criteria against which the performance of these services can be measured; they are numbered in 2000 and cover standards 2000 to 2600. There are seven performance standards: Managing the Internal Audit Activity (2000), Nature of Work (2100), Engagement Planning (2200), Performing the Engagement (2300), Communicating Results (2400), Monitoring Progress

(2500), and Resolution of Management's Acceptance of Risks (2600). Performance standards are as summarized below.

PS 2000: Managing the Internal Audit Activity

2010—Planning

2020—Communication and Approval

2030—Resource Management

2040—Policies and Procedures

2050—Coordination

2060—Reporting to Senior Management and the Board

2070—External Service Provider and Organizational Responsibility for Internal Auditing

PS 2100: Nature of Work

2110—Governance

2120—Risk Management

2130—Control

PS 2200: Engagement Planning

2201—Planning Considerations

2210—Engagement Objectives

2220—Engagement Scope

2230—Engagement Resource Allocation

2240—Engagement Work Program

PS 2300: Performing the Engagement

2310—Identifying Information

2320—Analysis and Evaluation

2330—Documenting Information

2340—Engagement Supervision

PS 2400: Communicating Results

2410—Criteria for Communicating

2420—Quality of Communications

2421—Errors and Omissions

2430—Use of "Conducted in Conformance with the International Standards for the Professional Practice of Internal Auditing"

2431—Engagement Disclosure of Nonconformance

2440—Disseminating Results

2450—Overall Opinions

PS 2500: Monitoring Progress

The chief audit executive must establish and maintain a system to monitor the disposition of results communicated to management.

> **2500.A1**—The chief audit executive must establish a follow-up process to monitor and ensure that management actions have been effectively implemented or that senior management has accepted the risk of not taking action.

2500.C1—The internal audit activity must monitor the disposition of results of consulting engagements to the extent agreed upon with the client.

PS 2600: Communicating the Acceptance of Risks

When the chief audit executive concludes that management has accepted a level of risk that may be unacceptable to the organization, the chief audit executive must discuss the matter with senior management. If the chief audit executive determines that the matter has not been resolved, the chief audit executive must communicate the matter to the board.

iii. **Implementation Standards (ISs)**

Implementation Standards are provided to expand upon the Attribute and Performance Standards, by providing the requirements applicable to assurance (A) or consulting (C) activities as follows:

a. Assurance services involve the internal auditor's objective assessment of evidence to provide an independent opinion or conclusions regarding an entity, operation, function, process, system, or other subject matter. The nature and scope of the assurance engagement are determined by the internal auditor. There are generally three parties involved in assurance services:

1. The person or group directly involved with the entity, operation, function, process, system, or other subject matter—the process owner
2. The person or group making the assessment—the internal auditor
3. The person or group using the assessment—the user

Examples of assurance services are review of payroll systems, internal controls, cash management systems, etc.

b. Consulting services are advisory in nature, and are generally performed at the specific request of an engagement client. The nature and scope of the consulting engagement are subject to agreement with the engagement client. Consulting services generally involve two parties:

1. The person or group offering the advice—the internal auditor
2. The person or group seeking and receiving the advice—the engagement client

Examples of consulting services are conducting training on risk management, closure of accounts using the International Public Sector Accounting Standards, etc.

8.2.3 IIA's Code of Ethics

Adherence to the code of ethics is essential to maintain the credibility of the internal audit profession and of individual auditors.

Sawyer (2012, as cited in Blume, 2014) considers ethics as key to the trust that clients and stakeholders place on internal audit. The violation of such rules of ethical behavior leads to penalties by peer and the professional body.

The code of ethics (simply termed the Code) applies to all internal audit professionals. It includes two essential components.

8.2.3.1 Fundamental Principles

All internal auditors are required to abide to the following principles:

i. **Integrity:** The integrity of internal auditors establishes trust and thus provides the basis for reliance on their judgment.
ii. **Objectivity:** Internal auditors exhibit the highest level of professional objectivity in gathering, evaluating, and communicating information about the activity or process being examined. Internal auditors make a balanced assessment of all the relevant circumstances and are not unduly influenced by their own interests or by others in forming judgments.
iii. **Confidentiality:** Internal auditors respect the value and ownership of information they receive and do not disclose information without appropriate authority, unless there is a legal or professional obligation to do so.
iv. **Competency:** Internal auditors apply the knowledge, skills, and experience needed in the performance of internal audit services.

8.2.3.2 Rules of Conduct

The rules of conduct amplify the above principles but are written such that they give specific guidance for each of the four principles in the form of *shall* and *shall not*.

8.3 International Organization of Supreme Audit Institutions (INTOSAI)

8.3.1 Introduction

INTOSAI is a worldwide affiliation of governmental entities. Its members are the Chief Financial Controller/Comptroller General/Auditor General Offices of nations.

INTOSAI was founded in 1953 in Havana, Cuba. Thirty-four audit organizations formed the group originally and as of 2010 the current membership includes 197 institutions (192 national institutions, the European Court of Auditors and 4 associated members).

INTOSAI relies on the Committee of Sponsoring Organizations of the Treadway Commission's (COSO's) integrated framework for internal control, and uses the COSO's definition of *internal control* and the IIA's definition of *internal audit*.

INTOSAI is a strong advocate for the establishment of an independent internal audit in public entities as stipulated in

- The International Standards of Supreme Audit Institutions (ISSAI 100, n.d.)—a benchmark for auditing public entities (External Audit Standards for public entities)
- ISSAI 1610—Using the Work of Internal Auditors

8.3.2 INTOSAI Guidance for Good Governance: INTOSAI GOVs 9100–9230

The guidance INTOSAI GOV 9100 states (p. 46), "The Supreme Audit Institution also has a vested interest in ensuring that strong internal audit units exist where needed. Those audit units constitute an important element of internal control by providing a continuous means for improving an organization's operations. In some countries, however, the internal audit units may lack independence, be weak, or be nonexistent. In those cases, the SAI should, whenever possible, offer assistance and guidance to establish and develop those capacities and to ensure the independence of the internal auditor's activities."—"The creation of an internal audit unit as part of the internal control system is a strong signal by management that internal control is important.

(…) For an internal audit function to be effective, it is essential that the internal audit staff be independent from management, work in an unbiased, correct and honest way and that they report directly to the highest level of authority within the organization.

(…) For professional guidance, internal auditors should use the Professional Practices Framework (PPF) of the Institute of Internal Auditors (IIA) (…) Additionally, internal auditors should follow the INTOSAI Code of Ethics."

8.3.3 ISSAI 1610 Using the Work of Internal Auditors (See Section 8.6)

8.4 Generally Accepted Government Auditing Standards (GAGAS) (GAO, 2011)

8.4.1 Summary

GAGAS, commonly referred to as the *Yellow Book*, are produced in the United States by the Government Accountability Office (GAO). The standards apply to both financial and performance audits of government agencies (GAO, 2011).

GAGASs are used by auditors who examine the federal government, including the GAO, various offices of inspectors general, and others. Many local government performance auditors also use the yellow book standards. In addition, Certified Public Accountant (CPA) firms that perform local government financial audits including an A-133 *single audit* must follow yellow book standards.

In addition to financial audits, the yellow book standards cover performance audits, which evaluate the performance of a program or project against defined objectives, such as objectives for efficiency and effectiveness.

8.4.2 Foundation and Ethical Principles

The ethical principles that guide the work of auditors who conduct audits in accordance with GAGAS are

a. Public interest
b. Integrity
c. Objectivity
d. Proper use of government information, resources, and positions
e. Professional behavior

8.4.3 Types of GAGASs

The types of audits that are covered by GAGAS, as defined by their objectives, are classified into three: financial audits, attestation engagements, and performance audits.

GAGAS requirements apply to the types of audits that may be performed in accordance with GAGAS as follows:

a. Financial audits: the requirements and guidance in Chapters 1 through 4 apply.
   – Financial statement audits
   – Other types of financial audits
b. Attestation engagements: the requirements and guidance in Chapters 1 through 3 and 5 apply.
   – Examination
   – Review
   – Agreed-upon procedures
c. Performance audits: the requirements and guidance in Chapters 1 through 3, 6, and 7 apply.
   – Program effectiveness and results audit objectives are frequently interrelated with economy and efficiency objectives.
   – Internal control audit objectives relate to an assessment of one or more components of an organization's system of internal control that is designed to provide reasonable assurance of achieving effective and efficient operations,

reliable financial and performance reporting, or compliance with applicable laws and regulations.
- Compliance requirements can be either financial or nonfinancial.
- Prospective analysis audit objectives provide analysis or conclusions about information that is based on assumptions about events that may occur in the future, along with possible actions that the entity may take in response to the future events.

8.4.4 General Standards

There are basically four general standards, as follows.

8.4.4.1 Independence

Independence comprises

a. Independence of mind
b. Independence in appearance

1. GAGAS Conceptual Framework Approach to Independence
   a. Identify threats to independence
   b. Evaluate the significance of the threats identified, both individually and in the aggregate
   c. Apply safeguards as necessary to eliminate the threats or reduce them to an acceptable level
2. Application of the Conceptual Framework
3. Government Auditors and Audit Organization Structure
   a. External Auditor Independence
   b. Internal Auditor Independence
4. Provision of Nonaudit Services to Audited Entities
   a. Requirements for Performing Nonaudit Services
   b. Consideration of Specific Nonaudit Services
      i. Management Responsibilities
      ii. Preparing Accounting Records and Financial Statements
      iii. Internal Audit Assistance Services Provided by External Auditors
      iv. Internal Control Monitoring as a Nonaudit Service
      v. Information Technology Systems Services
      vi. Valuation Services
      vii. Other Nonaudit Services (Non tax disbursement, Benefit plan administration, Investment, Corporate finance, Executive or employee personnel matters, Business risk consulting, etc.)
5. Documentation
6. Independence, Legal, and Ethical Requirements

8.4.4.2 Professional Judgment (Due Care)

Auditors must use professional judgment in planning and performing audits and in reporting the results. Professional judgment includes exercising reasonable care and professional skepticism. Reasonable care includes acting diligently in accordance with applicable professional standards and ethical principles. Professional skepticism is an attitude that includes a questioning mind and a critical assessment of evidence. Professional skepticism includes a mindset in which auditors assume that management is neither dishonest nor of unquestioned honesty.

8.4.4.3 Competence/Continuing Professional Education (CPE)

1. Technical Knowledge
2. Additional Qualifications for Financial Audits and Attestation Engagements
3. Continuing Professional Education
4. CPE Requirements for Specialists

8.4.4.4 Quality Control and Assurance

1. System of Quality Control
2. Leadership Responsibilities for Quality within the Audit Organization
3. Initiation, Acceptance, and Continuance of Audits
4. Human Resources
5. Audit Performance, Documentation, and Reporting
6. Monitoring of Quality
7. External Peer Review

8.4.5 Specific Standards

There are also four specific standards.

8.4.5.1 Standards for Financial Audits

This standard contains requirements, guidance, and considerations for performing and reporting on financial audits conducted in accordance with GAGAS.

1. Additional GAGAS Requirements for Performing Financial Audits
   a. Auditor communication
   b. Previous audits and attestation engagements
   c. Fraud, noncompliance with provisions of laws, regulations, contracts, and grant agreements, and abuse
   d. Developing elements of a finding
   e. Audit documentation

2. Reporting Auditors' Compliance with GAGAS
3. Reporting on Internal Control and Compliance with Provisions of Laws
4. Regulations, Contracts, and Grant Agreements
5. Communicating Deficiencies in Internal Control, Fraud, Noncompliance with Provisions of Laws, Regulations, Contracts, and Grant Agreements, and Abuse
   a. Deficiencies in internal control
   b. Presenting findings in the auditors' report
   c. Reporting findings directly to parties outside the audited entity
6. Reporting Views of Responsible Officials
7. Reporting Confidential and Sensitive Information
8. Distributing Reports
9. Additional GAGAS Considerations for Financial Audits
10. Materiality in GAGAS Financial Audits
11. Early Communication of Deficiencies

8.4.5.2 Standards for Attestation Engagements

This section contains requirements, guidance, and considerations for performing and reporting on attestation engagements conducted in accordance with GAGAS.

1. Examination Engagements
   i. Additional Fieldwork Requirements for Examination Engagements
       a. Auditor communication
       b. Previous audits and attestation engagements
       c. Fraud, noncompliance with provisions of laws, regulations, contracts, and grant agreements, and abuse
       d. Developing elements of a finding
       e. Examination engagement documentation
   ii. Additional GAGAS Reporting Requirements for Examination Engagements
       a. Reporting auditors' compliance with GAGAS
       b. Reporting deficiencies in internal control, fraud, noncompliance with provisions of laws, regulations, contracts, and grant agreements, and abuse
           ■ Deficiencies in internal control
           ■ Fraud, noncompliance with provisions of laws, regulations, contracts, and grant agreements, and abuse
           ■ Presenting findings in the examination report
           ■ Reporting findings directly to parties outside the audited entity
       c. Reporting views of responsible officials
       d. Reporting confidential and sensitive information
       e. Distributing reports

    iii. Additional GAGAS Considerations for Examination Engagements
        a. Materiality in GAGAS examination engagements
        b. Early communication of deficiencies
  2. Review Engagements
    i. Additional GAGAS Fieldwork Requirements for Review Engagements
        a. Communicating significant deficiencies, material weaknesses, instances of fraud, noncompliance with provisions of laws, regulations, contracts and grant agreements, and abuse
    ii. Additional GAGAS Reporting Requirements for Review Engagements
        a. Reporting auditors' compliance with GAGAS
        b. Distributing reports
    iii. Additional GAGAS Considerations for Review Engagements
        a. Establishing an understanding regarding services to be performed
        b. Reporting on review engagements
  3. Agreed-Upon Procedure Engagements
    i. Additional GAGAS Fieldwork Requirements for Agreed-Upon Procedure Engagements
        a. Communicating significant deficiencies, material weaknesses, instances of fraud, noncompliance with provisions of laws, regulations, contracts and grant agreements, and abuse
    ii. Additional GAGAS Reporting Requirements for Agreed-Upon Procedure Engagements
        a. Reporting auditors' compliance with GAGAS
        b. Distributing reports
    iii. Additional GAGAS Considerations for Agreed-Upon Procedure Engagements
        a. Establishing an understanding regarding services to be performed
        b. Reporting on agreed-upon procedure engagements

8.4.5.3 Fieldwork Standards for Performance Audits

This standard contains fieldwork requirements and guidance for performance audits conducted in accordance with GAGAS.

  1. Reasonable Assurance
  2. Significance in a Performance Audit
  3. Planning
  4. Nature and Profile of the Program and User Needs
  5. Internal Control
  6. Information Systems Controls
  7. Provisions of Laws, Regulations, Contracts, and Grant Agreements, Fraud, and Abuse
  8. Ongoing Investigations and Legal Proceedings

9. Previous Audits and Attestation Engagements
10. Previous Audits and Attestation Engagements
11. Assigning Staff and Other Resources
12. Communicating with Management, Those Charged with Governance, and Others
13. Preparing a Written Audit Plan
14. Obtaining Sufficient, Appropriate Evidence
15. Overall Assessment of Evidence
16. Developing Elements of a Finding
17. Early Communication of Deficiencies

8.4.5.4 Reporting Standards for Performance Audits

This section contains reporting requirements and guidance for performance audits conducted in accordance with GAGAS.

1. Reporting
2. Report Contents
3. Objectives, Scope, and Methodology
4. Fraud, Noncompliance with Provisions of Laws, Regulations, Contracts, and Grant Agreements, and Abuse
5. Reporting Findings Directly to Parties Outside the Audited Entity
6. Recommendations
7. Reporting Views of Responsible Officials
8. Reporting Confidential and Sensitive Information
9. Distributing Reports

GAGAS contain additional supplemental guidance for auditors and the audited entities to assist them in the implementation of GAGAS.

8.5 Comparison of IIA Standards and GAGAS

As stated earlier, GAGAS is commonly referred to as the *Yellow Book* and IIA Standards are commonly referred to as the *Red Book* (Hart-Fanta, 2013). The IIA provides a comparison of the IIA Standards and GAGAS on IIA's website, as shown in the references.

The following are the highlights of some of the most outstanding differences between the two standards:

■ Each of them starts from a different definition of auditing and auditors.
■ For GAGAS, the emphasis is on accountability, while the IIA emphasizes governance, risk, and controls to add value.

- The IIA requires an internal audit charter, whereas GAGAS does not.
- GAGAS discourages nonaudit consulting services, noting that they could compromise objectivity and independence; on the other hand, the IIA recognizes consulting as a service that internal auditors provide to their organizations or clients and have established *consulting standards* to that effect.
- Under GAGAS, auditors must document consideration of independence; the IIA has no formal requirement to document independence. However, the IIA Standards require internal auditors to have independence and state that an auditor "must have an impartial, unbiased attitude and avoid any conflict of interest." The Standards also require *organizational independence* and provides definitions of *independence* and *objectivity*.
- GAGAS require external peer reviews every three years; the IIA Standards require external peer reviews every five years.
- GAGAS define three types of assurance engagements: financial, attestation, and performance; the IIA Standards discuss assurance services but focus on the auditor's work and governance, risk assessment, and controls.
- The IIA Standards require the development of an audit universe and annual work plan; GAGAS have no such requirement.
- Under GAGAS, auditors write *findings* when fraud, abuse, internal control weaknesses, and noncompliance are found; the IIA Standards require auditors to "communicate engagement results and, where appropriate, the communication must contain the internal auditor's opinion and/or conclusions." These results must include issues of fraud, abuse, internal control weaknesses, and noncompliance. Each issue noted must include the condition, criteria, cause, and effect.
- GAGAS require 80 hours of CPE every two years; IIA Standards state, "Internal Auditors must enhance their knowledge, skills, and other competencies through continuing professional development," but it does not specify a required number of hours for noncertified members. However, Certified Internal Auditors are required to have a minimum of 40 hours of continuing education every year. Certified Government Auditing Professionals are required to have 25% of their hours in government related training.

8.6 ISA 610 (Revised 2013) and ISSAI 1610, Using the Work of Internal Auditors

8.6.1 Introduction and Scope of This ISA

The International Standards on Auditing (ISA) are professional standards for the performance of financial audit of financial statements. These standards are issued by the International Federation of Accountants (IFAC) through the International Auditing and Assurance Standards Board (IAASB).

The objective of the IAASB is to serve the public interest by setting high-quality auditing and assurance standards and by facilitating the convergence of international and national standards, thereby enhancing the quality and uniformity of practice throughout the world and strengthening public confidence in the global auditing and assurance profession.

This ISA 610 deals with the external auditor's responsibilities if using the work of internal auditors. This includes

a. Using the work of the internal audit function in obtaining audit evidence
b. Using internal auditors to provide direct assistance under the direction, supervision, and review of the external auditor

For purposes of this ISA 610, direct assistance means the use of internal auditors to perform audit procedures under the direction, supervision, and review of the external auditor.

Note: This ISA does not apply if the entity does not have an internal audit function.

Also, where the entity has an internal audit function, the requirements of ISA 610 relating to using the work of that function do not apply if

a. The responsibilities and activities of the function are not relevant to the external audit.
b. Based on the external auditor's preliminary understanding of the function obtained as a result of procedures performed under ISA 315 (Revised), "Identifying and Assessing the Risks of Material Misstatement through Understanding the Entity and Its Environment," the external auditor does not expect to use the work of the internal audit function in obtaining audit evidence.

Nothing in this ISA requires the external auditor to use the work of the internal audit function to modify the nature or timing, or reduce the extent, of audit procedures to be performed directly by the external auditor; it remains a decision of the external auditor in establishing the overall audit strategy.

Furthermore, nothing in ISA 610 relating to direct assistance compels the external auditor where it does not plan to use internal auditors to provide direct assistance.

In some jurisdictions, the external auditor may be prohibited, or restricted to some extent, by law or regulation from using the work of the internal audit function or using internal auditors to provide direct assistance. In this regard, ISA do not override laws or regulations that govern an audit of financial statements. Such prohibitions or restrictions will therefore not prevent the external auditor from complying with the ISA.

ISA 610 (Revised 2013), "Using the Work of Internal Auditors," should be read in conjunction with ISA 200, "Overall Objectives of the Independent Auditor and the Conduct of an Audit in Accordance with International Standards on Auditing."

In addition to the changes included in ISA 610 (Revised), ISA 610 (Revised 2013) now also includes requirements and guidance addressing the external auditor's responsibilities if using internal auditors to provide direct assistance under the direction, supervision, and review of the external auditor for purposes of the audit, where such assistance is not prohibited by law or regulation. The material in ISA 610 (Revised 2013) pertaining to direct assistance is effective for audits of financial statements for periods ending on or after December 15, 2014.

8.6.2 Relationship between ISA 315 (Revised) and ISA 610 (Revised 2013)

Many entities establish internal audit functions as part of their internal control and governance structures. The objectives and scope of an internal audit function, the nature of its responsibilities and its organizational status, including the function's authority and accountability, vary widely and depend on the size and structure of the entity and the requirements of management and, where applicable, those charged with governance.

ISA 315 (Revised) addresses how the knowledge and experience of the internal audit function can inform the external auditor's understanding of the entity and its environment and identification and assessment of risks of material misstatement. ISA 315 (Revised) also explains how effective communication between the internal and external auditors also creates an environment in which the external auditor can be informed of significant matters that may affect the external auditor's work.

Depending on whether the internal audit function's organizational status and relevant policies and procedures adequately support the objectivity of the internal auditors, the level of competency of the internal audit function, and whether the function applies a systematic and disciplined approach, the external auditor may also be able to use the work of the internal audit function in a constructive and complementary manner. ISA 610 addresses the external auditor's responsibilities when, based on the external auditor's preliminary understanding of the internal audit function obtained as a result of procedures performed under ISA 315 (Revised), the external auditor expects to use the work of the internal audit function as part of the audit evidence obtained. Such use of that work modifies the nature or timing, or reduces the extent, of audit procedures to be performed directly by the external auditor.

In addition, ISA 610 also addresses the external auditor's responsibilities if considering using internal auditors to provide direct assistance under the direction, supervision, and review of the external auditor.

There are instances where some individuals perform procedures similar to those of internal auditors; unless such procedures are performed by an objective and competent function that applies a systematic and disciplined approach, including quality control, such procedures would be considered internal controls and obtaining evidence regarding the effectiveness of such controls would be part of the auditor's responses to assessed risks in accordance with ISA 330.

8.6.3 The External Auditor's Responsibility for the Audit

It is important to note that the external auditor has sole responsibility for the expression of audit opinion, and that responsibility is not reduced by the external auditor's use of the work of the internal audit function or internal auditors to provide direct assistance on the engagement. Although internal auditors may perform audit procedures similar to those performed by the external auditor, neither the internal audit function nor the internal auditors are independent of the entity as is required of the external auditor in an audit of financial statements in accordance with ISA 200. ISA 610, therefore, defines the conditions that are necessary for the external auditor to be able to use the work of internal auditors. It also defines the necessary work effort that is needed to obtain sufficient appropriate evidence that the work of the internal audit function, or internal auditors providing direct assistance, is adequate for the purposes of the audit. The requirements are designed to provide a framework for the external auditor's judgments regarding the use of the work of internal auditors to prevent over or undue use of such work.

8.6.4 Objectives

The objectives of the external auditor, where the entity has an internal audit function and the external auditor expects to use the work of the function to modify the nature or timing, or reduce the extent of audit procedures to be performed directly by the external auditor, or use internal auditors to provide direct assistance, are

a. To determine whether the work of the internal audit function or direct assistance from internal auditors can be used, and if so, in which areas and to what extent; and having made that determination

b. If using the work of the internal audit function, to determine whether that work is adequate for purposes of the audit

c. If using internal auditors to provide direct assistance, to appropriately direct, supervise, and review their work

8.6.5 Requirements

8.6.5.1 Determining Whether and to What Extent to Use the Work of the Internal Auditors

The external auditor shall determine whether the work of the internal audit function can be used for purposes of the external audit by evaluating the following:

a. The extent to which the internal audit function's organizational status and relevant policies and procedures support the objectivity of the internal auditors
b. The level of competence of the internal audit function
c. Whether the internal audit function applies a systematic and disciplined approach, including quality control

Note that the external auditor shall not use the work of the internal audit function if the external auditor determines that

a. The function's organizational status and relevant policies and procedures do not adequately support the objectivity of internal auditors.
b. The function lacks sufficient competence.
c. The function does not apply a systematic and disciplined approach, including quality control.

8.6.5.2 Determining the Nature and Extent of Work of the Internal Audit Function That Can Be Used

As a basis for determining the areas and the extent to which the work of the internal audit function can be used, the external auditor shall consider the nature and scope of the work that has been performed, or is planned to be performed, by the internal audit function and its relevance to the external auditor's overall audit strategy and audit plan.

The external auditor shall make all significant judgments in the audit engagement and, to prevent undue use of the work of the internal audit function, shall plan to use less of the work of the function and perform more of the work directly:

a. The more judgment is involved in
    i. Planning and performing relevant audit procedures
    ii. Evaluating the audit evidence gathered
b. The higher the assessed risk of material misstatement at the assertion level, with special consideration given to risks identified as significant

   c. Also, the less the internal audit function's organizational status and relevant policies and procedures adequately support the objectivity of the internal auditors

   d. The lower the level of competence of the internal audit function

The external auditor shall also evaluate whether, in aggregate, using the work of the internal audit function to the extent planned would still result in the external auditor being sufficiently involved in the audit, given the external auditor's sole responsibility for the audit opinion expressed.

The external auditor shall, in communicating with those charged with governance, an overview of the planned scope, and timing of the audit in accordance with ISA 260, also communicate how the external auditor has planned to use the work of the internal audit function.

8.6.6 Using the Work of the Internal Audit Function

Where the external auditor plans to use the work of the internal audit function, the external auditor shall discuss the planned use of its work with the function as a basis for coordinating their respective activities.

The external auditor shall read the reports of the internal audit function relating to the work of the function that the external auditor plans to use to obtain an understanding of the nature and extent of audit procedures it performed and the related findings.

The external auditor shall perform sufficient audit procedures on the body of work of the internal audit function as a whole that the external auditor plans to use to determine its adequacy for purposes of the audit, including evaluating whether

   a. The work of the function had been properly planned, performed, supervised, reviewed, and documented.

   b. Sufficient appropriate evidence had been obtained to enable the function to draw reasonable conclusions.

   c. Conclusions reached are appropriate in the circumstances and the reports prepared by the function are consistent with the results of the work performed.

The nature and extent of the external auditor's audit procedures shall be responsive to the external auditor's evaluation of

   a. The amount of judgment involved

   b. The assessed risk of material misstatement

   c. The extent to which the internal audit function's organizational status and relevant policies and procedures support the objectivity of the internal auditors

   d. The level of competence of the function

   e. Shall include re-performance of some of the work

8.6.7 Determining Whether, in Which Areas, and to What Extent Internal Auditors Can Be Used to Provide Direct Assistance

8.6.7.1 Determining Whether Internal Auditors Can Be Used to Provide Direct Assistance for Purposes of the Audit

The external auditor may be prohibited by law or regulation from obtaining direct assistance from internal auditors; where this is the case, the use of an internal auditor to provide direct assistance to the external auditor does not apply in this standard.

Where the use of an internal auditor to provide direct assistance to the external auditor is permissive by regulations, the external auditor, where he/she plans to use the internal auditor in this capacity, shall evaluate the existence and significance of threat to objectivity and level of competence of the internal auditor through inquiries.

The external auditor shall not use an internal auditor to provide direct assistance if

a. There are significant threats to the objectivity of the internal auditor.
b. The internal auditor lacks sufficient competence to perform the proposed work.

8.6.7.2 Determining the Nature and Extent of Work That Can Be Assigned to Internal Auditors Providing Direct Assistance

In determining the nature and extent of work that may be assigned to internal auditors and the nature, timing and extent of direction, supervision, and review that is appropriate in the circumstances, the external auditor shall consider

a. The amount of judgment involved in
   i. Planning and performing relevant audit procedures
   ii. Evaluating the audit evidence gathered
b. The assessed risk of material misstatement
c. The external auditor's evaluation of the existence and significance of threats to the objectivity and level of competence of the internal auditors who will be providing such assistance

The external auditor shall not use internal auditors to provide direct assistance to perform procedures that

a. Involve making significant judgments in the audit
b. Relate to higher assessed risks of material misstatement where the judgment required in performing the relevant audit procedures or evaluating the audit evidence gathered is more than limited

c. Relate to work with which the internal auditors have been involved and which has already been, or will be, reported to management or those charged with governance by the internal audit function

d. Relate to decisions the external auditor makes in accordance with this ISA regarding the internal audit function and the use of its work or direct assistance

8.6.8 Using Internal Auditors to Provide Direct Assistance

Prior to using internal auditors to provide direct assistance for purposes of the audit, the external auditor shall

a. Obtain written agreement from an authorized representative of the entity that the internal auditors will be allowed to follow the external auditor's instructions, and that the entity will not intervene in the work the internal auditor performs for the external auditor

b. Obtain written agreement from the internal auditors that they will keep confidential specific matters as instructed by the external auditor and inform the external auditor of any threat to their objectivity

The external auditor shall direct, supervise, and review the work performed by internal auditors on the engagement in accordance with ISA 220. In so doing

a. The nature, timing, and extent of direction, supervision, and review shall recognize that the internal auditors are not independent of the entity and be responsive to the outcome of the evaluation of the amount of planning, audit procedure to be performed, assessment of audit evidence gathered, assessment of risk of material misstatement, and evaluation of the existence of threat to objectivity and level of competence of the internal auditor.

b. The review procedures shall include the external auditor checking back to the underlying audit evidence for some of the work performed by the internal auditors.

8.6.9 Documentation

Where the external auditor uses the work of the internal audit function, the external auditor shall include in the audit documentation

a. The evaluation of
   i. Whether the function's organizational status and relevant policies and procedures adequately support the objectivity of the internal auditors
   ii. The level of competence of the function
   iii. Whether the function applies a systematic and disciplined approach, including quality control

b. The nature and extent of the work used and the basis for that decision

c. The audit procedures performed by the external auditor to evaluate the adequacy of the work used

Where the external auditor uses internal auditors to provide direct assistance on the audit, the external auditor shall include in the audit documentation

a. The evaluation of the existence and significance of threats to the objectivity of the internal auditors, and the level of competence of the internal auditors used to provide direct assistance

b. The basis for the decision regarding the nature and extent of the work performed by the internal auditors

c. Who reviewed the work performed and the date and extent of that review in accordance with ISA 230

d. The written agreements obtained from an authorized representative of the entity and the internal auditors as provided under this standard

e. The working papers prepared by the internal auditors who provided direct assistance on the audit engagement

8.6.10 Application and Other Explanatory Materials

This involves the application of explanatory material of the above standards, which can be assessed publicly. They are as listed hereunder.

Definition of Internal Audit Function
■ Activities relating to governance
■ Activities relating to risk management
■ Activities relating to internal control

Determining Whether, in Which Areas, and to What Extent the Work of the Internal Audit Function Can Be Used
■ Evaluating the internal audit function
■ Objectivity and competence
■ Application of a systematic and disciplined approach

Circumstances When Work of the Internal Audit Function Cannot Be Used

Determining the Nature and Extent of Work of the Internal Audit Function That Can Be Used
■ Factors affecting the determination of the nature and extent of the work of the internal audit function that can be used
■ Judgments in planning and performing audit procedures and evaluating results
■ Assessed risk of material misstatement
■ Communication with those charged with governance

Using the Work of the Internal Audit Function
- Discussion and coordination with the internal audit function
- Procedures to determine the adequacy of work of the internal audit function
- Re-performance

Determining Whether, in Which Areas, and to What Extent Internal Auditors Can Be Used to Provide Direct Assistance
- Determining whether internal auditors can be used to provide direct assistance for purposes of the audit
- Determining the nature and extent of work that can be assigned to internal auditors providing direct assistance

Using Internal Auditors to Provide Direct Assistance

8.6.11 Additional Guidance on Public Sector Issues (ISSAI 1610)

On the other hand, ISSAI 1610 provides a supplementary guidance on ISA 610 and it is read together with the ISA. ISA 610, The Practice Note, provides additional guidance for public sector auditors related to

a. Overall considerations
b. Determining whether and to what extent to use the work of the internal auditors

ISSAI 1610 further stated that ISA 610 is applicable to auditors of public sector entities in their role as auditors of financial statements.

8.6.11.1 Overall Considerations

The objectives of a financial audit in the public sector are often broader than expressing an opinion whether the financial statements have been prepared, in all material respects, in accordance with the applicable financial reporting framework (i.e., the scope of the ISAs). Additional objectives may include audit and reporting responsibilities, for example, relating to reporting whether the public sector auditors found any instances of noncompliance with authorities, including budgets and accountability frameworks, and/or reporting on the effectiveness of internal control. Public sector auditors may find activities carried out by the internal audit function relating to the entity's noncompliance with authorities including budget and accountability and the entity's effectiveness of internal control relevant to the audit. In such cases, public sector auditors may use the work of the internal auditors to supplement the external audit work in these areas.

8.6.11.2 Determining Whether and to What Extent to Use the Work of the Internal Auditors

Public sector auditors in their determination of whether the work of the internal auditors is likely to be objective for the purposes of the audit, as noted in relevant paragraphs of ISA 610, consider any relevant INTOSAI guidance related to assessing the objectivity of the internal auditors and, if relevant, the existence and reports of any public sector internal audit function oversight body. However, where the internal audit function is established by legislation or regulation, and the following criteria are met, there is a strong indication that the internal audit function may be presumed to be objective:

a. Is accountable to top management, for example, the head or deputy head of the government entity, and to those charged with governance
b. Reports the audit results both to top management, for example, the head or deputy head of the government entity, and those charged with governance
c. Is located organizationally outside the staff and management function of the unit under audit
d. Is sufficiently removed from political pressure to conduct audits and report findings, opinions, and conclusions objectively without fear of political reprisal
e. Does not permit internal audit staff to audit operations for which they have previously been responsible for to avoid any perceived conflict of interest
f. Has access to those charged with governance

8.7 ISO 19011 2011 Auditing Standard

According to Praxiom Research Group Limited, ISO 19011 2011 is a standard for auditing management systems. It was developed by ISO Technical Committee 176, Subcommittee 3 (SC 3). ISO/TCC176176 is responsible for *quality management and quality assurance*, and SC 3 is responsible for *supporting technologies*. The official name of this standard is ISO 19011:2011 Guidelines for auditing management systems. They are referred to as guidelines because they are voluntary. They are not requirements or contractual obligations. These guidelines can be found in the following four sections of the document:

Part 4. Audit Principles
Part 5. Audit Program
Part 6. Audit Activities
Part 7. Auditor Competence

Part 4 outlines the principles that are (or should be) the foundation of management system auditing. They define the essential nature of auditing and should therefore influence how audit programs are designed, how audit activities are carried out, and how audit or competence is evaluated.

Part 5 explains how management system audit programs are designed and managed. It discusses how program objectives are established and how audit programs are developed, implemented, monitored, reviewed, and improved.

Part 6 explains how audit activities are planned and performed. It discusses how audits are initiated, how auditors prepare for audits, how they carry out audits, how audit results are reported, and how audits are completed.

Part 7 explains how the competence of management system auditors is evaluated. It discusses how competence requirements are defined, how auditor evaluation criteria are developed, how auditor evaluation methods are selected, and how competence is evaluated and improved. ISO 19011 2011 versus ISO 19011 2002: ISO first published this standard in 2002. This second edition was published on November 15, 2011. It cancels and replaces the first edition.

A detailed summary of ISO 19011 provided by Praxiom Research Group Limited is as follows.

8.7.1 Audit Principles

A. Have integrity and be professional.
– Comply with all applicable legal requirements.
– Withstand the pressures that may be exerted and the influences that may affect your professional judgment.

B. Present fair and truthful results.
– Make sure that audit results are fairly presented.
– Make sure that important concerns are reported.

C. Exercise due professional care.
– Perform auditing tasks with due care and diligence.
– Make reasoned judgments in all audit situations.

D. Care about confidentiality.
– Care about confidentiality and information security.
– Handle information with due care and discretion.
– Protect information that is sensitive or confidential.

E. Be independent and impartial.
– Be independent of the activities being audited.
– Be impartial and always be free of bias.

F. Use an evidence-based approach.
– Use an evidence-based approach to reach reliable and reproducible audit conclusions.

8.7.2 Audit Program

A. Create your audit program.
- Establish a management system audit program.
- Use your audit program to evaluate the overall effectiveness of your auditee's management systems.
- Monitor and measure the implementation of your management system audit program.
- Review your management system audit program in order to identify possible improvements.

B. Set your program objectives.
- Ensure that audit program objectives are established.
- Make sure that your audit program objectives support and are consistent with management system objectives.
- Consider all relevant information when you establish your audit program objectives.
- Use program objectives to ensure that your audit program is implemented and applied effectively.
- Use program objectives to direct audit planning.
- Use program objectives to direct audit activities.

C. Establish your audit program.
1. Perform audit program management tasks.
   - Clarify the extent of your audit program.
   - Define auditors' roles and responsibilities.
   - Develop procedures to manage audit program.
   - Determine the resources that program needs.
   - Implement and apply your audit program.
   - Establish records for your audit program.
   - Monitor your management system audit program.
   - Review your management system audit program.
   - Improve your management system audit program.
   - Discuss your audit program with top management.
2. Clarify manager's competence requirements.
   - Make sure that your audit manager is competent.
   - Make sure that audit manager has the competence to manage the program efficiently and effectively.
   - Make sure that your audit manager has the appropriate specialized knowledge and skills.
   - Ensure that audit manager continues to be competent.
   - Ensure that audit manager continues to carry out appropriate professional development activities.

3. Specify the extent of your audit program.
   - Establish the extent of your management system audit program (its focus and reach).
   - Consider the nature of your audits.
   - Consider the nature of your audit criteria.
   - Consider the nature of the auditee organization.
   - Consider the nature of the systems being audited.
   - Consider the nature and results of previous reviews.
4. Consider potential audit program risks.
   - Consider the risks that could potentially affect the achievement of your audit program objectives.
   - Identify and evaluate program planning risks.
   - Identify and evaluate program resource risks.
   - Identify and evaluate program staffing risks.
   - Identify and evaluate program implementation risks.
   - Identify and evaluate program record-keeping risks.
   - Identify and evaluate program monitoring risks.
   - Identify and evaluate program review risks.
5. Develop procedures to manage program.
   - Establish procedures to manage and control your management system audit program.
   - Use procedures to manage and control your management system audit program.
6. Identify program resource requirements.
   - Identify financial resource requirements.
   - Identify methodological resource requirements.
   - Identify technological resource requirements.
   - Identify human resource requirements.

D. Implement your audit program.
1. Apply your unique audit program.
   - Communicate and share pertinent information about the audit program with all relevant parties.
   - Define objectives for each individual audit.
   - Coordinate and control program activities.
   - Appoint competent audit team members.
   - Provide needed resources to audit teams.
2. Define the focus of each individual audit.
   - Define and document the objectives that each individual audit should achieve.
   - Define and document the scope of each audit.
   - Define and document the criteria that individual audits use to assess conformity.

3. Select methods for each individual audit.
   - Select and determine the methods that should be used to conduct audits.
   - Make sure that all audit managers agree on audit methods whenever two or more auditing organizations need to conduct a joint audit of the same auditee.
4. Appoint personnel for each individual audit.
   - Appoint audit team members for each separate audit.
   - Appoint an audit team leader for each separate audit.
   - Appoint technical experts for each separate audit.
5. Assign responsibility for individual audits.
   - Assign responsibility for an individual audit to a specific audit team leader.
   - Give the audit team leader enough time to plan the audit whenever audit assignments are allocated.
   - Give the audit team leader the information that he or she needs in order to carry out the audit.
6. Manage your audit program outcomes.
   - Ensure that audit program outcomes are managed efficiently and effectively.
   - Ensure that audit findings are evaluated.
   - Ensure that root-cause analyses are reviewed.
   - Ensure that remedial actions are reviewed.
   - Ensure that audit reports are reviewed.
7. Establish and maintain audit records.
   - Ensure that audit program records are established and maintained.
   - Ensure that a record of each individual audit is established and maintained.
   - Ensure that audit personnel records are established and maintained.

E. Monitor and modify your program.
   - Monitor the implementation of your program.
   - Modify your audit program whenever evidence indicates that change is required.

F. Review and improve your program.
   - Review your management system audit program.
   - Summarize your results and report to top management.
   - Improve your management system audit program.

8.7.3 Audit Activities

A. Manage your audit activities.
   - Perform audit activities that comply with your management system audit program (Part 5).

B. Initiate your audit activities.
1. Conduct and control audit activities.
   - Make sure that an audit team leader is appointed for each individual audit.
   - Make sure that audit team leaders initiate management system audits.
2. Establish initial contact with auditee.
   - Establish communications with the auditee.
   - Confirm your agreement with the auditee.
   - Share information with the auditee.
   - Gather information about the auditee.
   - Request access to documents and records.
   - Make arrangements to conduct the audit.
3. Determine the feasibility of the audit.
   - Make sure that you are reasonably confident that your audit objectives can be achieved.
   - Make sure that you have everything you need to plan and perform your audit.

C. Get ready for your audit.
1. Perform document review.
   - Select management system documentation for review.
   - Review auditee's management system documents.
   - Gather information to prepare for audit activities.
   - Establish an overview of system documentation.
2. Develop your audit plan.
   - i. Study source documents.
     - Allocate audit planning responsibility to team leader.
     - Consider how you plan to conduct your audit.
     - Think about how you intend to use your audit plan.
   - ii. Prepare official audit plan.
     - Prepare your management system audit plan.
     - Discuss your audit plan with the audit client.
     - Present your audit plan to the auditee.
   - iii. Assign work to audit team members.
     - Consult with audit team members before assigning roles and responsibilities.
     - Assign roles and responsibilities to each auditor.
     - Hold team meetings or briefings whenever work assignments need to be changed or reallocated.
   - iv. Prepare audit working papers.
     - Prepare appropriate audit working papers.
     - Use working papers to collect audit information.
     - Control your audit working papers and records.
     - Review your audit working papers and records.

D. Carry out your audit.
1. Establish audit sequence.
   - Conduct your opening audit meeting.
   - Review auditee's documents during your audit.
   - Communicate with participants during the audit.
   - Assign responsibilities to guides and observers.
   - Collect and verify information during the audit.
   - Develop and document your audit findings.
   - Discuss and prepare audit conclusions.
   - Present audit findings and conclusions.
2. Conduct opening meeting.
   - Plan your opening meeting.
   - Hold your opening meeting.
   - Introduce all participants.
   - Discuss communication channels.
   - Describe how the audit will be conducted.
   - Clarify your approach to risk management.
   - Explain how audit findings will be reported.
   - Confirm that support services will be available.
   - Specify the conditions that could cause the premature termination of the audit.
   - Identify feedback systems that the auditee could use to file a complaint or issue an appeal.
3. Perform document review.
   - Review relevant documents provided by the auditee.
   - Decide whether or not documents are adequate.
   - Use document review to gather relevant information.
   - Consider reviewing documents throughout the audit.
4. Communicate during audit.
   - Consider establishing formal communication arrangements that can be used during the audit.
   - Communicate with audit team members.
   - Communicate with auditee and audit client.
   - Communicate with external agencies (as required).
5. Assign guides and observers.
   - Consider asking or allowing guides and observers to accompany your audit team.
   - Assign roles and responsibilities to your audit guides and observers.
6. Collect and verify information.
   - Select your information-gathering methods.
   - Collect information to support your audit findings.

- Record evidence used to establish audit findings.
- Address unusual evidence discovered during audit.

7. Generate your audit findings.
   - Establish audit findings by evaluating your audit evidence and comparing it with your audit criteria.
   - Discuss your audit findings with audit team members whenever necessary or appropriate.

8. Prepare your audit conclusions.
   - Review audit findings and other related information.
   - Discuss and consider your audit conclusions.
   - Formulate and document your audit conclusions.
   - Prepare recommendations (if audit plan requires it).
   - Consider audit follow-up (whenever this is applicable).

9. Present findings and conclusions.
   - Plan your closing meeting.
   - Hold your closing meeting.
   - Explain your audit methods.
   - Present your audit findings.
   - Describe your audit conclusions.
   - Make recommendations (if appropriate).
   - Discuss diverging opinions (if any).
   - Develop a post-audit action plan.

E. Report your audit results.

1. Prepare your audit report.
   - Consider reporting options and plan your audit report.
   - Prepare your management system audit report.
   - Include or refer to your audit objectives.
   - Specify or refer to the scope of your audit.
   - Identify or refer to sponsors and participants.
   - Mention or refer to your audit agenda.
   - Discuss or reference your audit criteria.
   - Present or refer to your audit findings.
   - Document or refer to your audit conclusions.

2. Distribute your audit report.
   - Finalize your management system audit report in accordance with your audit program procedures.
   - Distribute your management system audit report in accordance with your audit procedures or audit plan.

F. Complete your audit.

- Verify that your audit has been completed.
- Protect audit documents and related information.
- Keep a record of lessons learned during the audit.

G. Follow-up on your audit.
- Consider whether remedial actions should be taken.
- Ask auditee to provide remedial action status reports.
- Verify that remedial actions were actually taken.

8.7.4 Auditor Competence

A. Establish an auditor evaluation process.
- Develop a process to evaluate audit team members.
- Plan the evaluation of your audit team members.
- Evaluate the competence of audit team members.
- Maintain the competence of audit team members.
- Improve the competence of audit team members.

B. Define auditor competence requirements.
1. Consider the work that auditors need to do.
   - Consider the work your auditors are expected to do when you think about the knowledge and skill they should have.
   - Consider the nature of your audit program.
   - Consider the organizations to be audited.
   - Consider the management systems to be audited.
   - Consider the requirements that must be met.
2. Be a professional and have good character.
   - Behave in a professional manner and exhibit good character whenever you are acting as an auditor.
   - Be ethical (be truthful and honest).
   - Be versatile (be adaptable and flexible).
   - Be perceptive (be attentive and watchful).
   - Be receptive (be willing to learn and improve).
   - Be observant (be aware of your surroundings).
   - Be collaborative (be capable of working with others).
   - Be open-minded (be willing to consider alternatives).
   - Be decisive (be able to draw timely conclusions).
   - Be tenacious (be persistent and focused).
   - Be self-reliant (be able to act independently).
   - Be diplomatic (be tactful and try to be discreet).
   - Be respectful (be sensitive to the auditee's culture).
3. Possess appropriate knowledge and skills.
   - i. Possess knowledge needed to achieve results.
     - Possess the knowledge and skill that you need in order to be able to achieve intended audit results.
     - Possess the knowledge and skill that you need in order to provide leadership to your audit team.

ii. Possess necessary generic knowledge and skills.
   a. Have generic auditing knowledge and skills.
      - Possess the knowledge and skill that you need in order to ensure that your audits are conducted in a systematic and consistent manner.
      - Be able to plan audits and organize work.
      - Be able to collect appropriate information.
      - Be able to prioritize and focus on important matters.
      - Be able to understand and use auditing knowledge.
      - Be able to understand and consider expert opinion.
      - Be able to verify accuracy of information collected.
      - Be able to use working papers to record activities.
      - Be able to evaluate the adequacy of audit evidence.
      - Be able to meet confidentiality and security needs.
      - Be able to document findings and conclusions.
      - Be able to communicate clearly and effectively.
      - Be able to stay on schedule and finish on time.
      - Be able to prepare appropriate audit reports.
      - Be able to comprehend auditing risks.
   b. Have management system knowledge and skills.
      - Possess the knowledge and skill that will ensure that you comprehend your audit scope and apply the audit criteria.
      - Understand and know how to use audit criteria.
      - Understand how management system standards have been applied by organizations in general.
      - Understand management system components and how they interact with one another.
      - Understand all relevant reference documents.
   c. Have organizational knowledge and skills.
      - Possess the knowledge and skill that will ensure that you comprehend the auditee organization's structure, business, and management practices.
      - Understand organizational types and functions.
      - Understand general business concepts and terms.
      - Understand cultural and social characteristics.
   d. Have relevant legal knowledge and skills.
      - Possess the knowledge and skill that will ensure that you are aware of, and will comply with, the auditee organization's legal and contractual requirements.
      - Understand relevant legal jurisdictions.
      - Understand relevant governing agencies.
      - Understand relevant legal concepts.
      - Understand relevant laws and regulations.

   iii. Possess specialized auditing knowledge and skills.
- Possess the discipline-specific and sector-specific knowledge and skill that you need in order to be able to audit specialized management systems and sectors; to evaluate auditee's activities, processes, and products; and to generate appropriate audit findings and reach valid conclusions.
- Understand management system concepts.
- Understand legal requirements and obligations.
- Understand the expectations of interested parties.
- Understand discipline-specific fundamentals.
- Understand risk management methodologies.

   iv. Possess team leadership knowledge and skills.
- Possess the additional management and leadership knowledge and skill that is needed in order to be able to ensure that audit teams are efficient and effective.
- Understand how to manage the audit process.
- Understand how to communicate with people.
- Understand how to balance the strengths and weaknesses of individual audit team members.
- Understand how to develop harmonious working relationships among audit team members.
- Understand how to help audit team members reach reliable audit conclusions.
- Understand how to prepare and complete accurate, clear, and concise audit reports.

   v. Possess multidisciplinary knowledge and skills.
- Possess the discipline-specific competence that you need in order to be able to audit multiple management systems that involve multiple disciplines.
- Possess the competence needed to audit at least one of the management systems and understand how the various management systems interact.

4. Get appropriate auditing knowledge and skills.
- Use formal education to acquire needed sector-specific and discipline-specific management system knowledge and skill.
- Use practical training services to acquire the appropriate auditing knowledge and skill.
- Use work experience to acquire general technical, managerial, and professional knowledge and skill.

5. Encourage team leaders to get experience.
- Acquire additional audit experience by working under the direction and guidance of other knowledgeable audit team leaders.

C. Develop auditor evaluation criteria.
- Select qualitative auditor evaluation criteria.
- Select behavior- and character-based criteria.
- Select knowledge- and skill-based criteria.
- Select quantitative auditor evaluation criteria.

D. Select auditor evaluation methods.
- Select two or more auditor evaluation methods.
- Consider using record reviews to evaluate auditors.
- Consider using feedback to evaluate auditors.
- Consider using interviews to evaluate auditors.
- Consider using observation to evaluate auditors.
- Consider using audit reviews to evaluate auditors.
- Consider using testing to evaluate auditors.

E. Evaluate the competence of auditors.
- Evaluate your management system auditors.
- Compare the information collected about the auditor against your particular auditor evaluation criteria.
- Help auditors to improve whenever they fail to meet your audit program's evaluation criteria.
- Encourage auditors to get more training.
- Encourage auditors to get more experience.

F. Maintain and improve auditor competence.
- Maintain and continually improve the competence of both auditors and audit team leaders.
- Update your professional development activities whenever relevant requirements change.
- Establish suitable evaluation mechanisms that you can use to continually evaluate the performance of both auditors and audit team leaders.

References

Blume, A. (2014). Internal Audit Techniques; Participants' Handbook. Deutsche GesellschaftfürInternationaleZusammenarbeit (GIZ) GmbH; Dar es Salaam, Tanzania, April 2014. Retrieved December 15, 2015, from: http://www.sulgo.or.tz/uploads/media/Internal_Audit_Participants_3.pdf.

GAO (2011). *Government Auditing Standards*. Comptroller General of the United States. United States Government Accountability Office, Washington, DC. Retrieved January 23, 2016, from: http://www.gao.gov/yellowbook.

Hart-Fanta, L. (2013). AASHTO Internal Audit Guide; 2.3—Comparison of IIA and GAGAS standards. Retrieved July 18, 2016, from: http://audit.transportation.org/Documents/2013%20Internal%20Audit%20Guide%20-%20DRAFT%20(2).pdf.

ISA 610 (Revised 2013). Using the Work of Internal Auditors (Effective for audits of financial statements for periods ending on or after December 15, 2014). IAASB, IFAC. Retrieved on August, 22, 2016 from: http://www.issai.org/media/115410/isa-610.pdf.

INTOSAI (2010). *ISSAI 1610—Using the Work of Internal Auditors*. Retrieved January 19, 2016, from: http://www.issai.org/media/13128/issai_1610_e_.pdf.

ISSAI 100. (n.d). Fundamental Principles of Public-Sector Auditing. INTOSAI Professional Standards Committee. PSC-Secretariat, Rigsrevisionen, Store Kongensgade 45, P.O. Box 9009, 1022 Copenhagen K, Denmark. Retrieved July 18, 2016 from: http://www.issai.org/media/69909/issai-100-english.pdf.

Praxiom Research Group Limited (2016a). *Executive Summary: ISO19011 2011*. Plain English. Copyright 2012–2013 by Praxiom Research Group Limited. Research Group Limited. All Rights Reserved. Retrieved January 25, 2016, from: http://www.praxiom.com/iso-19011-intro.htm.

Praxiom Research Group Limited (2016b). *ISO19011 2011, A Management System Auditing Standard*. Copyright 2012–2015 by Praxiom Research Group Limited. All Rights Reserved. Retrieved January 25, 2016, from: http://www.praxiom.com/iso-19011.htm.

The Institute of Internal Auditors (IIA) (2012). *International Standards for the Professional Practice of Internal Auditing (Standards)—ISPPIA*. pp. 1–18. Issued: October 2008. Revised: October 2012. Copyright 2012 The Institute of Internal Auditors (IIA).

Chapter 9

Internal Control Checklist

9.1 Introduction

The objective of the Internal Control Checklist is to provide any organization with a tool for evaluating their internal control structure and general compliance, while also promoting effective and efficient business practices. In this chapter, we shall make extensive use of a research document provided by Esmat (2011), a Cost Accountant and Plant Controller at Energizer, Egypt with over 36 years working experience. The effective utilization of this checklist will strengthen controls, improve compliance, and eliminate many potential audit comments.

9.2 Questions and Answers

A. What is internal control?

Internal control, in its broader sense, is defined as a process affected by an organization's board of directors, management, and other personnel, designed to provide reasonable assurance regarding the achievement of objectives in the following categories:
- Effectiveness and efficiency of operations
- Reliability of reporting
- Compliance with applicable rules, laws, and regulations

Internal control components include the control environment, risk assessment, control activities, information and communication, and monitoring.

Most of the time, the emphasis is on common control activities, which may include the following:
- Segregation of functional responsibilities to create a system of checks and balances

559

- A system of authorization and record procedures adequate to provide reasonable accounting control over assets, liabilities, revenues, and expenditures
- Development of policies and procedures for prescribing and documenting the business and control processes

This should consist of a well-thought-out strategy and be reviewed and adjusted periodically to reflect changes in the business and control environment.

B. What is legal/managerial compliance?

For purposes of this document, legal and managerial compliance is simply intended to refer to compliance with the various laws, rules, policies, directives, and procedures that prescribe the guidelines and parameters that we must operate within. Some of these are self-imposed to ensure effective business or control practices. Legal and managerial compliance requirements govern how we operate.

C. How can I operate more efficiently?

There is no fast answer to this question. Obviously, skilled, well-informed, and motivated faculty and staff is an important ingredient to an effective operation. Staff should be provided adequate training opportunities and understand what is expected of them. Good lines of communications are important.

With the fast pace of changes in technology, coupled with changes in regulatory compliance requirements and staff turnover, it is usually useful to review the various processes from time to time, asking why the various tasks are being performed and determining if the tasks add any value to the process, or if there is a better way to accomplish them.

Examining crises that have occurred in the past is often a useful way of preventing them in the future. Reviewing the structure or operations of similar organizations may also provide ideas on how to improve your organization.

   i. How do I use the checklist?

The checklist is simply a tool used by auditors if they were performing a review of a company department's internal controls. The checklist should be completed by management accountable for the particular business process. While *no* responses would normally indicate a potential weakness, this could be offset by *compensating* controls within the unit. It is difficult to make a statement regarding a particular control based on the response to just one question. Most internal control procedures are simply based on *common sense*; that is, the person having custody of the asset, such as cash, should not be solely responsible for accounting for it. No one person should be able to complete a requisition/payment transaction or personnel/payroll transaction from beginning to end without an appropriate monitoring or oversight. Incompatible duties should be segregated for a check and balance; laws and policies and directives are expected to be followed. Despite the fact that many internal controls are a simple matter of common sense, taking the time to periodically use this checklist to review the control processes can be a valuable tool in the process and help document your due diligence. The complete set of checklists should be available electronically at the company website for easy access, and complete by appropriate management levels.

    ii. What do we do if we identify potential control deficiencies or we have questions?

        Risks associated with potential control deficiencies may differ from unit to unit. The unit management is the first channel to address the implications of the deficiencies. Other resources may include the Controller's Office and the Office of Audit and Compliance Review.

        Remember, we all play a part in the organization's internal control system!

9.3 Committee of Sponsoring Organizations (COSO) of the Treadway Commission

According to Hart-Fanta (2014), internal control is a system implemented by an organization's governing body and management that helps ensure that the key financial, operational, and regulatory objectives are achieved. Internal control is affected by an entity's management and other personnel; it is not merely policy manuals and forms, but it also involves people at every level of the organization. Internal control is pervasive and impacts people, process, and technology. It can be expected to provide reasonable assurance—not absolute—assurance to an organization's management.

Under the COSO Framework (2013) as cited in Hart-Fanta (2014), internal control is broadly defined as a process effected by an entity's board of directors, management, and other personnel, designed to provide reasonable assurance, regarding the achievement of objectives in the following three COSO categories (Figure 9.1):

    i. *Reporting*—related to the internal and external financial and nonfinancial reporting to stakeholders, encompassing reliability, timeliness, transparency, or other elements as established by regulators, standard setters, or the entity's policies.

    ii. *Compliance*—adherence to the laws and regulations to which the entity is subject, where non-compliance could result in penalties, fines, or negative impacts to reputation.

    iii. *Operations*—addresses an entity's basic business objectives, including performance and goals and safeguarding of resources.

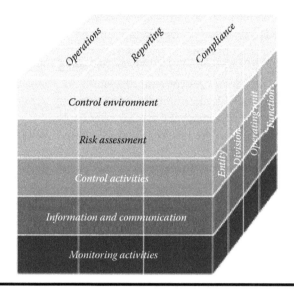

Figure 9.1 COSO internal control framework.

Management is responsible for designing and implementing the internal control system, which comprises five critical components:

a. Control environment;
b. Risk assessment;
c. Risk focused control activities;
d. Information and communication; and
e. Monitoring activities.

If designed and operating effectively, controls within these five components in totality provide a framework for internal control. The COSO (2013) framework, as cited in Hart-Fanta (2014), incorporates 17 principles that support these five components. For effective internal controls, the 2013 framework requires that each of the five components and 17 relevant principles be present and functioning, and that the five components must operate together in an integrated manner.

Note that *present* means that the components and relevant principles exist in the design and implementation of the system of internal control, whereas *functioning* means that the components and relevant principles continue to exist in the conduct of the system of internal control.

9.4 Five Components of COSO

9.4.1 Control Environment

The control environment sets the tone of an organization, influencing the control consciousness of its people. It is the set of standards, processes, and structures that provides the basis for carrying out internal control across the organization. This is the foundation for all other components of internal control, providing discipline and structure.

9.4.2 Risk Assessment

Every entity faces a variety of risks from external and internal sources that must be assessed. Risk assessment is the identification and analysis of relevant risks that could affect the achievement of the organization's objectives. It forms a basis for determining how the risks should be managed.

9.4.3 Control Activities

Control activities are the policies and procedures that help determine if management directives are carried out. They help facilitate the necessary actions required to address the risks to achieving of the entity's objectives. Control activities occur throughout the organization, at all levels and in all functions. They include a range of activities as diverse as approvals, authorizations, verifications, reconciliations, reviews of operating performance, security of assets, and segregation of duties.

9.4.4 Information and Communication

Pertinent information must be identified, captured, and communicated in a form and timeframe that enables people to carry out their responsibilities. Information systems produce reports containing operational, financial, and compliance-related information that makes it possible to run and control the business. They deal not only with internally generated data, but also with information about external reporting. Effective communication must also occur in a broader sense—flowing down, across, and up the organization. All personnel must receive a clear message from top management that control responsibilities must be taken seriously. They must understand their own role in the internal control system, as well as how individual activities relate to the work of others. They must have a means of communicating significant information upstream. There also needs to be effective communication with external parties, such as customers, suppliers, regulators and stakeholders.

9.4.5 Monitoring Activities

Internal control systems need to be monitored (a process that assesses the quality of the system's performance over time). This is accomplished through ongoing monitoring activities, separate evaluations, or a combination of the two. Ongoing monitoring occurs in the course of operations. It includes regular management and supervisory activities, and other actions personnel take in performing their duties. The 2013 Framework distinguishes between a management review control as a control activity and a monitoring activity. A management review control that is a control activity responds to a specified risk and is designed to detect and correct errors. However, a management review control that is a monitoring activity would ask why the errors exist, and then assign the responsibility of fixing the process to the appropriate personnel.

Managers establish policies, processes, and practices in these five components of management control to help the organization achieve the three specific objectives listed above. Internal auditors perform audits to evaluate whether the five components of management control are present and operating effectively, and if not, provide recommendations for improvement.

9.5 Control Objectives for Information and Related Technology (COBIT)

In a related development, while COSO is commonly accepted as the internal control framework for organizations, COBIT is the accepted internal control framework for the information technology (IT) environment. Released first in 1996 by the Information Systems Audit and Control Foundation (ISACF), it has been updated to include current IT governance principles and emerging international, technical, professional, regulatory, and industry-specific standards. The resulting control objectives have been developed for application to organization-wide information systems. In edition 4.1, COBIT is intended to meet the complex needs of management by bridging gaps between business risks, control needs and technical issues (COBIT 1996 framework as cited in Hart-Fanta, 2014).

9.6 Internal Control Principles

Company managers are charged with the responsibility of establishing a network of processes with the objective of controlling the operations of the company in a manner that provides the board of directors reasonable assurance that

- Data and information published either internally or externally are accurate, reliable, complete, and timely.
- The actions of administrators, officers, and employees are in compliance with the company's policies, standards, plans and procedures, and all relevant laws and regulations.
- The company's resources (including its people, systems, data/information bases, and client goodwill) are adequately protected.
- Resources are acquired economically and employed effectively; quality business processes and continuous improvement are emphasized.
- The company's internal controls promote the achievement of plans, programs, goals, and objectives.

Controlling is a function of management and is an integral part of the overall process of managing operations.

As such, it is the responsibility of managers at all levels of the company to

- Identify and evaluate the exposures to loss relating to their particular sphere of operations.
- Specify and establish policies, plans, and operating standards, procedures, systems, and other disciplines to be used to minimize, mitigate, or limit the risks associated with the exposures identified.
- Establish practical controlling processes that require and encourage administrators, officers, and employees to carry out their duties and responsibilities in a manner that achieves the control objectives outlined above.
- Maintain the effectiveness of the controlling processes established and foster continuous improvement to these processes.

The internal audit activity is charged with the responsibility for ascertaining that the ongoing processes for controlling operations throughout the organization are adequately designed and are functioning in an effective manner.

The Committee on Audit and Operations is responsible for monitoring, overseeing, and evaluating the duties and responsibilities of management, the internal audit activity, and the external auditors, as those duties and responsibilities relate to the organization's processes for controlling its operations. The committee is also responsible for determining that all major issues reported by the internal audit activity, the external auditor, and other outside advisors have been satisfactorily resolved. Finally, the committee is responsible for reporting to the full board significant matters pertaining to the company's internal control structure.

9.7 Principles of COSO

As pointed out earlier, the COSO (2013) framework, as cited in Hart-Fanta (2014), incorporates 17 principles that support five components. The 17 principles according to their categories are listed below:

a. Control environment; there are five principles relating to control environment:
  1. The organization demonstrates a commitment to integrity and ethical values.
  2. The board of directors demonstrates independence from management and exercises oversight of the development and performance of internal control.
  3. The management establishes—with board oversight—structures, reporting lines, and appropriate authorities and responsibilities in the pursuit of objectives.
  4. The organization demonstrates a commitment to attract, develop, and retain competent individuals in alignment with objectives.
  5. The organization holds individuals accountable for their internal control responsibilities in the pursuit of objectives.

b. Risk assessment; there are four principles relating to risk assessment:
  1. The organization specifies objectives with sufficient clarity to enable the identification and assessment of risks relating to objectives.
  2. The organization identifies risks to the achievement of its objectives across the entity and analyzes risks as a basis for determining how the risks should be managed.
  3. The organization considers the potential for fraud in assessing risks to the achievement of objectives.
  4. The organization identifies and assesses changes that could significantly affect the system of internal control.

c. Control activities; there are three principles relating to control activities:
  1. The organization selects and develops control activities that contribute to the mitigation, to acceptable levels, of the risks to achieving the objectives.
  2. The organization selects and develops general control activities over technology to support the achievement of objectives.
  3. The organization deploys control activities through policies that establish what is expected and in procedures that put policies into action.

d. Information and communication; there are three principles relating to information and communication:
   1. The organization obtains or generates and uses relevant, quality information to support the functioning of internal control.
   2. The organization internally communicates information, including objectives and responsibilities for internal control, that is necessary to support the functioning of internal control.
   3. The organization communicates with external parties about matters affecting the functioning of internal control.

e. Monitoring activities; there are two principles relating to monitoring activities:
   1. The organization selects, develops, and performs ongoing or separate evaluation to ascertain whether the components of internal control are present and functioning.
   2. The organization evaluates and communicates internal control deficiencies, in a timely manner, to those parties responsible for taking corrective action, including senior management and the board of directors, as appropriate.

9.8 Principles of COBIT

On the other hand, the COBIT framework is based on the following principle:

> To provide the information that the organization requires to achieve its objectives, the organization needs to invest in and manage and control IT resources using a structured set of processes to provide the services that deliver the required organization information.

The COBIT framework is structured in four principal domains. Each domain includes unique processes that sum to the 34 IT processes discussed hereunder. This framework identifies 34 IT processes and has an approach to provide control over these processes. It provides a generally applicable and acceptable standard (GAAS) for sound IT security and control practices to support management's needs in determining and monitoring the appropriate level of IT controls for their organizations (Hart-Fanta, 2014).

9.8.1 Plan and Organize (PO)

According to Hart-Fanta (2014), the PO domain covers strategy and tactics, and identifies how IT can best contribute to the achievement of the business objectives. The realization of the strategic vision needs to be planned, communicated, and managed for different perspectives. A proper organization as well as technological infrastructure should be put in place. The PO domain addresses the following processes:

- PO1—Define a strategic IT plan
- PO2—Define the information architecture
- PO3—Determine technological direction
- PO4—Define the IT processes, organizations, and relationships
- PO5—Manage the IT investment
- PO6—Communicate management aims and direction
- PO7—Manage IT human resources
- PO8—Manage quality
- PO9—Assess and manage IT risks
- PO10—Manage projects

9.8.2 Acquire and Implement (AI)

According to Hart-Fanta (2014), to realize the AI IT strategy, IT solutions need to be identified, developed or acquired, and implemented and integrated into the business process. In addition, changes in and maintenance of existing systems are covered by this domain to ensure that the solutions continue to meet business objectives. The AI domain addresses the following processes:

- AI1—Identify automated solutions
- AI2—Acquire and maintain application software
- AI3—Acquire and maintain technology infrastructure
- AI4—Enable operation and use
- AI5—Procure IT resources
- AI6—Manage changes
- AI7—Install and accredit solutions and changes

9.8.3 Delivery and Support

The delivery and support domain is concerned with the actual delivery of required services, which includes service delivery, management of security and continuity, service support for users, and management of data and operational facilities. It addresses the following processes:

- DS1—Define and manage service levels
- DS2—Manage third-party services
- DS3—Manage performance and capacity
- DS4—Ensure continuous service
- DS5—Ensure systems security

- DS6—Identify and allocate costs
- DS7—Educate and train users
- DS8—Manage service desk and incidents
- DS9—Manage the configuration
- DS10—Manage problems
- DS11—Manage data
- DS12—Manage the physical environment
- DS13—Manage operations

9.8.4 Monitor and Evaluate (ME)

According to Hart-Fanta (2014), all IT processes need to be regularly assessed over time for their quality and compliance with control requirements. The ME domain addresses performance management, internal control monitoring, regulatory compliance, and governance. It addresses the following processes:

- ME1—Monitor and evaluate IT performance
- ME2—Monitor and evaluate internal control
- ME3—Ensure compliance with external requirements
- ME4—Provide IT governance

9.9 Scope

The company will adopt the following principles.

Principles of Financial Management:

- Maintain accounting records in accordance with Generally Accepted Accounting Principles (GAAPs), which provide full disclosure of compliance with stewardship responsibilities of the company.
- Maintain an internal control environment that enhances sound business practices and clearly defines roles, responsibilities, and accountability.
- Ensure that applicable laws, regulations, and donor or sponsor requirements or restrictions are complied with, and those documentation standards provide assurances of such compliance.
- Provide accurate and relevant managerial financial reports. Standardized and cost-center-specific reports will be available as management tools for employees with delegated budgetary responsibilities. Higher-level reports will be provided to those employees with broader-level fiscal responsibilities.
- Utilize appropriate budgetary controls applicable to fund source to monitor variances and provide explanations of deviations.

- Maintain appropriate levels of financial transaction reviews and approvals by staff personnel responsible for budgetary entities.
- Involve both internal and external parties to provide periodic independent oversight of company financial activities. Such parties shall include accounting professionals within the entity, internal and external auditors, and governing bodies, as appropriate.
- Ensure all employees are aware of their responsibility to report suspected fraudulent or other dishonest acts and deviations from the Principles of Financial Management to their supervisor, or appropriate management level of audit and compliance.

9.10 Checklist Questions

9.10.1 Control Environment

☐ **Yes** ☐ **No** ☐ **N/S** ☐ **N/A**

☐☐☐☐ 1. Are appropriate company and staff members familiar with company policies, finance and accounting directives, and relevant operating and compliance requirements and guidelines?

☐☐☐☐ 2. Does management demonstrate the importance of integrity and ethical values, including the statement of core values to company and staff, and are they familiar with the code of ethics for public officers and employees?

☐☐☐☐ 3. Is good communication, collaboration, and team effort stressed?

☐☐☐☐ 4. Is management open to employee suggestions to improve productivity, service, and quality?

☐☐☐☐ 5. Do management and employees have the knowledge, training, and skills necessary to perform their jobs adequately and continue to take advantage of ongoing training opportunities?

☐☐☐☐ 6. Has management established a mission statement, set goals, and developed plans to meet its objectives?

☐☐☐☐ 7. Are plans and performance periodically assessed?

☐☐☐☐ 8. Are the unit's performance targets realistic and attainable?

☐☐☐☐ 9. Does integrity of financial and operational results take priority over reporting acceptable performance targets?

☐☐☐☐ 10. Is the unit's organizational structure and lines of authority clearly understood by employees?

☐☐☐☐ 11. Are employee job descriptions, desk procedures, and other internal operating procedures current?

☐☐☐☐ 12. Has the unit maintained an acceptable employee turnover rate?

☐☐☐☐ 13. Does employee morale appear to be at an acceptable level?

☐☐☐☐ 14. Does the unit have the time, tools, and resources to effectively accomplish its mission and objectives?

☐☐☐☐ 15. Has the unit established any benchmarks with peers to measure its resource use and outcomes?

☐☐☐☐ 16. Are records maintained in accordance with guidelines issued by the Office of the Provost?

☐☐☐☐ 17. Does the unit have a business continuation plan that addresses the absence of key employees and backup procedures for key business processes?

9.10.2 Budgeting, Accounting, and Financial Reporting

☐ **Yes** ☐ **No** ☐ **N/S** ☐ **N/A**

☐☐☐☐ 1. Is fiscal staff familiar with appropriate sections of Finance and Accounting Directives and Procedures?

☐☐☐☐ 2. Has fiscal staff been appropriately trained in the use of the accounting system, including the chart of accounts and edits?

☐☐☐☐ 3. Has fiscal staff been appropriately trained in the use of the systems reports and reporting tools?

☐☐☐☐ 4. Does fiscal staff possess basic accounting skills and knowledge necessary to adequately perform their responsibilities?

Reconciliations

☐☐☐☐ 5. Are departmental ledgers reviewed and reconciled to supporting documentation at least monthly?

☐☐☐☐ 6. Is the staff performing the reconciliation separate from the staff initiating and finalizing transactions?

☐☐☐☐ 7. Are reconciling differences, negative balances, or unsupported transactions investigated and corrected timely?

☐☐☐☐ 8. Does higher-level management review the reconciled ledgers and appropriate supporting documentation and appropriately document its review in a timely manner?

Fund Management

☐☐☐☐ 9. Are funds for large purchases, travel, etc., encumbered and set aside ahead of time to ensure that funds will be available when payment is due?

☐☐☐☐ 10. Are financial reports comparing budgeted balances with actual financial activity generated and reviewed by appropriate management?

☐☐☐☐ 11. If fund or cost center deficits are anticipated, are appropriate levels of management notified timely and appropriate corrective action taken?

☐ ☐ ☐ ☐   12. Does fiscal staff understand the rules associated with different fund types (E&G appropriations, grants, agency, auxiliary, direct support organizations, etc.)?

Comments/Compensating Controls:

_____

_____

_____

_____

_____

_____

_____

_____

9.10.3 Collections, Deposits, and Cash Funds

☐ Yes ☐ No ☐ N/S ☐ N/A

☐ ☐ ☐ ☐   1. Are staff members responsible for cash handling and deposits familiar with Finance and Accounting Directives and Procedures on cash handling and deposits?

☐ ☐ ☐ ☐   2. Is the collection and deposit preparation functions segregated from the accounting functions, including general ledger and accounts receivable maintenance?

☐ ☐ ☐ ☐   3. Has each cash collection point been approved to receive cash collections and or maintain petty cash change funds?

☐ ☐ ☐ ☐   4. Are receipts issued or mail logs receipts recorded immediately for all forms of collections received and at the earliest point of collection?

☐ ☐ ☐ ☐   5. Are cash register tapes or official company receipt forms (obtained from Treasury Management) issued each time a cash collection (including collection by check or credit card) is received over the counter?

☐ ☐ ☐ ☐   6. Are prenumbered receipts mail logs and cash register readings independently controlled, accounted for, and compared to validated deposit documentation by an individual with no cash handling responsibilities?

☐ ☐ ☐ ☐   7. Are all copies of voided receipt forms and cash register voids retained and accounted for or approved and documented?

☐ ☐ ☐ ☐   8. Are all collections required to be made payable to the proper payee, or the appropriate direct support organization party to the transaction?

☐☐☐☐   9. Are checks required to be restrictively endorsed upon receipt?

☐☐☐☐ 10. Are responsibilities for monies fixed at all times? (This would include prohibiting cash handlers from working out of the same cash drawer and requiring documentation of transfers of collections among employees.)

☐☐☐☐ 11. Are cash drawers or cash boxes secured when the cash custodian leaves his/her workstation?

☐☐☐☐ 12. Do cash registers have sufficient built-in control features to prevent the operator from backing out transactions without supervisory approval or resetting the cash register readings?

☐☐☐☐ 13. Are overages and shortages properly documented and appropriately explained?

☐☐☐☐ 14. Are deposits made timely?

☐☐☐☐ 15. Are receipts and deposits reconciled at least monthly with departmental ledgers?

☐☐☐☐ 16. Are funds physically stored in a safe or equally secure place?

☐☐☐☐ 17. Is knowledge of safe combinations or access to keys restricted to employees with a need-to-know or need-to-access privilege, and is the combination/keys to the safe changed when there are changes to the staff that have knowledge of the safe combination or who have had access to the safe keys?

☐☐☐☐ 18. Is the petty cash fund periodically counted by surprise?

☐☐☐☐ 19. Are deposits transmitted in locked bank bags?

☐☐☐☐ 20. Are staff and faculty prohibited from making loans from cash funds and from cashing personal checks from cash funds?

☐☐☐☐ 21. Are duties related to accounts receivable delegated so that no one individual can collect funds, update receivable records, and reconcile accounts receivable details?

☐☐☐☐ 22. Are accounts receivable billings issued at least monthly, or as required by an agreement?

☐☐☐☐ 23. Are accounts receivable aged regularly with older accounts receiving appropriate follow-up?

☐☐☐☐ 24. Is the write-off of delinquent accounts in compliance with company policy?

☐☐☐☐ 25. Are cases of suspected fraud or theft brought to the attention of area police, the Insurance Coordinator in Environmental Health and Safety, and Office of Audit and Compliance Review immediately upon discovery?

☐☐☐☐ 26. Does unit management periodically review data showing trends regarding the status of receivable balances and take appropriate action if needed?

☐☐☐☐ 27. Are sales taxes collected and properly remitted when appropriate?

☐☐☐☐ 28. If revenues are possibly subject to unrelated business income taxes, has the Company Tax Administration Office of Finance and Accounting been notified?

☐☐☐☐ 29. If the department accepts credit cards for payment, is the department following Finance and Accounting Directives and Procedures on credit cards?

This requires compliance with the Payment Card Industry Data Security Standards. These standards address appropriate security measures needed in place to secure customer information (i.e., credit card numbers, etc.), and may be found at the Visa Customer Information Security Program (CISP) website.

9.10.4 Asset Management

☐ Yes ☐ No ☐ N/S ☐ N/A

☐☐☐☐ 1. Are department property custodians familiar with the appropriate section of Finance and Accounting Directives and Procedures (1.4.9)?

☐☐☐☐ 2. Are Property Identification Decals placed in an easily scanned spot and maintained to make taking of inventory easier?

☐☐☐☐ 3. Is surplus equipment secured until properly surveyed and approved for removal by Asset Management?

☐☐☐☐ 4. Are equipment surveys and transfers recorded and submitted to Asset Management as soon as possible?

☐☐☐☐ 5. Is the surplus property website viewed or warehouse visited prior to making new equipment purchases?

☐☐☐☐ 6. Are all work areas and storerooms appropriately secured to deter unauthorized entry?

☐☐☐☐ 7. Are *attractive* items such as laptops, projectors, tools, and cameras, kept in a secure location when not being used?

☐☐☐☐ 8. Is furniture/equipment properly constructed at the company accounted for and included on the property records, when appropriate?

☐☐☐☐ 9. Is the use of property off-company properly accounted for and documented with an off-company certification form?

☐☐☐☐ 10. Is a control file maintained with the decals and descriptions of property that cannot have the decals affixed?

☐☐☐☐ 11. Is Asset Management notified when you receive government furnished equipment or donated equipment?

☐☐☐☐ 12. When moving equipment from one location to another within your department, is Asset Management notified in a timely manner using the online Movement of Property forms on Asset Management's website?

☐☐☐☐ 13. When transferring equipment to a different department or project, is an online Report of Transfer form completed in a timely manner?

☐☐☐☐ 14. Are adequate procedures in place to facilitate the annual inventory, including procedures to resolve discrepancies in a timely manner?

☐☐☐☐ 15. Is Asset Management notified of any errors or discrepancies on the equipment inventory report in a timely manner?

☐☐☐☐ 16. Is Company Police notified immediately of any stolen or missing property?

☐☐☐☐ 17. Are vehicle use records maintained for the use of company-owned vehicles?

☐☐☐☐ 18. Is vehicle use limited to personnel with valid driver's licenses and is this verified?

☐☐☐☐ 19. Are only appropriate employees allocated keys to the office and building?

☐☐☐☐ 20. Is the building secure and after hours access limited to appropriate employees?

☐☐☐☐ 21. Is a Property Update Document for equipment purchases completed and forwarded to Asset Management?

9.10.5 Payroll

☐ **Yes** ☐ **No** ☐ **N/S** ☐ **N/A**

☐☐☐☐ 1. Are staff members with responsibility for payroll familiar with the Finance and Accounting Directives and Procedures relating to Payroll?

☐☐☐☐ 2. Have employees charged with payroll and distribution responsibilities been appropriately trained?

☐☐☐☐ 3. Are the duties of approving job actions and approval of time segregated from the duties of distribution of the paychecks?

☐☐☐☐ 4. Are time and labor entries approved by the dean, director, unit head, or other supervisor who has supervisory responsibilities over the persons whose time or payment is being approved?

☐☐☐☐ 5. Does the payroll processor review the preliminary pay lists to ensure that employees will be paid correctly?

☐☐☐☐ 6. Does management review, sign, and date the Final Pay Lists to document that faculty and staff are paid according to wage contracts and terminated employees are not paid?

☐☐☐☐ 7. Is the Final Pay List reviewed in a timely manner so Payroll can be notified by the appropriate deadlines of any advices requiring EFT cancellation?

☐☐☐☐ 8. Are over- or underpayments dealt with promptly?

☐ ☐ ☐ ☐   9. Are payroll distributions properly approved and made timely and accurately?

☐ ☐ ☐ ☐   10. Are lump-sum payments and other types of additional pay properly documented?

☐ ☐ ☐ ☐   11. Are unclaimed paychecks returned to University Payroll Services after seven days?

☐ ☐ ☐ ☐   12. For employees required to maintain time cards for time worked, do the time records reflect the actual hours/minutes worked rather than the hours scheduled to work?

☐ ☐ ☐ ☐   13. Have procedures been implemented to ensure that overtime and compensatory time hours worked are appropriate and approved in advance by an employee's supervisor?

☐ ☐ ☐ ☐   14. Are payroll checks and earning statements properly secured prior to delivery?

☐ ☐ ☐ ☐   15. Is appropriate identification and authorization required if paychecks or earning statements are to be provided to individuals other than the employee? Additionally, if the employee is unknown to the paycheck distributor, is appropriate identification required before the paycheck is released?

9.10.6 Human Resource Management

☐ Yes ☐ No ☐ N/S ☐ N/A

☐ ☐ ☐ ☐   1. Have employees with HR administrative responsibilities attended training programs that are specific to their roles in the organization?

☐ ☐ ☐ ☐   2. Are hiring practices reflective of the company's nondiscrimination policy?

☐ ☐ ☐ ☐   3. Are the completed Recruitment Summaries being submitted prior to hire?

☐ ☐ ☐ ☐   4. Are the education or verification(s) and past work experience of the new employee(s) verified and documented?

☐ ☐ ☐ ☐   5. Are the appropriate criminal background checks being performed when required by position?

☐ ☐ ☐ ☐   6. Are I-9 forms being processed within three days of date of hire?

☐ ☐ ☐ ☐   7. Is the visa status of foreign national employees validated on a quarterly basis?

☐ ☐ ☐ ☐   8. Do new employees attend new employee orientation?

☐ ☐ ☐ ☐   9. Do new employees complete sexual harassment training within six months of date of hire?

☐ ☐ ☐ ☐   10. Are duties relating to processing and approving personnel actions segregated?

☐☐☐☐ 11. In addition to the central Human Resource Services file, does the unit maintain personnel files that include current job descriptions and performance appraisals?

☐☐☐☐ 12. Are personnel records maintained in accordance with retention schedules and access to confidential records limited to those with a *need to know*?

☐☐☐☐ 13. Are performance evaluations submitted on a timely basis with Human Resource Services?

☐☐☐☐ 14. Are employees who are covered by the Fair Labor Standards Act (nonexempt/hourly employees) compensated for overtime worked?

☐☐☐☐ 15. Are unit procedures in place to ensure that undergraduate student employees do not work more than 20 hours a week and do not work during scheduled classes without documentation that the class has been cancelled?

☐☐☐☐ 16. Are unit procedures in place to ensure that leave taken is properly approved and recorded?

☐☐☐☐ 17. Have supervisors and other staff members responsible for HR been properly trained on the Family and Medical Leave Act (FMLA)?

☐☐☐☐ 18. Are procedures in place to ensure awareness and compliance with the company's policy for reporting outside employment activities, and any potential conflicts of interest and nepotism?

☐☐☐☐ 19. Are terminations of appointments for employees separating from the company processed timely and the exit checklist reviewed?

9.10.7 Purchasing and Disbursements

☐ Yes ☐ No ☐ N/S ☐ N/A

☐☐☐☐ 1. Are staff responsible for requisition/purchasing and vendor payments and travel familiar with the Purchasing and Disbursement Sections of the Finance and Accounting Directives and Procedures?

☐☐☐☐ 2. Are the duties for initiating requisitions, receiving purchased items, processing of invoices for payment, and reconciliation of the departmental ledger separated between two or more employees?

☐☐☐☐ 3. Are contracts and leases approved by all appropriate parties prior to the effective date of the contract?

☐☐☐☐ 4. Does management review charges recorded on the departmental ledger and inquire about unfamiliar charges?

☐☐☐☐ 5. Is management's review of the departmental ledger, reconciliation, and supporting documentation appropriately documented?

☐☐☐☐ 6. Do unit procedures ensure that the best combination of quality, total price, and delivery are evaluated when acquiring goods or services?

☐☐☐☐ 7. Are purchase requisitions initiated and approved by employees specifically authorized to perform this task?

☐☐☐☐ 8. Are vendor invoices processed timely?

☐☐☐☐ 9. Are all invoices independently reviewed for completeness, accuracy, compliance with company directives, and agreement to supporting documentation (receiving reports and purchase orders) before approval for payment?

☐☐☐☐ 10. Do invoices receive appropriate supervisory approval before payment?

☐☐☐☐ 11. Are appropriate discounts offered being taken?

☐☐☐☐ 12. If the invoice inappropriately included taxes, were they deducted prior to payment?

☐☐☐☐ 13. Are encumbrances and disbursements reconciled with the departmental ledger?

☐☐☐☐ 14. Are returned purchases controlled in such a manner to ensure that the department receives the credit or refund due the department?

☐☐☐☐ 15. Are vendor invoices and travel reimbursements controlled in such a manner as to prevent duplicate payment?

☐☐☐☐ 16. Does the dean, director, or department head approve (by signature) the issuance of purchasing cards?

☐☐☐☐ 17. Does the department generate Monthly Paid Charges reports for each cardholder, and obtain supporting receipts and cardholder's signature?

☐☐☐☐ 18. Are purchasing card transactions authorized by an approver, reconciled timely, and signed by the cardholder?

☐☐☐☐ 19. Does the department management periodically review a list of departmental cardholders and their limits, to determine if changes need to be made?

☐☐☐☐ 20. Are originators adequately trained to ensure proper posting of travel related data?

☐☐☐☐ 21. Does the department create an Authorized Approver Request Form to authorize a designee to approve travel?

☐☐☐☐ 22. Does the approver verify that a Travel Authorization was created before the travel occurred?

☐☐☐☐ 23. Are Travel Authorizations compared to the traveler's budget balance to ensure that the traveler is still within the limits of his/her budget?

☐ ☐ ☐ ☐ 24. Are requests for travel reimbursements and related expenses submitted through the Travel and Expense module rather than the Accounts Payable Module?

☐ ☐ ☐ ☐ 25. Are travel advances made and approved through the Travel and Expense Module?

☐ ☐ ☐ ☐ 26. Are travel advances settled timely?

☐ ☐ ☐ ☐ 27. Are telephone bills reviewed and appropriately certified as to business use only?

☐ ☐ ☐ ☐ 28. Is a periodic review made of telephone lines and equipment to ensure that such telephone lines and equipment is needed?

☐ ☐ ☐ ☐ 29. Is the use of copy machines limited to official business use only?

☐ ☐ ☐ ☐ 30. Are maintenance agreements reviewed periodically, especially before they are renewed, to ensure that the equipment the maintenance agreement is intended to cover is still owned and used by the unit and that it is still in the unit's best interest to continue to carry the maintenance coverage?

☐ ☐ ☐ ☐ 31. Are the purchase, storage, and issuance of supplies properly controlled to prevent overpurchasing, pilferage, deterioration, and damage?

9.10.8 Contracts and Grants

☐ Yes ☐ No ☐ N/S ☐ N/A

☐ ☐ ☐ ☐ 1. Are staff members responsible for contracts and grants familiar with the Finance and Accounting Directives and Procedures relating to contracts and grants?

☐ ☐ ☐ ☐ 2. Have staff been provided sufficient training to understand the special requirements of expending contract and grant funds, effort reporting, and in general ensuring compliance with grant or contract terms and federal/local regulations?

☐ ☐ ☐ ☐ 3. Are appropriate procedures in place to ensure that all technical and progress reports are prepared by employees directly involved with the grant program or contract and are submitted to the sponsor or contractor in accordance with the terms of the agreement?

☐ ☐ ☐ ☐ 4. Are there policies and procedures to address circumstances when an award has not yet been accepted by the company (e.g., set up of temporary accounts), excess funds remain after completion of a project, and charges are in excess of allowed amounts?

☐ ☐ ☐ ☐ 5. Are costs directly charged to a grant or used as cost sharing reviewed to assure they are reasonable, allocable, consistently treated, and meet any restrictions that apply?

☐☐☐☐   6. Do fixed price contracts include all relevant expenditures?

☐☐☐☐   7. Are unit procedures in place to ensure travel is an allowable expense under sponsor terms, charged at allowable rates, and benefits the grant charged?

☐☐☐☐   8. Are salaries of administrative and clerical staff and nonsalary administrative items charged directly to a grant or sponsored project only if such services and expenses are explicitly budgeted for in the grant received?

☐☐☐☐   9. Is biweekly payroll distribution managed to assure that employee payroll is charged to sponsored projects consistent with employee's activities rather than budget or availability of funds?

☐☐☐☐ 10. Are payroll charges appropriately distributed and reported for employees whose compensation exceeds other budgetary restrictions?

☐☐☐☐ 11. Are unit procedures in place to ensure that staff effort is reported accurately and timely? Is documentation available to support the use of a suitable means of verification?

☐☐☐☐ 12. Is committed effort and assignments reviewed to verify that individual PIs are not *overcommitted* to current projects and report at least a minimum level of effort on his/her contract(s) or grant(s)?

☐☐☐☐ 13. Does the unit monitor if there are significant changes in an employee's committed research activities? If applicable, is there a process to ensure these changes are reported to the proper division or cost center?

☐☐☐☐ 14. Are polices and procedures in place to ensure payroll or other expenditure transfers are appropriate, approved, and processed timely and include required supporting documentation?

☐☐☐☐ 15. Are subgrants/subcontracts to other organizations routed to the proper division on the basis of properly completed and approved subaward proposals?

☐☐☐☐ 16. Are disbursements to subgrantees/subcontractors approved by principal proper manager based on properly completed reports or billings?

☐☐☐☐ 17. Except for capital grants, are purchases of fixed assets made prior to the end of the grant so the fixed assets can be used in accomplishment of the project objectives?

☐☐☐☐ 18. Are unit procedures in place to ensure expenditures are not charged after the grant period, and assist with the timely close-outs of awards?

☐☐☐☐ 19. Where projects require cost sharing or matching, does the unit compare regularly accumulated cost-shared amounts with grant cost-sharing requirements to see if it has met its cost-sharing goals?

☐☐☐☐ 20. Is there a control in place to ensure that expenses reported for purposes of cost sharing are not already charged directly to other sponsored projects unless specifically granted permission by both sponsors?

☐☐☐☐ 21. Are grant summary reports reviewed and reconciled to supporting documentation periodically to verify that balances agree to amounts reported in the system?

Comments/Compensating Controls:

_____

_____

_____

_____

_____

_____

_____

_____

9.10.9 *Information Technology*

☐ Yes ☐ No ☐ N/S ☐ N/A

☐☐☐☐ 1. Are appropriate faculty and staff members familiar with the Office of Information Technology Guidelines, Company IT Policies and Standards, and Basic Security Guidelines for Network Administrators?

☐☐☐☐ 2. Has a unit IT risk assessment been conducted within the past three years?

☐☐☐☐ 3. Have key IT positions been classified as positions of special trust?

☐☐☐☐ 4. Does a business continuation plan exist that identifies critical activities, backup files, programs, and alternative processing sites?

☐☐☐☐ 5. Have change management procedures been established, including patch management, for portable computers, workstations, and servers?

☐☐☐☐ 6. Are system security and application access logs enabled and reviewed periodically?

☐☐☐☐ 7. Are backups of operating systems, critical data, and key software programs made on a regular basis and stored at an off-site location?

☐☐☐☐ 8. Is access to the production systems authorized and documented through the use of standard forms or emails?

☐☐☐☐ 9. Are strong passwords for all production systems (interval change, minimum length, lock out, etc.) in place?

☐☐☐☐ 10. Are documented procedures in place for removing access to all production systems when an employee leaves the unit?

☐☐☐☐ 11. Is sensitive and restricted data managed by the unit (on networks, personal computers, and backup media) classified and protected by restricted access, encryption, or other controls?

☐☐☐☐ 12. Do policies provide for all personnel with a need to access critical applications (mainframe, networks, and personal computers) to have individual accounts and passwords and are they prohibited from sharing those passwords?

☐☐☐☐ 13. Are records of all software licensing agreements managed by the unit properly maintained?

☐☐☐☐ 14. Has the company policy on acceptable use of computer resources been effectively communicated to all employees including new hires?

☐☐☐☐ 15. Are antivirus software installed, operating and being updated for all computing resources (laptops, desktops, servers, etc.)?

☐☐☐☐ 16. Is system administrator access to the production systems restricted and based on need?

Comments/Compensating Controls:

_____

_____

_____

_____

_____

_____

_____

_____

Department _____

_____

Preparer(s) _____ Date _____

9.11 Understanding an Auditee's Internal Controls

According to Hart-Fanta (2014), the auditor needs to have a good understanding of the client's internal control system; the auditor can gain this knowledge through the following procedures:

- **Prior experience with the entity:** Recurring audits can be a major source of audit efficiency. Because systems and controls usually do not change frequently or significantly from year to year, information obtained by the auditor in previous audits of the entity/auditee can be updated and carried forward to the current year's audit.
- **Observation of client activities and procedures:** The auditor can observe client personnel in the process of preparing records and documents, and carrying out their assigned duties and control functions.
- **Inspection of documents and records:** By inspecting actual, completed documents and records, the auditor can have a better understanding of their application to the entity's internal control. The auditor may wish to obtain copies of sample documents used by the entity for inclusion in the permanent file.
- **Inquiries:** The auditor may inquire from management, supervisory, and staff personnel within the entity the types of documents used to process transactions and about control activities that have been put in operation for approving and/or authorizing, for example, a credit.
- **Entity's policy and system manuals:** This include both (1) policy manuals and documents, and (2) system manuals and documents, such as an accounting manual and an organization chart.

9.12 Documenting Internal Controls

It is essential that the auditors document their understanding of internal controls to:

- Provide evidence of the understanding of the design of significant processes
- Identify key risks within the process
- Identify controls that would prevent or detect errors from occurring within the process
- Identify control gaps and process improvement opportunities

The documentation may take several forms, such as

    i. Narrative—A document that describes a process or transaction flow using words rather than a pictorial representation. The purpose of a narrative is to:
- Provide evidence of understanding of a process.
- Identify and document key risks, controls and control gaps.
- Confirm understanding with the process owner.
- Provide knowledge that can be used in future years by other employees.

    ii. Flowchart—This is a diagram that shows the step-by-step progression through a procedure or system especially using connecting lines and a set of conventional symbols. The purpose of flowcharting is to
- Be a tool for analyzing processes
- Break down processes into individual events and activities, usually by the process or event owner
- Identify interdependencies across the business
- Link system and manual activities
- Identify control gaps, segregation of duties, problems and inefficiencies

    iii. Walkthrough—This is a document that traces one representative transaction through a process from beginning to end. The purpose of a walkthrough is to:
- Confirm understanding of the significant flow of transactions.
- Confirm understanding of the relevant controls.
- Confirm that relevant controls have been placed in operation.
- Confirm process documentation.

    iv. Internal control questionnaire—This is a questionnaire designed to identify basic control issues and used as a guide for improving or implementing good business practices and complying with policies and procedures.

9.13 Internal Control Weaknesses

There are many reasons why a control system may be weak. Understanding why internal control weaknesses occur in a system is one of the key components of the risk assessment process. Understanding these weaknesses helps management monitor for appropriate and effective internal controls. Internal audit should consider these factors and determine whether they exist as they walk through the risk assessment process with management. Some common reasons why internal control weaknesses occur may include the following (Hart-Fanta, 2014):

- Poorly designed or implemented internal control processes: In this situation, the process becomes routine due to overfamiliarity, and some steps in the process are overlooked.
- Poor communication: Information concerning a law, rule or procedure was not adequately communicated.
- Employees were not properly trained or instructed.
- Personnel are not knowledgeable about the importance of a step or process and its impact on another area.
- There is confusion over who is responsible (each area incorrectly thinks the other is handling the process).
- Time constraints.
- Inadequate resources devoted to the process.
- Employees unknowingly overlooked something.
- Personnel are comfortable with the current process and are resistant to change.
- Tone at the top.
- Size of the entity.

9.14 Evaluation of Internal Controls

According to Hart-Fanta (2014), auditors can verify if controls are being implemented as designed through testing, reviews, observations, and analytical procedures. Auditors can determine the validity and accuracy of transactions, as well as determine compliance with applicable rules, laws, and procedures, and assess the adequacy of existing controls. To perform the above tasks, the following evaluation tools are necessary:

- **Testing by statistical sampling**—This focuses on sampling techniques that provide assurance based on sampling risk that the auditor and stakeholders deem acceptable.
- **Testing by direct sampling**—This focuses more closely on specific transactions or certain types of transactions and can be used when the population under review is not homogeneous.
- **Reviews/interviews**—This is used when the performance of a process does not lend itself to normal testing procedures.
- **Observation**—This technique looks at actual practices to see if appropriate controls are actually in place and working.
- **Analytical procedure**—This technique takes information as a whole and applies some set standard, analysis or comparison.

	Magnitude of Misstatement (or Error) That Occurred or Could Occur		
Likelihood of Misstatement or Error	Inconsequential	More than inconsequential but less than material	Material
Remote	Not a significant deficiency or material weakness, and not likely to occur: Do not report	Significant deficiency or but not material weakness, and not likely to occur: Report informally, verbally, or via management letter	Significant deficiency or material weakness, but not likely to occur: Report informally, verbally, or via management letter
More than remote	Not a significant deficiency or material weakness but likely to occur: Report informally, verbally, or via management letter	Significant deficiency, not material but likely to occur: Report formally, via audit report	Significant and Material weakness and likely to occur: Report formally, via audit report

Figure 9.2 Internal control weakness reporting matrix. (Adapted and modified from Hart-Fanta, *AASHTO Internal Audit Guide*, 2014.)

9.15 Classifying Internal Control Weaknesses for Reporting

According Hart-Fanta (2014), upon determining that controls are inadequately designed implemented, auditors shall communicate the weakness to management based on the likelihood and magnitude or impact of the concern. This communication may be verbal, written via an informal management letter, or reported formally, such as in the audit report. The matrix in Figure 9.2 can help auditors determine how or where to report the weakness to management.

References

Esmat, F. (2011). Internal Control Checklist.
Hart-Fanta, L. (2014). *AASHTO Internal Audit Guide*; 2.3—Internal Control Overview. Retrieved July 18, 2016, from: http://audit.transportation.org/Documents/2013%20 Internal%20Audit%20Guide%20-%20DRAFT%20(2).pdf.

Glossary

Access controls: Procedures designed to restrict access to online terminal devices, programs, and data. Access controls consist of *user authentication* and *user authorization*. User authentication typically attempts to identify a user through unique log-on identifications, passwords, access cards, or biometric data. User authorization consists of access rules to determine the computer resources each user may access. Specifically, such procedures are designed to prevent or detect

a. Unauthorized access to online terminal devices, programs, and data
b. Entry of unauthorized transactions
c. Unauthorized changes to data files
d. Use of computer programs by unauthorized personnel
e. Use of computer programs that have not been authorized

Accounting estimate: An approximation of a monetary amount in the absence of a precise means of measurement. This term is used for an amount measured at fair value where there is estimation uncertainty, as well as for other amounts that require estimation. Where NSA 20 addresses only accounting estimates involving measurement at fair value, the term *fair value accounting estimates* is used.

Accounting records: The records of initial accounting entries and supporting records, such as checks and records of electronic fund transfers; invoices; contracts; the general and subsidiary ledgers, journal entries, and other adjustments to the financial statements that are not reflected in formal journal entries; and records such as worksheets and spreadsheets supporting cost allocations, computations, reconciliations, and disclosures.

Add value: The internal audit activity adds value to the organization (and its stakeholders) when it provides objective and relevant assurance, and contributes to the effectiveness and efficiency of governance, risk management, and control processes.

Adequate control: Present if management has planned and organized (designed) in a manner that provides reasonable assurance that the organization's risks have been managed effectively, and that the organization's goals and objectives will be achieved efficiently and economically.

Agreed-upon procedures engagement: An engagement in which an auditor is engaged to carry out those procedures of an audit nature to which the auditor and the entity and any appropriate third parties have agreed to report on factual findings. The recipients of the report form their own conclusions from the report by the auditor. The report is restricted to those parties that have agreed to the procedures to be performed since others, unaware of the reasons for the procedures, may misinterpret the results.

Analytical procedures: Evaluations of financial information through analysis of plausible relationships among both financial and nonfinancial data. Analytical procedures also encompass such investigation as is necessary of identified fluctuations or relationships that are inconsistent with other relevant information or that differ from expected values by a significant amount.

Annual report: A document issued by an entity, ordinarily on an annual basis, which includes its financial statements together with the auditor's report thereon.

Anomaly: A misstatement or deviation that is demonstrably not representative of misstatements or deviations in a population.

Applicable financial reporting framework: The financial reporting framework adopted by management and those charged with governance in the preparation of the financial statements that is acceptable in view of the nature of the entity and the objective of the financial statements or that is required by law or regulation. The term *fair presentation framework* is used to refer to a financial reporting framework that requires compliance with the requirements of the framework and

a. Acknowledges explicitly or implicitly that, to achieve fair presentation of the financial statements, it may be necessary for management to provide disclosures beyond those specifically required by the framework.
b. Acknowledges explicitly that it may be necessary for management to depart from a requirement of the framework to achieve fair presentation of the financial statements. Such departures are expected to be necessary only in extremely rare circumstances.

The term *compliance framework* is used to refer to a financial reporting framework that requires compliance with the requirements of the framework, but does not contain the acknowledgments in (a) or (b) above.

Application controls in information technology: Manual or automated procedures that typically operate at a business process level. Application controls can be preventative or detective in nature, and are designed to ensure the integrity of the accounting records. Accordingly, application controls relate to procedures used to initiate, record, process, and report transactions or other financial data.

Applied criteria: The criteria applied by management in the preparation of the summary financial statements.

Appropriateness (of audit evidence): The measure of the quality of audit evidence; that is, its relevance and its reliability in providing support for the conclusions on which the auditor's opinion is based.

Arm's length transaction: A transaction conducted on such terms and conditions as between a willing buyer and a willing seller who are unrelated and are acting independently of each other and pursuing their own best interests.

Assertions: Representations by management, explicit or otherwise, that are embodied in the financial statements, as used by the auditor to consider the different types of potential misstatements that may occur.

Assess: Analyze identified risks of material misstatement to conclude on their significance. *Assess*, by convention, is used only in relation to risk (also see **Evaluate**).

Association: See **Auditor association with financial information**.

Assurance (also see **Reasonable assurance**) **assurance engagement:** An engagement in which a practitioner expresses a conclusion designed to enhance the degree of confidence of the intended users other than the responsible party about the outcome of the evaluation or measurement of a subject matter against criteria. The outcome of the evaluation or measurement of a subject matter is the information that results from applying the criteria (also see **Subject-matter information**). Under the International Framework for Assurance Engagements, there are two types of assurance engagement a practitioner is permitted to perform: a reasonable assurance engagement and a limited assurance engagement.

Assurance services: An objective examination of evidence for the purpose of providing an independent assessment on governance, risk management, and control processes for the organization. Examples may include financial, performance, compliance, system security, and due diligence engagements.

Audit documentation: The record of audit procedures performed, relevant audit evidence obtained, and conclusions the auditor reached (terms such as *working papers* or *work papers* are also sometimes used).

Audit evidence: Information used by the auditor in arriving at the conclusions on which the auditor's opinion is based. Audit evidence includes both information contained in the accounting records underlying the financial statements and other information (also see **Sufficiency of audit evidence** and **Appropriateness of audit evidence**).

Audit file: One or more folders or other storage media, in physical or electronic form, containing the records that comprise the audit documentation for a specific engagement.

Audit firm: See **Firm**.

Audit nonconformance: An audit finding, substantiated by objective evidence, where there is a failure to meet the requirements of a procedure or work instruction.

Audit observation: An audit finding that, while not being a nonconformance, does give cause for concern, or may result in a nonconformance in the future.

Audit opinion: See **Modified opinion** and **Unmodified opinion**.

Audit risk: The risk of reaching invalid audit conclusions or providing faulty advice based on the audit work conducted. It is the risk that the auditor expresses an inappropriate audit opinion when the financial statements are materially misstated. Audit risk is a function of the risks of material misstatement and detection risk.

Audit sampling (sampling): The application of audit procedures to less than 100% of items within a population of audit relevance such that all sampling units have a chance of selection in order to provide the auditor with a reasonable basis on which to draw conclusions about the entire population.

Audit trail: A record of transactions in an accounting system that provides verification of the activity of the system. A complete audit trail allows auditors to trace transactions in a client's accounting records from original source documents into subsidiary ledgers through the general ledger and into basic financial statements and billings/invoices prepared and submitted by the entity.

Audit universe: An audit universe is the aggregate of all areas that are available to be audited within an enterprise.

Auditable units: Any organizational process or activity that can be audited. Internal auditors divide an organization into manageable auditable activities (auditable units) to define the audit universe, assess risk, and prioritize the use of audit resources.

Audited financial statements: Financial statements audited by the auditor in accordance with NSAs, and from which the summary financial statements are derived.

Auditee: The subsidiary, division, branch, department, business unit, group or other established subdivision of an organization that is the subject of an assurance engagement.

Auditor: *Auditor* is used to refer to the person or persons conducting the audit, usually the engagement partner or other members of the engagement team or as applicable, the firm. Where an NSA expressly intends that a requirement or responsibility be fulfilled by the engagement partner, the term *engagement partner* rather than *auditor* is used.

Auditor association with financial information: An auditor is associated with financial information when the auditor attaches a report to that information or consents to the use of the auditor's name in a professional connection.

Auditor's expert: An individual or organization possessing expertise in a field other than accounting or auditing, whose work in that field is used by the auditor to assist the auditor in obtaining sufficient appropriate audit evidence. An auditor's expert may be either an auditor's internal expert (who is a partner or staff, including temporary staff of the auditor's firm or a network firm) or an auditor's external expert.

Auditor's point estimate or auditor's range: The amount or range of amounts, respectively, derived from audit evidence for use in evaluating management's point estimate.

Auditor's range: See **Auditor's point estimate**.

Board: The highest level of governing body charged with the responsibility to direct or oversee the activities and management of the organization. Typically, this includes an independent group of directors (e.g., a board of directors, a supervisory board, or a board of governors, head of an agency, legislative body, board of governors, or trustees of nonprofit organization, or any other designated body of the organization). If such a group does not exist, the board may refer to the head of the organization. Board may refer to an audit committee to which the governing body has delegated certain functions and to whom the CAE reports to functionally.

Business process: A set of connected activities linked with each other for the purpose of achieving one or more business objectives.

Business risk: A risk resulting from significant conditions, events, circumstances, actions, or inactions that could adversely affect an entity's ability to achieve its objectives and execute its strategies or from the setting of inappropriate objectives and strategies.

Cause–effect relationship: The natural flow of business performance from a lower level to an upper level within or between perspectives. For example, training employees on customer relations leads to better customer service, which, in turn, leads to improved financial results. One side is a leader or driver, producing an end result or effect on the other side.

Change order: Document required when work is added to or deleted from the original scope of work of a contract which alters the original contract amount and/or completion date.

Chief audit executive (CAE): CAE is the head of the internal audit unit responsible for effectively managing the internal audit activity in accordance with the internal audit charter and the definition of internal auditing, the code of ethics, and the standards. The CAE reports functionally to the audit committee or board and administratively to the chief executive officer. The specific job title of the CAE may vary across organizations; in some quarters, he/she may be referred to as the auditor general, chief internal auditor, inspector general, or internal audit director, etc. The CAE or others reporting to the CAE will have appropriate professional certifications and qualifications.

Code of ethics: The code of ethics of the Institute of Internal Auditors (IIA) are principles relevant to the profession and practice of internal auditing, and rules of conduct that describe behavior expected of internal auditors. The code of ethics applies to both parties and entities that provide internal audit services. The purpose of the code of ethics is to promote an ethical culture in the global profession of internal auditing.

Comparative financial statements: Comparative information where amounts and other disclosures for the prior period are included for comparison with the financial statements of the current period but, if audited, are referred to in the auditor's opinion. The level of information included in those comparative financial statements is comparable with that of the financial statements of the current period.

Comparative information: The amounts and disclosures included in the financial statements in respect of one or more prior periods in accordance with the applicable financial reporting framework.

Compilation engagement: An engagement in which accounting expertise, as opposed to auditing expertise, is used to collect, classify, and summarize financial information.

Complementary user entity controls: Controls that the service organization assumes, in the design of its service, will be implemented by user entities and which, if necessary to achieve control objectives, are identified in the description of its system.

Compliance: Adherence to policies, plans, procedures, laws, regulations, contracts, or other requirements, such as the International Standards for the Professional Practice of Internal Auditing (Standards) and other relevant laws.

Compliance framework: See **Applicable financial reporting framework** and **General-purpose framework**.

Component: An entity or business activity for which group or component management prepares financial information that should be included in the group financial statements.

Component auditor: An auditor who, at the request of the group engagement team, performs work on financial information related to a component for the group audit.

Component management: Management responsible for the preparation of the financial information of a component.

Component materiality: The materiality for a component determined by the group engagement team.

Computer-assisted audit techniques (CAATs): Applications of auditing procedures using the computer as an audit tool.

Conflict of interest: Any relationship that is, or appears to be, not in the best interest of the organization. A conflict of interest would prejudice an individual's ability to perform his or her duties and responsibilities objectively.

Consulting services: Advisory and related client service activities, the nature and scope of which are agreed with the client, are intended to add value and improve an organization's governance, risk management, and control processes without the internal auditor assuming management responsibility. Examples include counsel, advice, facilitation, and training.

Contract modification: A change to an existing contract for a change in scope or other factors which must be agreed to by all parties of the contract.

Control: Any action taken by management, the board, and other parties to manage risk and increase the likelihood that established objectives and goals will be achieved. Management plans, organizes, and directs the performance of sufficient actions to provide reasonable assurance that objectives and goals will be achieved.

Control activities: Those policies and procedures that help ensure that management directives are carried out. Control activities are a component of internal control.

Control environment: Includes the governance and management functions and the attitudes, awareness, and actions of those charged with governance and management concerning the entity's internal control and its importance in the entity. The control environment is a component of internal control. The attitude, awareness, and actions of the board, management, owners, and others about the importance of control. This includes integrity and ethical rules, commitment to competence, board or audit committee participation, organizational structure, assignment of authority and responsibility, and human resource policies and practices.

Control processes: The policies, procedures (both manual and automated), and activities that are part of a control framework, designed and operated to ensure that risks are contained within the level that an organization is willing to accept.

Control risk: See **Risk of material misstatement**.

Corporate governance: See **Governance**.

Corresponding figures: Comparative information where amounts and other disclosures for the prior period are included as an integral part of the current period financial statements, and are intended to be read only in relation to the amounts and other disclosures relating to the current period (referred to as *current period figures*). The level of detail presented in the corresponding amounts and disclosures is dictated primarily by its relevance to the current period figures.

Cost center: A grouping of incurred costs identified with a specific final cost objective.

Criteria: The benchmarks used to evaluate or measure the subject matter, including, where relevant, benchmarks for presentation and disclosure. Criteria can be formal or less formal. There can be different criteria for the same subject matter. Suitable criteria are required for reasonably consistent evaluation or measurement of a subject matter within the context of professional judgment.

Customer: The subsidiary, division, branch, department, business unit group, individual, or other established subdivision of an organization that is the subject of a consulting engagement.

Date of approval of the financial statements: The date on which all the statements that comprise the financial statements, including the related notes, have been prepared and those with the recognized authority have asserted that they have taken responsibility for those financial statements.

Date of report (in relation to quality control): The date selected by the practitioner to date the report.

Date of the auditor's report: The date the auditor dates the report on the financial statements in accordance with NSA 29.

Date of the financial statements: The date of the end of the latest period covered by the financial statements.

Date the financial statements are issued: The date that the auditor's report and audited financial statements are made available to third parties.

Deficiency in internal control: This exists when

a. A control is designed, implemented, or operated in such a way that it is unable to prevent or detect and correct misstatements in the financial statements on a timely basis

b. A control necessary to prevent or detect and correct misstatements in the financial statements on a timely basis is missing

Detection risk: The risk that the procedures performed by the auditor to reduce audit risk to an acceptably low level will not detect a misstatement that exists and that could be material, either individually or when aggregated with other misstatements. The risk audit procedures will lead to a conclusion that material error does not exist when, in fact, such error does exist.

Direct cost: Any cost that is identified specifically with a particular final cost objective. Direct costs are not limited to items that are incorporated in the end product as material or labor. Costs identified specifically with a contract are direct costs of that contract. All costs identified specifically with other final cost objectives of the contractor are direct costs of those cost objectives. Direct costs can include labor, materials, and reimbursable expenses incurred specifically for an agreement.

Element: See **Element of a financial statement**.

Element of a financial statement: An element, account, or item of a financial statement.

Emphasis of matter paragraph: A paragraph included in the auditor's report that refers to a matter appropriately presented or disclosed in the financial statements that, in the auditor's judgment, is of such importance that it is fundamental to users' understanding of the financial statements.

Engagement: A specific internal audit assignment, task, or review activity, such as an internal audit, control self-assessment review, fraud examination, or consultancy. An engagement may include multiple tasks or activities designed to accomplish a specific set of related objectives.

Engagement documentation: The record of work performed, results obtained, and conclusions the practitioner reached (terms such as *working papers* or *work papers* are sometimes used).

Engagement letter: Written terms of an engagement in the form of a letter. A letter that represents the understanding between the client and the auditor about the engagement. The letter identifies the financial statements and/or schedules or function and describes the nature of procedures to be performed. It includes the objectives of the procedures, an explanation that the financial information and/or function is the responsibility of the company's management or auditee, and a description of the form of auditor's report.

Engagement objectives: Broad statements developed by internal auditors that define intended engagement accomplishments.

Engagement opinion: The rating, conclusion, or other description of results of an individual internal audit engagement, relating to those aspects within the objectives and scope of the engagement.

Engagement partner: The partner or other person in the firm who is responsible for the engagement and its performance, and for the report that is issued on behalf of the firm, and who, where required, has the appropriate authority from a professional, legal, or regulatory body.

Engagement quality control review: A process designed to provide an objective evaluation, on or before the date of the report, of the significant judgments the engagement team made and the conclusions it reached in formulating the report. The engagement quality control review process is for audits of financial statements of listed entities and those other engagements, if any, for which the firm has determined an engagement quality control review is required.

Engagement quality control reviewer: A partner, another person in the firm, suitably qualified external person, or a team made up of such individuals, none of whom is a party of the engagement team, with sufficient and appropriate experience and authority to objectively evaluate the significant judgments the engagement team made and the conclusions it reached in formulating the report.

Engagement risk: The risk that the practitioner expresses an inappropriate conclusion when the subject-matter information is materially misstated.

Engagement team: All partners and staff performing the engagement and any individuals engaged by the firm or a network firm who perform procedures on the engagement. This excludes external experts engaged by the firm or a network firm.

Engagement work program: A document that lists the procedures to be followed during an engagement, designed to achieve the engagement plan.

Enterprise risk management (ERM): A strategic business discipline that supports the achievement of an organization's objectives by addressing the full spectrum of its risks and managing the combined impact of those risks as an interrelated risk portfolio. It is the process of planning, organizing, leading, and controlling the activities of an organization in order to minimize the effects of risk on an organization's capital and earnings. Enterprise risk management expands the process to include not just risks associated with accidental losses, but also financial, strategic, operational, and other risks.

Committee of Sponsoring Organizations (COSO) defines ERM as "a process, effected by an entity's board of directors, management and other personnel, applied in strategy-setting and across the enterprise, designed to identify potential events that may affect the entity, and manage risk to be within its risk appetite, to provide reasonable assurance regarding the achievement of entity objectives."

Entity's risk assessment process: A component of internal control that is the entity's process for identifying business risks relevant to financial reporting objectives and deciding about actions to address those risks and the results thereof.

Entrance conference: A meeting between the auditor and the auditee during which the purpose and scope of the audit are discussed.

Environmental matters:

a. Initiatives to prevent, abate, or remedy damage to the environment, or to deal with conservation of renewable and nonrenewable resources (such initiatives may be required by environmental laws and regulations or by contract or they may be undertaken voluntarily)
b. Consequences of violating environmental laws and regulations
c. Consequences of environmental damage done to others or to natural resources
d. Consequences of vicarious liability imposed by law (e.g., liability for damages caused by previous owners)

Environmental performance report: A report, separate from the financial statements, in which an entity provides third parties with qualitative information on the entity's commitments toward the environmental aspects of the business, its policies and targets in that field, its achievement in managing the relationship between its business processes and environmental risk, and quantitative information on its environmental performance.

Environmental risk: In certain circumstances, factors relevant to the assessment of inherent risk for the development of the overall audit plan may include the risk of material misstatement of the financial statements due to environmental matters.

Error: An unintentional misstatement in financial statements, including the omission of an amount or a disclosure.

Estimation uncertainty: The susceptibility of an accounting estimate and related disclosures to an inherent lack of precision in its measurement.

Evaluate: Identify and analyze the relevant issues, including performing further procedures as necessary, to come to a specific conclusion on a matter. *Evaluation*, by convention, is used only in relation to a range of matters, including evidence, the results of procedures, and the effectiveness of management's response to a risk (also see **Assess**).

Exception: A response that indicates a difference between information requested to be confirmed or contained in the entity's records and information provided by the confirming party.

Exit conference: A meeting between the auditor and the auditee held after completion of the audit that generally focuses on preliminary audit findings, which could change based on further audit testing, supervisory review, and additional information submitted by the auditee.

Experienced auditor: An individual (whether internal or external to the firm) who has practical audit experience and a reasonable understanding of

a. Audit processes
b. NSAs and applicable legal and regulatory requirements
c. The business environment in which the entity operates
d. Auditing and financial reporting issues relevant to the entity's industry

Expert: See **Auditor's expert** and **Management's expert**.

Expertise: Skills, knowledge, and experience in a particular field.

External auditor: A registered public accounting firm, hired by the organization's board or executive management, to perform a financial statement audit providing assurance for the firm; issues, as a written attestation, a report that expresses an opinion about whether the financial statement are fairly presented in accordance with applicable Generally Accepted Accounting Principles (GAAPs).

External confirmation: Audit evidence obtained as a direct written response to the auditor from a third party (the confirming party), in paper form or by electronic or other medium.

External service provider: A person or firm outside of the organization that has special knowledge, skill, and experience in a particular discipline.

Fair presentation framework: See **Applicable financial reporting framework** and **General-purpose framework**.

Financial statements: A structured representation of historical financial information, including related notes, intended to communicate an entity's economic resources or obligations at a point in time or the changes therein for a period of time in accordance with a financial reporting framework.

The related notes ordinarily comprise a summary of significant accounting policies and other explanatory information. The term *financial statements* ordinarily refers to a complete set of financial statements as determined by the requirements of the applicable financial reporting framework, but it can also refer to a single financial statement.

Finding: Results from deficiencies in internal controls, fraud, illegal acts, violations of contract or grant provisions, and/or abuse. In accordance with GAGAS, as well as IIA standards, when documenting a finding, the auditor should include the condition, criteria, cause, effect, and a recommendation for correction. Generally, auditors include management responses to reportable findings within the final audit report.

Firm: A sole practitioner, partnership, or corporation or other entity of professional accountants.

Forecast: Prospective financial information prepared on the basis of assumptions as to future events that management expects to take place and the actions management expects to take as of the date the information is prepared (best-estimate assumptions).

Framework: A body of guiding principles that form a template against which organizations can evaluate a multitude of business practices. These principles comprise various concepts, values, assumptions, and practices intended to provide a yardstick against which an organization can assess or evaluate a particular structure, process or environment or a group of practices or procedures.

Fraud: An intentional act by one or more individuals among management, those charged with governance, employees, or third parties, involving the use of deception to obtain an unjust or illegal advantage. Or any illegal act characterized by deceit, concealment, or violation of trust. These acts are not dependent on the threat of violence or physical force. Frauds are perpetrated by parties and organizations to obtain money, property, or services; to avoid payment or loss of services; or to secure personal or business advantage.

Fraud risk factors: Events or conditions that indicate an incentive or pressure to commit fraud or provide an opportunity to commit fraud.

Fraudulent financial reporting: Involves intentional misstatements, including omissions of amounts or disclosures in financial statements, to deceive financial statement users.

General administrative expenses: Costs of operating a company that are incurred by, or allocated to, a business unit and are not directly linked to the company's products or services.

General IT controls: Policies and procedures that relate to many applications and support the effective functioning of application controls by helping ensure the continued proper operation of information systems. General IT controls commonly include controls over data center and network operations;

system software acquisition, change, and maintenance; access security; and application system acquisition, development, and maintenance.

Generally Accepted Accounting Principles (GAAP): Widely accepted set of rules, conventions, standards, and procedures for reporting financial information, as established by the Financial Accounting Standards Board (FASB).

Generally Accepted Auditing Standards (GAAS): The ten auditing standards adopted by the membership of the AICPA. Auditing standards differ from audit procedures in that "procedures" relate to acts to be performed, whereas "standards" pertain to the quality of the performance of those acts and the objectives of the procedures.

Generally Accepted Government Auditing Standards (GAGAS): Also known as the "Yellow Book," issued by the U.S. Government Accountability Office (GAO). GAGAS prescribe general procedures and professional standards that auditors must apply when performing government audits or attestation engagements.

General-purpose financial statements: Financial statements prepared in accordance with a general-purpose framework.

General-purpose framework: A financial reporting framework designed to meet the common financial information needs of a wide range of users. The financial reporting framework may be a fair presentation framework or a compliance framework. The term *fair presentation framework* is used to refer to a financial reporting framework that requires compliance with the requirements of the framework and

a. Acknowledges explicitly or implicitly that, to achieve fair presentation of the financial statements, it may be necessary for management to provide disclosures beyond those specifically required by the framework

b. Acknowledges explicitly that it may be necessary for management to depart from a requirement of the framework to achieve fair presentation of the financial statements

Such departures are expected to be necessary only in extremely rare circumstances. The term *compliance framework* is used to refer to a financial reporting framework that requires compliance with the requirements of the framework but does not contain the acknowledgements in (a) or (b) above.

Goal: An overall achievement that is considered critical to the future success of the organization. Goals express where the organizations want to be. What we must achieve to be successful.

Governance: Describes the role of person(s) or organization(s) with responsibility for overseeing the strategic direction of the entity and obligations related to the accountability of the entity. *Engagement partner* and *firm* are to be read as referring to their public sector equivalents where relevant.

Governance: The combination of processes and structures implemented by the board to inform, direct, manage, and monitor the activities of the organization toward the achievement of its objectives.

Group: All the components whose financial information is included in the group financial statements. A group always has more than one component.

Group audit: The audit of group financial statements.

Group audit opinion: The audit opinion on the group financial statements.

Group engagement partner: The partner or other person in the firm who is responsible for the group audit engagement and its performance, and for the auditor's report on the group financial statements that is issued on behalf of the firm. Where joint auditors conduct the group audit, the joint engagement partners and their engagement teams collectively constitute the group engagement partner and the group engagement team.

Group engagement team: Partners, including the group engagement partner and staff who establish the overall group audit strategy, communicate with component auditors, perform work on the consolidation process, and evaluate the conclusions drawn from the audit evidence as the basis for forming an opinion on the group financial statements.

Group financial statements: Financial statements that include the financial information of more than one component. The term *group financial statements* also refers to combined financial statements aggregating the financial information prepared by components that have no parent but are under common control.

Group management: Management responsible for the preparation of the group financial statements.

Group-wide controls: Controls designed, implemented, and maintained by group management over group financial reporting.

Historical financial information: Information expressed in financial terms in relation to a particular entity, derived primarily from that entity's accounting system, about economic events occurring in past time periods or about economic conditions or circumstances at points in time in the past.

Horizontal audit: Audits performed on a single process or procedure (such as document management, contract management, etc.) across the whole organization.

Impairment: Impairment to organizational independence and individual objectivity may include personal conflict of interest; scope limitations; restrictions on access to records, personnel, and properties; and resource limitations (funding).

Inconsistency: Other information that contradicts information contained in the audited financial statements. A material inconsistency may raise doubt about the audit conclusions drawn from audit evidence previously obtained and, possibly, about the basis for the auditor's opinion on the financial statements.

Independence: Comprises

    a. Independence of mind—the state of mind that permits the provision of an opinion without being affected by influences that compromise professional judgment, allowing an individual to act with integrity and exercise objectivity and professional skepticism.

    b. Independence in appearance—the avoidance of facts and circumstances that are so significant that a reasonable and informed third party, having knowledge of all relevant information, including any safeguards applied, would reasonably conclude a firm's or a member of the assurance team's integrity, objectivity, or professional skepticism had been compromised.

Independence: The freedom from conditions that threaten the ability of the internal audit activity to carry out internal audit responsibilities in an unbiased manner.

Indirect cost: Any cost that is not directly identified with a single, final cost objective, but is identified with two or more final cost objectives or an intermediate cost objective. Recipients recover their indirect costs in their overhead rate.

Ineligible cost: A cost that does not meet the terms of the agreement as well as federal and state statutes and regulations.

Information system relevant to financial reporting: A component of internal control that includes the financial reporting system, and consists of the procedures and records established to initiate, record, process, and report entity transactions (as well as events and conditions), and to maintain accountability for the related assets, liabilities, and equity.

Information technology controls: Controls that support business management and governance, as well as provide general and technical controls over information technology infrastructures such as applications, information, infrastructure, and people.

Information technology governance: Consists of the leadership, organizational structures, and processes that ensure that the enterprise's information technology supports the organization's strategies and objectives.

Inherent risk: See **Risk of material misstatement**.

Initial audit engagement: An engagement in which either

    a. The financial statements for the prior period were not audited.

    b. The financial statements for the prior period were audited by a predecessor auditor.

Initiatives: Planned actions to achieve objectives.

Inquiry: Inquiry consists of seeking information of knowledgeable persons, both financial and nonfinancial, within the entity or outside the entity.

Inspection: An audit procedure that involves the auditor's review of a document or record through physical examination to provide direct evidence of its content. This is a means of gathering direct evidence.

Inspection (as an audit procedure): Examining records or documents, whether internal or external, in paper form, electronic form, or other media, or a physical examination of an asset.

Inspection (in relation to quality control): In relation to completed engagements, procedures designed to provide evidence of compliance by engagement teams with the firm's quality control policies and procedures.

Intended users: The person, persons, or class of persons for whom the practitioner prepares the assurance report. The responsible party can be one of the intended users, but not the only one.

Interim financial information or statements: Financial information (which may be less than a complete set of financial statements as defined above) issued at interim dates (usually half yearly or quarterly) in respect of a financial period.

Internal audit activity: A department, division, team of consultants, or other practitioner(s) that provides independent, objective assurance and consulting services designed to add value and improve an organization's operations. The internal audit activity helps an organization accomplish its objectives by bringing a systematic, disciplined approach to evaluate and improve the effectiveness of governance, risk management, and control processes.

Internal audit charter: A formal document that defines the internal audit activity's purpose, authority, and responsibility. The internal audit charter establishes the internal audit activity's position within the organization; authorizes access to records, personnel, and physical properties relevant to the performance of engagements; and defines the scope of internal audit activities.

Internal audit function: An appraisal activity established or provided as a service to the entity. Its functions include, among other things, examining, evaluating, and monitoring the adequacy and effectiveness of internal control.

Internal auditors: Those individuals who perform the activities of the internal audit function. Internal auditors may belong to an internal audit department or equivalent function.

Internal control: The process designed, implemented, and maintained by those charged with governance, management, and other personnel to provide reasonable assurance about the achievement of an entity's objectives with regard to reliability of financial reporting, effectiveness, and efficiency of operations and compliance with applicable laws and regulations. The term *controls* refers to any aspects of one or more of the components of internal control.

International Financial Reporting Standards: The International Financial Reporting Standards issued by the International Accounting Standards Board.

International Professional Practices Framework: The conceptual framework that organizes the authoritative guidance promulgated by the IIA or other relevant body. The authoritative guideline comprises two categories: (1) mandatory and (2) strongly recommended.

Investigate: Inquire into matters arising from other procedures to resolve them.

IT environment: The policies and procedures that the entity implements and the IT infrastructure (hardware, operating systems, etc.) and application software that it uses to support business operations and achieve business strategies.

IT/ICT: Information technology/information communication technology.

Limited assurance engagement: Also see **Assurance engagement**. The objective of a limited assurance engagement is a reduction in assurance engagement risk to a level that is acceptable in the circumstances of the engagement, but where that risk is greater than for a reasonable assurance engagement, as the basis for a negative form of expression of the practitioner's conclusion.

Listed entity: An entity whose shares, stock, or debt are quoted or listed on a recognized stock exchange or are marketed under the regulations of a recognized stock exchange or other equivalent body.

Management: The person(s) with executive responsibility for the conduct of the entity's operations. For some entities in some cases, management includes some or all of those charged with governance, for example, executive members of a governance board or an owner–manager.

Management bias: A lack of neutrality by management in the preparation of information.

Management's expert: An individual or organization possessing expertise in a field other than accounting or auditing, whose work in that field is used by the entity to assist the entity in preparing the financial statements.

Management's point estimate: The amount selected by management for recognition or disclosure in the financial statements as an accounting estimate.

Measurement: A way of *monitoring* and *tracking* the *progress of strategic objectives*. Measurements can be *leading* indicators of performance (leads to an end result) or *lagging* indicators (the end results).

Measures: Indicators and monitors to track performance.

Misappropriation of assets: Involves the theft of an entity's assets and is often perpetrated by employees in relatively small and immaterial amounts. However, it can also involve management who are usually more capable of disguising or concealing misappropriations in ways that are difficult to detect.

Mission: Why we exist.

Misstatement: A difference between the amount, classification, presentation, or disclosure of a reported financial statement item, and the amount, classification, presentation, or disclosure that is required for the item to be in accordance with the applicable financial reporting framework. Misstatements can arise from error or fraud. Where the auditor expresses an opinion on whether the financial statements are presented fairly, in all material respects or give a true and fair view, misstatements also include those adjustments of amounts, classifications, presentation, or disclosures that, in the auditor's judgment, are necessary for the financial statements to be presented fairly, in all material respects or to give a true and fair view.

Misstatement of fact: Other information that is unrelated to matters appearing in the audited financial statements that is incorrectly stated or presented. A material misstatement of fact may undermine the credibility of the document containing audited financial statements.

Modified opinion: A qualified opinion, an adverse opinion, or a disclaimer of opinion.

Monitoring (in relation to quality control): A process comprising an ongoing consideration and evaluation of the firm's system of quality control, including a periodic inspection of a selection of completed engagements, designed to provide the firm with reasonable assurance that its system of quality control is operating effectively.

Monitoring of controls: A process to assess the effectiveness of internal control performance over time. It includes assessing the design and operation of controls on a timely basis and taking necessary corrective actions modified for changes in conditions. Monitoring of controls is a component of internal control.

Must: The Standards use the word *must* to specify an unconditional requirement.

Narrative: A written description of an internal control system, procedure, or process.

Negative confirmation request: A request that the confirming party respond directly to the auditor only if the confirming party disagrees with the information provided in the request.

Network: A larger structure

a. That is aimed at cooperation
b. That is clearly aimed at profit or cost sharing, or shares common ownership, control, or management; common quality control policies and procedures; common business strategy; the use of a common brand name or a significant part of professional resources

Network firm: A firm or entity that belongs to a network.

Noncompliance: Acts of omission or commission by the entity, either intentional or unintentional, which are contrary to the prevailing laws or regulations. Such acts include transactions entered into, or in the name of the entity or on its behalf, by those charged with governance, management, or employees. Noncompliance does not include personal misconduct (unrelated to the business activities of the entity) by those charged with governance: management or employees of the entity.

Nonresponse: A failure of the confirming party to respond or fully respond to a positive confirmation request or a confirmation request returned undelivered.

Nonsampling risk: The risk that the auditor reaches an erroneous conclusion for any reason not related to sampling risk.

Nuggets of gold: Chunks, bits, pieces, lumps, hunks and wads of valuable risk information.

Objective: What specifically must be done to execute the strategy. What is critical to the future success of the strategy. What the organization must do to reach its goal. Action statements linked to execution of strategy. Specific outcomes expressed in measurable terms (*not* activities).

Objectivity: An unbiased mental attitude that allows internal auditors to perform engagements in such a manner that they believe in their work product and that no quality compromises are made. Objectivity requires that internal auditors do not subordinate their judgment on audit matters to others.

Observation: Consists of looking at a process or procedure being performed by others, for example, the auditor's observation of inventory counting by the entity's personnel or of the performance of control activities. An audit procedure that involves the auditor seeing or experiencing something first hand. It could include having the auditee walk through a process while the auditor observes and monitors the activities, procedures, and steps performed and observes security practices. Through the performance of this activity, the auditor is able to obtain direct evidence.

Opening balances: Those account balances that exist at the beginning of the period. Opening balances are based on the closing balances of the prior period and reflect the effects of transactions and events of prior periods and accounting policies applied in the prior period. Opening balances also include matters requiring disclosure that existed at the beginning of the period, such as contingencies and commitments.

Other information: Financial and nonfinancial information (other than the financial statements and the auditor's report thereon) that is included, either by law, regulation or custom, in a document containing audited financial statements and the auditor's report thereon.

Other matter paragraph: A paragraph included in the auditor's report that refers to a matter other than those presented or disclosed in the financial statements that, in the auditor's judgment, is relevant to users' understanding of the audit, the auditor's responsibilities, or the auditor's report.

Outcome of an accounting estimate: The actual monetary amount that results from the resolution of the underlying transaction(s), event(s), or condition(s) addressed by the accounting estimate.

Overall audit strategy: Sets the scope, timing, and direction of the audit and guides the development of the more detailed audit plan.

Overall opinion: The rating, conclusion, or other description of results provided by the chief audit executive addressing, at a broad level, governance, risk management, or control processes of the organization. An overall opinion is the professional judgment of the chief audit executive based on the results of a number of individual engagements and other activities for a specific time interval.

Overhead expenses: All allowable general administrative expenses and fringe benefit costs not directly identified with a single final cost objective. Depending upon the size of the auditee, these costs may be separately identified on a schedule of overhead costs.

Overhead rate: A rate computed by adding together all of an entity's costs that cannot be associated with a single cost objective (e.g., general and administrative costs and fringe benefits costs), then dividing by a base value (usually direct labor cost). This rate is applied to direct labor, as incurred on projects, to allow an entity to recover the appropriate share of indirect costs allowable per the terms of the specific agreement.

Partner: Any individual with authority to bind the firm with respect to the performance of a professional services engagement.

Peer review: A quality control program in which the audit documentation of one STA audit group is periodically (three years for GAGAS, five years for IIA) reviewed by independent partners of other STA groups to verify that it conforms to the standards of the profession.

Performance materiality: The amount or amounts set by the auditor at less than materiality for the financial statements as a whole to reduce to an appropriately low level the probability that the aggregate of uncorrected and undetected misstatements exceeds materiality for the financial statements as a whole. If applicable, performance materiality also refers to the amount or amounts set by the auditor at less than the materiality level or levels for particular classes of transactions, account balances, or disclosures.

Permanent files: Files containing information of continuing importance to engagements covering an auditable unit.

Personnel: Partners and staff.

Perspectives: Different views that drive the organization. Perspectives provide a framework for measurement.

Pervasive: A term used, in the context of misstatements, to describe the effects on the financial statements of misstatements, or the possible effects on the financial statements of misstatements, if any, that are undetected because of an inability to obtain sufficient appropriate audit evidence. Pervasive effects on the financial statements are those that, in the auditor's judgment

a. Are not confined to specific elements, accounts, or items of the financial statements

b. If so confined, represent or could represent a substantial proportion of the financial statements

c. In relation to disclosures, are fundamental to users' understanding of the financial statements

Population: The entire set of data from which a sample is selected and about which the auditor wishes to draw conclusions.

Positive confirmation request: A request that the confirming party respond directly to the auditor indicating whether the confirming party agrees or disagrees with the information in the request or providing the requested information.

Practitioner: A professional accountant in public practice.

Preconditions for an audit: The use by management of an acceptable financial reporting framework in the preparation of the financial statements, and the agreement of management and those charged with governance to the premise on which an audit is conducted.

Predecessor auditor: The auditor from a different audit firm, who audited the financial statements of an entity in the prior period and who has been replaced by the current auditor.

Premise: Relating to the responsibilities of management and those charged with governance, on which an audit is conducted. That management and those charged with governance have acknowledged and understand that they have the following responsibilities that are fundamental to the conduct of an audit in accordance with NSAs. That is, responsibility

a. For the preparation of the financial statements in accordance with the applicable financial reporting framework, including, where relevant, their fair presentation

b. For such internal control as management and those charged with governance determine is necessary to enable the preparation of financial statements that are free from material misstatement, whether due to fraud or error

c. To provide the auditor with

    i. Access to all information of which management and those charged with governance are aware that is relevant to the preparation of the financial statements, such as records, documentation, and other matters

    ii. Additional information that the auditor may request from management and those charged with governance for the purpose of the audit

    iii. Unrestricted access to persons within the entity from whom the auditor determines it necessary to obtain audit evidence

    In the case of a fair presentation framework, (a) above may be restated as "for the preparation and fair presentation of the financial statements in accordance with the financial reporting framework" or "for the preparation of financial statements that give a true and fair view in accordance with the financial reporting framework." The "premise, relating to the responsibilities of management and those charged with governance, on which an audit is conducted" may also be referred to as the *premise*.

Professional accountant: An individual who is a member of an International Federation of Accountants member body.

Professional accountant in public practice: A professional accountant, irrespective of functional classification (e.g., audit, tax or consulting), in a firm that provides professional services. This term is also used to refer to a firm of professional accountants in public practice.

Professional judgment: The application of relevant training, knowledge, and experience, within the context provided by auditing, accounting, and ethical standards, in making informed decisions about the courses of action that are appropriate in the circumstances of the audit engagement.

Professional skepticism: An attitude that includes a questioning mind, being alert to conditions that may indicate possible misstatement due to error or fraud, and a critical assessment of evidence.

Programs: Major initiatives or projects that must be undertaken in order to meet one or more strategic objectives.

Project authorization and agreement: A contractual obligation of the federal government for payment of the federal share of project costs. The agreement will include a description of the project, the federal-aid project number, the work covered, total cost and amount of federal aid funds, the federal share of funds, signatures of state and federal officials, and any other provision set out by relevant law.

Projection: Prospective financial information prepared on the basis of

    a. Hypothetical assumptions about future events and management actions that are not necessarily expected to take place, such as when some entities are in a startup phase or are considering a major change in the nature of operations

    b. A mixture of best-estimate and hypothetical assumptions

Prospective financial information: Financial information based on assumptions about events that may occur in the future and possible actions by an entity. Prospective financial information can be in the form of a forecast, a projection, or a combination of both (see **Forecast** and **Projection**).

Public sector: National, regional (e.g., state, provincial, territorial), and local (e.g., city, town) governments, and related governmental entities (e.g., agencies, boards, commissions, and enterprises).

Reasonable assurance (in the context of assurance engagements, including audit engagements and quality control): A high but not absolute level of assurance.

Reasonable assurance engagement: Also see **Assurance engagement**. The objective of a reasonable assurance engagement is a reduction in assurance engagement risk to an acceptably low level in the circumstances of the engagement as the basis for a positive form of expression of the practitioner's conclusion.

Reasonable cost: A cost is reasonable if, in its nature and amount, it does not exceed that which would be incurred by a prudent person in the conduct of competitive business.

Recalculation: Consists of checking the mathematical accuracy of documents or records.

Reconcile (reconciliation): Efforts to prepare a schedule establishing agreement between separate sources of information, such as accounting records reconciled with the financial statements.

Related party: A party that is either

a. A related party as defined in the applicable financial reporting framework or
b. Where the applicable financial reporting framework establishes minimal or no related party requirements
 i. A person or other entity that has control or significant influence, directly or indirectly through one or more intermediaries, over the reporting entity.
 ii. Another entity over which the reporting entity has control or significant influence, directly or indirectly, through one or more intermediaries.
 iii. Another entity that is under common control with the reporting entity through having
  • Common controlling ownership
  • Owners who are close family members
  • Common key management

Related services: Comprise agreed-upon procedures and compilations.

Relevant ethical requirements: Ethical requirements to which the engagement team and engagement quality control reviewer are subject are contained in the Professional Code of Conduct and Guide for Members.

Reperformance: An audit procedure that involves the auditor redoing a certain activity or procedure to see if he or she arrives at the same results. The auditor's reperformance of a particular control provides direct evidence to support whether a control is operating effectively.

Report on the description and design of controls at a service organization: A report that comprises

a. A description, prepared by management of the service organization, of the service organization's system, control objectives, and related controls that have been designed and implemented as at a specified date
b. A report by the service auditor with the objective of conveying reasonable assurance that includes the service auditor's opinion on the description of the service organization's system, control objectives, and related controls and the suitability of the design of the controls to achieve the specified control objectives

Report on the description, design, and operating effectiveness of controls at a service organization: A report that comprises

a. A description, prepared by management of the service organization, of the service organization's system, control objectives and related controls, their design and implementation, at a specified date or throughout a specified period, and in some cases, their operating effectiveness throughout a specified period

b. A report by the service auditor with the objective of conveying reasonable assurance that includes

    i. The service auditor's opinion on the description of the service organization's system, control objectives and related controls, the suitability of the design of the controls to achieve the specified control objectives, and the operating effectiveness of the controls

    ii. A description of the service auditor's tests of the controls and the results thereof

Residual risk: The risk that exists after consideration of the controls management has been implemented to mitigate or transfer risk.

Resolution process: The process used to resolve findings. It may involve negotiating a corrective action, reimbursing funds, and improving procedures.

Responsible party: The person (or persons) who

a. In a direct reporting engagement, is responsible for the subject matter.

b. In an assertion-based engagement, is responsible for the subject-matter information (the assertion), and may be responsible for the subject matter. The responsible party may or may not be the party who engages the practitioner (the engaging party).

Review (in relation to quality control): Appraising the quality of the work performed and conclusions reached by others.

Review engagement: The objective of a review engagement is to enable an auditor to state whether, on the basis of procedures that do not provide all the evidence that would be required in an audit, anything has come to the auditor's attention that causes the auditor to believe that the financial statements are not prepared, in all material respects, in accordance with an applicable financial reporting framework.

Review procedures: The procedures deemed necessary to meet the objective of a review engagement, primarily inquiries of entity personnel and analytical procedures applied to financial data.

Risk: The possibility of an event occurring that will have an impact on the achievement of objectives. Risk is measured in terms of impact and likelihood.

Risk appetite: The level of risk that an organization is willing to accept. The amount of risk, on a broad level, that an entity is willing to accept in pursuit of its mission.

Risk assessment: A process used to identify and evaluate risk and its potential impacts/effects. The identification and analysis (typically in terms of impact and likelihood) of relevant risks to the achievement of organization's objectives, forming a basis for determining how the risks should be managed.

Risk assessment procedures: The audit procedures performed to obtain an understanding of the entity and its environment, including the entity's internal control, to identify and assess the risks of material misstatement, whether due to fraud or error, at the financial statement and assertion levels.

Risk culture: The set of shared values and beliefs that governs attitudes toward risk taking, care, and integrity, and determines how openly risk and losses are reported and discussed.

Risk factors: Conditions that can influence the frequency or magnitude and, ultimately, the business impact of an event/scenarios.

Risk management: A process to identify, assess, manage, and control potential events or situations to provide reasonable assurance regarding the achievement of the organization's objectives. According to ISO/IEC Guide 73:2002, risk management involves coordinated activities to direct and control an enterprise with regard to risk. In the international standard, the term *control* is used as a synonymous word for *measure*.

Risk of material misstatement: The risk that the financial statements are materially misstated prior to audit. This consists of two components, described as follows at the assertion level:

a. Inherent risk—The susceptibility of an assertion about a class of transactions, account balance, or disclosure to a misstatement that could be material, either individually or when aggregated with other misstatements, before consideration of any related controls. The risk that exists in an environment without the benefit of internal controls due to other factors such as the nature of transaction or activity, for example, complexity, frequent change, etc.

b. Control risk—The risk that a misstatement that could occur in an assertion about a class of transaction, account balance, or disclosure and that could be material, either individually or when aggregated with other misstatements, will not be prevented or detected and corrected on a timely basis by the entity's internal control.

Sample size: The number of items selected when a sample is drawn from a population.

Sampling: See **Audit sampling**.

Sampling error: The risk that the sample results will mislead the auditor, unless the auditor examines 100% of the population. The larger the sample, the lesser the risk of sampling error and the greater the reliability of the results.

Sampling risk: The possibility that conclusions drawn from the sample may not represent correct conclusions for the entire population. Sampling risk can lead to two types of erroneous conclusions:

a. In the case of a test of controls, that controls are more effective than they actually are, or in the case of a test of details, that a material misstatement does not exist when in fact it does. The auditor is primarily concerned with this type of erroneous conclusion because it affects audit effectiveness and is more likely to lead to an inappropriate audit opinion.

b. In the case of a test of controls, that controls are less effective than they actually are, or in the case of a test of details, that a material misstatement exists when in fact it does not. This type of erroneous conclusion affects audit efficiency, as it would usually lead to additional work to establish that initial conclusions were incorrect.

The possibility that conclusions drawn from the sample may not represent correct conclusions for the entire population.

Sampling unit: The individual items constituting a population.

Scope of a review: The review procedures deemed necessary in the circumstances to achieve the objective of the review.

Segregation of duties: Assigning to different people the responsibilities of authorizing transactions, recording transactions, and maintaining custody of assets. Segregation of duties reduces the opportunities for one person to both perpetrate and conceal errors or fraud.

Service auditor: An auditor who, at the request of the service organization, provides an assurance report on the controls of a service organization.

Service organization: A third-party organization (or segment of a third-party organization) that provides services to user entities that are part of those entities' information systems relevant to financial reporting.

Service organization's system: The policies and procedures designed, implemented, and maintained by the service organization to provide user entities with the services covered by the service auditor's report.

Service provider: A firm or person outside the organization, who provides assurance or consulting services to other organizations.

Should: The Standards use the word *should* where conformance is expected unless, when applying professional judgment, circumstances justify deviation.

Significance: The relative importance of a matter within the context in which it is being considered, including quantitative and qualitative factors, such as magnitude, nature, effect, relevance, and impact. Professional judgment assists internal auditors when evaluating the significance of matters within the context of the relevant objectives.

Significance: The relative importance of a matter, taken in context. The significance of a matter is judged by the practitioner in the context in which it is being considered. This might include, for example, the reasonable prospect of its changing or influencing the decisions of intended users of the practitioner's report; or as another example, where the context is a judgment about whether to report a matter to those charged with governance, whether the matter would be regarded as important by them in relation to their duties. Significance can be considered in the context of quantitative and qualitative factors, such as relative magnitude, the nature and effect on the subject matter, and the expressed interests of intended users or recipients.

Significant component: A component identified by the group engagement team that

a. Is of individual financial significance to the group
b. Due to its specific nature or circumstances, is likely to include significant risks of material misstatement of the group financial statements

Significant deficiency in internal control: A deficiency or combination of deficiencies in internal control that, in the auditor's professional judgment, is of sufficient importance to merit the attention of those charged with governance.

Significant risk: An identified and assessed risk of material misstatement that, in the auditor's judgment, requires special audit consideration.

Single audit: A rigorous, organization-wide audit or examination of an entity that expends $500,000 (currently) or more of federal assistance received for its operations. These are usually performed annually. The objective of a Single Audit is to provide assurance to the federal government as to the management and use of such funds by recipients such as states, cities, universities, and nonprofit organizations. These audits are typically performed by an independent certified public accountant (CPA) and encompass both financial and compliance components.

Smaller entity: An entity that typically possesses qualitative characteristics such as

a. Concentration of ownership and management in a small number of individuals (often a single individual—either a natural person or another enterprise that owns the entity provided the owner exhibits the relevant qualitative characteristics)
b. One or more of the following:
   i. Straightforward or uncomplicated transactions
   ii. Simple record keeping
   iii. Few lines of business and few products within business lines

iv. Few internal controls
v. Few levels of management with responsibility for a broad range of controls
vi. Few personnel, many having a wide range of duties

These qualitative characteristics are not exhaustive, they are not exclusive to smaller entities, and smaller entities do not necessarily display all of these characteristics.

Source documentation: Documents that support the costs recorded in an entity's records. Source documents can include timesheets, payroll registers, invoices, receipts, rental slips, cancelled checks, etc.

Special-purpose financial statements: Financial statements prepared in accordance with a special-purpose framework.

Special-purpose framework: A financial reporting framework designed to meet the financial information needs of specific users. The financial reporting framework may be a fair presentation framework or a compliance framework.

Staff: Professionals, other than partners, including any experts the firm employs.

Standard: A professional pronouncement promulgated by the Internal Audit Standards Board that delineates the requirements for performing a broad range of internal audit activities, and for evaluating internal audit performance.

Statistical sampling: An approach to sampling that has the following characteristics:

a. Random selection of the sample items
b. The use of probability theory to evaluate sample results, including measurement of sampling risk

A sampling approach that does not have these two characteristics is considered a nonstatistical sampling.

Strategic maps: A logical framework for organizing a collection of strategic objectives over the balanced scorecard (BSC) perspectives. Everything is linked to capture a cause and effect relationship. Strategy maps are the foundation for BSC.

Strategic theme (area): Strategic themes are the main, high-level business strategies that form the basis for the organization's business model. They apply to every part of the organization and define what major strategic thrusts the organization will pursue to achieve its vision. A major strategic thrust for the organization, such as maximizing shareholder value or improving the efficiency of operations.

Strategy: Refers to how management plans to achieve the organization's objectivity. It is an expression of what the organization must do to get from one reference point to another reference point. Strategy is expressed in terms of mission statements, vision, goals, and objectives. Strategy is usually developed by the top level of the organization and executed by lower levels in the organization.

Stratification: The process of dividing a population into subpopulations, each of which is a group of sampling units that have similar characteristics (often monetary value).

Subject-matter information: The outcome of the evaluation or measurement of a subject matter. It is the subject-matter information about which the practitioner gathers sufficient appropriate evidence to provide a reasonable basis for expressing a conclusion in an assurance report.

Subsequent events: Events occurring between the date of the financial statements and the date of the auditor's report, and facts that become known to the auditor after the date of the auditor's report.

Subservice organization: A service organization used by another service organization to perform some of the services provided to user entities that are part of those user entities' information systems relevant to financial reporting.

Substantive procedure: An audit procedure designed to detect material misstatements at the assertion level. Substantive procedures comprise

a. Tests of details (of classes of transaction account balances and disclosures)
b. Substantive analytical procedures

Sufficiency (of audit evidence): The measure of the quantity of audit evidence. The quantity of the audit evidence needed is affected by the auditor's assessment of the risks of material misstatement and also by the quality of such audit evidence.

Suitable criteria: See **Criteria**. Criteria that exhibit the following characteristics:

a. Relevance: Relevant criteria contribute to conclusions that assist decision making by the intended users.
b. Completeness: Criteria are sufficiently complete when relevant factors that could affect the conclusions in the context of the engagement circumstances are not omitted. Complete criteria include, where relevant, benchmarks for presentation and disclosure.
c. Reliability: Reliable criteria allow reasonably consistent evaluation or measurement of the subject matter, including, where relevant, presentation and disclosure, when used in similar circumstances by similarly qualified practitioners.
d. Neutrality: Neutral criteria contribute to conclusions that are free from bias.
e. Understandability: Understandable criteria contribute to conclusions that are clear, comprehensive, and not subject to significantly different interpretations.

Suitably qualified external person: An individual outside the firm with the competence and capabilities to act as an engagement partner, for example, a partner of another firm or an employee (with appropriate experience) of either a professional accountancy body whose members may perform audits and reviews of historical financial information, or other assurance or related services engagements, or of an organization that provides relevant quality control services.

Summary financial statements: Historical financial information that is derived from financial statements but that contains less detail than the financial statements, while still providing a structured representation consistent with that provided by the financial statements of the entity's economic resources or obligations at a point in time or the changes therein for a period of time.

Supplementary information: Information that is presented together with the financial statements that is not required by the applicable financial reporting framework used to prepare the financial statements, normally presented in either supplementary schedules or as additional notes.

Target: An expected level of performance or improvement required in the future. Desired level of performance and timelines.

Technology-based audit techniques: Any automated audit tool, such as generalized audit software, test data generators, computerized audit programs, specialized audit utilities, and computer-assisted audit techniques (CAATs) (The Institute of Internal Auditors [IIA], pp. 19–23).

Technology-based audit techniques: Any automated audit tool, such as generalized audit utilities, and computer-assisted audit techniques (CAAT).

Test: An audit procedure whereby the auditor reviews certain transactions and processes or attributes against established criteria. The auditor then decides whether the audited entity complied with the criteria, which are established standards, practices, laws, regulations, or requirements.

Tests of controls: An audit procedure designed to evaluate the operating effectiveness of controls in preventing or detecting and correcting material misstatements at the assertion level.

Those charged with governance: The person(s) or organization(s) (e.g., a corporate trustee) with responsibility for overseeing the strategic direction of the entity and obligations related to the accountability of the entity. This includes overseeing the financial reporting process. For some entities in some cases, those charged with governance may include management personnel, for example, executive members of a governance board of a private or public sector entity, or an owner–manager.

Tolerable misstatement: A monetary amount set by the auditor in respect of which the auditor seeks to obtain an appropriate level of assurance that the monetary amount set by the auditor is not exceeded by the actual misstatement in the population.

Total rate of deviation: A rate of deviation from prescribed internal control procedures set by the auditor in respect of which the auditor seeks to obtain an appropriate level of assurance that the rate of deviation set by the auditor is not exceeded by the actual rate of deviation in the population.

Tracing: An audit procedure that involves tracking information forward from one document to another subsequently prepared document or record. This test is performed as a means to test for the completeness of the document or record.

Unallowable cost: An item of cost that is ineligible for cost reimbursement.

Uncertainty: A matter whose outcome depends on future actions or events not under the direct control of the entity but that may affect the financial statements.

Uncorrected misstatements: Misstatements that the auditor has accumulated during the audit and that have not been corrected.

Unmodified opinion: The opinion expressed by the auditor when the auditor concludes that the financial statements are prepared, in all material respects, in accordance with the applicable financial reporting framework.

User auditor: An auditor who audits and reports on the financial statements of a user entity.

User entity: An entity that uses a service organization and whose financial statements are being audited.

Verifying: The act of tracing a transaction from one document to the original support document.

Vertical audit: Audits of a part of the organization or a specific project against all applicable procedures within the system.

Vision: What we want to be in the future. Our picture of the future or desired future state.

Vouching: An audit procedure that involves tracking information from one document or record back into a previously prepared document or record or to some other reliable source. This procedure is performed in order to determine the validity of the information.

Walkthrough: Procedure whereby an auditor follows a transaction from origination through the company's processes, including information systems, until it is reflected in the company's financial records, using the same documents and information technology that company personnel use.

Walkthrough test: Involves tracing a few transactions through the financial reporting system.

Written representation: A written statement by management provided to the auditor to confirm certain matters or to support other audit evidence. Written representations in this context do not include financial statements, the assertions therein, or supporting books and records.

Index

Page numbers followed by f and t indicate figures and tables, respectively.

For Product Safety Concerns and Information please contact our EU
representative GPSR@taylorandfrancis.com
Taylor & Francis Verlag GmbH, Kaufingerstraße 24, 80331 München, Germany

www.ingramcontent.com/pod-product-compliance
Ingram Content Group UK Ltd.
Pitfield, Milton Keynes, MK11 3LW, UK
UKHW021025180425
457613UK00020B/1054